P9-BEE-857

MAMMALS
of
CALIFORNIA

Tamara Eder

Lone Pine Publishing International

© 2005 by Lone Pine Publishing International Inc.
First printed in 2005   10 9 8 7 6 5 4 3 2 1
Printed in China

All rights reserved. No part of this work covered by the copyrights hereon may be reproduced or used in any form or by any means—graphic, electronic or mechanical—without the prior written permission of the publisher, except for reviewers, who may quote brief packages. Any request for photocopying, recording, taping or storage on information retrieval systems of any part of this work shall be directed in writing to the publisher.

Distributed by Lone Pine Publishing
1808 B Street NW, Suite 140
Auburn, WA, USA 98001

Website: www.lonepinepublishing.com

Library and Archives Canada Cataloguing in Publication
Eder, Tamara, 1974–
　　Mammals of California / Tamara Eder.
　　Includes index.
　　ISBN-13: 978-1-55105-344-8
　　ISBN-10: 1-55105-344-6

　　1. Mammals—California—Identification. I. Title.

QL719.C2E34 2005　　　599'.09794　　　C2005-902388-0

Technical Review: Christopher Conroy
Track & Print Illustrations: Ian Sheldon
Cover Photo: Mountain Lion, by Terry Parker
Scanning & Digital Film: Elite Lithographers Co.

The publisher and author thank Chris C. Fisher and Don Pattie for their previous contributions to the Mammal series.

Photo and Illustration Credits
All photographs are by Terry Parker, except as follows: Ken Balcomb 58; Renee DeMartin/West Stock 62, 66, 126; Tom/Pat Leeson/Image State 70; Corel 74; Leslie Degner 94; Mark Degner 104, 108; Wayne Lynch 112, 162; Tamara Eder 116, 142; Mark Newman/ West Stock 130; Eyewire 138

All illustrations are by Gary Ross, except as follows: Ian Sheldon 54–75, 129, 135, 137, 141, 143; Kindrie Grove 183, 198, 201, 203, 251, 258, 311

The photographs and illustrations in this book are reproduced with the generous permission of the copyright holders.

PC: P13

Contents

HOOFED MAMMALS

| American Bison
p. 32 | Bighorn Sheep
p. 34 | Pronghorn
p. 38 | Elk
p. 42 |

Mule Deer
p. 46

Wild Boar
p. 50

Horse
p. 52

WHALES, DOLPHINS & PORPOISES

Gray Whale
p. 56

Humpback Whale
p. 60

Orca
p. 64

Bottlenosed Dolphin
p. 68

Dall's Porpoise
p. 72

Mountain Lion
p. 78

Bobcat
p. 82

Western Spotted Skunk
p. 86

Striped Skunk
p. 88

American Marten
p. 90

Fisher
p. 92

Short-tailed Weasel
p. 96

Long-tailed Weasel
p. 98

American Mink
p. 100

Wolverine
p. 102

American Badger
p. 106

Northern River
Otter, p. 110

Sea Otter
p. 114

Ringtail
p. 118

Northern Raccoon
p. 120

Harbor Seal
p. 124

CARNIVORES

Northern Elephant Seal
p. 128

Northern Fur Seal
p. 132

Guadalupe Fur Seal
p. 134

Northern Sea-Lion
p. 136

California Sea-Lion
p. 140

American Black Bear
p. 144

Coyote
p. 148

Red Fox
p. 152

Kit Fox
p. 156

Common Gray Fox
p. 160

Island Gray Fox
p. 164

RODENTS

North American
Porcupine, p. 168

Western Jumping
Mouse, p. 172

Pacific Jumping
Mouse, p. 173

Western Harvest
Mouse, p. 174

Salt-marsh Harvest
Mouse, p. 175

Cactus Mouse
p. 176

California Mouse
p. 177

Deer Mouse
p. 178

Canyon Mouse
p. 180

Brush Mouse
p. 181

Pinyon Mouse
p. 182

Northern Grasshopper
Mouse, p. 183

Southern Grasshopper
Mouse, p. 184

Hispid Cotton Rat
p. 185

Bushy-tailed Woodrat
p. 186

White-throated Woodrat
p. 188

RODENTS

Desert Woodrat
p. 189

Dusky-footed
Woodrat, p. 190

House Mouse
p. 191

Norway Rat
p. 192

Black Rat
p. 193

Western Red-backed
Vole, p. 194

White-footed
Vole, p. 195

Sonoma Tree Vole
p. 196

Western Heather
Vole, p. 197

Montane Vole
p. 198

California Vole
p. 199

Townsend's Vole
p. 200

Long-tailed Vole
p. 201

Creeping Vole
p. 202

Sagebrush Vole
p. 203

Common Muskrat
p. 204

American Beaver
p. 206

Great Basin Pocket
Mouse, p. 210

White-eared Pocket
Mouse, p. 211

Little Pocket
Mouse, p. 212

San Joaquin Pocket
Mouse, p. 213

Long-tailed Pocket
Mouse, p. 214

Bailey's Pocket
Mouse, p. 215

Sonoran Desert Pocket
Mouse, p. 216

San Diego Pocket
Mouse, p. 217

California Pocket
Mouse, p. 218

Spiny Pocket
Mouse, p. 219

Dark Kangaroo
Mouse, p. 220

Pale Kangaroo
Mouse, p. 221

Ord's Kangaroo
Rat, p. 222

Chisel-toothed
Kangaroo Rat, p. 223

Panamint Kangaroo
Rat, p. 224

Stephen's Kangaroo
Rat, p. 225

Narrow-faced
Kangaroo Rat, p. 226

Agile Kangaroo
Rat, p. 227

Heermann's
Kangaroo Rat,
p. 228

California Kangaroo
Rat, p. 229

Giant Kangaroo Rat
p. 230

Merriam's Kangaroo Rat
p. 231

Fresno Kangaroo Rat
p. 232

Desert Kangaroo
Rat, p. 233

Northern Pocket
Gopher, p. 234

Western Pocket
Gopher, p. 235

Mountain Pocket
Gopher, p. 236

Botta's Pocket Gopher
p. 237

Townsend's Pocket Gopher
p. 238

Alpine Chipmunk
p. 239

Least Chipmunk
p. 240

Yellow-pine Chipmunk
p. 241

Yellow-cheeked
Chipmunk, p. 242

Allen's Chipmunk
p. 243

Siskiyou Chipmunk
p. 244

Sonoma Chipmunk
p. 245

Merriam's Chipmunk
p. 246

California Chipmunk
p. 247

Long-eared
Chipmunk, p. 248

RODENTS

Lodgepole Chipmunk
p. 249

Panamint Chipmunk
p. 250

Uinta Chipmunk
p. 251

Yellow-bellied
Marmot, p. 252

White-tailed Antelope
Squirrel, p. 254

Nelson's Antelope Squirrel
p. 255

Piute Ground Squirrel
p. 256

Belding's Ground Squirrel
p. 257

Rock Squirrel
p. 258

California Ground Squirrel
p. 259

Mohave Ground Squirrel
p. 260

Round-tailed
Ground Squirrel, p. 261

Golden-mantled
Ground Squirrel, p. 262

Eastern Gray Squirrel
p. 263

Western Gray Squirrel
p. 264

Douglas's Squirrel
p. 266

Northern Flying Squirrel
p. 268

Mountain Beaver
p. 270

Pygmy Rabbit
p. 274

Brush Rabbit
p. 275

Mountain Cottontail
p. 276

Desert Cottontail
p. 278

Snowshoe Hare
p. 280

Black-tailed
Jackrabbit, p. 283

RABBITS, HARES & PIKAS

White-tailed Jackrabbit
p. 284

European Rabbit
p. 285

American Pika
p. 286

BATS

Brazilian Free-tailed
Bat, p. 290

Pocketed Free-tailed
Bat, p. 291

Big Free-tailed Bat
p. 292

Western Mastiff
Bat, p. 293

Fringed Bat
p. 294

Long-eared Bat
p. 295

California Bat
p. 296

Western Small-footed
Bat, p. 297

Little Brown Bat
p. 298

Cave Bat
p. 299

Yuma Bat
p. 300

Long-legged Bat
p. 301

Southern Yellow
Bat, p. 302

Western Red Bat
p. 303

Hoary Bat
p. 304

Western Pipistrelle
p. 306

Silver-haired Bat
p. 308

Big Brown Bat
p. 309

Spotted Bat
p. 310

Pallid Bat
p. 311

Townsend's Big-eared
Bat, p. 312

California Leaf-
nosed Bat, p. 314

Mexican Long-
tongued Bat, p. 315

American Shrew
Mole, p. 318

Townsend's Mole
p. 319

Coast Mole
p. 320

Broad-footed Mole
p. 321

Mt. Lyell Shrew
p. 322

Preble's Shrew
p. 323

Vagrant Shrew
p. 324

Fog Shrew
p. 325

Montane Shrew
p. 326

Ornate Shrew
p. 327

Inyo Shrew
p. 328

Water Shrew
p. 329

Marsh Shrew
p. 330

Trowbridge's Shrew
p. 331

Merriam's Shrew
p. 332

Desert Shrew
p. 333

Virginia Opossum
p. 334

Introduction

Few things characterize wilderness as well as wild animals, and few animals are more recognizable than our fellow mammals. In fact, many people use the term "animal" when they really mean "mammal"—they forget that birds, reptiles, amphibians, fish and all the many kinds of invertebrates are animals, too.

Mammals come in a wide variety of colors, shapes and sizes, but they all share two important characteristics that distinguish them from the other vertebrates: only mammals have real hair, and only mammals nurse their young with milk from mammary glands (the feature that gives this group its name). Other, less well-known features that are unique to mammals include a muscular diaphragm, which separates the lower abdominal cavity from the cavity that contains the heart and lungs, and a lower jaw that is composed of a single bone on each side. The two lower jaw bones of a mammal are the left and right dentary bones; most other jawed vertebrates have five or six bones in their lower jaws. Additionally, a mammal's skull joins with the first vertebra at two points of contact—a bird's or reptile's skull has only one point of contact, which is what allows birds to turn their heads so far around. As well as setting mammals apart from all other kinds of life, these characteristics also identify humans as part of the mammalian group.

Whether you are enjoying a Northern River Otter play along a muddy bank, watching a Humpback Whale as it breaches or listening to the haunting sound of an Elk's bugle, the natural regions of California provide spectacular mammal-watching opportunities. Much has changed over the last 150 years, but the coast and interior of California remain internationally recognized destinations for visitors who are interested in rewarding natural experiences. To honor this treasure is to celebrate North America's intrinsic virtues, and this book is intended to provide readers with the knowledge needed to appreciate the rich variety of mammals in this region. Whether you are a naturalist, a photographer, a wildlife enthusiast or all three, you will find terrific opportunities in California to satisfy your greatest wilderness expectations.

The California Region

The natural region of California is an extremely biologically diverse area. Although this state represents only a small portion of the U.S., it encompasses a dramatic variety of landscapes. Lush coastal zones, rugged mountains, humid forests, wild backcountry, vast deserts and clear-blue lakes all contribute to the scenic beauty and ecological uniqueness of this region.

The wildlife and wildlife associations that occur in California are linked to the geological, climatic and biological influences of the region. Significant areas of this state, especially in the mountains, have been protected, and the value of that foresight is easily seen in the wealth of wildlife encounters granted to visitors. Even outside of protected areas, California has large areas of wilderness, and wildlife is never far. Coyotes, deer and foxes may be seen in some of our cities, while in more remote areas, you can see and hear Elk, American Black Bears and maybe even Mountain Lions. In the bays and inlets of the 1100 mi coastline we are frequently delighted by passing whales and other marine mammals. For those of us lucky enough to live in or visit California, we may be just minutes away from some of the most thrilling wildlife encounters in North America.

California is extremely varied in its biogeography. For simplification, this

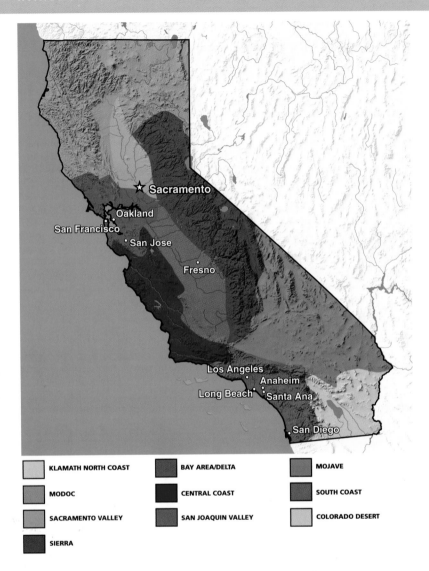

	KLAMATH NORTH COAST		BAY AREA/DELTA		MOJAVE
	MODOC		CENTRAL COAST		SOUTH COAST
	SACRAMENTO VALLEY		SAN JOAQUIN VALLEY		COLORADO DESERT
	SIERRA				

book divides the state into ten different bioregions—Klamath North Coast, Modoc, Sacramento Valley, Sierra, Bay Area/Delta, Central Coast, San Joaquin Valley, Mojave, South Coast and Colorado Desert. Looking at these natural regions in detail can lead to a better understanding of the mammals living here and how they interact with each other.

Klamath North Coast

Located in the northwestern part of the state, the Klamath North Coast Bioregion encompasses the rocky coastline, the coastal mountains and the southern region of the Cascade Mountains. Lush coastal and mountain forests characterize this region, as well as numerous lakes and rivers. The Klamath region receives the most rainfall of any part of the state. Winters near the coast are rainy and cool. This area is an active fog belt, and fog will cross the coastal zones at any time of the year. At higher elevations in the mountains, snow falls in the winter. The eastern interior part of this bioregion has less rain and hotter, drier summers than the coastal zones. Mixed coniferous forests dominate the Klamath North Coast Bioregion, although the overall vegetative mosaic includes grassland hills, oak woodlands, coastal prairie shrub and coastal dune communities. The major mixed forests include such trees as White Fir, Douglas-fir, Ponderosa Pine, Lodgepole Pine, Mountain Hemlock, cedars and redwoods. Redwood National Park, four national forests and several wilderness areas are found within this bioregion. Many mammals are present in good numbers in Klamath, including the Elk, Mountain Lion, American Black Bear, Red Fox, Common Gray Fox, Wolverine, Northern River Otter, Northern Flying Squirrel, Pomo Tree Vole, Coast Mole and Marsh Shrew.

Modoc

Interestingly, much of the Modoc Bioregion still looks as rugged and wild as when pioneers first crossed this area more than 150 years ago—perhaps attributable to having the lowest human population in all of California. The dramatic scenery of this northeastern wilderness includes high deserts, volcanic highlands, coniferous forests, rugged mountains and rich wetlands. In winter, high-elevation areas receive snow and low-elevation areas experience cool rains and frost. Summers throughout the bioregion are hot and dry. The Lassen Volcanic National Park contains numerous lakes and the towering 10,457 ft. Lassen Peak. The most recent volcanic activity in this park was in 1915. Elsewhere in this bioregion are the Modoc and Lassen national forests, and part of the Klamath National Forest. The dominant forest vegetation includes Yellow Pine, Jeffery Pine, White Fir, cedars and aspen. Mammals

that might be encountered while visiting natural areas of the Modoc Bioregion include the Pronghorn, Mule Deer, Bighorn Sheep, American Mink, Northern Grasshopper Mouse, Piute Ground Squirrel and White-tailed Jackrabbit.

Sacramento Valley

The Sacramento Valley is the watershed of the northern Sierra Nevada. Together with the San Joaquin Valley, these two bioregions make up California's Central Valley. The Sacramento Valley Bioregion is a unique system bordered by mountains to the north, east and west. Unlike the high-elevation mountain regions, winters here are cool, but snow rarely falls because the temperatures are usually above freezing. From about Thanksgiving through until the end of February the winter is frequently white from the heavy fogs that blanket most of the region. Summers fluctuate between heat waves at over 100° F, and cooling Delta Breezes that come in from the bay area. The two major rivers are the Sacramento and American rivers, and they carry water to the Sacramento–San Joaquin River Delta, which provides the water for two-thirds of California's population.

The Sacramento Valley Bioregion is a patchwork of natural areas including freshwater marshes, grasslands, oak forests and riparian forests. The marshlands here are an essential wintering habitat for many species of waterfowl, herons, egrets and birds of prey such as falcons and hawks. Many mammals live in the Sacramento Valley Bioregion, such as the Coyote, Bobcat, Northern River Otter, Ringtail, Common Muskrat, Western Pipistrelle and Desert Cottontail.

Sierra

The magnificent Sierra Nevada mountains—containing the headwaters that generate much of California's water supply—are the dominant feature of this bioregion. Rugged mountain peaks, coniferous and mixed forests, clear-blue lakes and swift rivers make the Sierra Bioregion both scenically beautiful and ecologically important. Mt. Whitney, at 14,496 ft., is not only the crown of the Sierra Bioregion, but it is the highest mountain in the contiguous United States. Because of the elevation difference throughout this region, the season can be very different from one place to the next. At high elevations, winters tend to be snowy and cold, while in areas of low elevation, winters are rainy and cool. Summers everywhere tend to be quite dry, but high elevations are still only cool to warm. The diversity of plants in the Sierra Bioregion is higher than in any other bioregion—this area contains more than half of the plant species known to occur in California. The typical forest has Ponderosa Pine, Sugar Pine, Black Oak, Red Fir, White Fir, Jeffrey Pine, Mountain Hemlock, Incense Cedar and Giant Sequoia. This bioregion boasts numerous state parks, eight national forests and three national parks: Yosemite, Kings Canyon and Sequoia. Like the plant diversity, the mammal diversity in this bioregion is also very high; up to two-thirds of California's mammals can be found here. The Bighorn Sheep, Mule Deer, American Black Bear, Wolverine, Fisher and Mountain Lion are some of the most charismatic species that live here, but other, smaller mammals are also abundant, including the Mountain Beaver, Long-eared Chipmunk, Golden-mantled Ground Squirrel, Spotted Bat and the rare Inyo Shrew.

Bay Area/Delta

This densely populated bioregion encompasses the San Francisco Bay Area and the Sacramento–San Joaquin River Delta. Much of this region has been altered by human development. Napa and Sonoma, two famous wine-producing counties, are found here. Year-round, the climate is humid. Summers tend to be warm or cool and sometimes foggy, and winters are usually cool but mild, and rainy. On very rare occasions, there may be wet, short-lived snowfalls. The different habitats in the Bay area include low coastal mountains,

salt marshes, redwood and mixed forests, coastal islands, freshwater marshes and coastal prairies. Oaks, redwoods, Douglas-fir, pine and manzanitas are just a few of the varied plant species found in this diverse landscape. The salt marshes and freshwater marshes are extremely important to migrating birds. All marsh zones—rich in bird diversity—are popular sites for birdwatchers and wildlife enthusiasts. The San Francisco Bay area boasts an increasing population of Sea Otters, thanks to an excellent recovery program. Other mammals that inhabit this region include the Harbor Seal, Common Gray Fox, Mule Deer, Bobcat, Virginia Opossum, Sonoma Chipmunk and Salt-marsh Harvest Mouse.

Central Coast

The Central Coast Bioregion is a unique and beautiful part of the state. Alas, this region also suffers many threats from increasing urbanization and industry. The marine environment here is extremely productive, but unsustainable harvesting and water contaminants pose major problems. The diverse landscape of this bioregion supports a large human population. Land usage includes agriculture, such as fruits, vegetables, vineyards and cattle ranching. The climate is mild, with seasonal rains and fog. Major landscape features include coastal mountains, dunes and interior forests. Chaparral, mixed hardwood forests, redwood forests and oak woodlands dominate, and Los Padres National Forest encompasses much of the southern parts of this bioregion. Introduced plant and animal species are numerous here, and many have become significant problems to resource managers and environmentalists alike. The Hearst Ranch, a major tourist destination, is found in the central coastal part of this bioregion and is home to many exotic species of mammals. Historically, the Hearst Ranch contained a private "zoo" where visitors could see animals in an open landscape. Unfortunately, long-term mismanagement resulted in several non-native species becoming naturalized and non-regulated residents. In the vicinity of Hearst Ranch are escaped Burchell's Zebras, Himalayan Tahrs, Sambar Deer, White Fallow Deer and Barbary Sheep, among others. Still, native mammals are predominant in this bioregion, and include the California Sea-Lion, Elk, Mountain Lion, Long-tailed Weasel, Dusky-footed Woodrat, Brush Rabbit and Western Mastiff Bat. Humpback and Gray whales are seasonally common along the coast as their migration takes them either north to colder, food-rich waters or south to warmer waters where they bear their calves.

San Joaquin Valley

The fertile San Joaquin Valley supports a major agriculture industry and is the leading fruit and vegetable producing region in the state. It was once rich in wetlands and wetland wildlife, but as much as 95 percent of this region dried as water was diverted for irrigation elsewhere. Perhaps more so here than in any other bioregion of California, human activity has resulted in a monumental change in the landscape and micro-climate. Remnants of grasslands with abundant ponds and marshes are protected in reserves and wildlife areas, but the overall habitat conversion evident in this valley is staggering. The Tule Elk State Reserve contains some natural habitat of the San Joaquin Valley, and provides a home for many threatened and endangered species. Also, the Kern National Wildlife Refuge has seasonal wetlands and provides habitat for a large variety of migrant and resident birds. Riparian areas, once abundant in this grassland-wetland habitat, are much reduced. As much as one-fifth of the remaining riparian areas are found in the South Fork Wildlife Area, in the southwestern part of the bioregion. The seasons in the San Joaquin Valley are more pronounced than in the Central Coast Bioregion, but milder than in the Sierra Bioregion to the east. Winters here tend to be moist with heavy fog, while summers are long, hot and dry. Mammals of this bioregion include the Bobcat, American Badger, Kit Fox, Fresno Kangaroo Rat, San Joaquin Pocket Mouse and Nelson's Antelope Squirrel.

Mojave

The dramatic landscape of the Mojave Bioregion is a mosaic of sweeping deserts, rugged peaks, outlandish Joshua Tree woodlands and verdant palm oases. Elevation here ranges from isolated peaks at up to 7000 ft. to 282 ft. below sea level, the lowest elevation in North America. Fully one-quarter of California—25 million acres—is represented in the Mojave Bioregion, a portion of an expansive desert system that also includes southern Nevada and a bit of southwestern Utah. The climate in the Mojave Bioregion is hot and dry in summer and cold in the winter. Winter may bring rainstorms that drench the area and create localized flash floods. The Joshua Tree and the California Fan Palm are the most distinctive trees in this region. Both are monocot trees, which puts them in a subgroup of flowering plants that also includes orchids and grasses. The California Fan Palm comprises the palm oases that are found here in the desert. These oases are rare; there are only 158 of them in North America. National parks and other protected areas are numerous in this bioregion. The three national parks here, Death Valley (encompassing the lowest elevation in North America), Joshua Tree and Mojave, attract wilderness and wildlife enthusiasts from around the world. Several of the small mammals found in this bioregion, such as the White-tailed Antelope Squirrel and Desert Kangaroo Rat, have special adaptations that allow them to live in dry desert habitats. Other mammals in the Mojave Bioregion include the Mule Deer, Bighorn Sheep, American Badger, Ringtail, Kit Fox, Coyote, Southern Grasshopper Mouse and Round-tailed Ground Squirrel.

South Coast

Discussion of the landscape of the South Coast Bioregion would not be complete without mention of the large, densely populated cities. Los Angeles, a legendary city of spaghetti junctions and skyscrapers, is a significant and unmistakable feature of the South Coast. The cities of this bioregion juxtapose the natural diversity of rugged coastal mountains, rolling hills, coastal sage scrub, woodlands and coastal marshlands. The negative effects of development on the ecosystem are especially apparent in this bioregion. The natural habitats here are endangered and shrinking, as industry and development encroach upon and alter the land. Proliferation of introduced species is another issue of major concern. With warm year-round temperatures, the environment is especially well-suited to the establishment of fair-weather species that find their way here either by accidental transportation or intentional introduction. This problem is not limited to mammalian species; exotic species in this region include plants, birds, terrestrial and marine invertebrates and even several amphibians and reptiles. Fortunately, many parks and reserves have been set up to protect natural habitats and the species that depend on them. Although the prime attractions in this region are probably Disneyland and Hollywood, there are numerous national wildlife refuges, and a surprising 29 percent of the region is national forest. Channel Islands National Park is home to the endemic Island Gray Fox, as well as marine mammals, such as the Harbor Seal, Northern Elephant Seal, Guadalupe Fur Seal and California and Northern Sea-Lions. In the waters around the islands are numerous dolphin, whale and porpoise species; whale-watching trips frequently encounter Gray Whales, Humpback Whales, Dall's Porpoises and dolphins. Terrestrial mammals that inhabit the South Coast Bioregion—especially in the national wildlife refuges—include the Mountain Lion, Bobcat, Ringtail, Desert Woodrat, Agile Kangaroo Rat, California Ground Squirrel and Townsend's Big-eared Bat.

Colorado Desert

As its name suggests, this small bioregion is largely delineated by the Colorado Desert, which is the western extreme of the Sonoran Desert that extends into Arizona and northwestern New Mexico. Overall, this desert is at a much lower elevation than the Mojave Desert to the north. Elevations here are mainly around 1000 ft., while the peaks reach only 3000 ft. The climate here is hot and dry in the summer and cool and moist in winter. The dominant habitats of the Colorado Desert Bioregion include sandy deserts, palm oases, small mountains, scrubby flatlands and alluvial slopes called bajadas. Most of this bioregion is under federal government management, and due to the lack of roads, much is inaccessible. This bioregion is an excellent destination for wildlife enthusiasts. Bird watching is at its best along the Colorado River and around Salton Sea. State parks and wildlife refuges such as the Picacho State Recreation Area, Salton Sea National Wildlife Refuge, Dos Palmas Preserve and Imperial National Wildlife Refuge (located mainly in Arizona) are some of this bioregion's best attractions. Among the varied wildlife of the desert are the Mule Deer, Bighorn Sheep, Coyote, Kit Fox, Bobcat, Black-tailed Jackrabbit, White-tailed Antelope Squirrel and California Leaf-nosed Bat.

Human-altered Landscapes

The impact of human activity on natural environments is visible throughout California. Cities, roadways, agricultural areas and forestry and mining sites are just a few examples of the impact we have had on the land. Many of the most common plants and animals in these altered landscapes were not present before the arrival of Europeans and modern transportation. In fact, California, Hawaii and Florida have the highest number of introduced species and ratio of introduced versus native species. The House Mouse, Norway Rat, Black Rat and Wild Boar are some of the most well established of the introduced species.

Seasonality

The seasons of California can influence the lives of mammals. Aside from bats and marine mammals, most species are confined to relatively slow forms of terrestrial travel. As a result, they have limited geographic ranges and must cope in various ways with the changing seasons.

With rising temperatures, reduced rain or snow and the greening of the landscape, spring brings renewal. At this time of year, many mammals bear their young. The abundance of food cycles through the food chain; lush new growth provides ample food for herbivores, and the numerous herbivore young become easy prey for the carnivorous mammals. While some small mammals, particularly the shrews and rodents, mature within weeks, offspring of the larger mammals depend on their parents for much longer periods.

In California, summers may be a time of growth and recovery from winter, or a time of stress from heat and aridity. In northern and mountain areas where winter is a sparse and cold season, some animals must eat vast quantities of food in the summer to build up fat reserves, while others work furiously to stockpile food caches in safe places. Elsewhere, especially in the south and along the coast, winter is a time of rain and is less stressful on animals.

For some of the more charismatic species, such as ungulates, fall is the time for mating. At this time of year, male Bighorn Sheep demonstrate extremes of aggression and vigilance. Many small mammals, however, such as voles and mice, mate every few months or even year-round.

An important aspect of seasonality is its effect on species composition. When you visit the northern mountain regions in winter, for example, you will see a different group of mammals than in summer. Many species, such as ground squirrels and American Black Bears, are dormant in winter. Conversely, many ungulates may be more visible in winter because they enter lowland meadows to find edible vegetation.

Watching Mammals

Many types of mammals are most active at night, so the best times for viewing are during the "wildlife hours" at dawn and at dusk. At these times of day, mammals are out from their daytime hideouts, moving through areas where they are more easily encountered. During winter, hunger may force certain mammals to be more active during midday. Conversely, in favorable seasons, some mammals may become less active and less visible.

Within the protected reserves and national parks of California, many of the larger mammals can be viewed easily from the safety of a vehicle. If you walk backcountry trails, however, you can find yourself right in the homes of certain mammals.

Although people have become more conscious of the need to protect wildlife, the pressures of increased human visitation have nevertheless damaged critical habitats, and some species have experienced frequent harassment. Modern wildlife viewing demands courtesy and common sense. While some of the mammals that are encountered in California appear easy to approach, it is important to respect your own safety as much as the safety of the animal being viewed. This advice seems obvious for the larger species (although it is ignorantly dismissed in some instances), but it applies equally to small mammals. Honor both the encounter and the animal by demonstrating a respect appropriate to the occasion. Here are some points to remember for ethical wildlife watching in the field:

• Confine your movements to designated trails and roads, wherever provided. This allows animals to adapt to human use in the area and also minimizes your impact on the habitat.

• Avoid dens and resting sites, and never touch or feed wild animals. Baby animals are seldom orphaned or abandoned, and it is against the law to take them away.

• Stress is harmful to wildlife, so never chase or flush animals from cover. Use binoculars and keep a respectful distance, for the animal's sake and often for your own.

• Leave the environment, including both flora and fauna, unchanged by your visits. Take home only pictures and memories.

• Pets are a hindrance to wildlife viewing. They may chase, injure or kill other animals, so control your pets or leave them at home.

• Take the time to learn about wildlife and the behavior and sensitivity of each species.

Top Mammal Watching Sites

Death Valley National Park

Despite its foreboding name, Death Valley can be an exciting place for a holiday. The national park covers over 3 million acres of western desert, and elevations range from the Badwater Basin saltpan at 282 ft. below sea level to the summit of Telescope Peak at 11,049 ft. This park includes many extreme zones such as saltpans, subalpine and even some regions that rank among the hottest and driest places on Earth. All of the species of animals and plants found here exhibit adaptations to help them survive in extreme conditions. Fifty-one species of native mammals live in the park, and although small mammals are more numerous than large mammals, keep your eyes open for Desert Bighorn, Bobcats, Mountain Lion, Mule Deer and, at night, Kit Foxes.

Yosemite National Park

Perhaps California's most famous national park, Yosemite is an excellent destination for visitors interested in dramatic scenery and unbeatable wildlife encounters. Located in the central Sierra Nevada, this park contains thousands of lake and ponds, rugged mountains, 1600 miles of streams and 800 miles of hiking trails. The park's bioregions include chaparral/oak woodlands, lower montane, upper montane, subalpine and alpine. As well, you may find yourself venturing into rare and magnificient sequoia groves. Eighty-five species of mammals are found within the boundaries of the park. While exploring Yosemite, you may be lucky enough to encounter Black Bears, Fishers, foxes and perhaps a Mountain Beaver (Aplodontia). Persistence might even lead you to the endemic Mount Lyell Shrew.

Klamath Basin National Wildlife Refuges

This union of six wildlife refuges encompasses extensive wetland, meadow and forest habitats. Three of the refuges are located in Oregon, while Lower Klamath, Tule Lake and Clear Lake Refuges are mostly in California.

MAMMAL-WATCHING SITES IN CALIFORNIA

1. Death Valley National Park
2. Yosemite National Park
3. Klamath Basin National Wildlife Refuges
4. Sequoia and Kings Canyon National Parks
5. Santa Monica Mountains National Recreation Area
6. Mojave National Preserve
7. Joshua Tree National Park
8. Redwood National and State Parks
9. Point Keyes National Seashore

The mixed habitat is home to a wide diversity of birds, amphibians and mammals. Seventy-eight species of mammals are known or suspected to occur on or near the Klamath refuges. Along with dozens of bird species, look for Yellow-Pine Chipmunks, Mountain Cottontails, Northern River Otters, Raccoons, Mule Deer and Rocky Mountain Elk.

Sequoia and Kings Canyon National Parks

Sequoia was California's first official national park. It was formed in 1890, exactly 50 years before its counterpart, Kings Canyon, was established. The two adjoining parks are managed as one. The park boasts an enormous elevation range, from 1360 ft. to 14,491 ft. This vast range encompasses a wide diversity of ecosystems and wildlife. The dominant plant communities include groves of giant sequoia, vast tracts of montane forests, spectacular alpine habitats and chaparral/oak woodlands. More than 70 species of mammals are found in the park, including Wolverines, Badgers, foxes, Martens, Golden-mantled Ground Squirrels, Black Bear, Pikas and Yellow-bellied Marmots.

Santa Monica Mountains National Recreation Area

Rising above Los Angeles, this national recreation area comprises 153,075 acres and is the world's largest urban national park. Furthermore, this park protects one of the world's last remaining examples of a relatively undisturbed Mediterranean-type ecosystem. The diverse geography in the park produces a wide variety of bioregions, including oak woodland, several types of chaparral, coastal sage scrub, valley oak savanna, grassland, riparian woodland, wetland and coastal marsh. Despite being so close to heavily impacted urban areas, the park has over 450 vertebrate species, including over 50 species of native mammals. Habitat fragmentation and encroachment of urban development threaten the species that still thrive here, but ongoing management strategies are committed to maintaining suitable habitat for species such as Mountain Lions, foxes, Badgers, Ringtails, Spotted Skunks and Long-tailed Weasels.

Mojave National Preserve

The Mojave National Preserve protects parts of the Mojave, Great Basin, and Sonoran deserts, three of the four major deserts that occur in North America. The park's geology is varied and beautiful; it includes ancient mountain ranges, sand dunes, giant mesas and remnants of volcanic domes and lava flows. This national preserve also boasts one of the largest Joshua tree forests. Other vegetative regions include white fir stands, chaparral, and communities of cactus. Many of the vertebrates here are nocturnal in order to avoid the daytime temperature extremes. Mammals you may encounter here include Mountain Lions, Bighorn Sheep, skunks and Kit Fox. Nocturnal small mammals, such as bats, kangaroo mice and pocket mice, are numerous.

Joshua Tree National Park

Joshua Tree National Park protects nearly 800,000 acres of land, including three main ecosystems: the Colorado Desert, the Mojave Desert and the Little San Bernadino Mountains. This park contains a vast variety of desert plants, and Joshua trees can be found throughout much of the park. Scarcity of food in the desert zones limits the number of large mammals that can be supported, but small mammals are common. Small mammals of the desert tend to live in burrows, where they can avoid the heat of the day and the desiccating, dry air. Hiking and exploring this park is exciting; landscape features include rugged mountains, granitic monoliths and earthquake faults. While trying to avoid the six species of rattlesnakes found in the park, you may encounter any of the 52 mammal species that live here. The most desirable mammals to see include desert Bighorn Sheep, Kit Foxes, Bobcats and Mountain Lions. Look for Bighorn Sheep and Mule Deer close to a water source such as a spring.

Redwood National and State Parks

The Redwood parks comprise several parks united as one protected area. The parks include Prairie Creek Redwoods State Park, Del Norte Coast Redwoods State Park, Jedediah Smith Redwoods State Park, and Redwood National Park. Together these parks are a World Heritage Site and an International Biosphere Reserve. The Redwood parks protect 45 percent of all the old-growth redwood forest remaining in California. Redwood trees can live to be 2000 years old and stand over 300 ft. Protecting these trees has other conservation benefits; this park contains over

104,000 acres of land, including prairie and oak woodlands. The Redwood parks also protect the coast and seaside submerged area, totaling nearly 6000 acres. At least 75 species of mammals are represented in the park, including both terrestrial and marine mammals. Mountain Lions, Black Bears and Roosevelt Elk are among the largest of the terrestrial mammals, while on the coast the California Sea Lions, Harbor Seals and Gray Whales are among the most visible marine mammals.

Point Reyes National Seashore

The spectacularly beautiful Point Reyes National Seashore encompasses rugged coastline, open beaches and rolling mountains that resemble a Mediterranean ecosystem. Forests within the park include bishop pine and Douglas-fir communities. At least 80 species of mammals occur in the park, including a variety of marine mammals. Up to 20 species of dolphins and whales can sometimes be seen from the mainland. Point Reyes is an excellent place for viewing and photographing Northern Elephant Seals, which have made a comeback here since 1970. Prior to 1970, hunting had decimated their populations. When hiking through the park, you may encounter River and Sea Otters, Mountain Beaver (Aplodontia), Virginia Opossum, Long-tailed Weasels, Fallow Deer and the rare Tule Elk.

About This Book

This guide has full accounts for 178 species of wild and feral mammals that have been reported in California. Domestic farm animals, such as cattle, sheep and llamas, are not described here, nor are many of the introduced species. Although many whales, dolphins and porpoises are known to occur in the waters off California, only those that are most common and most likely to be encountered near shore are included. Humans, a member of the order Primates, have lived in this region at least since the end of the last Pleistocene glaciation, but the relationship between our species and the natural world is well beyond the scope of this book.

Organization

Biologists divide mammals (class Mammalia) into a number of subgroups, called orders, which form the basis for the organization of this book. Nine mammalian orders have wild or feral representatives in California: even-toed hoofed mammals (Artiodactyla); odd-toed hoofed mammals (Perissodactyla); whales, dolphins and porpoises (Cetacea); carnivores (Carnivora); rodents (Rodentia); hares and pikas (Lagomorpha); bats (Chiroptera); insectivores (Insectivora) and marsupials (subclass Marsupialia, order Didelphimorphia). In turn, each order is subdivided into families, which group together the more closely related species. For example, within the carnivores, the Wolverine and the American Mink, which are both in the weasel family, are more closely related to each other than either is to the Striped Skunk, which is in its own family.

Mammal Names

Although the international zoological community closely monitors the use of scientific names for animals, common names—which change with time, local language and usage—are more difficult to standardize. In the case of birds, the American Ornithologists' Union has been very effective in standardizing the common names used by professionals and recreational naturalists alike. There is, as yet, no similar organization to oversee and approve the common names of mammals in North America, which can lead to some confusion.

For example, many people apply the name "mole" to pocket gophers, burrowing mammals that leave loose cores of dirt in fields and reminded early settlers of the moles they knew in the East and in Europe. To add to the confusion, most people use the name "gopher" to refer not to pocket gophers, but to the more observable ground squirrels. If you consider non-mammalian species, it would get even worse. The name gopher is used in many parts of North America to denote a species of snake and even a tortoise!

You may think that such confusion is limited to the less charismatic species of animals, but even some of the best-known mammals are victims of human inconsistency. Most people clearly know the identities of the Moose and the Elk, but these names can cause great confusion for European visitors. The species that we know as the Elk, *Cervus elaphus*, is called the Red Deer in Europe, while "Elk" is the name Europeans use for *Alces alces* ("elk" and "alces" come from the same root), which is known as the Moose in North America. The blame for this confusion falls on the early European settlers, who misapplied the name "Elk" to populations of *Cervus elaphus*. In an as-yet-unsuccessful attempt to resolve the confusion, many naturalists use the name "Wapiti" for the species *Cervus elaphus* in North America.

Despite the lack of an "official" list of mammal common names, there are some widely accepted standards, such as the "Revised checklist of North American mammals north of Mexico, 1997" (Jones et al. 1997, Occasional Papers, Museum of Texas Tech University, No. 173), *The Smithsonian Book of North American Mammals* (Wilson and Ruff 1999) and *Common Names of Mammals of the World* (Wilson and Cole 2000). This book follows these sources for the scientific names of mammals and, for the most part, for common names as well.

Range Maps

Mapping the range of a species is a problematic endeavor: mammal populations fluctuate, distributions expand and shrink, and dispersing individuals are occasionally encountered in unexpected areas. The range maps included in this book are intended to show the distribution of breeding/sustaining populations in the region, and not the extent of individual specimen records. Full color intensity on the map indicates a species' presence; pale areas show its absence. Within the full-color range, the species may be found in its suitable habitat. For species with especially small ranges, arrows are used to help locate the range. A question mark may be used to indicate uncertainty about the presence of a species.

Similar Species

Before you finalize your decision on the species identity of a mammal, check the "Similar Species" section of the account; it briefly describes other mammals that could be mistakenly identified as the species you are considering. By concentrating on the most relevant field marks, the subtle differences between species can be reduced to easily identifiable traits. As you become more experienced at identifying mammals, you might find you can immediately short-list an animal to a few possible species. By consulting this section you can quickly glean the most relevant field marks to distinguish between those species, thereby simplifying the identification process.

The MAMMALS

HOOFED MAMMALS

These mammals include the "megaherbivores" of California: they all fall into the largest size class of terrestrial mammals and most eat plants exclusively. All of the native hoofed mammals in the region belong to the order Artiodactyla (even-toed hoofed mammals). Wild Pigs can be found in scattered populations in the United States, and although they are not native here, they are Artiodactyls. All even-toed hoofed mammals have either two or four toes on each limb. If there are four toes, the outer two, which are called dewclaws, are always smaller and higher on the leg, touching the ground only in soft mud or snow. Horses, which are not native to North America, belong to the order Perissodactyla (odd-toed hoofed mammals) and have just a single toe on each foot. Another difference between the two orders of hoofed mammals is in the structure of their ankle bones. The ankle bones of all even-toed hoofed mammals are grooved on both their upper and lower surfaces, which enables these animals to rise from a reclined position with their hindquarters first. This ability means that the large hindleg muscles are available for fight or flight more quickly than in odd-toed hoofed mammals, such as horses, which must rise front first. Additionally, the native even-toed hoofed mammals have incisors only on the lower jaw; they have a cartilaginous pad at the front of the upper jaw instead of teeth. Nearly all hoofed mammals are strict herbivores. The Wild Pig is the only hoofed mammal in California that is omnivorous and that has upper incisors and canines.

In California, several of the native hoofed mammals are divided into well-known subspecies. Three subspecies of Elk, for example, inhabit the state: the Tule Elk, Roosevelt Elk and Rocky Mountain Elk. Also, the Black-tailed Deer is a subspecies of the Mule Deer and is common in the coastal ranges. Although these subspecies have distinct appearances, they are not genetically different enough to be considered as separate species. For example, the subspecies are capable of interbreeding and producing viable offspring.

Cattle Family (Bovidae)

Native bovids are distinguished by the presence of true horns in both the male and female. The horns are never shed, nor are they branched, and they grow throughout the animal's life. They consist of a keratinous sheath (keratin is the main type of protein in our fingernails and hair) over a bony core that grows from the frontal bones of the skull. Like the deer and allies, bovids are cud chewers, and they have complex, four-chambered stomachs to digest their meals.

Bighorn Sheep

Pronghorn Family (Antilocapridae)

This exclusively North American family contains just the one species. The Pronghorn has only two toes (no dew-claws), and (like the other native artiodactyls) it lacks upper canine teeth (as well as upper incisors). Both sexes have true horns, but unlike bovids, the Pronghorn sheds and regrows the keratinous sheath each year (the bony core is not shed). The darkly colored sheath (but not the bony core) is branched, hence the name *pronghorn*.

Pronghorn

Deer Family (Cervidae)

Mule Deer

In North America, all adult male cervids (and female Caribou) have antlers, which are bony outgrowths of the frontal skull bones that are shed and regrown annually. In males with an adequate diet, the antlers generally get larger each year. New antlers are soft and tender, and they are covered with "velvet," a layer of skin with short, fine hairs and a network of blood vessels to nourish the growing antlers. The antlers stop growing in late summer, and as the velvet dries the deer rubs it off. Cervids are also distinguished by the presence of scent glands in pits just in front of the eyes. Like all native artiodactyls, their lower canine teeth look like incisors, so there appear to be four pairs of lower incisors.

Swine Family (Suidae)

The Old World Swine includes eight species that originated in Eurasia and Africa. All eight still thrive in only these countries, except for the Domestic Pig (*Sus scrofa*), which has been widely introduced in most areas of human habitation. Despite its name, the Domestic Pig now ranges free in many parts of North America, and these feral populations can become quite large. These free ranging pigs are now called Wild Pigs or Feral Pigs, and they are the same species as the European Wild Boar. Wild Boar were also introduced, and these two varieties of swine sometimes hybridize in North America. Wild Pigs are the only artiodactyls here to have upper incisors and upper canines; also, the canines are modified as tusks.

Wild Boar

Horse Family (Equidae)

Horse

All members of this family, which also includes zebras and donkeys, have a single toe on each limb, a bushy dorsal mane and a long, well-haired tail. Although horse-like animals were once native to North America, they disappeared from our continent more than 10,000 years ago. The herds of feral Horses and burros that are now found in several places throughout the western United States are descended from domestic animals.

American Bison
Bison bison

Historically, millions of American Bison lived in North America. Evidence of their once-great presence can still be found, even where bison no longer roam. Stained bones spill yearly from riverbanks, and large isolated boulders are often smoothly polished and set in shallow pits from thousands of years of itchy bison rubbing their hides for relief.

California never had a large population of bison, compared to that of the central states, and natural populations were extirpated from the state. Reintroduced populations live on Santa Catalina Island and on the mainland around Camp Pendelton, San Diego County.

Similarly, bison elsewhere in North America live primarily in isolated or protected areas and on private ranches. Since grasslands—their primary habitat—have been converted almost completely to agricultural fields, bison have become more common in mountain parks. Montane regions are marginal habitat for these large herbivores, but mountain parks now provide some of the best habitat and protection for these indigenous bovines. Yellowstone National Park may hold the largest herds today.

The bison, a truly majestic animal, has become symbolic of the difficulties involved in trying to "manage" nature. Many bison are carriers of the disease brucellosis, which, if transmitted to domestic cattle, causes cows to miscarry. There has never been a confirmed case of brucellosis transmission from wild bison to domestic cattle—cattle would have to come into contact with either infected birthing material or a wet newborn calf of an infected bison to contract the disease—but many populations of bison are subject to culling and even slaughter if they leave protected area boundaries. Understandably, debates rage between advocates of bison protection and those people worried about brucellosis transmission to cattle.

ALSO CALLED: American Buffalo.

DESCRIPTION: The head and forequarters are covered with long, shaggy, woolly, dark brown hair that abruptly becomes shorter and lighter brown behind the shoulders. The head is massive and appears to be carried low because of the high shoulder hump and massive forequarters. Both sexes have short, round, black horns that curve upward. The legs are short and clothed in shaggy hair. The long tail has a tuft of hair at the tip. A bison calf is reddish at birth but becomes darker by its first fall.

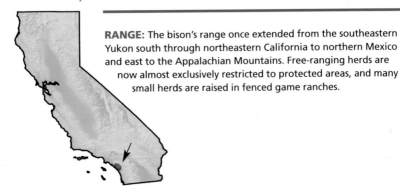

RANGE: The bison's range once extended from the southeastern Yukon south through northeastern California to northern Mexico and east to the Appalachian Mountains. Free-ranging herds are now almost exclusively restricted to protected areas, and many small herds are raised in fenced game ranches.

Total Length: 6¹⁄₂–13 ft.
Shoulder Height: 3¹⁄₄–6¹⁄₂ ft.
Tail Length: 12–28 in.
Weight: 790–2400 lb.

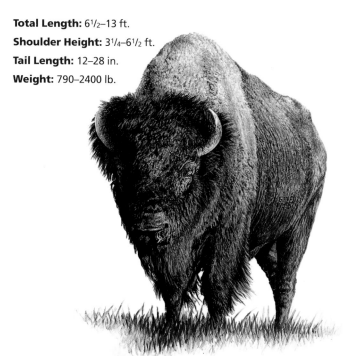

HABITAT: Although the American Bison was historically most abundant in grasslands, it also inhabited alpine tundra, areas of montane and boreal forest and aspen parkland with abundant short vegetation.

FOOD: Most of the diet is made up of grasses, sedges and forbs. In sparse seasons, the American Bison sometimes browses on shrubs, cattails and lichens, but grasses are still the primary food.

DEN: Bison typically bed down at night and during the hottest part of the day to ruminate. After a herd has been in an area for a while, it will leave behind wallows—dusty, saucer-like depressions where the bison rolled and rubbed repeatedly.

YOUNG: After a gestation of 9 to 10 months, a cow bison typically gives birth to a single 40-lb. precocial calf in May. It begins to graze at about one week, but it is not weaned until it is about seven months old. A cow typically mates for the first time at two or three years old. A bull is sexually mature then, too, but competition from older males normally prevents him from breeding until he is seven to eight years old.

SIMILAR SPECIES: No other native mammal resembles an American Bison. The only other native bovid, the **Bighorn Sheep** (p. 34) looks very different and lives in a different habitat.

DID YOU KNOW?

If bison are caught by a storm away from shelter, they face into the wind, relying on the woolly coat of their head and shoulders to block the chill.

Bighorn Sheep
Ovis canadensis

One of the most recognizable symbols of North American wilderness is the male Bighorn Sheep. In California, this handsome native bovine inhabits rocky mountainous regions. Although Bighorn Sheep have a well-developed sense of balance and are at home on distant steep slopes and rocky ledges, they are also sometimes seen along roadsides in parks and wildlife areas.

Bighorn Sheep numbers in California are stable, but their numbers are not high. Recent population decline caused by hunting has been curtailed, but the bighorn numbers still show little sign of increase. Every year, however, people visiting natural areas are rewarded with sightings of bighorns. Provided that people are unobtrusive and non-aggressive, they can catch glimpses of the sheep's natural behavior amidst the beautiful mountain scenery. As friendly and quiet as a Bighorn Sheep appears, however, always remember that it is a wild animal and should be treated as such.

Bighorn lambs that are too young and too small to have mastered the sanctuary of cliffs are particularly vulnerable to predation by carnivores. Newborn lambs occasionally become prey for eagles, Mountain Lions and Bobcats. Provided they survive their first year, most Bighorns live long lives—few of their natural predators can match the Bighorn Sheep's sure-footedness and vertical agility.

The magnificent courtship battles between Bighorn rams have made these animals favorites of TV wildlife specials and corporate advertising. During October and November, adult rams establish a breeding hierarchy that is based on the relative sizes of their horns and the outcomes of their impressive head-to-head combats. In battle, opposing rams rise on their hindlegs, run a few steps toward one another and smash their horns together with a magnificent bang. Once the breeding hierarchy has been established, mating takes place, after which the rams and ewes tend to split into separate herds. For the most part, the rams abandon their head blows until the next fall, but broken horns and ribs are reminders of their clashes.

ALSO CALLED: Mountain Sheep.

DESCRIPTION: This robust, brownish sheep has a bobbed tail and a large, white rump patch. The belly, the insides of the legs and the end of the muzzle are also white. The brown coat is darkest in fall, gradually fading with winter wear. It looks motley in June while the new coat

RANGE: From the Rocky Mountains of Alberta and west-central British Columbia, the Bighorn Sheep's range extends east to the Dakotas and south through California and New Mexico into northern Mexico.

Total Length: 5–6 ft.
Shoulder Height: 30–45 in.
Tail Length: 3¹/₄–5 in.
Weight: 120–340 lb.

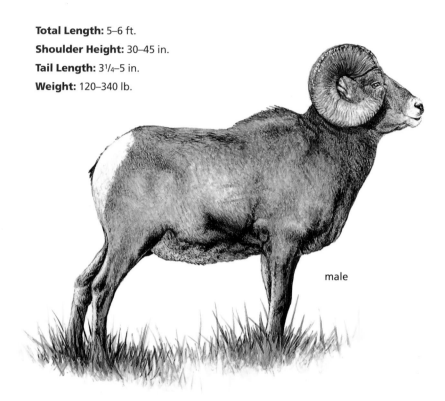

male

grows in. "Bighorn" is a well-deserved name, because the circumference of a ram's horns can be as much as 18 in. at the base. The curled horns can be over 43 in. long and spread 26 in. from tip to tip. Heavy ridges, the pattern of which is unique to each individual, run transversely across the horn. A deep groove forms each winter, which makes it possible to determine a sheep's age from its horns. A ewe's horns are shorter and noticeably more flattened from side to side than a ram's. Also, a ewe's horns never curl around to form even a half circle, whereas an older ram's horns may form a full curl or more.

HABITAT: Although it is most common in non-forested, mountainous areas where cliffs provide easy escape routes, the Bighorn Sheep can thrive outside the mountains as long as precipitous slopes are present in the vicinity of appropriate food and water. Some populations live along steep riverbanks and even in the gullied badlands of more arid environments.

FOOD: The diet consists primarily of broad-leaved, non-woody plants and grasses. Exposed, dry grasses on windswept slopes provide much of the winter food. The Bighorn Sheep exhibits a

DID YOU KNOW?

Bighorn rams occasionally interbreed with domestic ewes. The hybrids, which have the economically inferior, coarse hair of Bighorns, are a concern to wool ranchers as well as conservationists.

hoofprint

walking trail

ruminant's appetite for salt. To fulfill this need, herds may travel miles, even through dense forests, to reach natural salt licks. They often lick and eat the salty soil along roadways. This activity unfortunately increases the number of collisions with vehicles.

DEN: A Bighorn Sheep typically beds down for the night in a depression that is about 4 ft. wide and up to 1 ft. deep. The depression usually smells of urine and is almost always edged with the sheep's small droppings.

YOUNG: Typically, a ewe gives birth to a single precocial lamb in seclusion on a remote rocky ledge in late May or early June, after a gestation of about six months. The ewe and her lamb rejoin the herd within a few days. Initially, the lamb nurses every half hour; as it matures, it nurses less frequently, until it is weaned at about six months. Lambs are extremely agile and playful: they jump and run about, scale small cliffs, engage in mock fights and even leap over one another. These activities prepare them for escaping predators later in life.

Mule Deer

SIMILAR SPECIES: The **Mule Deer** (p. 46) also has a large, whitish rump patch and an overall brown color, but bucks have branched antlers, and does have no head protrusions (other than their ears).

Pronghorn

Antilocapra americana

Through the heat-blurred light of a grassland afternoon, the shape of a Pronghorn emerges from the brown landscape to stand and stare. Just as suddenly, it turns and retreats into the open plains. The Pronghorn superficially resembles a deer, and it is often called an antelope, but it has no close living relatives—it is the sole member of an ancient family of hoofed mammals that dates back 20 million years. This animal's unique, pronged horns are neither antlers nor true horns; only the outer keratinous sheath is shed each year, not the bony core.

In open landscape, the Pronghorn's phenomenal eyesight serves it well in detecting predators. The Pronghorn's large eyes protrude so far out from the sides of its head that it has stereoscopic vision to the rear as well as in front. A Pronghorn is rarely seen first.

Should danger press, a Pronghorn will erect the hairs of its white rump patch to produce a mirror-like flash that is visible at a great distance. Speed, which comes easily and quickly to the Pronghorn, is this animal's chief defense, and even three-day-old fawns are quite capable of outrunning a human. The Pronghorn is the swiftest of North America's land mammals, and is among the fastest in the world. With its efficient metabolism, powered by an extremely large heart and lungs for its body size, the Pronghorn can run at about 55 mph. for several minutes at a time. Its lack of dewclaws is also thought to be a result of its adaptation for speed.

For all its speed, the Pronghorn is a poor jumper, and its numbers declined rapidly with the fencing of rangelands throughout the west. In the 1800s Pronghorns were believed to have numbered in the millions, but by the early 1900s the total population in the United States was about 20,000. This decline was caused by a combination of restricted movement from fences and over-hunting. Pronghorn are still considered a game animal, and some hunting occurs. Fortunately, the efforts of government and private programs have helped increase their numbers.

The fences still remain on rangeland, but many people now construct fences suitable for a Pronghorn to fit underneath. Running Pronghorns surprise many passing motorists when, one after another, they hardly break stride to deftly dip beneath the lowest strand of barbed wire in a fence.

DESCRIPTION: The upperparts, legs and tail are generally tan. The belly, lower sides and lower jaw are white, and there

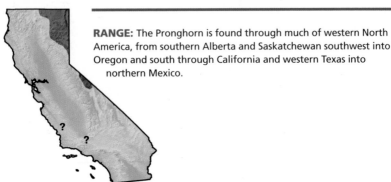

RANGE: The Pronghorn is found through much of western North America, from southern Alberta and Saskatchewan southwest into Oregon and south through California and western Texas into northern Mexico.

Total Length: 4–4³/₄ ft.
Shoulder Height: 32–41 in.
Tail Length: 3³/₈–6 in.
Weight: 70–140 lb.

are two broad white bands across the throat and a large white rump patch. There is a short, black-tipped mane on the nape of the neck. There are no dewclaws on the legs. Both sexes may have horns, but those of the doe are never as long as her ears and do not have the ivory-colored tips occasionally seen on the buck's. The buck's horns are straight near the base, and then bear a short branch or "prong" before they usually curve backward or inward to sharp tips. The muzzle is black, and on the buck the black extends over the face to the horn bases. The buck also has a broad black stripe running from the ear base to behind the lower jaw.

HABITAT: The Pronghorn is a staunch resident of relatively treeless areas. It inhabits open, often arid grasslands, grassy brushlands and semi-deserts and avoids woodlands.

FOOD: The winter diet is composed almost exclusively of sagebrush, bitterbrush and other woody shrubs. In spring, the diet switches to snowbrush, snowberry, rabbitbrush and sagebrush for 67 percent of the intake; forbs make up 17 percent, alfalfa and crops about 15 percent and grasses only 1 percent.

DID YOU KNOW?

Although Pronghorns typically give humans a wide berth, they can display an extreme curiosity, and a piece of plastic or a rag caught on a fence and waving in the breeze can often entice individuals to approach.

hoofprint

walking trail

DEN: Because it is a roaming animal that remains active day and night—it alternates short naps with watchful feeding—the Pronghorn does not maintain a home bed.

YOUNG: Forty percent of does bear a single precocial fawn with their first pregnancies, but 60 percent of first births and nearly all subsequent pregnancies result in the birth of twins. In June, a doe finds a secluded grassy spot to give birth, following a gestation period of $7^{1}/_{2}$ to 8 months. Fawns lie hidden in the grass at first, and their mothers return to nurse them about every $1^{1}/_{2}$ hours. The does gradually reduce the frequency of nursings, and when a fawn is about two weeks old and capable of outrunning most potential predators, mother and young rejoin the herd. Some does may breed during the short, mid- to late September breeding season of their first year, but most do not breed until their second year.

Mule Deer

SIMILAR SPECIES: The **Mule Deer** (p. 46) has a white rump, but it is larger, and the bucks have antlers, not black horns. Deer also lack the white throat bands and white lower sides of the Pronghorn.

Elk
Cervus elaphus

The bugle of the bull Elk is as much a symbol of fall as golden leaves and the first frost. The Elk has likely always held some form of fascination for humans, as evidenced by native hunting and lore, but it is another of North America's large mammals that suffered widespread extirpation during the time of settlement and agricultural expansion across the continent.

The dramatic decline of Elk in North America during the 19th century prompted wide-scale conservation efforts for remnant populations and far-reaching reintroduction programs to form new herds. Even the great numbers of Elk currently seen in mountain parks owe their presence to mitigative human efforts.

In California there are three subspecies of Elk, the Rocky Mountain Elk, the Roosevelt Elk and the Tule Elk. The Roosevelt Elk subspecies (*C. e. roosevelti*) is usually darker in color and the males tend to develop a "cup" on the royal tine of their antlers. This cup gives the tip of the antlers a slightly palmate appearance. Roosevelt Elk live in coastal mountains and can be found in northwestern California. The Rocky Mountain Elk subspecies (*C. e. nelsoni*) inhabits parts of Shasta county, and has been introduced into Kern and San Luis Obispo counties. The Tule Elk (*C. e. nannodes*) is the smallest of the three subspecies and is found in a few scattered populations in central and southern counties.

Elk form breeding harems to a greater degree than most other deer. A bull Elk that is a harem master expends a considerable amount of energy during the fall rut—his fierce battles with rival bulls and the upkeep of cows in his harem demand more work than time permits—and he frequently starts winter in a weakened state. Once the rut is over, however, bulls fatten up by as much as a pound a day. Cows and young Elk, on the other hand, usually see the sparse winter season while they are fat and healthy. This disparity makes sense in evolutionary terms: many cows enter winter pregnant with the next generation for the Elk population, whereas, once winter arrives, the older bulls' major contributions are past.

Fortunately for Elk, much of their inhabited areas in California have become more accessible to grazing, even during winter. Artificially lush golf courses and agricultural fields supply high-quality forage throughout the year, while roads, townsites and other human activity have eliminated most major predators—except, of course, humans.

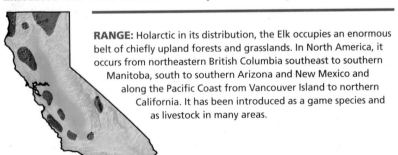

RANGE: Holarctic in its distribution, the Elk occupies an enormous belt of chiefly upland forests and grasslands. In North America, it occurs from northeastern British Columbia southeast to southern Manitoba, south to southern Arizona and New Mexico and along the Pacific Coast from Vancouver Island to northern California. It has been introduced as a game species and as livestock in many areas.

Total Length: 6½–8½ ft.
Shoulder Height: 4–5 ft.
Tail Length: 4¾–7 in.
Weight: 400–1100 lb.

male

In wilder areas, Elk are typically most active during the daytime, particularly near dawn and dusk, but they often become nocturnal in areas of high human activity where hunting occurs.

ALSO CALLED: Wapiti.

DESCRIPTION: The summer coat is generally golden brown. The winter coat is longer and grayish brown. Year-round, the head, neck and legs are darker brown, and there is a large yellowish to orangish rump patch bordered by black or dark brown fur. The oval metatarsal glands on the outside of the hocks are outlined by stiff yellowish hairs. A bull Elk has a dark brown throat mane, and he starts growing antlers in his second year. By his fourth year, the bull's antlers typically bear six points to a side, but there is considerable variation both in the number of points a bull will have and the age when he acquires the full complement of six. A bull rarely has seven or eight points. The antlers are usually shed in spring. New ones begin to grow by late spring, becoming mature in August.

HABITAT: Although the Elk prefers upland forests and grasslands, it sometimes ranges into high altitude zones,

---

DID YOU KNOW?

By the end of the 1800s Elk had disappeared from eastern North America, and two subspecies became extinct. From an estimated low of perhaps 41,000 for the entire continent, the species has since recovered to probably over 1 million. Elk are becoming popular livestock animals, so their numbers may increase still more.

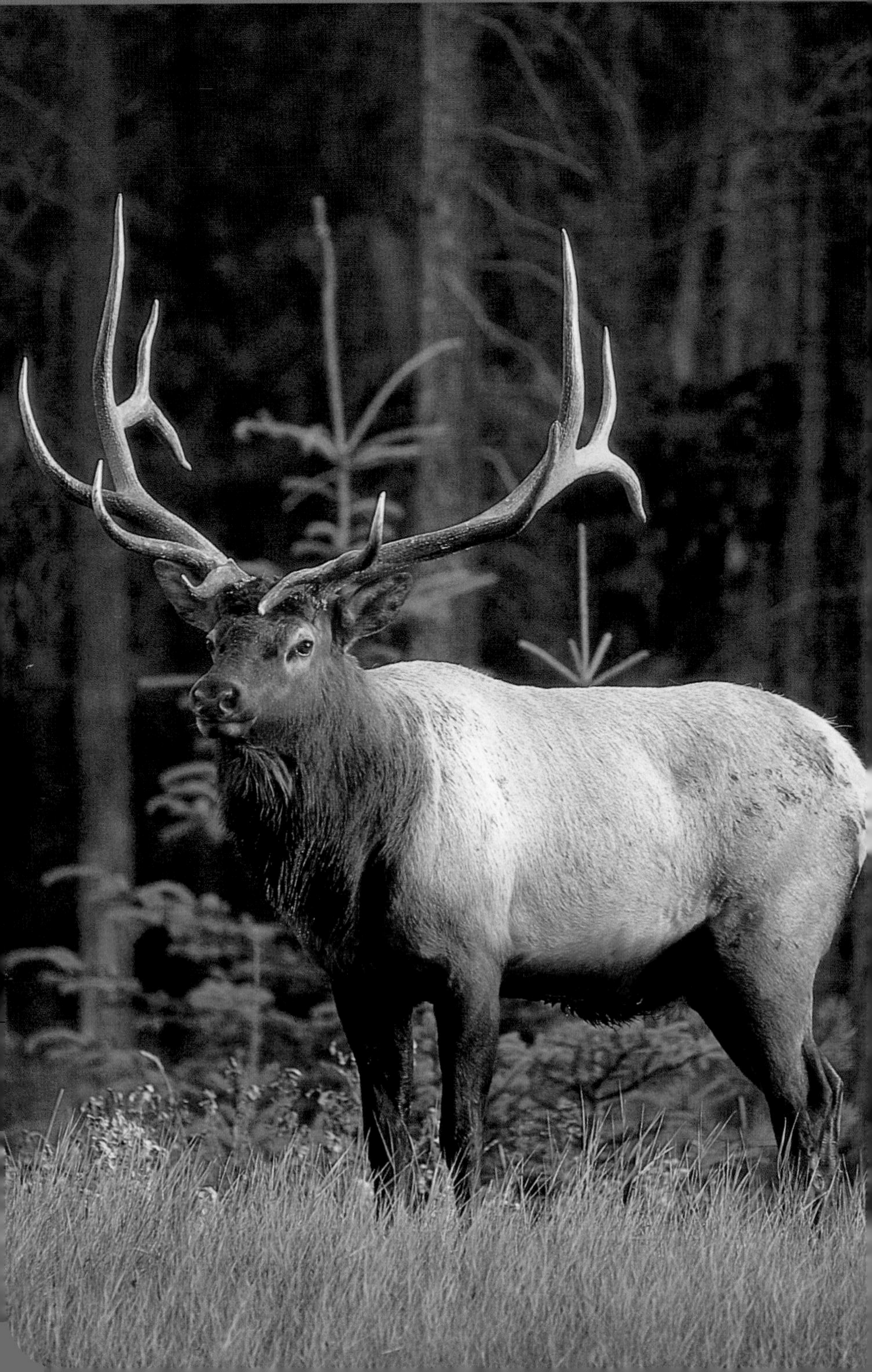

hoofprint

walking trail

coniferous forests or brushlands. Elk often exhibit altitudinal migrations; they move to higher elevations in spring and lower elevations in fall. Coastal populations enjoy the lush vegetation and do not exhibit such pronounced seasonal movements.

FOOD: Elk are some of the most adaptable of grazers. Woody plants and fallen leaves frequently form much of their fall and winter diet. Sedges and grasses frequently make up 80 to 90 percent of the diet in spring and summer. Salt is a necessary dietary component for all animals that chew their cud, and Elk may travel vast distances to devour salt-rich soil.

DEN: The Elk does not keep a permanent den, but it often leaves flattened areas of grass, leaves or snow where it has bedded down during the day.

YOUNG: A cow Elk gives birth to a single precocial calf between late May and early June, following a gestation period of 8 to $8^1/_2$ months. The young stand and nurse within an hour, and within two to four weeks the cow and calf rejoin the herd. The calf is weaned in fall.

SIMILAR SPECIES: The **Mule Deer** (p. 46) has a whitish, rather than yellowish or brownish, rump patch and is smaller. Also, Mule Deer bucks have smaller racks of antlers.

Mule Deer

Mule Deer

Odocoileus hemionus

The Mule Deer, an inhabitant of this region since prehistoric times, continues to thrive in the mountains and in fragmented landscapes. If you want an intimate encounter with a large deer in the wild, there may be no better candidate than the Mule Deer. It tends to frequent open areas in parks and other protected areas, and it can be bold, conspicuous and quite tolerant of human visitors. Hikers in California are not the only people to frequently encounter this native cervid; in some parts of the state, such as the Bay Area, they are abundant even in residential neighborhoods.

One of the Mule Deer's best-known characteristics is its bouncing gait, which is known as "stotting" or "pronking." When it stots, a Mule Deer bounds and lands with all four legs simultaneously. This fascinating gait allows the deer to move safely and rapidly across and over the many obstructions it encounters in the complex brush and hillside areas it typically inhabits. Although stotting is characteristic of the Mule Deer, this animal also walks, trots and gallops perfectly well. When disturbed, a retreating Mule Deer will often stop for a last look at whatever disturbed it before it disappears completely from view.

Mule deer feed at dawn, at dusk and well into the night. They have great difficulty traveling through snow that is more than knee deep, so they are unable to occupy high mountainous areas of interior and northeastern California in winter. To avoid the snow, they migrate to lower elevations at the onset of winter, sometimes even into towns. Here they find the extra vegetation needed through the winter.

During the mating season, Mule Deer bucks compete for the does that are in estrus. Two bucks will tangle with their antlers, trying to force each other's head lower than their own. The weaker of the two eventually surrenders and usually leaves the area. Rarely, the antlers of two bucks become locked during these competitions, and if they are unable to free themselves, both bucks inevitably perish from starvation, predation or battle wounds. Mating season usually ends in November, but in some populations it may continue until as late as January.

Of the six subspecies of Mule Deer found in California, the most widespread and abundant are the Black-tailed or Columbian Deer (*O. h. columbianus*) and the California Mule Deer (*O. h. californicus*). The other subspecies are the Peninsula Mule Deer (*O. h. peninsulae*), the Cedros Island Mule

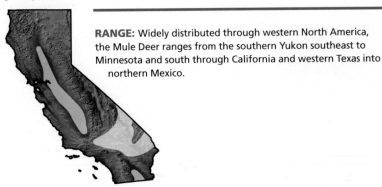

RANGE: Widely distributed through western North America, the Mule Deer ranges from the southern Yukon southeast to Minnesota and south through California and western Texas into northern Mexico.

Total Length: 4½–5½ ft.
Shoulder Height: 35–41 in.
Tail Length: 4¾–8¾ in.
Weight: 68–470 lb.

male

Deer (*O. h. cerrosensis*), the Inyo Mule Deer (*O. h. inyoensis*) and the Southern Mule Deer (*O. h. fuliginatus*).

DESCRIPTION: The Mule Deer gets its name from its large, mule-like ears. It has a large, whitish rump patch that is divided by a short, black-tipped tail. (The Black-tailed Deer has a smaller white rump patch and an almost fully black tail.) The dark forehead contrasts with both the face and upperparts, which are tan in summer and dark gray in winter. There is a dark spot on each side of the nose. The throat and insides of the legs are white year-round. A buck has fairly heavy, upswept antlers that are equally branched into forked tines. The metatarsal glands on the outside of the lower hindlegs are 4–6 in. long.

HABITAT: This deer's summer habitats vary from dry brushlands to high tundra zones. Bucks tend to remain at higher elevations where they form small bands; does and fawns remain at lower elevations. In drier regions, both sexes are often found in streamside situations. The Mule Deer thrives in the early successional stages of forests, so it is often found where fire or logging removed the canopy a few years before.

DID YOU KNOW?

Although the Mule Deer is usually silent, it can snort, grunt, cough, roar and whistle. A fawn will sometimes bleat. Even people who have observed deer extensively may be surprised to encounter one that is vocalizing.

hoofprint

FOOD: Grasses and forbs form most of the summer diet. In fall, the Mule Deer consumes both the foliage and twigs of shrubs. The winter diet makes increasing use of twigs and woody vegetation, and grazing occurs in hayfields adjacent to cover.

DEN: The Mule Deer leaves oval depressions in grass, moss, leaves or snow where it lies down to rest or chew its cud. It typically urinates upon rising. A doe usually steps to one side first, but a buck will urinate in the middle of the bed before leaving.

YOUNG: Following a gestation of 6$^1/_2$ to 7 months, a doe gives birth to one to three (usually two) fawns in May or June. The birth weight is 7$^3/_4$–8$^1/_2$ lb. A fawn is born with light dorsal spots, which it retains until the fall molt in August. The fawn is weaned when it is four to five months. Does become sexually mature at 1$^1/_2$ years, bucks at 2 or 2$^1/_2$ years.

walking trail

Elk

SIMILAR SPECIES: The **Elk** (p. 42) is much larger, has a dark mane on the throat and has a yellowish or orangish rump patch. The **Bighorn Sheep** (p. 34) has large, curled horns. The **Pronghorn** (p. 38) has black "horns" and two white bands around its neck.

Wild Boar

Sus scrofa

When we enter wildlife areas and national parks and think of potentially dangerous animals therein, the first animals that conjure up some fear in us are American Black Bears and Mountain Lions. Oddly enough, one of the most ferocious animals is the Wild Boar. When a boar is wounded, with young, or cornered, it can become a very dangerous forest animal. Keep this in mind as you walk along nature trails. If you see distinctive patches of torn up earth where a boar has been rooting around, be cautious, as the boar may still be in the vicinity. Wild Boar do not have good eyesight, but their hearing is acute and they will know of your presence long before you know of theirs.

Wild Boar are the same species as the domestic pigs that are raised for food in great numbers. The wild, pure-blood boar (European Wild Boar) are different in appearance to the farm raised variety, but they are able to interbreed. When Wild Boar were introduced into North America from Europe, they were first contained in preserves for hunting purposes. Of course, the boar escaped, and many cross-bred with existing domestic varieties. As a result, many populations are entirely hybrids, but a few pure-blooded lines of Wild Boar are well established in the southern and western states. In the west, the boar populations in Oregon are likely all hybrids, while some of the ones in California are the pure-blooded line that is native to Europe and Asia.

ALSO CALLED: Wild Pig, Domestic Pig, Feral Pig, Wild Hog

DESCRIPTION: Wild Boar are medium-sized hoofed mammals, just slightly shorter in height than Mule Deer (p. 46). Like domestic pigs, they have a sensitive, flexible disk at the end of the snout. They have coarse, dense fur, and in winter they have a thick under coat. Usually they are gray, brown or black in color, but some individuals may be mottled with white. Along the ridge of the back are long, dark bristly hairs. Their tails are sparsely furred and hang straight down. They have tusks, or modified canines, that continue growing throughout their lives. The upper tusks curl out and up over the mouth and may be up to 9 in. long. The lower tusks are much smaller and curl slightly outward from the mouth. Unlike the native artiodactyls, Wild Boar have both upper and lower incisors.

HABITAT: Wild Boar inhabit a variety of regions, such as forested mountain areas,

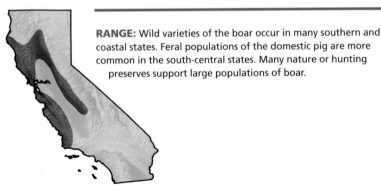

RANGE: Wild varieties of the boar occur in many southern and coastal states. Feral populations of the domestic pig are more common in the south-central states. Many nature or hunting preserves support large populations of boar.

Total Length: 4$^2/_5$–6 ft.
Tail Length: up to 12 in.
Weight male: 165–440 lb.
Weight female: 77–330 lb.

brushy areas, marshes, swamps, ravines and ridges.

DEN: At night, boar sleep in hollowed out depressions or places of trampled vegetation. Pregnant sows hollow out a shallow "nest" in the ground and line it with grass.

FOOD: Wild Boar eat like pigs—that is, they are omnivores and eat almost anything. In nut-bearing forests in the fall, they dine heavily on acorns, walnuts, and pecans. At other times of the year—or in other habitats—green vegetation, roots, tubers, fruit, crayfish, frogs, salamanders, eggs, fledgling birds, rabbits, newborn fawns and carrion are all eaten.

YOUNG: Mating occurs throughout the year, but there are two seasonal peaks. Dominant males mate first, followed by young and subordinate males. Gestation is 16 weeks, whereupon females give birth to a litter of 3 to 12 young. Young are born in a grass-lined depression made by the sow. The piglets have several longitudinal stripes along each side, but they lose these by the time they are six weeks old. Young are weaned when they are three months old. A sow and her young often feed together as a family group, and in some places, families join and form herds of up to 50 individuals.

SIMILAR SPECIES: Feral Pigs from domestic stocks have a different appearance: their fur is finer and sparser, they have rounder bodies and heads, their legs are shorter, their tails often curl, and they lack tusks. Hybrids of the two varieties (Wild Boar and domestic pig) have intergrading characteristics. It is unlikely to confuse the pig with any other species in this region.

DID YOU KNOW?

Wild Boar have an extremely well-developed sense of smell. For this reason, pigs are famous for their ability to "sniff-out" truffles, a fungal delicacy that grows underground. The pigs that are used to find truffles are muzzled, so they can locate the truffle but cannot eat it.

Horse
Equus caballus

Feral Horses in North America are descended from domesticated populations, and they have lived in the West for centuries. These wild Horses can usually be distinguished from their domestic kin by their much longer manes and tails, and their patterns of behavior.

Horse herds can have a different assortment of males and females, depending on the herd type. One type of herd is an accumulation of young bachelors. Males, usually over the age of two, leave their parent herd and may band together for a while, because no herd stallion will permit them near his mares. They stay together until either they find mares of their own or they are strong enough to steal mares from older stallions. Another common type of herd is the mixed herd, in which a number of mares, a single adult stallion, a few young males and foals live and forage together. The mares in a herd like this are closely guarded by the stallion and are not free to come and go, but they are the ones that decide where the herd is going and what they are going to do each day.

In some harems there are two stallions, a number of subordinate mares and perhaps a few foals. In this grouping, the subdominant, usually younger, stallion exhibits "champing" behavior, in which it approaches the dominant stallion nose to nose with its ears forward in a gesture of friendly respect. As he matures and becomes the dominant stallion's equal, this champing behavior may become more threatening. Ultimately, a duel occurs. The two stallions face each other with their ears back, necks arched and tails high. They fight standing side-by-side, biting, kicking and pushing each other off balance. Eventually, one stallion is beaten and runs off, perchance to find other mares to make a new harem. Mares of the harem stay together and accept the control of the victorious stallion. Only very rarely does a mare leave a harem to join a different herd.

ALSO CALLED: Mustang.

DESCRIPTION: Because of domestication in their recent history, wild Horses are extremely variable in size and color. They may be a solid color ranging from black to white or they may be spotted or bay or have various other color patterns. There are often white markings on the face, such as a star or blaze. They have both upper and lower incisors and small (if any) canines. They generally have a long mane and a long tail. Their hooves are semi-circular and uncloven, and they lack dewclaws.

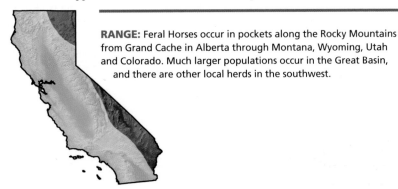

RANGE: Feral Horses occur in pockets along the Rocky Mountains from Grand Cache in Alberta through Montana, Wyoming, Utah and Colorado. Much larger populations occur in the Great Basin, and there are other local herds in the southwest.

Total Length: up to 7 ft.
Shoulder Height: 3¹/₂–5¹/₂ ft.
Tail Length: up to 3 ft.
Weight: 590–860 lb.

HABITAT: Horses prefer areas of abundant vegetation beside watercourses, but they are so adaptable that they may be found from deserts to alpine tundra.

FOOD: As grazers, Horses spend as much as 80 percent of daytime hours grazing. Even at night they sleep only about 50 percent of the time—the rest of the night they are still grazing. Horses are herbivores, and they consume mainly grasses and forbs during the summer months. In winter, they eat woodier vegetation, such as the twigs or the bark of shrubs.

DEN: Feral Horses make no den for sleeping, but if they lie down a "bed" is visible where the grass was flattened. Although Horses might lie down, they usually sleep standing up. While standing, the Horse falls asleep and a highly specialized tendon in each leg locks the knee and prevents the leg from collapsing. When the Horse wakes, the tendon is released and it can move.

YOUNG: A mare gives birth to one foal a year after a gestation of 11 months. Mating may occur during spring, summer or fall, often just a few days after a mare delivers her foal. The foal is precocious, and within a few hours of birth it is able to run with its mother and the rest of the herd. The foal is weaned shortly before the next foal is born.

SIMILAR SPECIES: No other animal has the same combination of a long-haired mane and tail and a single, uncloven hoof on each foot. Unlike the native ungulates, Horses have neither antlers nor horns.

DID YOU KNOW?

Domestic Horse breeds vary greatly in size from generations of selective breeding. The smallest are considerably less than 2 ft. high at the shoulders, while the largest work horses are up to 6 ft. tall. Feral Horses are usually medium to large sized.

WHALES, DOLPHINS & PORPOISES

All whales belong to the order Cetacea, and they are distinguished from other mammals by their nearly hairless bodies, blowholes on the tops of their heads, paddle-like forelimbs, lack of hindlimbs, fusiform bodies and powerful tail flukes. There are at least 80 species worldwide, classified into two suborders according to whether they have teeth (suborder Odontoceti) or baleen (suborder Mysticeti). The toothed whales are far more numerous and diverse, with some 70 species worldwide: the porpoises, dolphins, sperm whales, beaked whales, Narwhal and Beluga. There are only 11 species of baleen whales worldwide, but this group comprises the largest cetaceans: the rorquals, Gray Whale, Bowhead Whale and right whales.

The coast of California has some of the best whale-watching areas in North America. About 30 species regularly occur in these waters, of which 22 are odontocetes and 8 are mysticetes. The most well-known and commonly seen cetaceans in the region are Gray Whales, Humpback Whales, Orcas and Bottlenosed Dolphins. The little Dall's Porpoises are less frequently seen, but sightings of them are delightful, memorable events. With luck, and in the right locations, any of these five species can be viewed from land while they feed in bays and inlets or pass by on their annual migrations. For this reason, only these five cetaceans are included here. Other species may be encountered unexpectedly at any time, especially if you take a boat trip into open waters.

While whale-watching, you may be lucky enough to see any of a number of whale displays. In a "breach," some or all of the whale's body rises out of the water and splashes back in. "Lob-tailing" refers to a whale forcefully slapping its tail flukes on the surface of the water—not to be confused with "fluking," which refers to the flukes rising clear above the water before a dive. Whales are "spy-hopping" when they rise almost vertically out of the water, just far enough to have a look around. "Logging" is a form of rest; individuals float at the surface alone or in a close group, all facing the same direction.

Gray Whale Family (Eschrichtiidae)

The unique Gray Whale is the sole member of this family. This whale shares some characteristics with the rorqual whales, but it is dissimilar enough to be classified on its own. Like the rorquals, the Gray Whale has throat pleats that expand when food-rich water is drawn into the mouth, but the Gray's throat pleats are fewer (only two to four) and much less effective. Each Gray Whale typically has at least two pleats, although three to seven are not uncommon. Gray Whales have a heavy appearance, an arched mouth, yellowish brown baleen and two distinct blowholes. The species is believed to carry more creatures, such as barnacles and whale lice, than any other whale.

Gray Whale

Rorqual Family (Balaenopteridae)

Rorquals, numbering only a few species worldwide, represent some of the largest whales on earth—including the Blue Whale, the largest animal on this planet. The name "rorqual" is derived from the Norwegian word *rorhval,* meaning "furrow," and refers to the numerous pleats or folds in the skin of the throat. These pleats unfold and allow the throat to distend to an enormous balloon-like shape when the whale gulps a massive volume of food-rich water into its mouth. The whale does not swallow the water; the pleats contract and the tongue moves up and forward to effectively push the water out through the baleen, and any crustaceans or fish are trapped inside the mouth to be swallowed whole.

Humpback Whale

Rorquals are easily identified by their pointed snouts, flattened heads, long, slender bodies and relatively small dorsal fins that protrude about two-thirds down the length of their body. When a rorqual's mouth is open, the short, black baleen, which is continuous around the forward point of the jaw, is visible. All of the rorquals have two distinct blowholes.

Ocean Dolphin Family (Delphinidae)

Aquariums, movies and anecdotal accounts have made Bottlenosed Dolphins and Orcas world-famous. Although many people call the Orca a whale, it is actually the largest dolphin in the world. All delphinids have a sleek fusiform shape and are generally free of callosities and barnacles. Many delphinids exhibit high brain to body size ratios (encephalization quotients) and are considered the most intelligent of the cetaceans. Bottlenosed Dolphins top the scales with the highest encephalization quotient—a ratio similar to that of chimpanzees. All toothed whales (including porpoises) have only one external blowhole.

Orca

Porpoise Family (Phocoenidae)

The porpoises, which number only six species worldwide, are often mistakenly referred to as small dolphins. The largest porpoise rarely reaches more than $6^1/_2$ ft. in length, and the smallest is just less than 5 ft., making porpoises some of the smallest cetaceans in the world. Unlike dolphins, which have conical teeth for holding and biting prey, the porpoises have flattened, spade-shaped teeth that slice their prey. They do not have a distinct beak, and their heads are quite rounded. Their body shape is a bit more robust than the streamlined dolphins, and their flippers are typically small and stubby. Viewing porpoises in the wild can be a challenge because they are generally shy and timid. When they surface for air, they rise only long enough for a quick breath and then roll rapidly back in.

Dall's Porpoise

Gray Whale
Eschrichtius robustus

Gray Whales, some of the most frequently observed whales, are famous for their extensive migrations—among the longest of any mammal. In their voyages, these whales travel back and forth between the cold Arctic seas where they spend summers and the warm Mexican waters where they spend winters. Each year, almost the entire world population of Gray Whales performs this cycle, amounting to over 12,400 mi of travel along the western coast of North America.

During their summers in Arctic or near-Arctic seas, Grays feed on the abundant bottom-dwelling crustaceans known as amphipods. These whales eat enormous quantities of food during their five to six months in the north. During their migration and especially their stay in southern waters, they eat very little and may even fast completely. Having lost as much as 30 percent of their body weight, they are slim and hungry when they return to the rich Arctic waters.

The Gray Whales' journey to winter waters takes 2 to 2^1/$_2$ months: they leave the Arctic waters by late September and arrive in the warm waters off California and Mexico by late December. This southward migration coincides with the reproductive activity of the whales, and

once in warm waters, a female either mates or gives birth. If she mates, her journey south the next year will be to give birth, because gestation is about 13^1/$_2$ months. Conversely, if she gives birth, she will court and mate the next year.

By late February or March, Gray Whales begin their return to northern waters. Mothers with new calves may postpone their journey a bit longer to ensure the young have the strength for the journey. The whales arrive in the Arctic again by May or June.

The best time to view passing Gray Whales in California is from December to March. Many whale-watching sites are found along the coast, and nearby towns usually have an abundance of boat tour companies. The west coast of Baja and California is perhaps the most famous place in the world for viewing Gray Whales. Here they relax, play, mate and raise their young.

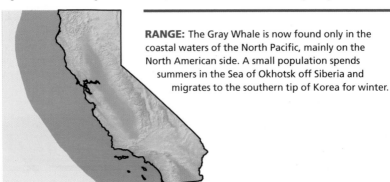

RANGE: The Gray Whale is now found only in the coastal waters of the North Pacific, mainly on the North American side. A small population spends summers in the Sea of Okhotsk off Siberia and migrates to the southern tip of Korea for winter.

Total Length: up to 50 ft.; average 45 ft.
Total Weight: up to 45 tons; average 35 tons
Birth Length: about 15 ft.
Birth Weight: 1000 lb.

Gray Whales, which once inhabited both the Atlantic and Pacific oceans, have been close to extinction at least twice in history and now live only in Pacific waters. Grays were particularly vulnerable to whalers because they live mainly in shallow waters. As a result of many years of protection, these whales have now recovered their numbers in the eastern Pacific.

Aside from man, the only predator of Gray Whales is the Orca, which might take young or weak individuals.

ALSO CALLED: Devilfish, Mussel-digger, Scrag Whale.

DESCRIPTION: The Gray Whale is easily distinguished from other whales by its mottled gray appearance and narrow, triangular head. Between the eye and the tip of the snout, the head is slightly arched, and the jaw line usually has a similar arch. Over most of the body there are many yellow, orange or whitish patches of barnacles and "whale lice" (actually a crustacean, not true lice); these are especially prominent on the head. There is no dorsal fin, but this whale does have one bump where the dorsal fin should be, and then a series of smaller bumps or "knuckles" continuing along the dorsal ridge to the tail. In a dive, these bumps are visible, as are the distinctly notched tail and pointed flukes. The small flippers are wide at the base but taper to a pointed tip. Female Grays are typically 3–4 ft. longer than males.

BLOW: When seen from the front or the rear, the blow of Gray Whales appears bushy, heart-shaped and may be up to 15 ft. high. In some cases, the

DID YOU KNOW?

Gray Whales are favorites among whale-watchers because they can be very friendly and may even approach boats. In extraordinary encounters, Grays seem to enjoy the occasional back rub from willing admirers.

blow looks V-shaped. From the side, it appears bushy but not distinctive.

OTHER DISPLAYS: Gray Whales exhibit breaching, spy-hopping and fluking. They will breach anywhere in their range, but most often in breeding lagoons in the south. They rise nearly vertically out of the water, come down with an enormous splash and then repeat the breach two or three times in a row. Spy-hopping is also common, and they may keep their heads out of the water for 30 seconds or more. In shallow water individuals have been observed "cheating" by resting their flukes on the bottom so they can keep their heads above water with minimal effort. Before a deep dive, they raise their flukes clear above the surface of the water.

GROUP SIZE: Generally these whales are seen in groups of only one to three individuals. They may migrate in groups of up to 15, and food-rich areas in the north can attract dozens or hundreds of Gray Whales at a time.

FOOD: Unlike other baleen whales, the Gray Whale is primarily a bottom-feeder. Its food consists of benthic

dive sequence

amphipods and other invertebrates. A feeding whale dives down to the bottom and rolls onto one side, sticking out its lower lip and sucking in great volumes of food, water and muck. Once its mouth is full, it uses its powerful tongue to push the silty water out through the baleen, trapping the crustaceans inside to be swallowed whole. Most Gray Whales are "right-lipped," they way humans are mainly right-handed, meaning they prefer to feed using the right side of the mouth. A close-up look at a Gray's face will determine its preference, because the side it uses will have numerous white scars and no barnacles. Inside the whale's mouth, the same uneven wear is evident; on right-lipped whales the baleen plates on the right side are shorter and more worn than the plates on the left.

YOUNG: Male Gray Whales are sexually mature when they are just over 36 ft. long, and females are when they are nearly 38 ft. long (from 5 to 11 years of age for both sexes). Mating occurs in December or January, and a single calf is born $13^1/_2$ months later—in the following January or February. The young start their journey northward with their mothers when they are only two months old and they continue nursing until they are six to nine months old.

blow

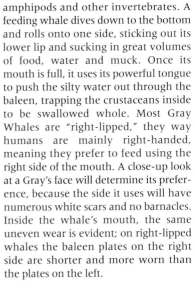

Humpback Whale

SIMILAR SPECIES: The **Humpback Whale** (p. 60) is usually darker in color, with "knuckles" and bumps on its head and unmistakably long flippers that bear unique dark and light markings on their undersides.

Humpback Whale
Megaptera novaeangliae

Humpback Whales are renowned for their extensive migrations and haunting songs. These whales are commonly spotted by whale-watchers, and they seem to enjoy performing for their boat-bound admirers.

In the summer, Humpbacks are seen feeding and socializing off California. In winter, they migrate south to Mexican or Costa Rican waters where they mate and calve. There are two other major populations of Humpback Whales. One whale population summers in British Columbian and Alaskan waters, and migrates to Hawaiian waters for winter. The other population also winters in Hawaiian waters, but migrates to Aleutian waters for summer feeding. In general, each population migrates between high latitude summer feeding waters and lower latitude mating and calving waters. These populations are not absolutely distinct; there are small numbers of Humpbacks that may alternate destinations in different years.

A Humpback's impressive underwater song can last from a few minutes to half an hour, and the entire performance can go on for several days with only short breaks between each song. While the true meaning of their song eludes us, we know that only males sing and that they perform mainly during the breeding season, implying that the main purpose is courtship.

Humpbacks breed in tropical waters in winter. Here the males become very aggressive toward each other and battle to determine dominance. A dominant male becomes the escort to a female with a calf. Presumably, a female with a calf is one who is, or will soon be, receptive to mating.

Other than the brief bouts of fighting between males during the breeding season, Humpback Whales have gentle and docile natures. They feed primarily on schooling fish or krill, using "lunge-feeding" or "bubble nets" to concentrate their prey. When lunge-feeding, a whale approaches a school of fish and surges forward, gulping into its greatly stretched throat a large volume of both fish and water. The thick baleen permits

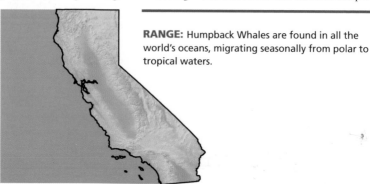

RANGE: Humpback Whales are found in all the world's oceans, migrating seasonally from polar to tropical waters.

Total Length: up to 62 ft.; average 45 ft.
Total Weight: up to 53 tons; average 30 tons
Birth Length: 13–16 ft.
Birth Weight: 1–2 tons

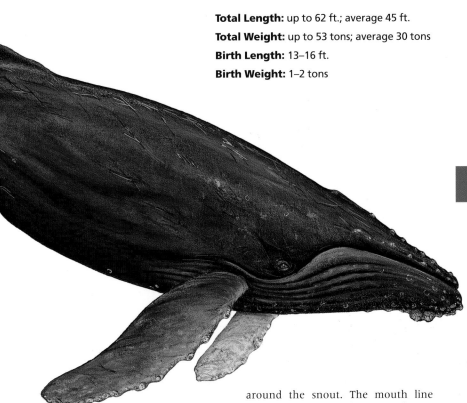

water to be squeezed out of the whale's mouth, while the fish remain to be swallowed. When bubble-netting, one or more whales circle a school of fish or krill from below while releasing a constant stream of bubbles. The bubbles rise and momentarily trap the confused fish, and the whales surge up inside the cylindrical "net" and gulp the fish into their mouths.

DESCRIPTION: This species is slightly more robust in the body than other rorquals. Body color is either dark gray or dark slate blue, and the undersides may be the same as the back or nearly white. A Humpback's head is slender, with numerous knobs and projections around the snout. The mouth line arches downward to the eye, and 12 to 36 grooves are visible on the pale throat. The flippers are distinctively long and knobby, with a varying pattern of white markings. The tail flukes are strongly swept back and have irregular trailing edges. Like the flippers, the flukes have unique white markings that can be used to identify individuals. The dorsal fin can be small and stubby or high and falcate, and several small knuckles are visible on the dorsal ridge between the fin and tail. Humpbacks

DID YOU KNOW?

A Humpback's song is composed of trills, whines, snores, wheezes and sighs, resulting in one of the loudest and most mysterious sounds produced by any animal.

often carry barnacles and whale lice. A female Humpback is longer than a male.

BLOW: The Humpback Whale makes a thick, orb-shaped blow that can reach up to 10 ft. high and is visible at a great distance. From directly in front or behind, the blow may appear slightly heart-shaped.

OTHER DISPLAYS: An acrobatic whale, the Humpback dazzles whale-watchers with high breaches that finish in a tremendous splash. Other behaviors that it may repeat several times include lob-tailing, flipper-slapping and spy-hopping. Humpbacks are often inquisitive, and they may approach boats if boaters are non-harassing. When they breathe and dive, they roll through the water and show a strongly arched back. The tail flukes are lifted high only on deep dives.

dive sequence

GROUP SIZE: Humpbacks commonly live in small groups of two or three members, but some groups may have 15 members, and occasionally one whale is seen on its own. Good feeding and breeding waters usually draw large groups.

FOOD: Humpbacks feed only in summer, and after their winter in the tropics they are slim and hungry. This whale may feed by either lunging or bubble-netting, with much individual variation enhancing each technique. Major foods include krill, herring, sardines and anchovies.

YOUNG: Courtship between Humpbacks is elaborate and involves lengthy bouts of singing by the males. Mating usually occurs in warm waters, and single calves are born following a gestation of about $11^1/_2$ months. The calves stay close to their mothers and nurse for about one year. Females reach sexual maturity when they are about 40 ft. long and males when they are at least 38 ft. long (about five years of age for both).

blow

SIMILAR SPECIES: The **Gray Whale** (p. 56) is slimmer and has mottled gray skin with numerous patches of barnacles and whale lice. As well, the Gray Whale has shorter flippers that lack distinctive markings.

Gray Whale

Orca

Orcinus orca

The Orca, with its striking colors and intelligent eyes, has fascinated humankind for centuries. Once revered by indigenous peoples of the Pacific Northwest, this black-and-white giant now symbolizes everything from biodiversity protection to nonhuman intelligence.

Orcas are one of the most widely distributed mammals on earth; they live in every ocean of the world, from cold polar seas to warm equatorial waters. Uncontested as the top marine predator, Orcas feed on a wider variety of creatures than any other whale. They are regarded as intelligent yet fearsome creatures—they are the lions that rule the seas.

Studies on the northern Pacific coast indicate that there are three distinct forms of Orcas. The two common groups are the "transients" and the "residents," distinguishable by appearance and behavior. Transient Orcas tend to be larger than residents, and they have taller, straighter dorsal fins. The transients live in smaller pods, from one to seven individuals, and they have large home ranges; resident Orcas have seasonally small ranges and travel along predictable routes. Transients are more likely to feed on other sea mammals, they dive for up to 15 minutes, they make erratic direction changes while traveling and they do not vocalize as much as residents. Resident Orcas, on the other hand, feed mainly on fish, rarely dive longer than three or four minutes and are highly vocal. Recently, researchers have identified a new class of Orca: the "offshore" Orcas resemble the residents in appearance, but they usually live farther out at sea. Much more research is needed to accurately describe this group.

Unlike the rorqual whales, Orcas have never been hunted heavily by humans. Some hunting has taken place in the past several decades, but it has not threatened the total population. Unfortunately, live hunting for the aquarium trade has taken many Orcas and their close cousins, the Bottlenosed Dolphins, from the wild. These activities cause

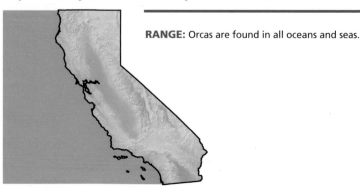

RANGE: Orcas are found in all oceans and seas.

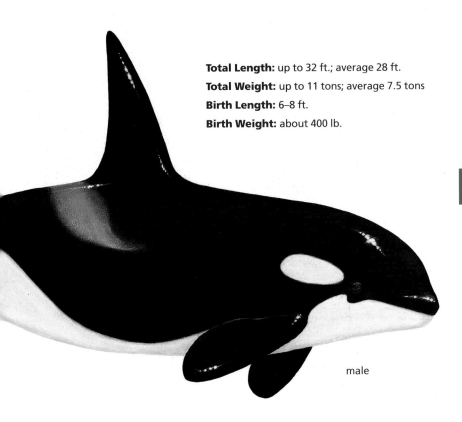

Total Length: up to 32 ft.; average 28 ft.
Total Weight: up to 11 tons; average 7.5 tons
Birth Length: 6–8 ft.
Birth Weight: about 400 lb.

male

male

female

much controversy, because whales are intelligent animals and many people feel that to keep them confined in an aquarium is unjust. Much of what we have learned about cetacean intelligence and biology, however, comes from aquarium studies, and this knowledge helps us to better understand and protect whales in the wild.

ALSO CALLED: Killer Whale, Great Killer Whale, Grampus.

DESCRIPTION: The Orca is unmistakable; its body is jet black, but with white undersides and a white lower jaw as well as white patches behind the eyes

DID YOU KNOW?

Orcas have been known to eat land animals—there are records of pods killing and eating Moose and Caribou that swim across narrow channels and river mouths in northern Canada and Alaska.

and on its sides. Its large flippers are paddle-shaped, and its dorsal fin is tall and triangular. An old male may have a fin as tall as 6 ft., and the fins of some old individuals may be wavy when seen straight on. The female's dorsal fin is smaller and more curved than the male's. Behind the dorsal fin there is often a gray or purplish "saddle." Each whale's dorsal fin and saddle patch has a unique shape, and the fin often bears scars; scientists and whale-watchers can identify individual Orcas by these characteristics. The eye is below and in front of the white facial spot, and the snout tapers to a rounded point. The flukes are dark on top and whitish below, with pointed tips, concave trailing edges and a distinct notch in the middle. The male Orca is longer than the female.

BLOW: In cool air, the blow of the Orca is low and bushy.

OTHER DISPLAYS: Orcas are extremely acrobatic for their size. They are inquisitive and often approach boats, apparently to get a better look at the humans on board. They are often seen breaching clear out of the water, lob-tailing,

dive sequence

flipper-slapping, logging and spy-hopping. They may speed-swim, or porpoise, with their entire body leaving the water at each breath. Sub-surface beaches of rounded pebbles attract many Orcas, and they seem to enjoy rubbing their bodies on the smooth stones.

GROUP SIZE: Orcas travel in pods of 3 to 25 individuals. Certain social gatherings may attract several pods at one time.

FOOD: Orcas feed on a wider variety of animals than any other whale, partly because of their global distribution. Several hundred species are potential prey to these top predators of the sea, including, but not limited to, fish of all kinds, seals, other cetaceans, dugongs, sea turtles and birds.

YOUNG: Mating is believed to occur between individuals of a pod, but superpods occasionally form and paternity is difficult to ascertain. Males reach maturity when they are about 19 ft. long and females when they are about 16 ft. long; females first give birth at about the age of 15. Winter appears to be the peak calving season, and gestation is believed to be 12 to 16 months.

blow hole

Dall's Porpoise

SIMILAR SPECIES: Along the coast, the **Dall's Porpoise** (p. 72) may be mistaken as a baby Orca. The **False Killer Whale** (*Pseudorca crassidens*) is entirely black and lacks the large dorsal fin.

Bottlenosed Dolphin
Tursiops truncatus

The familiar Bottlenosed Dolphin rivals only the Orca as the most well-recognized cetacean species in the world. This fame is owed in part to aquarium performances and TV shows (such as *Flipper*) but also to the species' natural curiosity and friendliness towards humans. All over the world the Bottlenosed Dolphin is reported to hobnob with swimmers and perform acrobatics for admiring whale-watchers. Of all cetaceans, this species is one of the best studied, especially in the fields of behavioral ecology, intelligence and communication.

The issue of non-human intelligence is loaded with misconceptions and biases. The main problem is that humans have no guaranteed means of assessing intelligence in other animals. Scientists can study their behavior and conduct performance tests, but there always seems to be a margin of doubt and error in every method we use. Nevertheless, it is clear that Bottlenosed Dolphins are among the most intelligent of all mammals.

A close look at the brain of a dolphin reveals information about the potential intelligence of the creature. Second only to humans, a dolphin's brain is very large for its body size—a ratio called encephalization quotient—and the only

other creature to exhibit such a high ratio is the chimpanzee. (On performance tests, however, Bottlenosed Dolphins routinely figure problems out much faster than chimpanzees. When switches are used for correct answers, for example, chimpanzees routinely make random pokes at the switch before figuring out the purpose. Dolphins, on the other hand, manage to trigger switches correctly with few, if any, random attempts.) Another characteristic of a Bottlenosed Dolphin's brain is the extremely well-developed cerebral cortex. The cerebral cortex is involved with the precise echolocation used by the dolphin, but this part of the brain is also responsible for intellect, thought, language and memory.

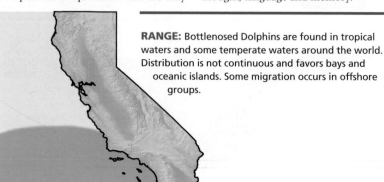

RANGE: Bottlenosed Dolphins are found in tropical waters and some temperate waters around the world. Distribution is not continuous and favors bays and oceanic islands. Some migration occurs in offshore groups.

Total Length: up to 12¾ ft.; average 10 ft.
Total Weight: up to 650 lb.; average 440 lb.
Birth Length: about 3½ ft.
Birth Weight: about 50 lb.

Worldwide, three different subspecies of Bottlenosed Dolphins have been described: *T. t. truncatus* in the Atlantic, *T. t. gilli* in the Pacific and *T. t. aduncus* in the Indian. Some researchers argue that they may even be distinct species. As well as subspecies, there appears to be two different varieties: the small and slender inshore dolphins, and the larger and more robust offshore dolphins. These two varieties also exhibit social and behavioral differences. Offshore Bottlenosed Dolphins appear to undergo slight seasonal migrations. The inshore Bottlenosed Dolphins are year-round residents, and they can be found along most of California, Baja and in good numbers in the Gulf of California.

ALSO CALLED: Bottle-nosed Dolphin, Atlantic/Pacific Bottlenose Dolphin, Gray Porpoise, Gray Dolphin, Cowfish.

DESCRIPTION: This robust dolphin is mainly bluish gray, with subtle markings on the face such as bands of darker gray from the eye to the flipper or from the eye to the top of the rostrum. The facial markings vary greatly between individuals and populations. Normally the undersides are light gray or whitish. Its forehead is rounded, and there is a crease separating the short but prominent beak. The dorsal fin is falcate and sometimes slightly hooked at the tip. Its flippers are dark colored on both sides, and they are broad at the base but taper

DID YOU KNOW?

Bottlenosed Dolphins have "signature whistles" for individuals in their group, which are probably like human names. Signature whistles are usually accompanied by a small string of bubbles released from the blowhole.

to a long, slender point. The tail stock is thick, giving the dolphin a powerful appearance. Its flukes are distinctly notched with swept-back tips. Offshore groups tend to be more robust than the inshore groups.

BLOW: This dolphin does not make a distinct blow, but the sharp puffing sound is clearly audible at short range.

OTHER DISPLAYS: The Bottlenosed Dolphin is famous for its acrobatics. It will frequently bow-ride and lobtail, and when it breaches it often clears the water completely, sometimes adding a twist or somersault. Groups are highly active and play extensively at the surface. Inshore individuals rarely dive longer then 5 minutes, but offshore dolphins may remain submerged for as long as 15 minutes.

GROUP SIZE: Group size can vary regionally and between populations. Offshore groups are larger, numbering

up to 25 individuals, whereas inshore groups rarely number over 10. At times, up to 500 of these dolphins have been sighted in open waters.

FEEDING: The Bottlenosed Dolphin feeds on a surprising variety of creatures such as fish, squid, octopus, eels, rays, shrimp, crabs and even small sharks. In areas of Baja this dolphin has been seen herding fish onto shore, where it grabs the fish as they wriggle on land. After consuming the fish, the dolphin slides or inches its way back into the water.

REPRODUCTION: Reproduction is well-studied for this species. A female gives birth only every two or three years. Gestation is 12 months and nursing lasts from 12 to 18 months. The age of first reproduction is not the same as sexual maturity, because social dynamics may influence mating. Sexual maturity may occur at five years (or later) for females and about 10 or 11 years for males. The lifespan in the wild is up to 35 or 40 years.

Risso's Dolphin

SIMILAR SPECIES: The **Spinner Dolphin** (*Stenella longirostris*) is smaller and more slender and has a longer beak; an adult **Risso's Dolphin** (*Grampus griseus*) always shows many long white scars over its body.

Dall's Porpoise
Phocoenoides dalli

The second-smallest cetacean in the region (Harbor Porpoises, *Phocoena phocoena,* are smaller), Dall's Porpoises are a welcome sight for boaters and whale-watchers. They are high-speed swimmers that frequently provide hours of delight for human spectators. Fortunately, they are very tolerant of human company, and the approach of boats rarely startles them.

Despite their name, these animals do not actually "porpoise" through the water the way dolphins and other small cetaceans do. Instead, they surface only long enough for a quick breath and in doing so create the distinctive conical splashes of water that are typical of the species.

Dall's Porpoises appear to undergo short migrations along the West Coast. In summer they tend to move northward, and in winter they move farther south. There may also be some inshore/offshore migration, perhaps in response to food availability. In some years, for unexplained reasons, mass assemblies of a few thousand individuals have been monitored moving through passages near Alaska and northern British Columbia.

Like all dolphins and porpoises, Dall's Porpoises can sleep with half of the brain at a time, allowing them to be continuously vigilant for danger. The major natural enemies of Dall's Porpoises are Orcas and sharks.

Worldwide efforts to protect whales have had many admirable results. Unfortunately, Dall's Porpoises are still being hunted on a massive scale. Several

countries take a total of at least 14,000—and have taken as many as 45,000—in a year. Several thousand more are accidentally killed in fishing nets they cannot detect. It is not known how long the species may be able to sustain such losses; the Dall's Porpoise is not currently classed as endangered, but few reliable population estimates are available.

ALSO CALLED: Spray Porpoise, True's Porpoise, White-flanked Porpoise.

DESCRIPTION: Often mistaken for a baby Orca, the Dall's Porpoise is colored distinctly black and white. Its head is black, and it tapers to a narrow mouth.

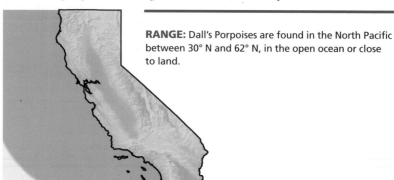

RANGE: Dall's Porpoises are found in the North Pacific between 30° N and 62° N, in the open ocean or close to land.

Total Length: up to 8 ft.; average 6 ft.

Total Weight: up to 490 lb.; average 300 lb.

Birth Length: 2½–3 ft.

Birth Weight: unknown

Dalli-type

The "lips" of its small mouth are usually black, but on some individuals they are white. There are numerous, closely spaced spade-shaped teeth. The black body is extremely robust for its length, and there is a large white patch on the belly and sides. Two forms of this porpoise occur: the Truei-type, which has a white patch that stretches from in front of the flippers to the tail stock, and the Dalli-type, which has a smaller white patch on its sides beginning about one-third down its body. The black, triangular dorsal fin has a hooked tip, and it is usually light gray or white on the trailing half. The small flippers lie close to the head, and they are dark black above and below. When viewed from above, the flukes are shaped like a wide ginkgo leaf and have a white or gray trailing edge.

BLOW: This porpoise does not make a visible blow. As it swims and breaks the surface, a V-shaped cone of water comes off its head and this cone is referred to as a "rooster-tail." Many boaters look for this rooster-tail—it can be seen from a much greater distance than the porpoise itself.

DID YOU KNOW?

Dall's Porpoises are among the fastest cetaceans, often clocked at speeds up to 35 mph.

OTHER DISPLAYS: Dall's Porpoises are not acrobatic and do not leap out of the water. Nevertheless, they are exceptionally fast and even seem hyperactive as they dart and zig-zag about. They appear to love bow riding, and they zoom toward a fast-moving boat like a black-and-white torpedo. If a Dall's Porpoise comes to the bow of your boat, don't slow down for a better look because it will quickly lose interest in a boat going slower than 12 mph.

GROUP SIZE: Dall's Porpoises are commonly found in groups of 10 to 20 individuals, but aggregations of hundreds may occur in some waters.

FOOD: Dall's Porpoises feed at the surface or in deep water, and their primary foods include squid, lanternfish, hake, mackerel, capelin and other schooling fish. Maximum feeding depth has been estimated at about 1600 ft. These porpoises have high metabolic rates and

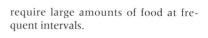

require large amounts of food at frequent intervals.

YOUNG: Two peaks in calving seem to occur, one in February-March and again in July-August. Peak mating must have a similar split, because gestation is about $11^1/_2$ months. Males reach sexual maturity when they are about 6 ft. long (four to five years) and females when they are $5^1/_2$ ft. long (three to four years).

Pacific White-sided Dolphin

SIMILAR SPECIES: The **Pacific White-sided Dolphin** (*Lagenorhynchus obliquidens*) is much grayer overall and is slimmer relative to its length. A baby **Orca** (p. 64) looks similar, but it would never be seen unattended by its mother.

CARNIVORES

This group of mammals is aptly named because, while some members of the order Carnivora are actually omnivorous (and eat a great deal of plant material), most of them prey on other vertebrates. Here in California, these "meat-eaters" vary greatly in size and form, from the small Short-tailed Weasel to the enormous Northern Elephant Seal.

Cat Family (Felidae)

Excellent and usually solitary hunters, all cats have long, curved, sharp, retractile claws. Like dogs, cats walk on their toes—they have five toes on each forefoot and four toes on each hindfoot—and their feet have naked pads and furry soles. As anyone with a housecat knows, the top of a cat's tongue is rough with spiny, hard, backward-pointing papillae, which are useful to the cat for grooming its fur.

Mountain Lion

Skunk Family (Mephitidae)

Biologists previously placed skunks in the weasel family, but recent DNA research has led taxonomists to group the North American skunks (together with the stink badgers of Asia) in a separate family. Unlike most weasels, skunks are usually boldly marked, and when threatened, they can spray a foul-smelling musk from their anal glands.

Striped Skunk

Weasel Family (Mustelidae)

Long-tailed Weasel

Most weasels are lithe predators with short legs and elongated bodies. They have anal scent glands that produce an unpleasant-smelling musk, but, unlike skunks, they use it to mark territories more than for defense. Most species have been trapped for their valuable, long-lasting fur.

Raccoon Family (Procyonidae)

Raccoons are small to mid-sized omnivores that, like bears (and humans), walk using their entire foot, from heel to toe (plantigrade). They are good climbers. Raccoons are best known for their long, banded, bushy tails and distinctive black facial masks. The Ringtail, also a member of this family, is more slender than a Northern Raccoon, it has semi-retractile claws and when it walks there is no contact between the heel and the ground (subdigitigrade).

Northern Raccoon

Hair Seal Family (Phocidae)

The hair seals are also known as "true seals," and they are believed to share a common ancestor with the mustelids. These seals have hindflippers that permanently face backwards; they cannot rotate their hips and hindlegs to support the weight of their bodies. Their flippers are covered with hair, and there are claws on all five digits. There are no external ear flaps (pinna). The elephant seal is the largest carnivore of all.

Northern Elephant Seal

Eared Seal Family (Otariidae)

Eared seals include the fur seals and sea-lions, and all are believed to share a common ancestor with bears. These seals can rotate their hindlegs forward to help support their weight when they are on land. Their flippers are hairless, and only the hindflippers have nails on the middle three digits. As their name suggests, these seals have external ear flaps (pinna). Hair seals (Phocidae) and eared seals (Otariidae) are collectively referred to as pinnipeds.

Northern Sea-Lion

Bear Family (Ursidae)

The three North American members of this family (only one of which occurs in this region) include the world's largest terrestrial carnivores. All bears are plantigrade—they walk on their heels—and they have powerfully built forelegs and a short tail. Although most bears sleep through the harshest part of winter, they do not truly hibernate—their sleep is not deep and their temperature drops only a couple of degrees. Contrary to popular belief, bears may rouse during winter and even come out of their dens on milder days.

American Black Bear

Dog Family (Canidae)

This family of dogs, wolves, Coyotes and foxes is one of the most widespread terrestrial, non-flying mammalian families. The typically long snout houses a complex series of bones associated with the sense of smell, which plays a major role in finding prey and in communication. Members of this family walk on their toes, and their claws are blunt and non-retractile.

Kit Fox

77

Mountain Lion
Puma concolor

A pug-mark in mountain snow or a heavily clawed tree trunk are two powerful reminders that some places in California are still wild enough for the Mountain Lion. Widespread but uncommon, there may be as many 5000 individuals in the state, and their numbers appear to be increasing. These large cats were once found throughout much of North America, but conflicts with settlers and their stock animals resulted in extensive removal of this great feline. Still, it is one of the most widespread, if not abundant, carnivores in both North and South America. Its alternate common names reflect this distribution: "puma" is derived from the name used by the Incas of Peru; "cougar" comes from Brazil.

The Mountain Lion is generally a solitary hunter, except when a mother is accompanied by her young. When the young are old enough, they follow their mother and sometimes even help her kill—a process that teaches the young how to hunt for themselves. Although the Mountain Lion is capable of great bursts of speed and giant bounds, it often opts for a less energy-intensive hunting strategy. Silent and nearly motionless, a cat will wait in ambush in a tree or on a ledge until prey approaches. By leaping onto the shoulders of its prey and biting deep into the back of the neck while attempting to knock the prey off balance, the Mountain Lion can take down an adult Elk.

These big cats need the equivalent of about one deer a week to survive, and their densities in the wild tend to correlate with ungulate densities. Mountain Lions are adaptable creatures that may hunt by day or night. Hunting by day is quite common in the wilderness, but in areas close to human development the cats are active only at night.

One of the most charismatic animals of North America, the Mountain Lion is a creature every naturalist hopes to see. This elusive cat is a master of living in the shadows, but if you spend enough time in the wilderness of central California, you may one day see a streak of burnished brown flash through your peripheral vision. If this streak was actually a Mountain Lion, you can count yourself among the extremely lucky. Few people—even biologists—ever get more than a fleeting glimpse of these graceful felines. If you startle one, which is quite improbable—it usually knows of your presence long before you know of its—it will quickly disappear from sight. Only the young may come for a closer look at you. Young Mountain Lions, like most young carnivores,

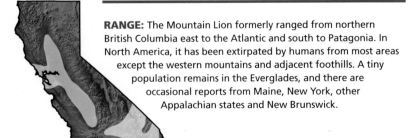

RANGE: The Mountain Lion formerly ranged from northern British Columbia east to the Atlantic and south to Patagonia. In North America, it has been extirpated by humans from most areas except the western mountains and adjacent foothills. A tiny population remains in the Everglades, and there are occasional reports from Maine, New York, other Appalachian states and New Brunswick.

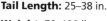

Total Length: 6–9 ft.
Shoulder Height: 26–32 in.
Tail Length: 25–38 in.
Weight: 70–190 lb.

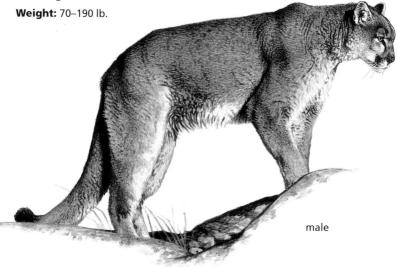

male

are extremely curious and don't yet realize that humans are best avoided.

ALSO CALLED: Cougar, Puma.

DESCRIPTION: This handsome feline is the only remaining large, long-tailed native cat in California (the Jaguar, *Panthera onca*, once lived here, but it is now extirpated). Its body is mainly buffy gray to tawny or cinnamon in color, with pale buff or nearly white undersides. Its body is long and lithe, and its tail is almost one third of its total length. The head, ears and muzzle are all rounded. The tip of the tail, sides of the muzzle and backs of the ears are black. Some individuals have prominent facial patterns of black, brown, cinnamon and white.

HABITAT: Mountain Lions are found most frequently in remote, wooded, rocky places, usually near an abundant supply of deer. In California, they inhabit mainly the mountain and riparian regions, although they may venture into brushlands or alpine regions, depending on food availability.

FOOD: Here in California, Mountain Lions rely mainly on Mule Deer (p. 46). Additional prey species include other hoofed mammals, rabbits, porcupines, skunks, Coyotes and American Beavers. Even mice, birds, adult Bobcats and domestic dogs and cats may be consumed. In harsh winters, Mountain Lions feed easily on animals weakened by starvation.

DID YOU KNOW?

During an extremely cold winter, a Mountain Lion can starve if the carcasses of its prey freeze solid before it can get more than one meal. This cat's jaws are designed for slicing, and it has trouble chewing frozen meat.

DEN: A cave or crevice between rocks usually serves as a den, but a Mountain Lion may also den under an overhanging bank, beneath the roots of a wind-thrown tree or even inside a hollow tree.

YOUNG: A female Mountain Lion may give birth to a litter of one to six (usually two or three) kittens at any time of the year after a gestation of just over three months. The tan, black-spotted kittens are blind and helpless at birth, but their eyes open at two weeks. Their mottled coats help camouflage them when their mother leaves to find food. As the kittens mature, they lose their spots and their blue eyes turn brown or hazel. They are weaned at about six weeks, by which time they weigh about $6^1/_2$ lb. Young Mountain Lions may stay with their mother for up to two years.

walking trail   foreprint

SIMILAR SPECIES: The **Bobcat** (p. 82), the other native cat in the region, is much smaller and has a mottled coat and bobbed tail.

Bobcat

Bobcat
Lynx rufus

For those of us who are naturalists as well as feline enthusiasts, our chances of seeing a Bobcat in the wild are much greater than seeing a Mountain Lion. Bobcats seem to be more tolerant of human presence; their territories may even border on developed land. Night drives through wild areas, especially chaparral regions, offer some of the best opportunities for seeing Bobcats, although, at best, the experience is a mere glimpse of the cat bobbing along in the headlights. Bobcats are occasionally seen in areas close to cities and farmlands.

The Bobcat looks like a large version of a housecat, but it has little of the housecat's domestication. A wildcat in every sense of the word, it impresses observers with its lightfootedness, agility and stealth, usually leaving the momentary experience forever etched in the viewer's mind.

Over the past two centuries, Bobcat populations have fluctuated greatly because of this feline's adaptability to human-wrought change and its vulnerability to our resentment. Less restricted in diet than the Canada Lynx, the Bobcat may vary its diet of hares with any number of small animals, including an occasional turkey or chicken . . . or two. Its farmyard raids did not go over well with early settlers, and for more than 200 years the Bobcat was considered vermin. Even today, this striking native feline remains on the "varmint" list in some areas.

Despite its small size, the Bobcat is a ferocious hunter that can take down animals much larger than itself. Tales from long ago that told of Bobcats killing deer were considered by the uninformed to be either tall tales or cases of mistaken identity. But this remarkable feat is indeed possible for a surreptitious Bobcat that waits motionless on a rock or ledge for a deer to approach. The Bobcat leaps onto the neck of the unsuspecting animal and then maneuvers to the lower side of the neck to deliver a suffocating bite to the deer's throat. Bobcats may resort to such rough tactics in late winter when food is scarce, but they usually dine on simpler prey, such as rabbits, birds and rodents. Most of their prey, big or small, is caught at night in an ambush. During the day, Bobcats rest in any handy shelter, such as rock crevices, hollow logs, snags, stumps and dense brush.

Finding Bobcat tracks in soft ground may be the easiest way to determine the presence of this small cat in an area. Unlike Coyote or fox prints, Bobcat (and lynx) prints rarely show any claw marks,

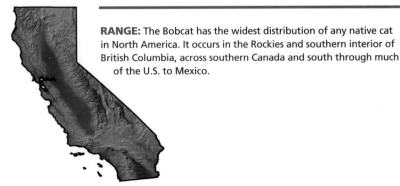

RANGE: The Bobcat has the widest distribution of any native cat in North America. It occurs in the Rockies and southern interior of British Columbia, across southern Canada and south through much of the U.S. to Mexico.

Total Length: 30–49 in.
Shoulder Height: 17–21 in.
Tail Length: 5–6¾ in.
Weight: 15–29 lb.

and there is one cleft on the front part of the main foot pad and two on the rear. A Bobcat's print is like a large version of a housecat's, except that it tends to be found much farther from human structures. Like all cats, Bobcats bury their scat, and their scratches and scrapings can help confirm their presence.

DESCRIPTION: The coat is generally tawny or yellowish brown, although it varies slightly with the seasons. The winter coat is usually dull gray with faint patterns. In summer, the coat often has a reddish tinge to it (the source of the scientific name *rufus*). A Bobcat's sides are spotted with dark brown, and there are dark, horizontal stripes on the breast and outsides of the legs. There are two black bars across each cheek and a brown forehead stripe. The ear tufts are less than 1 in.

long. The chin and throat are whitish, as is the underside of the bobbed tail. The upper surface of the tail is barred, and the tip of the tail is black on top.

HABITAT: The Bobcat occupies open coniferous and deciduous forests and brushy areas. It especially favors riparian areas, which offer excellent cover for its clandestine hunting. In California it lives in all parts of chaparral country.

> **DID YOU KNOW?**
>
> Most cats have long tails, which they lash out to the side to help them corner better when in pursuit of prey. The Bobcat, however, typically hunts in brushy areas, and a short, or "bobbed," tail won't get caught in branches.

foreprint

FOOD: The Bobcat feeds mainly on rabbits and hares, but rodents, skunks, birds, reptiles, amphibians and invertebrates are also eaten. When necessary, it scavenges the kills of other animals, and it may even take down its own large prey, such as a deer. A Bobcat may also consume substantial amounts of vegetation, mostly fruits and grasses.

DEN: Bobcats do not keep a permanent den. During the day, they use any available shelter. Female Bobcats prefer rocky crevices for the natal den, but they may also use hollow logs or the cavity under a fallen tree. The mothers do not provide a soft lining in the den for the kittens.

YOUNG: Bobcats typically breed in February or March, giving birth to one to seven (usually three) hairy, gray kittens in April or May, but they sometimes breed at other times of the year. The kittens' eyes open after nine days. They are weaned at two months, but they remain with the mother for three to five months. Female Bobcats become sexually mature at one year old and males at two.

walking trail

SIMILAR SPECIES: The only other native cat in the region is the **Mountain Lion** (p. 78), but it is much larger and has a longer tail.

Mountain Lion

Western Spotted Skunk
Spilogale gracilis

To watch the antics of a Western Spotted Skunk as it prepares to spray is almost worth the putrid penalty. When agitated and fearing for its safety, the Western Spotted Skunk resorts to the practice that has made this family infamous. If foot stamping and tail raising do not convey sufficient warning, the next stage certainly will.

Unlike the more familiar Striped Skunk, which sprays in a *U* position with its feet planted, the Western Spotted Skunk literally goes over the top when it sprays. Like a contortionist in a sideshow circus, this little skunk faces the threat and performs a handstand, letting its tail fall toward its head. The skunk can maintain this balancing act for more than five seconds, which is usually sufficient time to take aim and expel a well-placed stream of fetid fluid into the face of the intruder. Many animals may attempt to kill and eat this skunk before it sprays, but few are successful.

Throughout diverse habitats, including wilderness and urban areas, a common occurrence is the odor of skunk in the air. While this lingering odor may be from a skunk spraying in defense, it is all too often from a road-killed skunk. Road fatalities are a major cause of death among skunks, despite the weasel-like agility and dexterity of these animals.

The Western Spotted Skunk is especially nimble; with surprising ease, it can climb up to holes in hollow trees or to bird nests, where it finds shelter or food.

DESCRIPTION: This small skunk is mainly black with a white forehead spot and a series of four or more white stripes broken into dashes on the back. The pattern of white spots is different on each individual. The tail is covered with long, sparse hairs, and the tip of the tail is white with a black underside. The ears are small, rounded and black, and the face strongly resembles a weasel's. This skunk may walk, trot, gallop or make a series of weasel-like bounds. At night, its eyeshine is amber.

HABITAT: Western Spotted Skunks are found in woodlands, riparian zones, rocky areas, open grasslands or scrublands. They do not occupy marshlands or very wet areas. Farmlands make an excellent home. They are mainly nocturnal, and even in prime habitat they are seldom seen.

FOOD: This omnivorous mammal feeds on great numbers of insects, berries, eggs, nestling birds, small rodents, lizards and frogs. Animal matter usually accounts for a larger part of its diet than vegetation

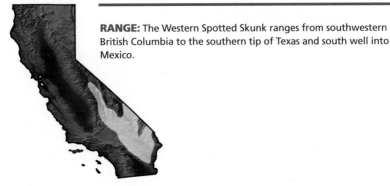

RANGE: The Western Spotted Skunk ranges from southwestern British Columbia to the southern tip of Texas and south well into Mexico.

Total Length: 12¹/₂–23 in.
Tail Length: 4–8¹/₄ in.
Weight: 1–2 lb.

does. The Western Spotted Skunk is an opportunistic forager, and it will eat nearly anything that it finds or can catch. Insects, especially grasshoppers and crickets, are the most important food in summer, and small mammals are significant in fall and spring.

DEN: The Western Spotted Skunk is nomadic by comparison to the Striped Skunk. It rarely makes a permanent den, preferring to hole up temporarily in almost any safe spot: rock crevices, fallen logs, buildings, woodpiles, abandoned burrows of other mammals and even tree cavities. The natal den is used for a longer period than other den spaces, and it differs primarily in the grass and leaves with which the female lines the inside for comfort. In parts of California in winter, several skunks may den together to conserve energy and wait out inclement weather.

YOUNG: Two to six (usually four) young are born in May or June. The

eyes and ears are closed at birth. The young skunks are covered with fine fur that betrays their future pattern. The eyes open after one month, and the young begin playing together at 36 days. By two months they are weaned. The family frequently stays together through fall, and it may overwinter in the same den, not dispersing until the following spring.

SIMILAR SPECIES: The **Striped Skunk** (p. 88) is the only other animal in the region with a black-and-white coat. As its name suggests, however, its white markings are in broad stripes.

DID YOU KNOW?

Spotted skunks become sexually mature at a very young age. A male may be able to mate when he is just five months old, and a female usually mates in September or October of her first year.

Striped Skunk
Mephitis mephitis

In nature, many of the best-dressed creatures are poisonous or unsafe in some way. Poisonous snakes, frogs and insects often bear striking colors and patterns that warn intruders of their dangerous characteristics. The same is true for skunks; their bold black and white patterns convey a clear warning to stay away. Anyone not heeding this warning will likely receive a face full of foul, repugnant fluid.

Butylmercaptan is responsible for the stink. Seven different sulfide-containing "active ingredients" have been identified in the musk, which not only smells bad, but also irritates the skin and eyes. A distressed Striped Skunk will turn its body into a *U* prior to spraying, placing all four feet on the ground and having its tail and head both facing the threat. If a skunk successfully targets the eyes, there is intense burning, copious tearing and sometimes a short period of blindness. From a distance, a whiff of a skunk's musk may be tolerable, but at point blank range it is strong enough to induce nausea.

Despite all these good reasons to avoid close contact with the Striped Skunk, the species is surprisingly tolerant of observation from a discreet distance, and watching a skunk can be very rewarding—its gentle movements contrast with the hyperactive behavior of its weasel cousins. The Striped Skunk's activity begins at sundown, when it emerges from its daytime hiding place. It usually forages among shrubs, but it often enters open areas, where it can be seen with relative ease. The Striped Skunk is an opportunistic predator that feeds on whatever animal matter is available. During winter, its activity is much reduced, and skunks spend the coldest periods in communal dens.

A regular predator of the Striped Skunk is the Great Horned Owl. Lacking a highly developed sense of smell, this owl does not seem to mind the skunk's odor—nor do the few other birds that commonly scavenge road-killed skunks.

DESCRIPTION: This cat-sized, black-and-white skunk is familiar to most people. Its basic color is glossy black. A narrow white stripe extends up the snout to above the eyes, and two white stripes begin at the nape of the neck, run back on either side of the midline and meet again at the base of the tail. The white bands often continue on the tail, ending in a white tip, but there is much variation in the amount and distribution of the white markings. The foreclaws are long and are used for digging. A pair of perineal musk glands on

RANGE: The Striped Skunk is found across most of North America, from Nova Scotia to Florida in the East and from the southwestern Northwest Territories to northern Baja California in the West. It is absent from parts of the deserts of southern Nevada, Utah and eastern California.

Total Length: 21¹/₂–31¹/₂ in.

Tail Length: 8–14 in.

Weight: 4¹/₄–9¹/₄ lb.

either side of the anus discharge the foul-smelling yellowish liquid for which skunks are famous.

HABITAT: The Striped Skunk seems to prefer streamside woodlands, groves of hardwood trees, semi-open areas, brushy grasslands and valleys. It also regularly occurs in cultivated areas, around farm-steads and even in the hearts of cities, where it can be an urban nuisance that eats garbage and raids gardens.

FOOD: All skunks are omnivorous. Insects, including bees, grasshoppers, beetles and various larvae, make up about 40 percent of the spring and sum-mer diet. To get at bees, skunks will scratch at a hive entrance until the bees emerge and then the skunks chew up great gobs of mashed bees, thus incur-ring the bee-keeper's wrath. The rest of the diet is composed of bird eggs and nestlings, amphibians, reptiles, grains, green vegetation and particularly in fall, small mammals, fruits and berries. Car-rion, especially roadkill, can also make up a sizable portion of a skunk's diet.

DEN: In most instances, the Striped Skunk builds a bulky nest of dried leaves and grasses in an underground burrow or beneath a building. Winter and maternal dens are underground.

YOUNG: A female Striped Skunk gives birth to 2 to 10 (usually 5 or 6) blind, helpless young in April or May, after a gestation of 62 to 64 days. The typical black-and-white pattern of a skunk is present on the skin at birth. The eyes and ears open at three to four weeks. At five to six weeks, the musk glands are functional. Weaning follows at six to seven weeks. The mother and her young will forage together into the fall, and they often share a winter den.

SIMILAR SPECIES: Only the small **Western Spotted Skunk** (p. 86) also bears a black-and-white pattern, but its white areas are a series of spots or thin stripes, not the broad white stripes of the Striped Skunk. The **American Badger** (p. 106) has a white stripe running up its snout, but it is larger and squatter and has a grizzled, yellowish gray body.

DID YOU KNOW?

Fully armed, the Striped Skunk's scent glands contain about 1 oz. of noxious, smelly fluid. The spray has a maximum range of about 20 ft., and a skunk is accurate for half that distance.

American Marten
Martes americana

Ferocity and playfulness are perfectly blended in the American Marten. This quick, active, agile weasel is equally at home on the forest floor or among branches and tree trunks. Its fluid motions and attractive appearance contrast with its swift and deadly hunting tactics. A keen predator, the American Marten sniffs out voles, takes bird eggs, nabs fledglings and acrobatically pursues tree squirrels.

Unfortunately, this animal's playfulness, agility and insatiable curiosity are not easily observed because it tends to inhabit wilder areas. The American Marten has been known to occupy human structures for short periods of time, should a food source be near, but more typical marten sightings are restricted to flashes across roadways or trails. Human pursuit of a marten rarely leads to a satisfying encounter—this weasel's mastery of the forest is ably demonstrated in its elusiveness.

A close relative of the Eurasian Sable (*M. zibellina*), the American Marten is widely known for its soft, lustrous fur, and it is still targeted on traplines in remote wilderness areas. As with so many species of forest mammals, populations seem to fluctuate markedly every few years—a cyclical pattern revealed by trappers' records. Some scientists attribute these cycles to changes in prey abundance, whereas some trappers suggest that marten populations simply migrate from one area to another.

The American Marten is often used as an indicator of environmental conditions because it depends on food found in mature coniferous forests. The loss of such forests has led to declining populations and even extirpation from many areas of the U.S. Hopefully, modern methods of forest management will maintain adequate habitat for the American Marten and prevent its further decline.

ALSO CALLED: Pine Marten.

DESCRIPTION: This slender-bodied, fox-faced weasel has a beautiful pale yellow to dark brown coat and a long, bushy tail. The feet are well furred and equipped with strong, non-retractile claws. The conspicuous ears are $1^3/_8$–$1^3/_4$ in. long. The eyes are dark and almond-shaped. The breast spot, when present, is usually orange but sometimes whitish or cream, and it varies in size from a small dot to a large patch that occupies the entire region from the chin to the belly. A male is about 15 percent larger than a female. There is a well-defined scent gland, about 3 in. long and 1 in. wide, on the center of the abdomen.

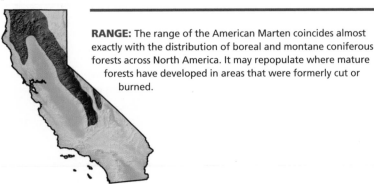

RANGE: The range of the American Marten coincides almost exactly with the distribution of boreal and montane coniferous forests across North America. It may repopulate where mature forests have developed in areas that were formerly cut or burned.

Total Length: 19³/₄–26³/₄ in.
Tail Length: 7–9 in.
Weight: 1–2³/₄ lb.

HABITAT: The marten prefers mature, particularly coniferous, forests that contain numerous dead trunks, branches and leaves to provide cover for its rodent prey. It does not occupy recently burned or fully cut-over areas. In California, slash piles that harbor Golden-mantled Ground Squirrels and other rodents can attract numerous martens.

FOOD: Although voles make up most of the diet, the American Marten is an opportunistic feeder that will eat squirrels, hares, bird eggs and chicks, insects, carrion and occasionally berries and other vegetation. In summer, it may enter the alpine zones to hunt pikas and marmots. This active predator hunts both day and night. Martens have been known to raid garbage cans and dumpsters of mountain cabins and ski lodges.

DEN: The preferred den site is a hollow tree or log that the female lines with dry grass and leaves.

YOUNG: Breeding occurs in July or August, but with delayed implantation of the embryo, so the litter of one to six (usually three or four) young is not born until March or April. The young are blind and almost naked at birth and weigh just 1 oz. The eyes open at six to seven weeks, at which time the young are weaned from a diet of milk to one of mostly meat. The mother must quickly teach her young to hunt, because when they are only about three months old she will reenter estrus, and, with mating activity, the family group disbands. Young female martens have their first litter at about the time of their second or third birthdays.

SIMILAR SPECIES: The **Fisher** (p. 92) is more than twice as large, with a long black tail and often frosted or grizzled-gray to black fur. It seldom has an orange chest patch. The **American Mink** (p. 100) has a white chin and irregular white spots on the chest, but it has shorter ears, shorter legs (it does not climb well) and a much less bushy, cylindrical tail.

DID YOU KNOW?

Although the American Marten, like most weasels, is keenly carnivorous, it has been known to consume an entire apple pie left cooling outside a window and to steal doughnuts off a picnic table.

Fisher

Martes pennanti

For the lucky naturalist, meeting a wild Fisher is a once-in-a-lifetime opportunity. The rest of us must content ourselves with the knowledge that this reclusive animal remains a top predator in coniferous wildlands. Historically, the Fisher was more numerous, and it once ranged throughout the northern boreal forest, the northeastern hardwood forests and the forests of the Rocky Mountains and the Pacific ranges.

The Fisher is an animal of deep, untouched wilderness, and it often disappears shortly after development begins. Forest clearing, habitat destruction, fires and over-trapping resulted in its decline or extirpation over much of its range, but there have been a few reintroductions and a gradual recovery in some areas over the past two decades.

The Fisher is among the most formidable of predators here, and it could probably be considered the most athletic of this region's carnivores. Fishers are particularly nimble in trees, and the anatomy of their ankles allows the feet to rotate sufficiently so that they can descend trees headfirst. Making full use of its athleticism during foraging, the Fisher incorporates any type of ecological community into its extensive home range, which can reach 75 mi across.

According to Ernest Thompson Seton, a legendary naturalist of the 19th century, as fast as a squirrel can run through the treetops, a marten can catch and kill it, and as fast as the marten can run, a Fisher can catch and kill it.

The Fisher is a good swimmer, but, despite its name, it rarely eats fish. Perhaps this misnomer arose because of confusion with the similar-looking, though much smaller, American Mink (p. 100), which does regularly feed on fish. These two weasels are quickly distinguished by their preferred habitats: the American Mink inhabits riparian areas; Fishers prefer deep forests.

Few of the animals on which the Fisher preys can be considered easy picking; the most notable example is the Fisher's famed ability to hunt North American Porcupine (p. 168). What the porcupine lacks in mobility, it more than makes up for in defensive armory, and it requires all the Fisher's speed, strength and agility to mount a successful attack. This hunting skill is far less common than wilderness tales suggest, however, and Fishers do not exclusively track porcupines; rather, they opportunistically hunt whatever crosses their trails. Most of a Fisher's diet consists of rodents, rabbits, grouse and other small animals.

RANGE: Fishers occur across the southern half of Canada (except the Prairies) and into the northeastern U.S. In the West they are found through the Cascades and Sierra Nevada and through the Rockies to Wyoming.

Total Length: 31–47 in.
Tail Length: 12–16 in.
Weight: 4$\frac{1}{2}$–12 lb.

DESCRIPTION: The Fisher has a face that is fox-like, with rounded ears that are more noticeable than those on other large weasels. In profile, its snout appears distinctly pointed. The tail is dark and more than half as long as the body. The coloration over its back is variable, ranging from frosted gray or gold to black. The undersides, tail and legs are dark brown. There may be a white chest spot. A male has a longer, coarser coat than a female, and he is typically 20 percent larger.

HABITAT: In California they are found in the northwest, where they prefer dense coniferous forests, but they avoid redwood regions. Fishers are not found in young forests or where logging or fire has thinned the trees. They are most active at night and thus are seldom seen. Fishers have extensive home ranges, and they may only visit a particular part of their range once every two to three weeks.

FOOD: Like other members of the weasel family, the Fisher is an opportunistic hunter, killing squirrels, hares, mice, muskrats, grouse and other birds. Unlike almost any other carnivore, however, the Fisher may hunt porcupines, which it kills by repeatedly attacking the head. It also eats berries and nuts, and carrion can be an important part of its diet. Here in California they also eat false truffles (a type of fungus).

DEN: Hollow trees and logs, rock crevices, brush piles and cavities beneath boulders all serve as den sites. Most dens are only temporary lodging,

DID YOU KNOW?

The scientific name *pennanti* honors Englishman Thomas Pennant. In the late 1700s, he predicted the decline of the American Bison and postulated that Native Americans entered North America via a Bering land bridge.

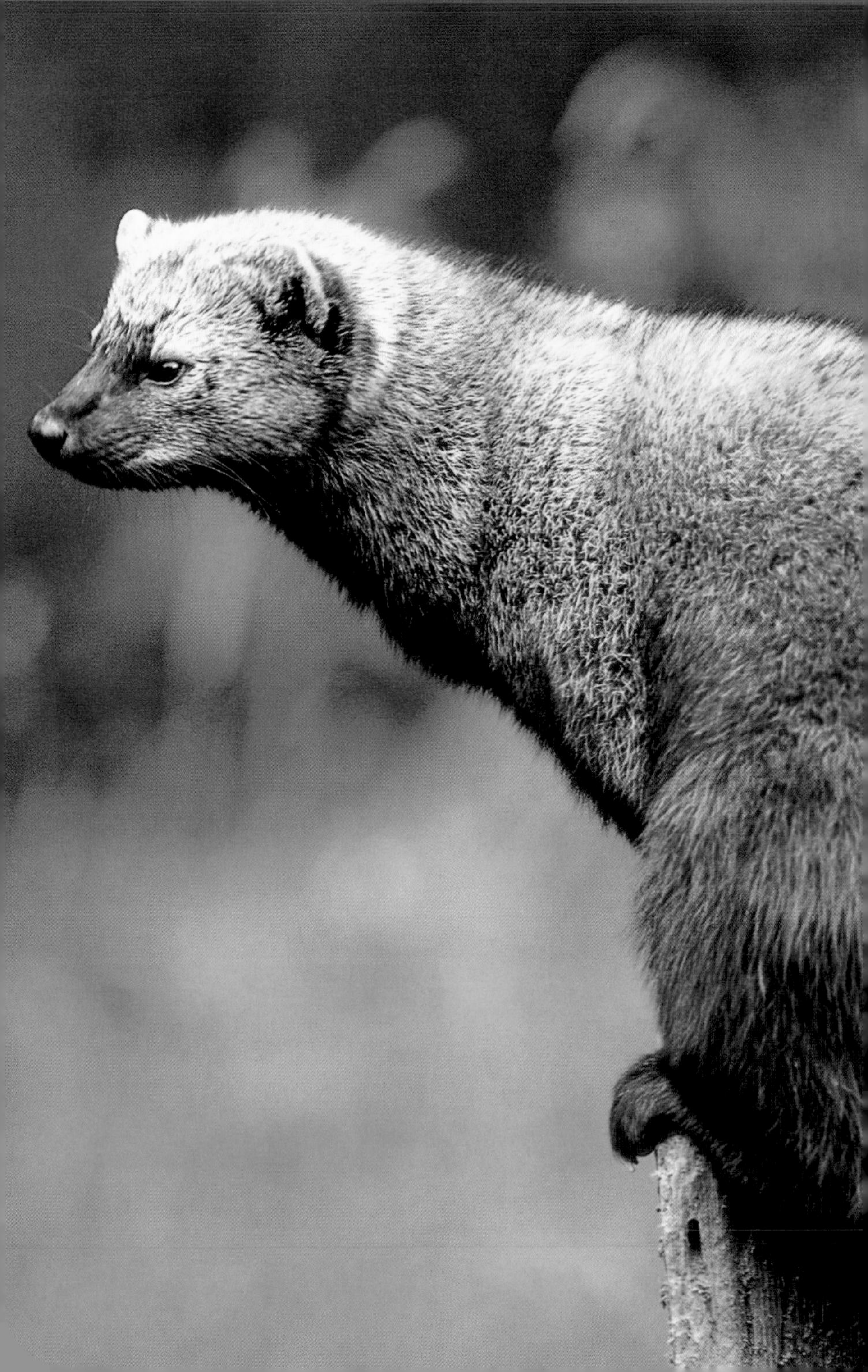

because the Fisher is always on the move throughout its territory. The natal den is more permanent, and it is usually located in a safe place, such as a hollow tree. A Fisher may excavate its winter den in the snow.

YOUNG: A litter of one to four (usually two or three) young is born in March or April. The mother will breed again about a week after the litter is born, but implantation of the embryo is delayed until January of the following year. During mating, the male and female may remain coupled for up to four hours. The helpless young nurse and remain in the den for at least seven weeks, after which time their eyes open. When they are three months old, they begin to hunt with their mother, and by fall they are independent. The female is usually sexually mature when she is two years old.

walking trail   foreprint

American Marten

SIMILAR SPECIES: The **American Marten** (p. 90) is smaller and lighter in color, and it usually has a buff or orange chest spot. The **American Mink** (p. 100) is smaller and has shorter ears, shorter legs and a cylindrical, much less bushy tail. The Fisher typically has a more grizzled appearance than either the marten or mink.

Short-tailed Weasel
Mustela erminea

In English, the name "weasel" is often used to describe pointy-nosed villains or to characterize dishonest cheats. Unfortunately, these connotations give weasels a bad reputation. Although weasels have pointed noses, they are neither villainous nor deceitful. Inarguably, though, weasels are efficient predators with an exceptional talent for hunting.

The Short-tailed Weasel is a relatively common carnivore in California, primarily in the Sierra Nevada, Klamath and North Coast Ranges. Despite its abundance in these regions, the Short-tailed Weasel is not commonly seen. Like all weasels, it is somewhat nocturnal (intermittently active both day and night) and inhabits areas with heavy cover.

When Short-tailed Weasels roam about their ranges, they explore every hole, burrow, hollow log and brush pile for potential prey. Where there is snow in winter, they travel both above and below the snow in their search for prey. Once a likely meal is located, it is seized with a rush, and then the weasel wraps its body around the animal and drives its needle-sharp canines into the back of the skull or neck. If the weasel catches an animal larger than itself, it seizes the prey by the neck and strangles it.

The Short-tailed Weasel's dramatic change between its winter and summer coats led Europeans to give it two different names: an animal wearing the dark summer coat is called a "stoat"; in the white winter pelage it is known as an "ermine." In California, two weasel species alternate between white in winter and brown in summer, so the stoat and ermine labels are best avoided to prevent confusion. Moreover, in areas lacking winter snow the weasels do not change color.

ALSO CALLED: Ermine.

DESCRIPTION: This weasel's short summer coat has brown upperparts and creamy white underparts, often suffused with lemon yellow. The feet are snowy white, even in summer, and the last third of the tail is black. The short, oval ears extend noticeably above the

winter coat

RANGE: A holarctic species, this weasel occurs in North America throughout most of Alaska and Canada and south to northern California and northern New Mexico in the West and northern Iowa and Pennsylvania in the East.

elongated head. The eyes are black and beady. The long neck and narrow thorax make it appear as if the forelegs are positioned farther back than on most mammals, giving the weasel a snake-like appearance. Starting in October and November in mountain regions, these animals become completely white, except for the black tail tip. The lower belly and inner hindlegs often retain the lemon yellow wash. In late March or April, the weasel molts back to its summer coat.

HABITAT: The Short-tailed Weasel is most abundant in coniferous or mixed forests and streamside woodlands. In summer, it may often be found in the alpine tundra, where it hunts on rockslides and talus slopes.

FOOD: The diet appears to consist almost entirely of animal prey, including mice, voles, shrews, chipmunks, pocket gophers, pikas, rabbits, bird eggs and nestlings, insects and even amphibians. These weasels are quick, lithe and unrelenting in their pursuit of anything they can overpower. They often eat every part of a mouse except the filled stomach, which may be excised with surgical precision and left on a rock.

DEN: Short-tailed Weasels commonly take over the burrows and nests of mice, ground squirrels, chipmunks, pocket gophers or lemmings and modify them for weasel occupancy. They line the nest with dried grasses, shredded leaves and the fur and feathers of prey. Sometimes a weasel accumulates the furs of so many animals that the nest grows to a diameter of 8 in. Some nests are located in hollow logs, under buildings or in an abandoned cabin that once supported a sizable mouse population.

YOUNG: In spring, the female gives birth to 4 to 12 (usually 6 to 9) blind, helpless young that weigh just $1/16$ oz. each. Their eyes open at five weeks, and

Total Length: $8^3/_4$–13 in.
Tail Length: $1^5/_8$–$3^1/_2$ in.
Weight: $1^5/_8$–$3^3/_4$ oz.

summer coat

soon thereafter they accompany the adults on hunts. At about this time, a male has typically joined the family. In addition to training the young to hunt, he impregnates the mother and all her young females, which are sexually mature at two to three months. Young males do not mature until the next February or March—a reproductive strategy that reduces interbreeding among littermates.

SIMILAR SPECIES: The **Long-tailed Weasel** (p. 98) is generally larger and has orangish underparts, generally lighter upperparts and yellowish to brownish feet in summer.

DID YOU KNOW?

These weasels typically mate in late summer, but after little more than a week, the embryos stop developing. In early spring, up to eight months later, the embryos implant in the uterus and the young are born about one month later.

Long-tailed Weasel
Mustela frenata

On a sunny winter day, there may be no better wildlife experience than to follow the tracks of a Long-tailed Weasel. This curious animal zig-zags as though it can never make up its mind which way to go, and every little thing it crosses seems to offer a momentary distraction. The Long-tailed Weasel seems continuously excited, and this bountiful energy is easily read in its tracks.

Long-tailed Weasels hunt wherever they can find prey: along wetland edges, on and beneath mountain snow, in burrows and even occasionally in trees. They can overpower smaller prey, such as mice, large insects and snakes, and kill them instantly. Larger prey species, up to the size of a rabbit, they grab by the throat and neck and wrestle to the ground. As the weasel wraps its snake-like body around its prey in an attempt to throw it off balance, it tries to kill the animal with bites to the back of the neck and head.

Unlike the Short-tailed Weasel (p. 96) and the more northerly Least Weasel (*M. nivalis*), the Long-tailed Weasel only occurs in North, Central and South America (only into Bolivia). With the conversion of native grasslands to farmland, the Long-tailed Weasel has declined to a point where it is now regarded as a species of concern in much of its range. Still, in some native grasslands that teem with ground squirrels, the Long-tailed Weasel can be found bounding about during the daytime, continually hunting throughout its waking hours.

DESCRIPTION: The summer coat is a rich cinnamon brown on the upperparts and usually orangish or buffy on the underparts. The feet are brown in summer. The tail is half as long as the body, and the terminal quarter is black. Where there is snow in winter, the coat is entirely white, except for the black tail tip and sometimes an orangish wash on the belly. The body is long and slender—the forelegs appear to be positioned well back on the body—and the head is hardly wider than the neck.

HABITAT: The Long-tailed Weasel is an animal of open country. It may be found in agricultural areas, on grassy slopes and in the alpine tundra. Sometimes, in places where the Short-tailed Weasel is rare or absent, it forages in deciduous woodlands, intermontane valleys and open forests.

FOOD: Although the Long-tailed Weasel can successfully subdue larger prey than can its smaller relative, voles and mice

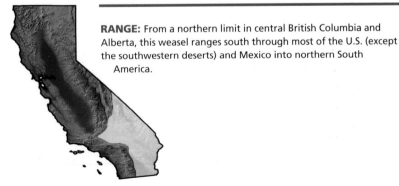

RANGE: From a northern limit in central British Columbia and Alberta, this weasel ranges south through most of the U.S. (except the southwestern deserts) and Mexico into northern South America.

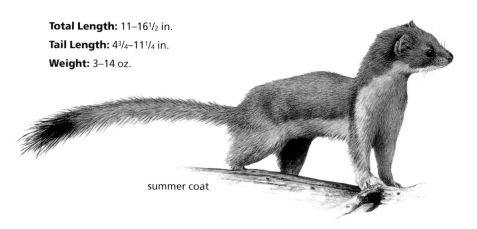

Total Length: 11–16^1/$_2$ in.
Tail Length: 4^3/$_4$–11^1/$_4$ in.
Weight: 3–14 oz.

summer coat

still make up most of its diet. It also preys on ground squirrels, woodrats, tree squirrels, rabbits and shrews, and it takes the eggs and young of ground-nesting birds when it encounters them.

DEN: These weasels usually make their nests in the burrow of a small mammal they have eaten. Nest cavities are lined with soft materials such as hair from prey. The female makes a maternal den in the same manner, either in a burrow, in a hollow log or under an old tree stump.

YOUNG: Long-tailed Weasels typically mate in mid-summer, but, through delayed implantation of the embryos, the young are not born until April or May. The litter contains four to nine (usually six to eight) blind, helpless young. They are born with sparse white hair, which becomes a fuzzy coat by one week and a sleek coat in two weeks. At 3^1/$_2$ weeks the young begin to supplement their milk diet with meat; they are weaned when their eyes open, just after seven weeks. By six weeks, there is a pronounced difference in size, with young males weighing about 3^1/$_2$ oz. and females 2^1/$_2$ oz. At about this time, a mature male weasel typically joins the group to breed with the mother and the young females as they become sexually

mature. The group travels together, and the male and female teach the young to hunt. The group disperses when the young are 2^1/$_2$ to 3 months old.

SIMILAR SPECIES: The **Short-tailed Weasel** (p. 96) is typically smaller, has a relatively shorter tail and has a white to lemon yellow (not orangish) belly and white feet in summer.

winter coat

DID YOU KNOW?

Weasel sign is not uncommon if you know what to look for: the tracks typically follow a paired pattern, and the twisted, hair-filled droppings, which are about the size of your pinkie finger, are often left atop a rock pile.

99

American Mink
Mustela vison

To many people, the fluid undulations of a bounding mink are more valuable than its much-prized fur. The American Mink is a lithe weasel that was described by naturalist Andy Russel as "moving . . . like a brown silk ribbon." Indeed, like most weasels, the mink seems to move with the unpredictable flexibility of a toy Slinky in a child's hands.

Minks are tenacious hunters, following scent trails left by potential prey over all kinds of obstacles and terrain. Almost as aquatic as otters, these opportunistic feeders routinely dive to depths of 10 ft. or more in pursuit of fish. Their fishing activity tends to coincide with breeding aggregations of fish in spring and fall, or during winter, when low oxygen levels force fish to congregate in oxygenated areas. It is along watercourses, therefore, that minks are most frequently observed, and their home ranges often stretch out in linear fashion, following rivers for up to 3 mi.

The American Mink is active throughout the year, and it is often easiest to follow by trailing its tracks in muddy water edges. The paired prints left by its bounding gait trace the inquisitive animal's adventures as it comes within sniffing distance of every burrow, hollow log and bush pile. This active forager always seems to be on the hunt; scarcely any feeding opportunities are passed up. Minks may kill more than they can eat, and surplus kills are stored for later use. A mink's food caches are often tucked away in its overnight dens, which are typically dug into riverbanks, beneath rock piles or in the home of a permanently evicted muskrat.

DESCRIPTION: The sleek coat is generally dark brown to black, usually with white spots on the chin, chest and sometimes the belly. The legs are short. The tail is cylindrical and only somewhat bushy. A male is nearly twice as large as a female. The anal scent glands produce a rank, skunk-like odor.

HABITAT: The American Mink is almost never found far from water. It frequents wet zones in coniferous or hardwood forests, brushlands and streamside vegetation in the foothills and even some grassy lowlands.

FOOD: Minks are fierce predators of muskrats, but in their desire for nearly any meat they also take frogs, fish, waterfowl and their eggs, mice, voles, rabbits, snakes and even crayfish and other aquatic invertebrates.

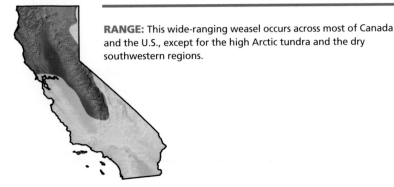

RANGE: This wide-ranging weasel occurs across most of Canada and the U.S., except for the high Arctic tundra and the dry southwestern regions.

Total Length: 18¹/₂–27¹/₂ in.
Tail Length: 5–8¹/₄ in.
Weight: 1¹/₄–3 lb.

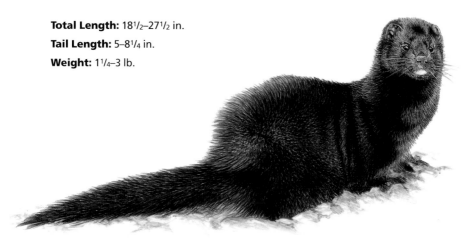

2 x 2 loping trail

YOUNG: Minks breed any time between late January and early April, but because the period of delayed implantation varies in length (from one week to 1¹/₂ months), the female almost always gives birth in spring. The actual gestation is about one month. There are 2 to 10 (usually 4 or 5) helpless, blind, pink, wrinkled young in a litter. Their eyes open at 24 to 31 days, and weaning begins at five weeks. The mother teaches the young to hunt for two to three weeks, after which they fend for themselves.

SIMILAR SPECIES: The **American Marten** (p. 90) has a bushier tail, longer legs and an orange or buff throat patch, and it is not as sleek looking. The **Fisher** (p. 92) is much larger and inhabits forests. The **Northern River Otter** (p. 110) is much larger and has a tapered tail and webbed feet.

DID YOU KNOW?

"Mink" is from a Swedish word that means "stinky animal." Although not as aromatic as skunks, minks are the smelliest of the weasels. The anal musk glands can release the stinky liquid, but not aim the spray, when a mink is threatened.

DEN: The den is usually in a burrow close to water. A mink may dig its own burrow, but more frequently it takes over a muskrat or beaver burrow and lines the nest with grass, feathers and other soft materials.

Wolverine
Gulo gulo

The Wolverine is one of the most poorly understood mammals in North America. It is an elusive animal of deep wilderness, as well as a creature of many myths and tall tales. More recently, the Wolverine has become a symbol of deep, pristine wilderness. Although most of us will never see a Wolverine, the knowledge that it maintains a hold in remote forests may reassure us that expanses of wilderness still exist.

Tales of the Wolverine's gluttony—its reputation rivals that of hyenas in Africa—have lingered in forest lore for centuries. Pioneers warned their children against the dangers of the forests, and often they meant Wolverines. The Wolverine is an efficient and agile predator: it can crush through bone in a single bite; it has long, semi-retractile foreclaws that allow it to climb trees; and it is ferocious enough to challenge a lone bear or wolf. What we rarely hear about is this animal's intelligence, its uniqueness among its weasel relatives and its sheer vigor and beauty.

From the few behavioral studies of Wolverines, their character emerges as being less vicious and more clever. Even simple observations of a Wolverine standing on its hindlegs and scanning the surroundings with a paw at its forehead to shield its eyes from the sun are indicative of intelligent behavior we are only now starting to understand. Nevertheless, some of the Wolverine's reputation is well deserved. True to its nickname "skunk bear," the Wolverine produces a stink that rivals skunks in foulness. The abundant, stinky scent is produced in glands beside the anus and is primarily used to mark territory.

The Wolverine's habitat preferences seem to vary as its diet shifts with seasons. In summer, it eats mostly ground squirrels and other small mammals, birds and berries; in winter it lives on carrion, mainly hoofed mammals, most of which it scavenges from wolves or roadkills. Like a vulture, the Wolverine can detect carcasses from far away.

The largest weasel of all, the Wolverine has one of the mammal world's most powerful sets of jaws, which it uses to tear meat off frozen carcasses or to crunch through bone to get at the rich, nourishing marrow inside. Few other large animals are able to extract as much nourishment from a single carcass.

DESCRIPTION: Although the head is small and weasel-like, the long legs and long fur look like they belong on a small bear. But unlike a bear, the Wolverine

RANGE: In North America, the Wolverine is a species of the coniferous forests and tundra of Alaska and northern Canada. It follows the montane coniferous forests from Alaska to as far south as California and Colorado.

Total Length: 27½–43 in.
Tail Length: 6¾–10 in.
Weight: 15–35 lb.

has an arched back and a long, bushy tail. The coat is mostly a shiny, dark cinnamon brown to nearly black. There may be yellowish-white spots on the throat and chest. A buffy or pale brownish stripe runs down each side from the shoulder to the flank, where it becomes wider. These stripes meet just before the base of the tail, leaving a dark saddle.

HABITAT: The Wolverine prefers large areas of remote wilderness in the high Sierra Nevada, where it frequently occupies wooded foothills and mountains. In summer, it forages into the alpine tundra and hunts along slopes. In winter, it drops to lower elevations and may disperse somewhat from the mountains. The Wolverine's enormous territory encompasses a great variety of habitats; this agile, determined predator is likely able to conquer almost any wild terrain.

FOOD: Prey includes marmots, ground squirrels, gophers, mice, deer carcasses, other vertebrates, berries and insects. Wolverines may kill large snowbound prey, but most large prey is scavenged carrion. Although Wolverines are generally thought to avoid human habitations, they are known to break into wilderness cabins and meat caches to eat or destroy everything within.

DEN: A Wolverine may maintain several dens throughout its territory, ranging in quality from makeshift cover under tree

DID YOU KNOW?

The Wolverine's lower jaw is more tightly bound to its skull than most other mammals' jaws. The articulating hinge that connects the upper and lower jaws is wrapped by bone in adult Wolverines, and in order for the jaws to dislocate this bone would have to break.

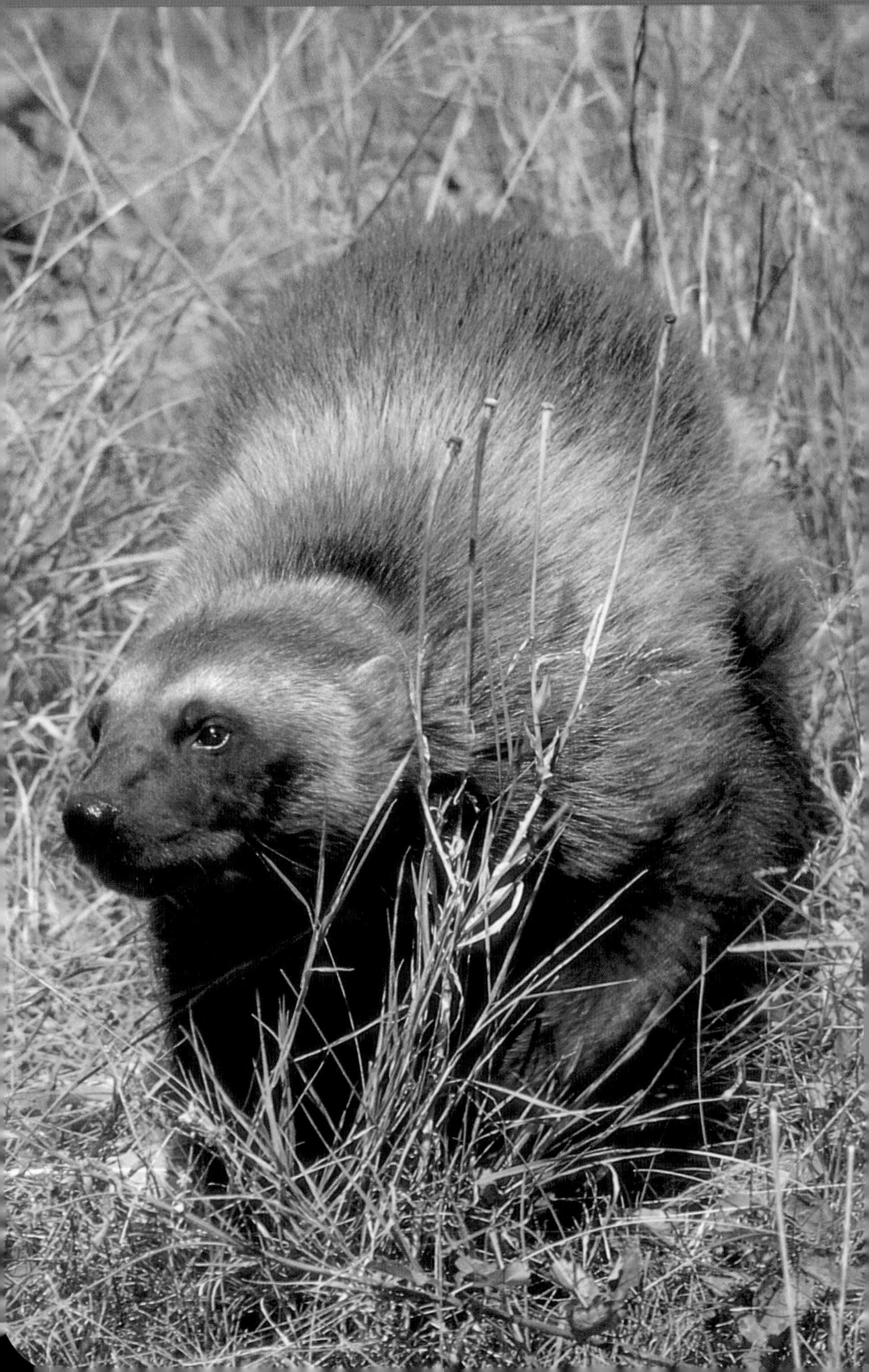

branches to a permanent underground dugout. The den may be among the roots of a fallen tree, in a hollow tree butt, in a rocky crevice or even in a semi-permanent snowbank. The natal den is often underground, and it is lined with leaves by the mother.

YOUNG: Wolverines breed between late April and early September, but the embryos do not implant in the uterine wall until January. Between late February and mid-April the female gives birth to a litter of one to five (generally two or three) cubs. The stubby-tailed cubs are born with their eyes and ears closed and with a fuzzy white coat that sets off the darker paws and face mask. They nurse for eight to nine weeks; then they leave the den and their mother teaches them to hunt. The mother and her young typically stay together through the first winter. The young disperse when they become sexually mature in spring.

walking trail   foreprint

American Badger

SIMILAR SPECIES: The **American Badger** (p.106) is squatter, with a distinctive vertical stripe on its forehead and without the lighter side stripes of a Wolverine. The **American Black Bear** (p.144) is much larger, has an inconspicuous tail, and lacks the light buffy stripe along each side.

American Badger
Taxidea taxus

In low-elevation meadows and open woodlands throughout most of California, a lucky observer may spy an American Badger. Badgers, with their flair for remodelling, are nature's roto-tillers and backhoes. The large holes left by badgers are of critical importance as den sites, shelters and hibernacula for dozens of species, from Coyotes to Black-widow Spiders. When badgers are eliminated from an area, the populations of many of these burrow-dependent animals eventually decline.

The badger enjoys a reputation for fierceness and boldness that was acquired in part from a not-very-closely-related mammal bearing the same name in Europe. While it is true that a cornered American Badger will put up an impressive show of attitude, like most animals it prefers to avoid a fight. When it is severely threatened or in competition, the badger's claws, strong limbs and powerful jaws make this animal a dangerous opponent. In spite of its impressive arsenal, the badger routinely kills only ground squirrels and other small rodents. However, rare occasions are known where badgers have taken Coyote pups. Likewise, a group of Coyotes may defeat a badger.

Pigeon-toed and short-legged, the American Badger is not much of a sprinter, but its heavy front claws enable it to move large quantities of earth in short order. Although a badger's predatory nature is of benefit to landowners, its natural digging skills have led many badgers to be killed by ranchers, as cattle and horses have been known (very rarely) to break their legs when stepping carelessly into badger excavations.

Badgers usually spend inclement winter weather sleeping in their burrows, but they do not enter a full state of hibernation like their European relatives, or like the ground squirrels upon which they feed. In some interior mountain regions of California, American Badgers may stay in their burrow for long periods.

In spite of low population densities, almost all sexually mature female badgers are impregnated during the nearly three months that they are sexually receptive. As with most members of the weasel family, once the egg is fertilized further embryonic development is delayed until the embryos implant, usually in January, which will result in a spring birth.

DESCRIPTION: Long, grizzled, yellowish-gray hair covers these short-legged,

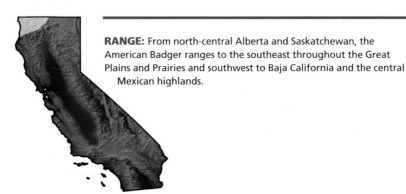

RANGE: From north-central Alberta and Saskatchewan, the American Badger ranges to the southeast throughout the Great Plains and Prairies and southwest to Baja California and the central Mexican highlands.

Total Length: 31–33 in.
Tail Length: 5–6¼ in.
Weight: 11–24 lb.

muscular members of the weasel family. The hair is longer on the sides than on the back or belly, which adds to the flattened appearance of the body. A white stripe originates on the nose and runs back onto the shoulders or sometimes slightly beyond. The top of the head is otherwise dark. A dark, vertical crescent, like a badge, runs between the short, rounded, furred ears and the eyes. The sides of the face are whitish or very pale buff. The short, bottlebrush tail is more yellowish than the body, and the lower legs and feet are very dark brown, becoming blackish at the extremities. The three central claws on each forefoot are greatly elongated for digging. Older American Badgers sometimes have the "wrap-around" jaw articulation seen in older Wolverines.

HABITAT: Essentially an animal of open places, the badger shuns forests. It is usually found in association with ground squirrels, typically in grasslands and open parkland. In the mountains, it forages on treeless alpine slopes or in riparian meadows. It may visit alpine areas in summer in search of pocket gophers and other burrowing prey.

FOOD: Burrowing mammals fill most of the badger's dietary needs, but it also eats eggs, young ground-nesting birds, mice, carrion, insects and snails.

DEN: An American Badger may dig its own den or take over and refurbish a ground squirrel's burrow. The den may approach 30 ft. in length and have a diameter of about 1 ft. It builds a bulky grass nest in an expanded chamber near or at the end of the burrow. A large pile of excavated earth is generally found to one side of the burrow entrance.

DID YOU KNOW?

Badgers make an incredible variety of sounds: adults hiss, bark, scream and snarl; in play, young badgers grunt, squeal, bark, meow, chirr and snuffle; and the front claws clatter when a badger runs on a hard surface.

YOUNG: One to five (usually four) naked, helpless young are born between late April and mid-June. Their eyes open after a month, and at two months their mother teaches them to hunt. In early evening they leave the burrow, trailing their mother. The babies investigate every grasshopper or beetle they encounter, but the mother directs the expedition to ground squirrel burrows. She often cripples a ground squirrel and then leaves it for her young to kill. The young disperse in fall, when they are three-quarters grown. Some of the young females may mate in their first summer, but most badgers are not sexually mature until they are a year old. Delayed implantation of the embryo is characteristic.

walking trail

foreprint

Wolverine

SIMILAR SPECIES: The larger **Wolverine** (p. 102) does not have the "flattened" appearance of a badger, and it lacks the thin white stripe on its nose. Also, Wolverines lope, whereas badgers trot. The **Striped Skunk** (p. 88) is smaller and has distinct black and white markings. The **Northern Raccoon** (p. 120) has a black "mask" and ringed tail.

Northern River Otter
Lontra canadensis

It may seem too good to be true, but all those playful characterizations of the Northern River Otter are actually based on fact. Otters often amuse themselves by rolling, sliding, diving or "body surfing," and they may also push and balance floating sticks with their noses or drop and retrieve pebbles for minutes at a time. They seem particularly interested in playing on slippery surfaces—they leap onto wet grass or mud with their forelegs folded close to their bodies for a streamlined and slippery ride. Unlike most members of the weasel family, river otters are social animals, and they will frolic together in the water and take turns sliding down banks.

With their lithe bodies, rudder-like tails, webbed toes and valved ears and nostrils, river otters are well adapted for aquatic habitats. Even when they emerge from water to clamber over rocks, there is a serpentine appearance to their progression. Although they spend lots of time at play, otters are diligent hunters and efficient at catching prey when it is plentiful. Otters generally cruise along slowly in the water by paddling with all four feet, but they can dart after prey with the ease of a seal. When an otter swims quickly, it propels itself mainly with vertical undulations of its body, hindlegs and tail. Otters can hold their breath for as long as five minutes, and, if so inclined, they could swim the breadth of a small lake without surfacing.

Because of all their activity, Northern River Otters leave many signs of their presence when they occupy an area. Their slides are the most obvious and best-known evidence—but be careful not to mistake the slippery beaver trails that are common around beaver ponds for otter slides. Despite their other aquatic tendencies, otters always defecate on land. Their scat is simple to identify—it is almost always full of fish bones and scales.

River otters may make extensive journeys across land, even through forested areas. Although a river otter looks clumsy on land, it can easily outrun a human with its humped, loping gait. On slippery surfaces, such as wet grass or mud, the otter glides along, usually on its belly with its legs tucked either back or forward to help steer and push. On flat ground, slides are sometimes pitted with blurred footprints where the otter has given itself a push for momentum. In mountain regions otters make slides in the snow and on ice.

In the past, the Northern River Otter's thick, beautiful, durable fur was sought after, and excessive trapping greatly

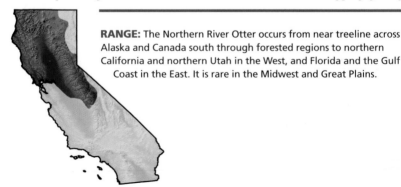

RANGE: The Northern River Otter occurs from near treeline across Alaska and Canada south through forested regions to northern California and northern Utah in the West, and Florida and the Gulf Coast in the East. It is rare in the Midwest and Great Plains.

Total Length: 3½–4½ ft.
Tail Length: 12–20 in.
Weight: 10–24 lb.

diminished the otter's continental population. Trapping has since been reduced, and the otter seems to be slowly recolonizing parts of North America from which it has been absent for decades. Even in areas where it is known to occur, however, it is infrequently seen, but its marks of playfulness remind us that we are not alone in our ability to have fun.

DESCRIPTION: This large, weasel-like carnivore has dark brown upperparts that look black when wet. It is paler below, and the throat is often silver gray. The head is broad and flattened, and it has small eyes and ears and prominent, whitish whiskers. The feet are webbed. The long tail is thick at the base and gradually tapers to the tip. The male is the larger gender. Otters do not hibernate, and where ice forms in winter, they still chase fish under the ice.

HABITAT: Year-round, river otters live primarily in or along wooded rivers, deltas, ponds and lakes. Although they rarely forage far from water, dispersing individuals may be seen far from water as they search for new territory. In northern California they are common on the coast, where they eat crabs, mussels and saltwater fish and are often mistaken for Sea Otters. They may be active day or night, but tend to be more nocturnal close to human activity. The Northern River Otter often inhabits lakes or ponds where beavers are active.

DID YOU KNOW?

When a troupe of agile river otters travel single file through the water, their undulating, lithe bodies combine to form a very serpent-like image—perhaps with enough similarity to give rise to the rumors of lake-dwelling sea-monsters.

foreprint

loping trail

FOOD: Crayfish, turtles, frogs and fish form the bulk of the diet, but otters occasionally depredate bird nests and eat small mammals such as mice, young muskrats and young beavers, and sometimes even insects and earthworms.

DEN: The permanent den is often in a bank, with both underwater and above-water entrances. During a journey for new territory, an otter rests under roots or overhangs, in hollow logs, in the abandoned burrows of other mammals or in abandoned beaver or muskrat lodges. Natal dens are often abandoned muskrat, beaver or even Woodchuck dens.

YOUNG: The female bears a litter of one to six blind, fully furred young in March or April. The young are 5 oz. at birth. They first leave the den at three to four months, and leave their parents at six to seven months. Otters become sexually mature at two years. The mother breeds again soon after her litter is born, but delayed implantation of the embryos puts off the birth until the following spring.

SIMILAR SPECIES: The **Sea Otter** (p. 114) is found only in saltwater and it rarely comes to shore. The **American Beaver** (p. 206) is more stout and has a wide, flat, hairless, scaly tail. The **American Mink** (p. 100) is smaller, its feet are not webbed, and its tail is cylindrical, not tapered.

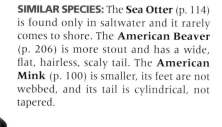

Sea Otter

Sea Otter
Enhydra lutris

For many animal enthusiats, the playful and intelligent Sea Otter is among the most desired animals to see while visiting the coast of California. This fully aquatic carnivore has such a buoyant body and curious demeanor that watching one is not only comical but mesmerizing. When two Sea Otters are playing, they turn somersaults at the surface and wrestle together as if trying to dunk each other under. When they are resting, they lounge on their backs at the surface and rub their faces with curled-up paws, much like cats do when grooming. Sea Otters are even neighborly, and they regularly hobnob with the local sea-lions and seals.

To tell the difference between Sea Otters and Northern River Otters on the coast is easy—with the right information. Sea Otters do not venture more than 1 1/4 mi from shore or into water more than 100 ft. deep. Typically, they stay close to rocky shores with abundant kelp beds. They also prefer open coastline and are therefore rarely seen in passages or sheltered water. River otters, on the other hand, are frequently seen in sheltered waters and deltas. Also, river otters are well known for their travels, and an otter seen several miles from shore or one that is swimming long distances from island to island is a Northern River Otter. Any otter seen moving or eating on land is, again, a river otter. Sea Otters are very clumsy on land, and their locomotion is limited to an ungainly, heavy lope, an awkward, slow walk or an even slower, body-dragging slide. Being so limited on land, Sea Otters rarely come out of the water; they may haul out onto rocks to rest only during rough or stormy weather.

At night, or for daytime rest, Sea Otters wrap themselves in kelp at the surface. The kelp is attached underwater and prevents the otter from drifting while it sleeps.

The Sea Otter does not have a layer of insulating blubber like other marine mammals; it relies on its high metabolism and thick coat to keep warm. Its full coat is both a blessing and a curse: Sea Otters were hunted for their pelts almost to extinction. Although some populations are slowly increasing, others are in decline and the species is still listed as threatened. The current decline of some Sea Otter populations is probably attributable to habitat disturbance and Orca predation.

DESCRIPTION: The stout-bodied Sea Otter has a short tail and rounded head. Its slightly flattened tail is no more than

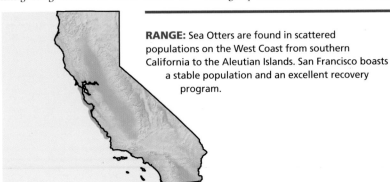

RANGE: Sea Otters are found in scattered populations on the West Coast from southern California to the Aleutian Islands. San Francisco boasts a stable population and an excellent recovery program.

Total Length: 30–65 in.
Tail Length: 10–16 in.
Total Weight: 50–100 lb.

one-third the length of its body. Its fur may be a variety of colors including light brown, reddish brown, yellowish gray or nearly black, and the fur is very thick, especially on the throat and chest. It has two "pockets," each formed from a fold of skin between its chest and each underarm. Often the head is lighter than the body; in old males the head may be nearly white. Its tiny ears may appear pinched, but are otherwise inconspicuous. All four feet are webbed and the hindfeet resemble flippers. Male Sea Otters are larger than females.

HABITAT: This species lives almost its entire life in shallow coastal waters, favoring areas of kelp beds or reefs with nearby or underlying rocks.

FOOD: The Sea Otter feeds primarily on sea urchins, crustaceans, shellfish and fish. An otter dives underwater for up to five minutes and returns to the surface with its prey and a stone, using its underarm pockets to carry its load. One

otter was seen unloading six urchins and three oysters from its "cargo holds." To unload its pockets and eat, the otter rests on its back. It places the stone on its chest and uses it as an anvil on which to bash the shell of the urchin, shellfish or crustacean repeatedly until it breaks, exposing the flesh inside. Unlike the Northern River Otter, the Sea Otter does not come onto shore to eat its meal.

YOUNG: Mating occurs in the water, usually in late summer. The female gives birth to one pup $6^1/_2$ to 9 months later, a gestation that probably includes a period of delayed implantation. On rare occasions, a female has two pups.

DID YOU KNOW?

Sea Otters caught in oil spills have extremely low chances of survival. The oil slicks their coat and destroys the insulating and waterproofing qualities of the fur.

She gives birth in the water, and to nurse her young she floats on her back and allows the pup to sit on her chest. The pup also plays and naps on its mother's chest. It is weaned at one year but may stay with its mother for several more months, even if she gives birth again. If the mother senses danger, such as an approaching shark or Orca, she will hold her pup under her forelegs and dive into a kelp bed until the danger passes.

foreprint

walking trail

hindprint

SIMILAR SPECIES: The **Northern River Otter** (p. 110) has a longer tail and hindlegs that are not flipper-like; it is, almost invariably, any otter seen on land. **Seals** and **sea-lions** (pp. 124–43) have different body shapes and their forelegs are flippers instead of paws.

Northern River Otter

117

Ringtail

Bassariscus astutus

With the face of a fox, the body of a weasel, the tail of a lemur, the claws of a cat and the eyes of an owl, the striking Ringtail is one of the most unique animals in the region. Such mythical descriptions are perhaps the best way to describe the Ringtail, as it seems to have many of the best qualities of other animals. Less obvious, it also has extraordinary dexterity, keen hearing and acute eyesight, all of which contribute to a superb nighttime hunter. Although seeing the Ringtail in the wild is a memorable experience, its distribution in California is patchy. In some areas it is locally common, while in other parts it is absent. Like raccoons, it favors habitats near water, and it tends to avoid high elevations.

People seldom see the Ringtail because it forages almost exclusively at night. It hunts with a style similar to that of a cat. It waits in ambush and as unsuspecting prey approaches, it readies itself and pounces onto the animal. The Ringtail tries to knock its prey off balance and pin it down to deliver a fatal bite to the neck. This hunting style and the Ringtail's impressive mousing skill are responsible for its alternate common name, Cacomistle. This name is derived from the language of the Mexican Nahuatl people; it means "half Mountain Lion."

Unlike the Mountain Lion, however, the Ringtail is quite small and hunts mainly rodents, reptiles and amphibians.

Occasionally Ringtails are seen in the headlights of a car, particularly where roads pass over streams and rivers in the foothills. It is also well known for sneaking into camps and backyards and carrying off food items. The Ringtail is remarkably surreptitious, because it seems to equally excel in secrecy as it does in light-footed nimbleness. A Ringtail uses its semi-retractile, cat-like claws to cling onto almost sheer surfaces, and it can scale trees or nearly vertical cliffs to get at bird nests, reptiles and rodents.

ALSO CALLED: Cacomistle, Miner's Cat, Ring-tailed Cat, Civet Cat

DESCRIPTION: Looking like a slender, big-eared, fox-faced cat, the Ringtail is gray or yellowish gray above and buff beneath. Its most noticeable characteristic is the long, bushy tail that is alternately banded black and white. This extremely agile animal almost appears to flow through the rocky terrain it inhabits.

HABITAT: The Ringtail generally occupies rocky slopes and valleys in the foothills regions, usually near water.

RANGE: Ringtails occur from southern Oregon east to southern Wyoming and south into southern Mexico.

Total Length: 24–32 in.
Tail Length: 12–17 in.
Weight: 1³/₄–2¹/₂ lb.

Areas with logs, snags, rock crevices and other good cover are particularly good Ringtail habitats. It has been found as high as 8500 ft., but it normally prefers much lower elevations. There is a population in the Sierra Buttes.

FOOD: The omnivorous Ringtail eats insects and other invertebrates, small mammals, reptiles, amphibians, bird eggs and nestlings, carrion and fruit.

DEN: The den has a tiny entrance. It is generally found in rocky debris or in natural caves, but sometimes a hollow tree or the space beneath an abandoned building is used.

YOUNG: After mating in late February or March, one to five (usually three to four) blind, helpless, 1-oz. babies are born, usually in May, but sometimes as late as July. Their eyes and ears open and the teeth erupt when they are one month old. At this time, they also switch from a milk diet to animal food brought in by both parents. The mother trains her offspring to hunt, and they disperse when they reach adult size by early winter. Ringtails are sexually mature before their first birthdays.

SIMILAR SPECIES: Only the **Northern Raccoon** (p. 120) has a banded tail like that of the Ringtail, but the raccoon is much stockier and sports a humped back.

DID YOU KNOW?

In remote mining operations, miners found the Ringtail's superb mousing ability so necessary that they put out food to encourage these nocturnal predators. Although cats are famous mousers, the Ringtail is better still.

Northern Raccoon
Procyon lotor

The Northern Raccoon is famous for its black bandit mask and ringed tail. The mask suits the raccoon, because it is well known as a looter of people's gardens, cabins, campsites and, yes, even garbage cans. A raccoon is likely to investigate tasty bits of food and any shiny object it finds. For all its roguish behavior, however, the Northern Raccoon is rarely associated with ferociousness or savagery—it is mainly a playful and docile animal unless it is cornered or threatened. Testing a raccoon's ferocity is an unnecessary and simple-minded act. Raccoons have been known to wound and even kill attacking dogs.

Raccoons are among the most frequently encountered wild carnivores in many parts of the region. When raccoons are seen, which is usually at night, they quickly bound away, effectively evading flashlight beams and slipping into burrows or climbing to tree retreats. Should their sanctuary be found, raccoons remain still at a safe distance, waiting for the invasive experience to end.

Northern Raccoons tend to frequent muddy environments, a characteristic that allows people to find their diagnostic tracks along the edges of wetlands and waterbodies. Like humans and bears, raccoons walk on their heels, so they leave unusually large tracks for their body size. They will methodically circumnavigate wetlands in the hopes of finding duck nests or unwary amphibians upon which to dine.

The manner in which raccoons typically feel their way through the world has long been recognized. In fact, our word "raccoon" is derived from the Algonquian name for this animal, *aroughcoune*, which means "he scratches with his hands." One of the best-known characteristics of the Northern Raccoon is its habit of dunking its food in water before eating it. People once thought that the raccoon was washing its food—the scientific name *lotor* is Latin for "washer"—but biologists now believe that a raccoon's sense of touch is enhanced by water, and that it is actually feeling for inedible bits to discard (which may, by some, be considered as washing).

Cold winters are an ecological barrier to the dispersal of this animal, because it does not hibernate and so requires year-round food availability. Over the past century, however, raccoons have been moving into colder climes, perhaps because of increasing human habitation in these areas. Raccoons benefit from the heated buildings and year-round food-scraps and garbage produced by humans. As urban "wildlife,"

RANGE: The Northern Raccoon occurs from southern Canada south through most of the U.S. and Mexico. It is absent from parts of the Rocky Mountains, central Nevada, Utah and Arizona.

Total Length: 26–38 in.
Tail Length: 7½–16 in.
Weight: 12–31 lb.

raccoons may become nuisances when they search for food.

DESCRIPTION: The coat is blackish to brownish gray overall, with lighter, grayish-brown underparts. The bushy tail, with its four to six alternating blackish rings on a yellowish-white background, makes the raccoon one of the most recognizable North American carnivores. There is a black "mask" across the eyes, bordered by white "eyebrows" and a mostly white snout, and a strip of white fur separates the upper lip from the nose. The ears are relatively small. Northern Raccoons are capable of producing a wide variety of vocalizations: they can purr, growl, snarl, scream, hiss, trill, whinny and whimper.

HABITAT: Raccoons prefer edge habitats between forested regions and wetlands such as streams, lakes and ponds. They are not typically found high in the mountains, but they may be locally common in foothill regions and low montane forests.

FOOD: The Northern Raccoon fills the role of medium-sized omnivore in the food web. Besides eating fruits, nuts, berries and insects, it avidly seeks out and eats clams, frogs, fish, eggs, young birds and rodents. Just as a bear does, the raccoon consumes vast amounts of food in fall to build a large fat reserve that will help sustain it over winter.

DEN: The den is often located in a hollow tree, but raccoons are increasingly using sites beneath abandoned buildings or under discarded construction materials. In the foothills, dens can sometimes be found in rock crevices, where grasses or leaves carried in by the female may cover the floor.

DID YOU KNOW?

Raccoons have thousands of nerve endings in their "hands" and "fingers." It is an asset they constantly put to use, probing under rocks and in crevices for food.

YOUNG: After about a two-month gestation, females bear a litter of two to seven (typically four) young sometime between March and May. The young weigh just 2 oz. at birth. Their eyes open at about three weeks, and when they are six to seven weeks old they begin to feed outside the den. At first, the mother carries her young about by the nape of the neck, as a cat carries kittens. About a month later, she starts taking them on extended nightly feeding forays. Some young disperse in fall, but others remain until their mother forces them out when she needs room for her next litter.

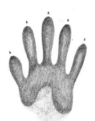

walking trail

foreprint

Ringtail

SIMILAR SPECIES: The **Ringtail** (p. 118) lacks the black mask, has a longer and bushier tail and is slimmer and more weasel-like. The **American Badger** (p. 106) could be confused with a raccoon, but a badger is much squatter; its facial markings are vertically oriented, unlike the horizontal "mask" of a raccoon; and its shorter, thinner tail doesn't have the raccoon's distinctive rings.

Harbor Seal
Phoca vitulina

The inquisitive Harbor Seal is a well-known resident of the western coast. These seals bespeckle the rocky coastline at almost any time of day throughout the year. They bask on shore either alone or in large groups.

Harbor Seals are frequently referred to as sociable or gregarious, but this notion is not entirely true. Although many seals may bask on rocks together, they pay very little attention to their neighbors and seldom interact. Only during the pupping season is there interaction, and it is primarily between females. Mothers with newborn pups may congregate in a "nursery" in shallow water where the pups can sleep. These nursery groups are not truly social; they form solely as a protective measure against possible predation. While most of the females and pups sleep, some are likely to be awake and watchful for danger.

The same is true for hauled-out seals. Where several seals are together, chances are good that there is always at least one individual awake and wary of an approaching Orca or other threat.

Harbor Seals cannot sleep at the surface like sea-lions and Sea Otters. During the day, they can sleep underwater in shallow coastal water by resting vertically just above the bottom. Young pups commonly rest in this manner. They can go without breathing for nearly 30 minutes, and although they sometimes wake up to breathe, they frequently rise to the surface and take a breath without awakening, and then sink back to the bottom. At night when the tide is out, they sleep high and dry in their preferred haul-out site. They frequently rest with their heads and rear flippers

RANGE: Harbor Seals are found along the northern coasts of North America, Europe and Asia. They inhabit the entire coast from Alaska to California.

Total Length: 4–6 ft.
Total Weight: 110–310 lb.

lifted above the rock. Along the coast, Harbor Seals can often be seen sleeping on offshore rocks during the day.

Harbor Seals tend to be wary of humans, and if you approach them they are likely to dive immediately into the water. On the other hand, many kayakers and boaters have enjoyed watching inquisitive individuals that approach their boats for a better look. This kind of experience is controlled by the seal; if it wants to see you, it will come closer. If the seal is afraid of you, it will leave. Do not approach a seal that has tried to flee you, because it can cause unnecessary stress to the animal.

DESCRIPTION: A Harbor Seal is typically dark gray or brownish gray with light, blotchy spots or rings. The reverse color pattern is also common—light gray or nearly white with dark spots. The undersides are generally lighter than the back. The outer coat is composed of stiff guard hairs about $3/8$ in. long, and this characteristic is what gives seals in this family the name "hair seals." The guard hairs cover an insulating undercoat of sparse curly hair about $1/4$ in. long. Pups bear a spotted silvery or gray-brown coat at birth. The head is large and round and there are no visible ears. Each of the short front flippers bears long narrow claws. The male is the larger gender in this species.

DID YOU KNOW?

Sometimes these seals follow fish several hundred miles up major rivers; there are even permanent populations in some inland lakes.

HABITAT: This nearshore species is frequently found in bays and estuaries. Harbor Seals inhabit kelp forest regions, where they are the top predator. Common haul-out sites include intertidal sandbars, rocks and rocky shores, and favored spots are used by Harbor Seals generation after generation.

FOOD: Harbor Seals feed primarily on fish, such as rockfish, cod, herring, flounder and salmon. To a lesser extent, they also feed on mollusks, such as clams, squid and octopus, and crustaceans, such as crabs, shrimp and crayfish. Newly weaned pups seem to consume more shrimp and mollusks than do adults. Adult Harbor Seals have been seen taking fish from nets and some have even entered fish traps to feed, making a clean getaway afterwards.

YOUNG: The breeding season for Harbor Seals varies geographically. The farther north a population, the later the breeding and pupping. Gestation lasts 10 months, and in California the peak pupping season is April and May. The pups are weaned when 4 to 6 weeks old—after they have tripled their birth weight on their mothers' milk, which is more than 50 percent fat. Within a few days of weaning their pups, females mate again. Harbor Seals become sexually mature at 3 to 7 years. Captive seals have lived more than 35 years, although the typical life span for males is 20 years and for females is 30 years.

foreprint

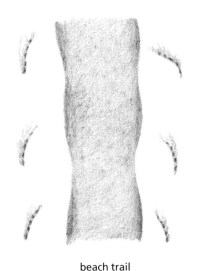

beach trail

SIMILAR SPECIES: The **Northern Fur Seal** (p. 132) and the **sea-lions** (pp. 136–43) are usually larger and have long, hairless hindflippers that can rotate under the body to support its weight. As well, they have longer muzzles, small pinnae and more dog-like faces than the Harbor Seal. The **Northern Elephant Seal** (p. 128) is much larger and has a distinctively large snout.

Northern Fur Seal

Northern Elephant Seal
Mirounga angustirostris

The enormous Northern Elephant Seal is one of the largest of all seals. Only its Southern Hemisphere counterpart, the Southern Elephant Seal (*M. leonina*), averages slightly larger.

Elephant seals are famous for their incredible diving capabilities. Their dives normally last for about 20 minutes at depths between 1000 and 2100 ft., but a few recorded dives lasted 2 hours and reached depths up to 5000 ft. Of mammals, only the Sperm Whale and some of the beaked whales can dive deeper or longer than this.

Northern Elephant Seals are also known for their long migrations—two per year. Sometime between December and late February the adults arrive at sandy beaches in California or Mexico, where females give birth and mate. Afterwards, the adults and the young of the year depart for good feeding waters. Adult males and some juveniles may venture as far north as the Gulf of Alaska and the Aleutian Islands, where they feast on the abundant sea life. Most females and young of the year do not travel quite as far; they prefer feeding in waters between 40° N and 45° N.

After feeding for two to five months, Northern Elephant Seals return to the sandy shores of Mexico and California to molt—females and juveniles come ashore sometime between April and June, and males sometime between July and August. When elephant seals molt, they shed the short, dense, yellowish-gray pelage along with large patches of old skin. During both the mating and molting seasons elephant seals fast and lose up to 36 percent of their body weight. After the molting season, they once again venture out to food-rich waters to replenish their bodies before mating.

Adult males who travel twice a year to waters around Alaska tally up more travel miles than any other mammal, even more than the renowned Gray Whale. Each year, a male Northern Elephant Seal may cover 13,000 mi. and spend from 250 to 300 days at sea.

Commercial harvest for oil during the heavy whaling years reduced the number of Northern Elephant Seals to somewhere between 100 and 1000, with local populations completely extirpated. These seals are now fully protected under the Marine Mammal Protection Act and their numbers have increased dramatically. More sightings off the coast of California are now being reported.

RANGE: These enormous seals are found from coastal Baja California to the Gulf of Alaska. They probably disperse within a few hundred miles from the coast during the non-breeding season.

Total Length: Males 12–16 ft., females 7–12 ft.

Total Weight: Males up to 5070 lb., females up to 2000 lb.

male

female

DESCRIPTION: The sheer size of the Northern Elephant Seal gives away its identity. If you have any doubt, however, a closer look at its nose will confirm it. Both sexes of this large seal have a nose that extends past the mouth, but an adult male has a pendulous, inflatable, foot-long snout that resembles a trunk. This seal is mainly gray or light brown in color, with similarly colored sparse hair. Its hindflippers appear to be lobed on either side and have reduced claws. The tough skin of the male's neck and chest is covered with creases, scars and wrinkles, a feature absent in females. Pups are born black but molt to silver at one month.

HABITAT: The Northern Elephant Seal lives in the temperate waters off the West Coast. It migrates between northern feeding waters and southern breeding and molting beaches twice a year. During the breeding and molting seasons, Northern Elephant Seals haul out onto sandy beaches. They do not haul out onto rocks, but they may cross over

> **DID YOU KNOW?**
>
> When on land, Northern Elephant Seals are very noisy—the males produce a series of loud rattling snorts, and females make sounds resembling monstrous belches.

rocks if necessary to reach a sandy beach. These seals rarely haul out during the feeding season; instead, they rest at the surface of the water and can stay offshore for months at a time.

FOOD: Northern Elephant Seals feed on a variety of sea creatures including squid, octopus, small sharks, rays, pelagic red crabs and large fish. Adult males feed on larger prey than do females and pups.

YOUNG: The breeding range for this species includes the coasts of Baja, California and southern Oregon. These seals are polygamous, but not strongly territorial. During the breeding season from December to March, males arrive on shore first and battle fiercely for status in the social hierarchy; a high status means they can have a large harem. The females come to shore a couple of weeks after the males, and within a few

days each female gives birth to a pup conceived in the previous breeding season. Gestation is 11 months, and nursing takes place for no more than one month, during which time the mothers fast. Just a few days before their pups are to be weaned, the females mate, and then after weaning they leave. Females are sexually mature at 2 to 5 years and males at about 5 years, but males typically cannot win a harem until they are at least 8 years old.

SIMILAR SPECIES: The **Harbor Seal** (p. 124) and **sea-lions** (pp. 136–43) in the region are much smaller, and none have the distinctive snout of the Northern Elephant Seal.

Harbor Seal

Northern Fur Seal
Callorhinus ursinus

Completely at home in the ocean, the Northern Fur Seal almost never comes to shore, except during its breeding season. The rest of the year, this seal is pelagic off the coast of California and neighboring regions.

In general, these seals are not gregarious; they are either alone or in a group of no more than three individuals. Even during the breeding season, when large groups gather on rocky islands, interaction is limited to courtship and mating. The bulls savagely defend their territories, and although the females are less aggressive, they still keep to themselves. When the females have finished nursing their young, they depart the rocky shores and leave the pups to fend for themselves. Many pups die of disease within the first month or two after birth, but many of those that make it to weaning will survive even though they never see their mothers again.

The Northern Fur Seal travels more at sea than almost any other seal or sealion; only the Northern Elephant Seal covers more miles each year. Including the distance it covers feeding at sea, and its migrations to and from breeding islands, a Northern Fur Seal tallies about 6000 mi. of travel each year.

DESCRIPTION: The Northern Fur Seal has a small head with long whiskers, small external ears, large eyes and a short, pointed nose. Its tail is very short, but the flippers are extremely large in relation to the size of the body. When the seal is wet it is sleek and black. When dry, the male is mostly dark grayish black, while the female shows a brownish or reddish throat and often some silvery-gray underparts. Adult males have a thickened neck and are more than twice the weight of females. Newborn pups are black, and male pups are larger than female pups.

HABITAT: Northern Fur Seals are pelagic for 7 to 10 months of the year. They come ashore only to breed, mainly on rocky beaches of the Pribilof and Commander islands.

FOOD: Northern Fur Seals feed mainly on squid, along with herring, capelin and pollack up to 10 in. long. Almost all feeding takes place at night, when fish are closer to the surface. These seals may dive in search of food; the maximum recorded dive depth is 755 ft., but most seals forage at depths of 230 ft. or less.

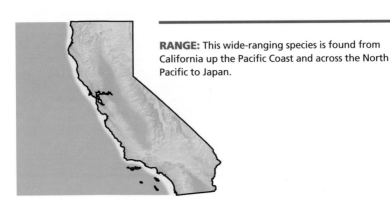

RANGE: This wide-ranging species is found from California up the Pacific Coast and across the North Pacific to Japan.

Total Length: Males 6–7½ ft., females 3½–5 ft.

Tail Length: 2 in.

Total Weight: Males 330–620 lb., females 84–120 lb.

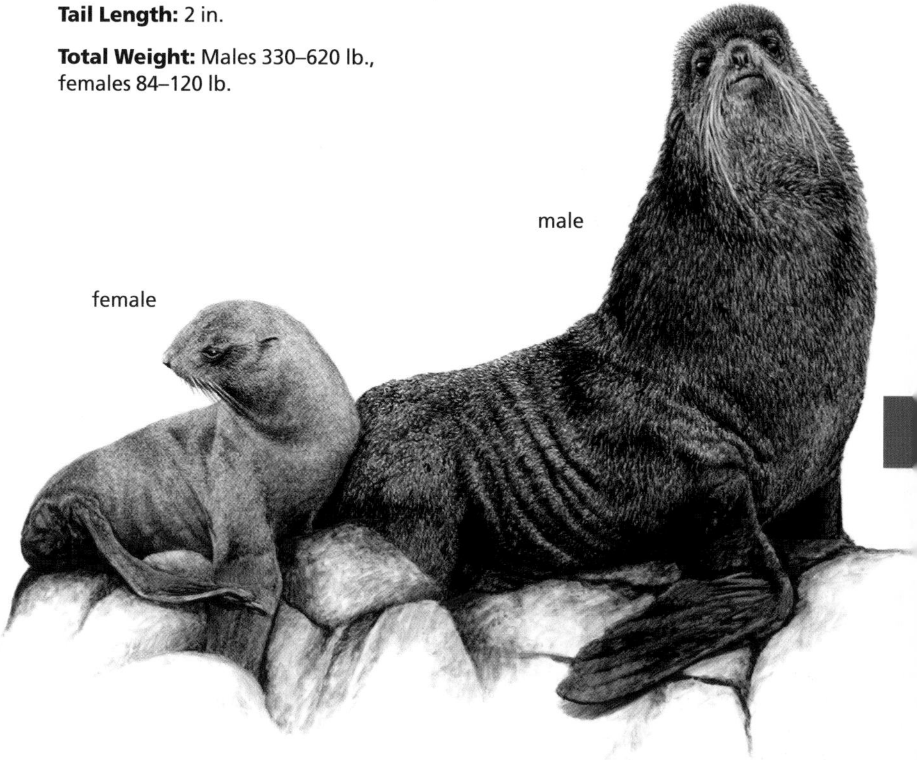

male

female

YOUNG: Males come to shore in late May and June and battle to establish their territories. Females come to shore in mid-June or July, and within two days they give birth to a pup conceived the previous summer. Mating occurs 8 to 10 days later. The pup nurses for four or five months.

SIMILAR SPECIES: The **Harbor Seal** (p. 124) is a true seal that does not rotate its hindflippers under its body, and it usually has spots. The **Guadalupe Fur Seal** (p. 134) has a limited range. The **Northern Sea-Lion** (p. 136) is larger, and the **California Sea-Lion** (p. 140), which is usually larger, has relatively shorter hindflippers.

DID YOU KNOW?

When this seal is resting in the water, it often keeps one hindflipper straight up and waving in the wind. No one knows why the seal does this, but it does make the animal easy to spot from a boat.

Guadalupe Fur Seal
Arctocephalus townsendi

The history of the Guadalupe Fur Seal has been an unfortunate combination of anonymity and devastation. Prior to 1892, this fur seal was unknown to science, and yet its total population was nearly eradicated by hunting for its pelts. At the end of the 1800s, just a handful of seals remained. Charles Haskins Townsend, sent in 1892 by the U.S. Fish Commission to report on this unknown fur seal, saw only seven fur seals alive, and he took discarded skulls from Guadalupe Island to be studied by the Smithsonian Institute. Later, in 1894, seal hunters found a group of 15 fur seals on Guadalupe Island and killed all of them for their pelts. At the turn of the century the species was believed to be extinct. In 1949, a single fur seal was spotted on one occasion, and later, 14 more were confirmed. These sightings proved that this species that was thought to be extinct, and which had not been documented for more than 20 years, had survived. With the protection of Guadalupe Island in 1975, and local awareness of the plight of these fur seals, their numbers began to rise. Today, they have been seen as far north as San Miguel Island, and their numbers may be between 7000 and 9000.

DESCRIPTION: This rare seal (actually a misnomer, it is really a type of sea-lion) has very thick, grizzled fur that is mainly rich brown in color. The head and face are bear-like, and it has big eyes and distinct narrow ears. Its muzzle is somewhat narrow and conical. The darkly colored front flippers are conspicuously larger than the hindflippers—a characteristic unique to fur seals and useful for field identification. Its hindflippers are also darkly colored.

HABITAT: This seal belongs to a family that is primarily a Southern Hemisphere family. Only two members of this family can be found north of the equator, the Guadalupe Fur Seal, and the Galapagos Fur Seal (*A. galapagoensis*). The Guadalupe Fur Seal hauls out to breed on just two rocky islands off Baja. They also haul out on other islands, but rocks and crevices are a habitat requirement. (Because these seals have such thick fur, the shade provided by rocks is necessary to avoid over-heating when on land.)

FEEDING: Studies of a few individuals have revealed that many types of fish and squid are the primary prey species. Some shrimp is also consumed.

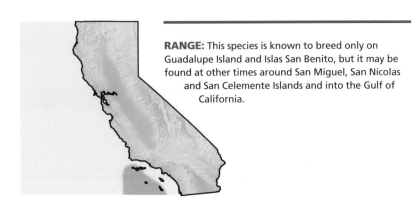

RANGE: This species is known to breed only on Guadalupe Island and Islas San Benito, but it may be found at other times around San Miguel, San Nicolas and San Celemente Islands and into the Gulf of California.

Total Length: males up to 6¼ ft, females up to 4½ ft.

Tail Length: 2 in.

Total Weight: males up to 350 lb, females up to 100 lb.

REPRODUCTION: The males are unusual in that they defend territories in rocky habitats that include caves and crevices. Females usually aggregate into harems during the breeding season. Mating and pupping occurs in May, June and July. Females mate 7 to 10 days after they give birth to a pup conceived the previous year. Not much else is known about the reproductive history. Guadalupe Island has been declared a sanctuary as the breeding ground for this species.

SIMILAR SPECIES: The **Harbor Seal** (p. 124) is a true seal that does not rotate its hindflippers under its body, and it usually has spots. The **Northern Fur Seal** (p. 132) has a much broader range. The **Northern Sea-Lion** (p. 136) is larger, and the **California Sea-Lion** (p. 140), which is usually larger, has relatively shorter hindflippers.

DID YOU KNOW?

The population recovery for this species has been good, but El Niño events adversely affect these fur seals. Until the population is large and stable, these fur seals will continue to be threatened by El Niño conditions.

Northern Sea-Lion
Eumetopias jubatus

Once common in California, the Northern Sea-Lion population in this state has declined dramatically since the early 1900s. Even in the past few years pup production has declined by 30 percent. Causes of the decline are unknown, but water quality, water temperature and poaching may all be factors.

During the breeding and pupping season, sea-lions congregate at rookery sites used generation after generation. Several rookeries can still be found in California, most notably Año Nuevo Island, Farallon Islands, Pt. Saint George, Sugarloaf on Cape Mendocino and a few on San Miguel Island. In a rookery, mature bulls make a roaring sound, and when this is combined with the grumbles and growls of the others, the resulting cacophony can be heard more than a mile away. Outside the pupping season, the "bachelors," young of the year, some barren cows and the odd mature bull form loose colonies, feeding together and otherwise interacting.

Adult male Northern Sea-Lions are the largest of the eared seals. There is great sexual dimorphism, with adult males three to four times as heavy as the females. A large difference in weight is characteristic of pinnipeds with territorial males that hold a harem. Females form loose aggregations with their pups within a male's territory, and they are far faster and more agile than the males.

Northern Sea-Lions are well known for their curiosity and playfulness. They are very active, sometimes leaping clear out of the water and occasionally throwing rocks back and forth. They have even been seen jumping over surfaced whales. Their smaller cousins, the California Sea-Lions (p. 140), share this playfulness and are commonly seen performing tricks in marine park shows.

For many years, sea-lions were killed because it was believed that they fed on commercially valuable fish. Research indicates, however, that they feed opportunistically on any readily available sea creatures—commonly octopus, squid and "scrap" fish such as herring and greenling. Although intentional killing has decreased, sea-lion populations have declined by as much as 80 percent of historic numbers.

A unique characteristic of sea-lions is that they frequently swallow rocks as large as 5 in. across. Although no one knows for sure, the most likely explanation is that, as in birds, the stones help

RANGE: Northern Sea-Lions are found near shore from southern California up to Alaska and the Aleutian Islands, and across to Siberia and Japan.

Total Length: Males 8½–11 ft., females 6–6½ ft.

Total Weight: Males up to 2200 lb., females 600–790 lb.

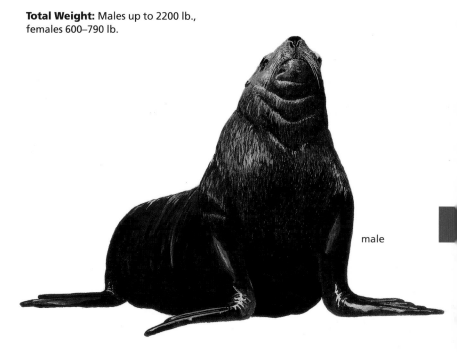

male

pulverize food inside their stomachs. Sea-lions' teeth are ill suited for chewing, and these mammals regularly swallow large chunks of meat and whole fish.

ALSO CALLED: Steller Sea-Lion.

DESCRIPTION: Adults are light buff to reddish brown when dry, and brown to nearly black when wet. These sea-lions have a thick blubber layer. Adult males develop a huge neck that supports a mane of long, coarse hair. Females are sleek, without the massive neck. During the breeding season adult males evicted from the colony often bear huge cuts and tears on the neck and chest, reminders of the vicious battles waged

over a territory. The hindflippers are drawn forward under the body and—like all eared seals—Northern Sea-Lions can jump and clamber up steep rocky slopes at an amazing rate.

HABITAT: Northern Sea-Lions live mainly in coastal waters near rocky shores, although they are less common in inshore waters than the California Sea-Lion. During the breeding season

DID YOU KNOW?

Although Northern Sea-Lions are saltwater mammals, they have been known to swim up major rivers in search of lamprey and salmon.

they occupy rocky, boulder-strewn beaches or rock ledges. Sea-lions may rest in the water in a vertical position with their heads above the surface. They prefer to stay in the water during inclement weather, but when the sun shines they usually haul out and bask on the rocks.

FOOD: These sea-lions feed primarily on blackfish, hake, rockfish and anchovies. Others foods include squid, octopus, shrimp, clams, salmon and bottom fish. Males do not eat for one to two months while defending a territory.

YOUNG: Males come to shore in early May and battle to establish their territories. Females come to shore in mid-May or June, and within three days give birth to a pup conceived during the previous summer. Females form loose aggregations with their pups in a male's territory and mating occurs within two weeks after the pups are born. Pups nurse for about one year, but some have been known to nurse as long as three years. Females may live to be 30 years old and are sexually mature at three to seven years. Males probably do not breed before age 10.

SIMILAR SPECIES: The **Northern Fur Seal** (p. 132) and the more common **California Sea-Lion** (p. 140) are both smaller. The **Northern Elephant Seal** (p. 128) is much larger and has a distinctively long snout. The **Harbor Seal** (p. 124) is much smaller and lacks the ability to rotate its hindflippers under its body.

Northern Fur Seal

California Sea-Lion
Zalophus californianus

The famous California Sea-Lion has received both our admiration and our persecution. Each year, thousands of children and adults sit in theme parks and watch in awe as these sea-lions flip in the air and perform stunts with hoops and big red beach balls. Sea-lions are major attractions at marine aquariums around the world, and at best, these performances leave lasting impressions of the talent and special intrigue of our fellow mammals. Unfortunately, these good feelings are not always shared by the animal, and many sea-lions in captivity die of health problems or accidents.

Interestingly, these sea-lions come by their playfulness naturally; it is not something humans can credit themselves for teaching them. In the wild, females and young pups frequently play and cavort in the water, and they are even known to play with other species. Flinging a piece of kelp around in the water and hitting the wild waves for some good body surfing are just part of the daily routine. A sea-lion's true grace is apparent underwater, where it turns sinuous loops and spirals in an aquatic ballet that belies its terrestrial ancestry. Many visitors to coastal areas are rewarded with sightings of this sea-lion, and lucky individuals have even had personal encounters. Kayakers and even swimmers have been approached by juveniles and females that want to play. The behavior of juveniles and females is rarely aggressive, and most circumstances of play involve friendly splashes and eager somersaults underwater.

Despite being much adored by children and tourists, California Sea-Lions in the wild often suffer harsh judgements. Because these sea-lions potentially feed on many fish valuable to fisheries, there is widespread interaction between them and fishermen. California Sea-Lions, like all other marine mammals, are protected by law, and killing them is punishable. In the 19th and early 20th centuries, California Sea-Lions were killed in great numbers for oil (from their blubber) and hides. Later in the 20th century, they were also killed for the pet food industry. This kind of killing is now unlawful, but each year thousands of sea-lions still die. Most of these deaths are attributable to fishing nets, discarded net material and fibrous garbage, all of which entrap and drown sea-lions. Because of intentional and accidental deaths, the California Sea-Lion population is much reduced from historical numbers, and the species may never fully recover.

RANGE: This sea-lion inhabits coastal waters of the North Pacific from Mexico to Vancouver Island. There are also good numbers in the Galapagos Islands and three small, isolated populations in the Sea of Japan.

Total Length: male 6¹/₂–8 ft.,
female 4¹/₂–6¹/₂ ft.

Total Weight: male 440–860 lb.,
female 100–250 lb.

On the coast of California, wintering California Sea-Lions may be encountered from August to April. The breeding season lasts from May to July, but their breeding grounds are much farther south. Many seal-lions leave their southern breeding territories and move northward to feed in the food-rich waters. Some females may stay near their breeding grounds year-round, while younger males are more likely to be found at the northern limits of their range during winter. These sea-lions do not stay at sea for extended periods during their winter feeding; they are frequently observed at well-used haul out sites.

DESCRIPTION: The California Sea-Lion has a slender, elongated body, a blunt snout and a short but distinct tail. The adult male is brown, while the female is tan with the chest and abdomen slightly darker. An adult male develops a noticeably raised forehead that helps distinguish it from the Northern Sea-Lion. The front flippers are long and bear distinct claws. California Sea-Lions have coarse guard hair that covers only a small amount of underfur. They are a noisy bunch—the males produce a honking bark, the cows wail and the pups bleat.

HABITAT: California Sea-Lions are common in coastal waters around islands with rocky or sandy beaches. Preferred haul-out sites include sandy or boulder-strewn beaches below rocky cliffs, and they may even congregate in large numbers on piers. In some places they occupy sea caverns. They tend to avoid the rocky islets preferred by Northern Sea-Lions.

FEEDING: These sea-lions eat a wide variety of foods, including at least 50 species of fish and many types of squid,

DID YOU KNOW?

The name "pinniped," which refers to all seals and sea-lions, literally means "feather-footed"—an apt description of their fan-shaped flippers.

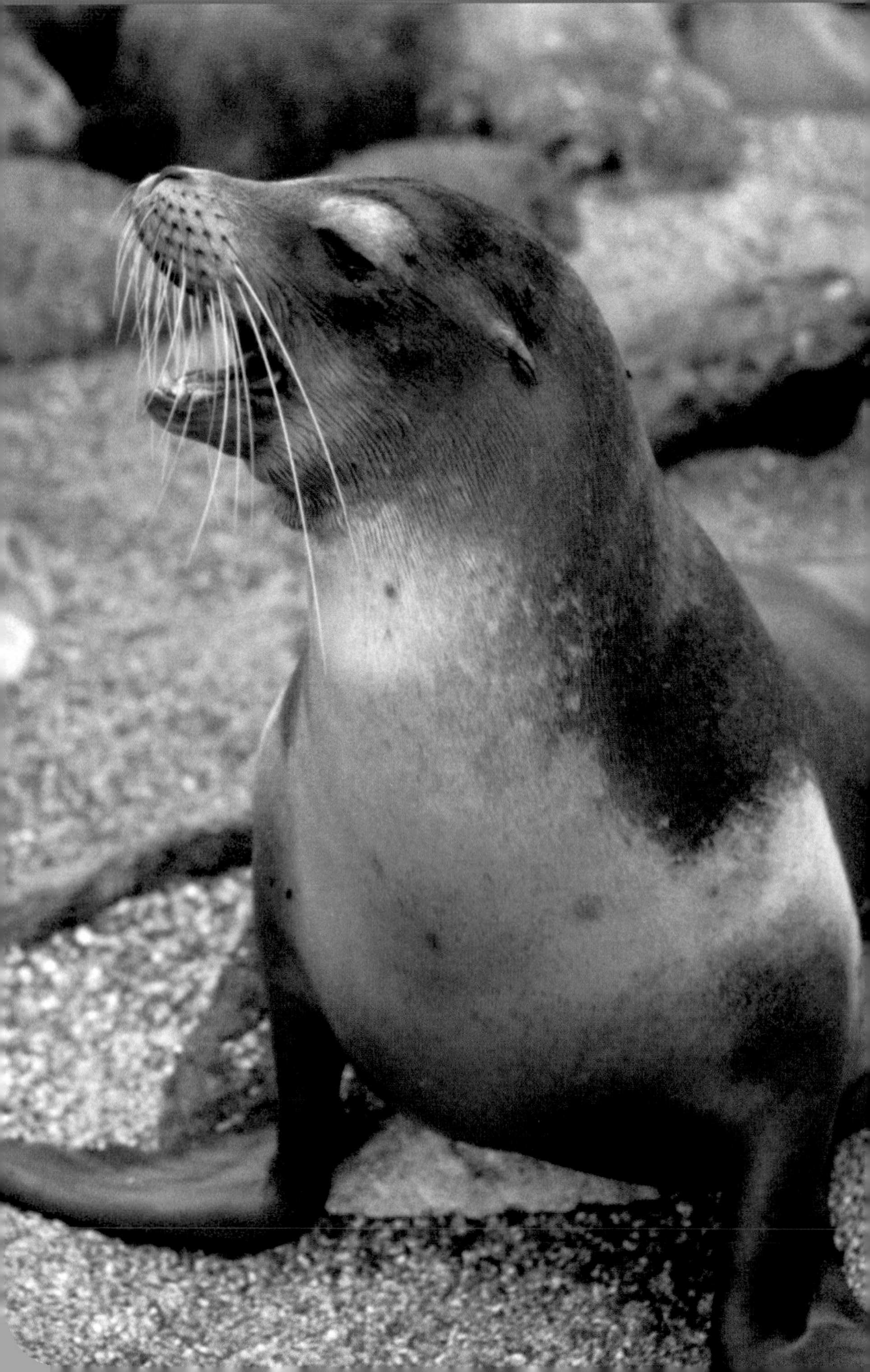

octopus and other mollusks. In some regions, such as Seattle, sea-lions are known to feed on commercially valuable and even endangered species of fish. Although some agencies support killing these sea-lions, there are widespread efforts for non-lethal management, such as relocating the sea-lions to distant waters.

YOUNG: Males establish their territories on rocky or sandy beaches in May, June or July. Females arrive on the breeding grounds in May or June. If a female conceived the previous year, she will give birth to a pup, and within one month she mates again. Females with pups form colonies. When a mother leaves her pup to feed, it is no easy task finding her pup amidst dozens of look-alike youngsters when she returns. First she lets out a loud, distinctive wail, and her pup will answer with a lamb-like bleat. She follows this bleat until she finds the pup, and she confirms it is hers by smell. Most pups are weaned by eight months, but a few may nurse for a year or more. Pups begin eating fish before they are weaned.

SIMILAR SPECIES: The **Northern Sea-Lion** (p. 136) is larger and paler. The **Northern Fur Seal** (p. 132) is smaller and often more reddish on its undersides. The **Northern Elephant Seal** (p. 128) is much larger and has a distinctive snout. The **Harbor Seal** (p. 124) is smaller and, like the Northern Elephant Seal, lacks the ability to rotate its hindflippers under its body.

Northern Sea-Lion

American Black Bear
Ursus americanus

The black bear, an inhabitant of most forested regions of California, is often feared by city dwellers who come to wilderness parks to appreciate the scenery and wilderness. People who are more experienced with the wild forest and with animal behavior tend to regard the black bear with a healthy respect, but perhaps less apprehension.

Contrary to popular belief and their classification as a carnivore, black bears do not readily hunt large animals. They are primarily opportunistic foragers and feed on what is easy and abundant—usually berries, horsetails, other vegetation and insects, although they won't turn up their noses at fish, young fawns or another carnivore's kill. Black bear sows with young cubs are the most likely to attack young deer and Elk.

In the past few decades, the ubiquitous dandelion has become increasingly abundant in the mountains along roadsides and swaths cut into the forests, especially in central interior regions. As a result, black bears are now more frequently seen along roadsides, and if a bear glances up at your passing car, it will betray its new favorite food. With dandelion leaves sticking out of its mouth and the puffy seeds stuck over its face and muzzle, the bear looks like a little kid covered in its favorite ice cream. Unfortunately, together with an increase in bear sightings along roadsides, vehicle collisions that may claim bears' lives are also increasing.

Within its territory, a black bear has favorite feeding places and follows well-travelled paths to these sites. Keep in mind that the trails you hike in the mountains may be used not only by humans, but also by bears en route to lush meadows or rich berry patches.

Normally, black bears are reclusive animals that will flee to avoid contact with humans if they hear you coming. If you surprise a bear, however, back away slowly. In particular, heed its warning of a foot stamp, a throaty "huff" or the champing sound of its teeth. The bear is agitated and probably does not like you, and it is giving you a clear warning to retreat from its territory in respect of its dominance. Many cases of bear attacks occur when these warning signals are not understood by a person who instead remains frozen in place. The bear likely interprets such behavior as a challenge.

One grim threat to bears throughout the world is the illegal trade in body parts. Bear paws and gall bladders have high black-market values, and poaching occurs in both Canada and the United States, but fortunately to a lesser extent than elsewhere. As populations of many

RANGE: Across North America, the black bear occurs nearly everywhere there are forests, swamps or shrub thickets. It avoids grasslands and deserts.

Total Length: 4½–6 ft.
Shoulder Height: 3–3¾ ft.
Tail Length: 3–7 in.
Weight: 88–595 lb.

bears around the world shrink, however, North American bears face an increasing threat. With bear numbers dwindling and black market values increasing, it is feared that the generally well-protected animals in the mountains may become prime targets of the trade.

DESCRIPTION: The coat is long and shaggy and ranges from black to brown to honey colored. The body is relatively short and stout, and the legs are short and powerful. The large, wide feet have sharp, curved black claws. The head is large and has a straight profile. The eyes are small, and the ears are short, rounded and erect. The tail is very short. An adult male is about 20 percent larger than a female.

HABITAT: Black bears are primarily forest animals, and their sharp, curved foreclaws enable them to easily climb trees, even as adults. In spring, they often forage in natural or roadside clearings.

FOOD: Away from human influences, up to 95 percent of the black bear's diet is plant material: leaves, buds, flowers, berries, fruits, truffles and roots are all consumed. This omnivore also eats animal matter, including bees (and honey) and other insects; even young hoofed mammals may be killed and eaten. Carrion and garbage are eagerly sought out.

DEN: The den, which is only used during winter, may be in a cave or hollow tree, beneath a fallen log or under the roots of a windthrown tree, or even in a haystack. The bear usually carries in a few mouthfuls of grass to lie on during its sleep. It will not eat, drink, urinate or defecate during its time in the den. The hibernation is not deep; instead, it is as if the bear is very groggy or heavily drugged. A bear may rouse from this torpor and leave its den on mild winter days.

DID YOU KNOW?

During its winter slumber, a black bear loses 20 to 40 percent of its body weight. To prepare for winter, the bear must eat thousands of calories a day during late summer and fall.

YOUNG: Black bears mate in June or July, but the embryos do not implant and begin to develop until the sow enters her den in November. The number of eggs that implant seems to be correlated with the female's weight and condition—fat mothers have more cubs. One to five (usually two or three) young are born in January, and they nurse while the sow sleeps. Their eyes open and they become active when they are five to six weeks old. They leave the den with their mother when they weigh $4^1/_2$–$6^3/_4$ lb., usually in April. The sow and her cubs generally spend the next winter together in the den, dispersing the following spring. Black bears typically bear young in alternate years, as the physical drain on the female is too great to allow conception in consecutive years.

walking trail   hindprint   foreprint

SIMILAR SPECIES: The larger **Grizzly Bear** (*Ursus arctos*) is no longer found in California. The **Wolverine** (p. 102) looks a little like a very small black bear, but it has a long tail, an arched back and pale side stripes.

Grizzly Bear

Coyote
Canis latrans

A chorus of yaps, whines, barks and howls complements the darkening skies in wild areas of California. Although Coyote calls are most intense during late winter and spring, corresponding to courtship, these excited sounds can be heard during suitable weather at any time of the day or year. Often initiated by one animal, many family groups soon join in and the calls pour from the valleys, making it obvious to all that these animals relish joining together and making noise.

Two centuries ago, the early explorers of this continent made frequent references in their journals to foxes and wolves, but they seldom mentioned Coyotes. Coyotes have increased their numbers across North America in the past century in response to the expansion of agriculture and forestry and the reduction of wolf populations. Despite widespread human efforts to exterminate them, they have thrived.

One of the few natural checks on Coyote abundance is the Gray Wolf (*C. lupus*). As the much larger and more powerful canids of the wilderness neighborhood, wolves typically exclude Coyotes from their territories. Since the extirpation of wolves in California, the conditions have favored Coyotes. They are now so widely distributed and comfortable with human development that almost every valley, and even many cities, holds a healthy population.

Because of its relatively small size, the Coyote typically preys on small animals. Its preferred prey here in California appears to be rabbits and hares, but it also takes mice, voles, ground squirrels and birds, and it may even kill young Bighorn Sheep and deer. Although they usually hunt alone, Coyotes occasionally form packs, especially if they hunt hoofed mammals during winter. The Coyotes may split up, with some waiting in ambush while the others chase the prey toward them, or they may run in relays to tire their quarry—the Coyote, which is the best runner among the North American canids, typically cruises at 25–30 mph.

Coyotes owe their modern-day success to their varied diet, early age of first breeding, high reproductive output and flexible living requirements. They consume small and medium-sized mammals throughout the year, but they also feed on such diverse offerings as eggs, birds, insects, carrion, fruits and berries. Their variable diet and nonspecific habitat choices allow them to adapt to just about any region of North America.

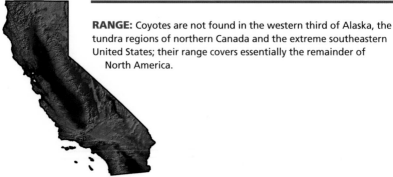

RANGE: Coyotes are not found in the western third of Alaska, the tundra regions of northern Canada and the extreme southeastern United States; their range covers essentially the remainder of North America.

Total Length: 3½–4½ ft.
Shoulder Height: 23–26 in.
Tail Length: 12–16 in.
Weight: 18–44 lb.

DESCRIPTION: Coyotes look like gray, buffy or reddish-gray, medium-sized dogs. The nose is pointed and there is usually a gray patch between the eyes that contrasts with the rufous top of the snout. The long, bushy tail has a black tip. The underparts are light to whitish. When frightened, a Coyote runs with its tail tucked between its hindlegs. Coyotes in the northern part of California tend to be slightly larger than those in the south.

HABITAT: Coyotes are found in all terrestrial habitats in North America, except the barren tundra of the far north and the humid southeastern forests. They have greatly expanded their range, in part because of Gray Wolf extirpations and in part because forest clearing has brought about favorable changes in habitat for Coyotes.

Plains and open country are excellent places to see Coyotes.

FOOD: Although primarily carnivorous, feeding on rabbits, ground squirrels, mice, birds, amphibians and reptiles, Coyotes will sometimes eat cactus fruits, melons, berries and vegetation. Most ranchers dislike Coyotes because they have been known to take young sheep, calves and pigs that are left exposed. They may even attack and consume dogs and cats.

DID YOU KNOW?

Coyotes can, and do, interbreed with domestic dogs. The "coydog" offspring often become nuisance animals, killing domestic livestock and poultry.

DEN: The den is usually a burrow in a slope, frequently an American Badger hole that has been expanded to 1 ft. in diameter and about 10 ft. deep. Rarely, Coyotes have been known to den in an abandoned car, a hollow tree trunk or a dense brush pile.

YOUNG: A litter of 3 to 10 (usually 5 to 7) pups is born in April, after a gestation of about two months. The furry pups are blind at birth. Their eyes open after about 10 days, and they leave the den for the first time when they are three weeks old. Young Coyotes fight with each other and establish dominance and social position at just three to four weeks of age.

walking trail   foreprint

Gray Wolf

SIMILAR SPECIES: The larger **Gray Wolf** (*Canus lupus*) is no longer found in California. The **Red Fox** (p. 152) is generally smaller, much redder, and has a white tail tip and black forelegs. The smaller **Common Gray Fox** (p. 160) has a crest of black hairs on the top of its tail and a black spot on each side of the muzzle. **Coyote-like domestic dog breeds** generally have more bulging foreheads and are stockier.

151

Red Fox

Vulpes vulpes

More than other native canids, the Red Fox has received some favorable representations in literature and modern culture. From Aesop's Fables to sexy epithets, the fox is often symbolized as a diabolically cunning, intelligent, attractive and noble animal. Many people favor having foxes nearby because of this species' skill at catching mice. Foxes have a well-deserved nickname, "reynard," from the French word for fox, *renard,* which is used for someone who is unconquerable owing to their cleverness. The fox's intelligence, undeniable comeliness and positive impact upon most farmlands have endeared it to many people who otherwise might not appreciate wildlife.

Foxes at work in their natural habitat embody playfulness, roguishness, drama and stealth. Young fox kits at their den wrestle and squabble in determined sibling rivalry. If its siblings are busy elsewhere, a young kit may amuse itself by challenging a plaything, such as a stick or piece of old bone, to a bout of aggressive mock combat. An adult out mousing will sneak up on its prey rustling in the grass and jump stiff-legged into the air, hoping to come down directly atop the unsuspecting rodent. If the fox misses, it stomps and flattens the grass with its forepaws, biting in the air to try to catch the mouse. Usually the fox wins, but, if not, it will slip away with stately composure as though the display of undignified abandon never occurred.

Oddly enough, Red Foxes exhibit both feline dexterity and a feline hunting style. Foxes hunt using an ambush style, or they creep along in a crouched position, ready to pounce on their prey. Another un-dog-like characteristic is the large gland above the base of the tail, which gives off a strong musk somewhat resembling the smell of a skunk. This scent is what allows foxhounds to easily track their quarry. Foxes are territorial, and the males, like other members of the dog family, mark their territorial boundaries with urine.

Despite its vast range, the Red Fox is rarely seen. Its primarily nocturnal activity is probably the main reason, but a fox's keen senses of sight, hearing and smell enhance its elusive nature. Winter may be the best time to see a fox: it is more likely to be active during the day and its color stands out when it is mousing in an open field in daylight. Red Foxes have adapted to human activity, and many of them live in agricultural areas and even in the outskirts of cities. There are two subspecies of Red Fox in California. The native (*V. v. necator*) is found in montane and highland areas of

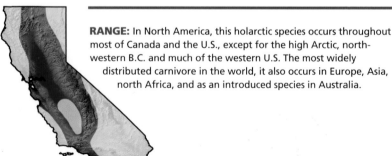

RANGE: In North America, this holarctic species occurs throughout most of Canada and the U.S., except for the high Arctic, north-western B.C. and much of the western U.S. The most widely distributed carnivore in the world, it also occurs in Europe, Asia, north Africa, and as an introduced species in Australia.

Total Length: 35–44 in.
Shoulder Height: 15–16 in.
Tail Length: 14–17 in.
Weight: 8–15 lb.

Siskiyou County, and from Lassen to Tulare Counties. The other subspecies is presumably introduced from central plains populations, and is found in the lowlands and coastal areas of southern California.

DESCRIPTION: This small, slender, dog-like fox has an exceptionally bushy, long tail. Its upperparts are usually a vivid reddish orange, with a white chest and belly, but there are many color variations: a Coyote-colored phase; the "cross fox," which has darker hairs along the back and across the shoulder blades; and the "silver fox," which is mostly black with silver-tipped hairs. In all color phases, the tail has a white tip and the backs of the ears and fronts of the forelegs are usually black.

HABITAT: The Red Fox prefers open habitats interspersed with brushy shelter year-round. It avoids extensive areas of dense, coniferous forest.

FOOD: This opportunistic feeder usually stalks its prey and then pounces on it or captures it after a short rush. In winter, small rodents, rabbits and birds make up most of the diet, but dried berries are also eaten. In more moderate seasons,

DID YOU KNOW?

The Red Fox's signature feature—its white-tipped, bushy tail—provides balance when the fox is running or jumping, and during cold weather a fox wraps its tail over its face.

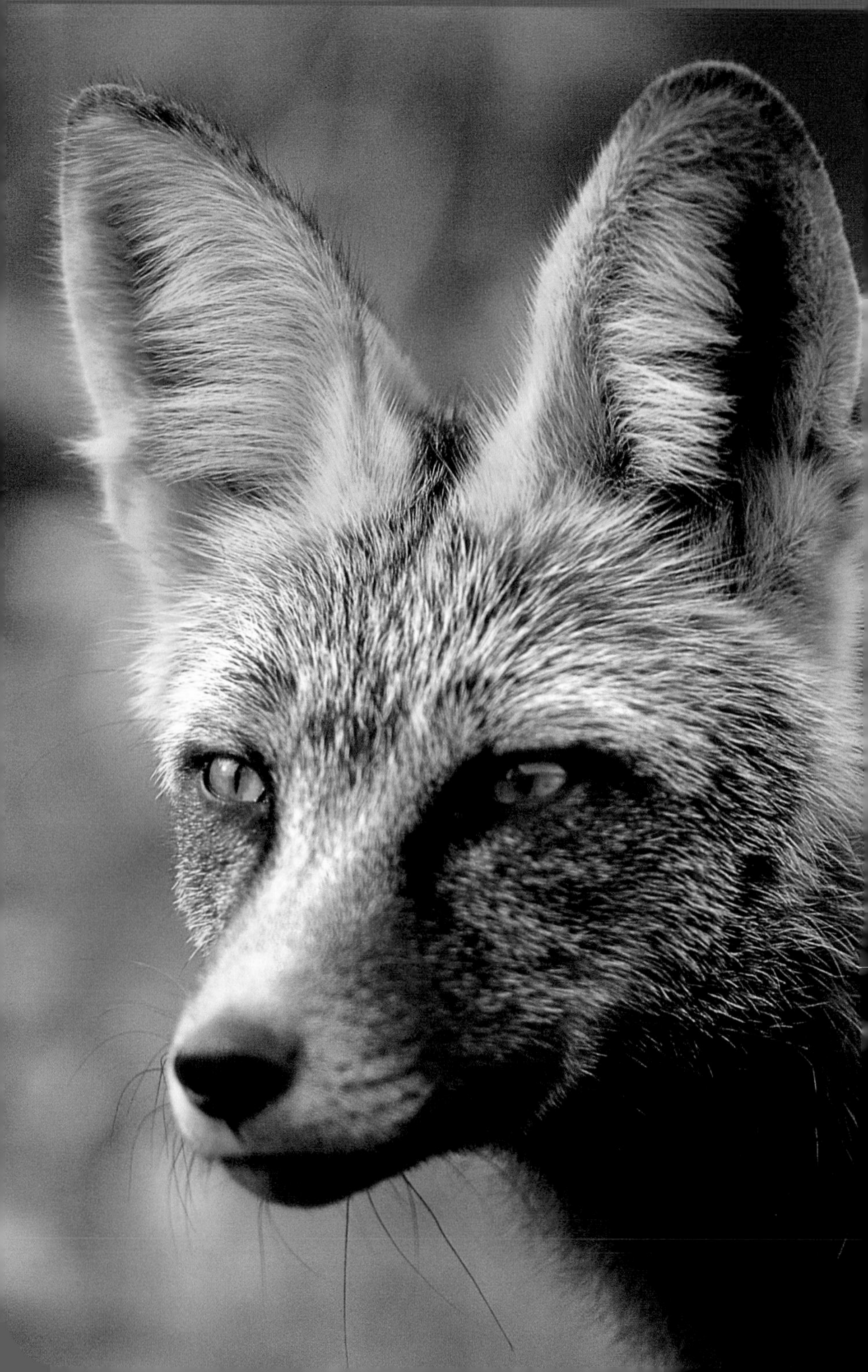

foreprint

walking trail

invertebrates, birds, eggs, fruits and berries supplement the basic small-mammal diet.

DEN: The Red Fox generally dens in a burrow, which the vixen either digs herself or, more usually, makes by expanding a badger hole. The den is sometimes located in a hollow log, in a brush pile or beneath an unoccupied building.

YOUNG: A litter of 1 to 10 kits is born in April or May after a gestation of about 7½ weeks. The kits weigh about 3½ oz. at birth. Their eyes open after nine days, and they are weaned when they are one month old. The parents first bring the kits dead food and later crippled animals. The father may bring back to the den several voles, or perhaps a hare and some mice, at the end of a single hunting trip. After the kits learn to kill, the parents start taking them on hunts. The young disperse when they are three to four months old; they become sexually mature well before their first birthdays.

Coyote

SIMILAR SPECIES: The larger **Coyote** (p. 148) has a dark-tipped tail and does not have black forelegs. The smaller **Common Gray Fox** (p. 160) usually has less red overall and has a crest of black along the top of the black-tipped tail.

Kit Fox
Vulpes macrotis

The cat-sized Kit Fox has a history of misnomers, persecution and unfortunate decline. It has long been debated whether or not the Swift Fox (*V. velox*) and the Kit Fox are the same species or two different ones. Much evidence supports their distinct status, but research has shown that there is some geneflow in eastern New Mexico and western Texas. Nevertheless, many mammalogists agree to treat them separately—as they are herein. The Latin name of the Kit Fox aptly describes the animal. *Vulpes* is Latin for "fox," and *macrotis* is Greek, derived from the words *makros* for "long" and *ōtos* for "ear." Translated, the name means "the fox with long ears." Not surprisingly, its ears are proportionately the longest of any canid in North America.

For many years, Kit Foxes were exterminated as "vermin," along with Gray Wolves, Coyotes, other foxes and birds of prey. Vermin were animals that could potentially kill a domestic animal, or that preyed upon a wild animal that humans wanted to hunt, such as deer. The result of this massive extermination effort is that very few canids exist now in the United States. Kit Foxes are now known to be extremely valuable in the ecosystem, as they feed primarily on small rodents and insects. In areas where Kit Foxes have been extirpated, rodents such as kangaroo rats, pocket mice and others increase in numbers to such an extent that they may pose serious threats to agriculture, grazing and health.

Although we now understand the importance of Kit Foxes in the ecosystem, they are still unfortunate victims of poaching, hunting and poisoning. Some are killed because of out-dated ideas of vermin, some are hunted for their fur, and others are killed accidentally either by poisoned meat intended for other animals, or by consuming rodents that have been poisoned. The Jan Joaquin Kit Fox, here in California, is endangered because of heavy agricultural development in the valley that renders the habitat unsuitable for Kit Foxes.

The behavior of Kit Foxes is unlike the behavior of Swift Foxes. Swift Fox populations that have been recently studied indicate the animals are very sociable and often live in groups. Kit Foxes are primarily solitary, except during times of breeding. In the mating season, males may return to their previous mate, and some have been known to have the same mate throughout their life (the same is true for Swift Foxes). During the remainder of the year, the males prefer a solitary lifestyle. Once the

RANGE: The Kit Fox is found in southeastern Oregon, much of Nevada, central and southern California, western Utah, much of Arizona and New Mexico, southwestern Colorado, and eastern Texas.

Total Length: 24–33 in.
Shoulder Height: 11³/₄ in.
Tail Length: 9–13 in.
Weight: 3¹/₈–6 lb.

young disperse from the female, she also hunts alone. Calls of the Kit Fox are quite variable. Their repertoire includes a shrill yap, whines, growls and a rumbling purr.

DESCRIPTION: This small fox is mainly grayish yellow above, sometimes with flecks of rusty- or black-colored hairs. They are whitish or buff below, their feet are similarly light-colored, and their tails are black-tipped. On some individuals there is a black spot also at the upper base of the tail. The tail makes up almost 40 percent of their total length. The soles of their feet are well-haired, perhaps an adaptation that gives greater traction on desert sand. Their large triangular ears are dark behind and whitish inside. In between their eyes and nose, on either side of the muzzle, are nearly black patches of fur.

HABITAT: Inhabitants of deserts and arid regions, Kit Foxes are associated with sagebrush flats and creosote/grass communities. They may hunt in sand dunes, but are generally found in areas of some ground cover on light, sandy desert soils.

DEN: Kit Foxes dig burrows similar to those of the Red Fox only somewhat smaller. As a rule, the Kit Fox spends the heat of the day in its cool den, and comes out in the evenings and at night.

DID YOU KNOW?

Although they are wary of intruders and human disturbance, Kit Foxes can be unusually indifferent to us. On many occasions, campers have been surprised by a Kit Fox walking into their campfire circle and helping itself to a choice cut of meat.

Kit Fox burrows could be mistaken for those of a badger, but the badger's burrow is elliptical or flattened, much like the overall shape of the badger itself. A pregnant vixen cleans and arranges several possible den sites before she chooses the one that suits her needs best.

FOOD: In many parts of the southwestern states, the Kit Fox is an important predator of small rodents. Normal Kit Fox populations keep in check the numbers of rodents on pasture and cultivated land. Their primary prey species include kangaroo rats, pocket mice, and rabbits. Other species that are consumed to a lesser extent include reptiles, ground-nesting birds and insects.

YOUNG: Males join company with a female in October or November, and mating occurs in December. Like Swift Foxes, Kit Foxes are monogamous and may mate for life. Gestation ranges from 49 to 56 days, whereupon a litter of four or five altricial pups are born. The pups nurse for the first few weeks, and as they are weaned the males bring in fresh food for them. The pups emerge when they are one month old, and begin hunting when they are three or four months old. In October, the young of the year disperse.

foreprint

walking trail

Common Gray Fox

SIMILAR SPECIES: The **Swift Fox** (*Vulpes velox*) is very similar and is often considered as the same species. Studies have shown they interbreed in some areas where their ranges meet. The **Common Gray Fox** (p. 160) is larger and has more red in its coat, as well as a distinctive black crest on the tail.

Common Gray Fox
Urocyon cinereoargenteus

Truly a crafty fox, the Common Gray Fox is known to elude predators by taking the most unexpected of turns—running up a tree. Unlike other canids, this fox seems comfortable in a tree, and it may climb into the branches to rest and sleep. There are even records of these foxes denning in natural tree cavities, and raising their litters as high as 20 ft. off the ground. It is the only North American member of the dog family that can climb.

The Common Gray Fox's tendency to live in areas of tree cover means it is less frequently seen other foxes. Furthermore, the majority of its activity occurs during the dark or twilight hours, enhancing its clandestine nature. As its name suggests, this species is by far the most common fox in California, and your chances of seeing one in the evening are very good. Remember, you may have to turn your eyes skyward and scan the trees, especially those with thick, heavily forked trunks or leaning branches.

After the mating season, the male stays with the female and helps with raising the young. His primary role after the female gives birth is to bring her food, because she must remain with the young constantly for several days. Gray foxes often cache their food, especially large kills that cannot be consumed at once. Small kills may be buried right near the den during the whelping season, partly to provide the female with ready food but also to stimulate the interest of the pups. Large cache sites are made either in heaped up vegetation or in holes dug into loose dirt.

Many of the fox populations in North America suffered great losses during the peak of the fur trade. To most foxes, Coyotes and wolves, humans are the worst enemy. Fortunately for the Common Gray Fox, its pelt is of lower quality (to humans, that is—the fox certainly appreciates it). Its beautifully patterned, grizzled fur is very stiff, rather than soft and long like the winter coat of a Red Fox, so it was trapped less. The Common Gray Fox has also suffered less persecution from farmers, because it is quite shy and rarely hunts domestic animals. Unlike many other canids, Common Gray Foxes are not inclined toward chickens. They prefer to hunt the mice that abound around a henhouse, and their mousing ability is so good that they are even considered welcome visitors to a barnyard.

DESCRIPTION: This handsome fox has an overall grizzled appearance because of the long, grayish fur over its back. Its

RANGE: Common Gray Foxes have an extensive distribution in the U.S. They range through most of the eastern states, and from Texas west to California and up the West Coast through most of Oregon. Some populations can be found in Colorado and Utah.

Total Length: 31–44 in.
Shoulder Height: 14–15 in.
Tail Length: 11–17 in.
Weight: 7½–13 lb.

undersides are reddish in color, as are the back of the head, throat, legs and feet. Sometimes the belly may be mostly white with only reddish highlights. The tail, which always has a black crest and a black tip, is otherwise grayish with reddish undersides. The ears are pointed and mainly gray in color, with patches of red on the back side. A distinct black spot is present on either side of the muzzle.

HABITAT: The Common Gray Fox inhabits a variety of different environments, always near trees or ground cover. This fox prefers foraging in wooded areas rather than open environments.

DEN: This fox's den can be found in a variety of places. Most commonly, it is on a ridge or rocky slope or under brush cover in a woodland, but it may also be underground. If necessary, a fox digs a burrow itself, but more often it refurbishes the abandoned burrow of another animal, such as an American Badger.

FOOD: Gray foxes are more omnivorous than other foxes. They consume a variety of small mammals, such as rabbits, rodents and birds, as well as large amounts of insects and other invertebrates. Late in summer, grasshoppers, crickets and other agricultural pests make

DID YOU KNOW?

Although this fox is quite small, it can run very quickly over short distances. In one record, a Common Gray Fox topped 28 mph.

161

walking trail

up much of the diet. A significant part of the diet is vegetable matter, such as fruits and grasses. Favorite items include apples, grapes, persimmons and nuts.

YOUNG: Mating occurs in January or February, and after a gestation of about 53 days, one to seven young are born. They are born blind and almost hairless, and for the first several days they require constant care by the mother. After 12 days their eyes open, and they venture out of the den when they are 1 1/2 or 2 months old. When they are four months old, they learn how to hunt and accompany their parents while foraging. By the fifth month, they have dispersed to start their own dens.

foreprint

Kit Fox

SIMILAR SPECIES: The **Kit Fox** (p. 156) is smaller, less reddish overall and lacks the black crest and tip on the tail. The **Red Fox** (p. 152) is much redder overall and has a white-tipped tail. The **Coyote** (p. 148) is larger and lacks the black spots on either side of the muzzle. The **Island Gray Fox** (p. 164) is identical, but smaller, and lives only on six of the Channel Islands.

Island Gray Fox
Urocyon littoralis

This tiny inhabitant of the Channel Islands is the only canid to be found off the mainland in California. Although it looks very similar to its mainland cousin, the Common Gray Fox (*U. cinereoargenteus*), it is only about one half to two-thirds the size. Like other island animals that have few predators, this gray fox is tolerant of human activity and is easy to see and photograph. As well, it is often active during daylight and evening hours, unlike its mainland counterpart. The only real predators of the Island Gray Fox are large birds of prey such as hawks and eagles, but these birds are not common over the islands.

On Santa Cruz, Santa Rosa, and San Clemente Islands this fox is quite common. Nevertheless, it is a species of concern in California and is listed as threatened. Populations of these gray foxes are vulnerable to habitat degradation from human activity on the islands, competition for resources with domestic and feral cats, exotic species introduced on the islands and infectious canine diseases.

DESCRIPTION: Like its larger mainland cousin, this diminutive fox has an overall grizzled-gray appearance. Its undersides are ochraceous, as are the back of the head, throat, legs and feet. The reddish undersides may have buffy patches. The grayish tail has ochraceous highlights, a black crest, and a black tip. The large, pointed ears are mainly gray, with buffy orange at the base and on the back side. Like many other foxes, there are distinct black spots on either side of the muzzle.

HABITAT: The Island Gray Fox is considered a habitat generalist, and it is generally distributed in all habitats over the entire islands on which it occurs.

DEN: This fox dens in any available shelter such as a rock crevice, bushes or in or under a building. Most other fox species will excavate a burrow, but this fox does not.

FOOD: The Island Gray Fox feeds mainly on deer mice, grasshoppers, beetles, lizards, some birds, and many varieties of fruits and berries such as prickly pear, toyon, saltbrush, ice plant and manzanita.

YOUNG: Mating occurs in February or March, and a small litter (usually two) is born in April or May. Like other canids, young are born blind and almost hairless, and for the first several days they

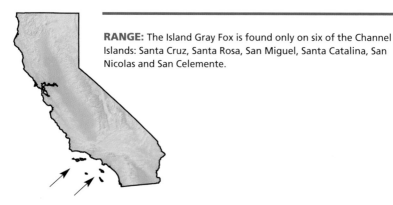

RANGE: The Island Gray Fox is found only on six of the Channel Islands: Santa Cruz, Santa Rosa, San Miguel, Santa Catalina, San Nicolas and San Celemente.

Total Length: 23–31 in.
Shoulder Height: 4³/₄–6 in.
Tail Length: 4¹/₂–11¹/₂ in.
Weight: 3¹/₂–5¹/₂ lb.

require constant care. Both parents care for the young, and the male also brings food to the female when she is nursing. By two weeks they are well-furred and their eyes are open, and when they are three to four months old they accompany their parents while foraging. The young will disperse to start their own dens by their first winter.

SIMILAR SPECIES: The **Common Gray Fox** (p. 160) is identical, but larger. This is the only fox to inhabit the Channel Islands; all other foxes live on the mainland.

DID YOU KNOW?

These foxes are thought to have arrived on the Channel Islands by swimming or rafting from the mainland. Their arrival pre-dates the arrival of the Chumash people, Native Americans who are believed to have been the first people on the Islands and who colonized them 9000 to 10,000 years ago.

RODENTS

In terms of sheer numbers, rodents are the most successful group of mammals in California. Because we usually associate rodents with rats and mice, the group's most notorious members, many people look on all rodents as filthy vermin. You must remember, however, that the much more endearing chipmunks, marmots, beavers and squirrels are also rodents. Most small rodents are important prey species for a wide variety of reptiles, birds and other mammals.

A rodent's best-known features are its upper and lower pairs of protruding incisor teeth, which continue to grow throughout the animal's life. These four teeth have pale yellow to burnt orange enamel only on their front surfaces; the soft dentine at the rear of each tooth is worn away by the action of gnawing, so that the teeth retain knife-sharp cutting edges. Most rodents are relatively small mammals, but beavers and porcupines can grow quite large. Of the rodents, porcupines and beavers give birth to precocial young, and as a result their litter sizes are smaller on average than the other rodents, which have altricial young.

Porcupine Family (Erethizontidae)

The stocky-bodied North American Porcupine has some of its hairs modified into sharp-pointed quills that it uses for defense. Its sharp, curved claws and the rough soles of its feet are adapted for climbing.

North American Porcupine

Jumping Mouse Family (Dipodidae)

Jumping mice are named for the long leaps they make when they are startled. The hindlegs are much longer than the forelegs, and the tail, which is longer than the combined length of the head and body, serves as a counterbalance during jumps. Jumping mice are almost completely nocturnal.

Western Jumping Mouse

Cactus Mouse

Mouse Family (Muridae)

This diverse group of rodents is the largest and most successful mammal family in the world. Its members include the familiar rats and mice, as well as voles and lemmings. The representatives of this family in California vary in size from the tiny Western Harvest Mouse to the Common Muskrat.

Beaver Family (Castoridae)

The American Beaver is one of the two species worldwide in its family, and the only representative on our continent. It is the largest North American rodent. After humans, it is probably the animal with the greatest ability to impact the wilderness landscape in our region.

American Beaver

Pocket Mouse Family (Heteromyidae)

Little Pocket Mouse

Pocket mice, kangaroo mice and kangaroo rats make up a group of small to medium-sized rodents that are somewhat adapted to a subterranean existence. They feed mainly on seeds, and they use their external, fur-lined cheek pouches to transport food to caches in their burrows. Typically denizens of dry environments, many of them can live for a long time without drinking water. Most members of this family make two-footed leaps when moving quickly (known as ricochetal locomotion).

Pocket Gopher Family (Geomyidae)

Almost exclusively subterranean, all pocket gophers have small eyes, tiny ears, heavy claws, short, strong forelegs and a short, sparsely haired tail. Their fur-lined cheek pouches, or "pockets," are primarily used to transport food. The lower jaw is massive, and the incisor teeth are used in excavating tunnels.

Northern Pocket Gopher

Squirrel Family (Sciuridae)

Merriam's Chipmunk

This family, which includes chipmunks, tree squirrels, flying squirrels, marmots and ground squirrels, is considered the second-most structurally primitive group of rodents. All its members, except the flying squirrels, are active during the day, so they are seen more frequently than other rodents.

Mountain Beaver Family (Aplodontidae)

The Mountain Beaver is the sole living member of its family, and it is usually considered the most primitive rodent. A Mountain Beaver resembles a small, stout marmot with a tiny tail. The name "Mountain Beaver" is misleading; other than being a fellow rodent it has no relation to the American Beaver.

Mountain Beaver

North American Porcupine
Erethizon dorsatum

Although it lacks the charisma of large carnivores and ungulates, the North American Porcupine is famous for its unsurpassed defensive mechanism. A porcupine's formidable quills, numbering about 30,000, are actually stiff, modified hairs with overlapping, shingle-like barbs at their tips. Contrary to popular belief, a porcupine cannot throw its quills, but if it is attacked it will lower its head in a defensive posture and lash out with its tail. The loosely rooted quills detach easily, and they may be driven deeply into the attacker's flesh. The barbs swell and expand with blood, making the quills even harder to extract. Quill wounds may fester, or, depending on where the quills strike, they can blind an animal, prevent it from hunting or eating and even puncture a vital organ.

Porcupines are strictly vegetarian, and they are frequently found feeding in agricultural fields, willow-edged wetlands and forests. The tender bark of young branches seems to be a porcupine delicacy, and although you wouldn't think it from their size, porcupines can move far out on very thin branches with their deliberate climbing. Accomplished, if slow, climbers, porcupines use their sharp, curved claws, the thick, bumpy soles of their feet, and the quills on the underside of the tail in climbing. These large, stocky rodents often remain in individual trees and bushes for several days at a time, and when they leave a foraging site, the gnawed, cream-colored branches are clear evidence of their activity.

The North American Porcupine is mostly nocturnal, and it often rests by day in a hollow tree or log, in a burrow or in a treetop. It is not unusual to see a porcupine during the day, however, either in an open field or in a forest. It often chews bones or fallen antlers for calcium, and the sound of a porcupine's gnawing can sometimes be heard at a considerable distance.

Unfortunately for the North American Porcupine, its armament is no defense against vehicles—highway collisions are a major cause of porcupine mortality—and most people only see porcupines as roadkill.

DESCRIPTION: This large, stout-bodied rodent has long, light-tipped guard hairs surrounding the center of the back, where abundant, long, thick quills crisscross one another in all directions. The young are mostly black, but adults are variously tinged with yellow. The upper surface of the powerful, thick tail is amply supplied with dark-tipped, white to yellowish quills. The front claws are curved

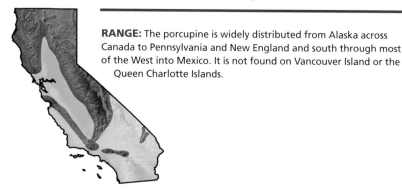

RANGE: The porcupine is widely distributed from Alaska across Canada to Pennsylvania and New England and south through most of the West into Mexico. It is not found on Vancouver Island or the Queen Charlotte Islands.

Total Length: 21–37 in.
Tail Length: 5½–9 in.
Weight: 7¾–40 lb.

and sharp. The skin on the soles of the feet is strongly dimpled, like the soles of deck shoes. There may be gray patches on the cheeks and between the eyes.

HABITAT: Porcupines occupy a variety of habitats ranging from montane forests to riparian zones and even some meadows adjacent to treed areas.

FOOD: Completely herbivorous, the North American Porcupine is like an arboreal counterpart of the American Beaver. It eats leaves, buds, twigs and especially young bark or the cambium layer of both broad-leaved and coniferous trees and shrubs. During spring and summer, it eats considerable amounts of herbaceous vegetation. The porcupine typically puts on weight during spring and summer and loses it during fall and winter. It seems to have a profound

fondness for salt, and it will chew wood handles, boots and other material that is salty from sweat or urine.

DEN: Porcupines prefer to den in caves or shelters along watercourses or under rocks, but they sometimes move into abandoned buildings, especially in winter in cold areas of the state. They are typically solitary animals, denning alone, but they may share a den during particularly cold weather. Sometimes a porcupine

DID YOU KNOW?

The name "porcupine" comes from the Latin *porcospinus*, meaning "spiny pig," and underwent many variations (Shakespeare used the word "porpentine") before its current spelling was established in the 17th century.

foreprint

walking trail

will sleep in a treetop for weeks, avoiding any den site, while it completely strips the tree of bark.

YOUNG: The porcupine's impressive armament inspires many questions about how it manages to mate. The female does most of the courtship, although males may fight with one another, and she is apparently stimulated by having the male urinate on her. When she is sufficiently aroused, she relaxes her quills and raises her tail over her back so that mating can proceed. Following mating in November or December and a gestation of $6^1/_2$ to 7 months—unusually long for a rodent—a single precocious porcupette is born in May or June. The young porcupine is born with quills, but they are not dangerous to the mother—the baby is born headfirst in a placental sac with its soft quills lying flat against its body. The quills harden within about an hour of birth. Porcupines have erupted incisor teeth at birth, and although they may continue to nurse for up to four months, they begin eating green vegetation before they are one month old. Porcupines become sexually mature when they are $1^1/_2$ to $2^1/_2$ years old.

Northern Raccoon

SIMILAR SPECIES: No other animal in California closely resembles the porcupine, but there is a small chance that the **Northern Raccoon** (p. 120) could be mistaken for a porcupine.

Western Jumping Mouse
Zapus princeps

Total Length: 8¹/₂–10 in.

Tail Length: 5–6³/₈ in.

Weight: ¹/₂–1¹/₄ oz.

True to its name, a jumping mouse is capable of exceptional leaps, powered by its large hindfeet and balanced by its long tail. Unfortunately, the two species of jumping mice in California are virtually indistinguishable from each other in the field, and this resemblance may create some confusion in areas where their ranges overlap. Their hopping escape maneuvers and supremely long tails, however, are sufficiently distinctive for even novice naturalists to distinguish them from most other rodents.

DESCRIPTION: A broad, dark, longitudinal band extends from the nose to the rump. This dorsal stripe is primarily dull brown, with some blackish hairs. The sides of the body are yellowish olive, often with some orangish hairs. The belly is a clear creamy white. The flanks and cheeks are golden yellow. The nearly naked tail is olive-brown above and whitish below. The hindfeet are greatly elongated, relative to the body size.

RANGE: This western species is found from the southern Yukon southeast to North Dakota and south to central California and northern New Mexico.

HABITAT: This jumping mouse prefers areas of tall grass, often near streams, that have sparse brush or trees. In the mountains, it ranges from valley floors up to treeline and even into tundra sedge meadows. It frequently enters the water and appears to swim well, diving as deep as 3¹/₂ ft.

FOOD: In spring and summer, berries, tender vegetation, insects and a few other invertebrates are eaten. As fall approaches, grass seeds and forb fruits are taken more frequently. Subterranean fungi are also favored.

DEN: The hibernation nest, made of finely shredded vegetation, is 1–2 ft. underground in a burrow that is 3¹/₂–10 ft. long. The breeding nest is typically built among interwoven broad-leaved grasses or in sphagnum moss in a depression.

YOUNG: Breeding takes place within a week after the female emerges from hibernation. Following an 18-day gestation, four to eight young are born in late June or early July. The eyes open after two to five days. The young nurse for one month. Some females have two or even three litters a year.

SIMILAR SPECIES: The **Pacific Jumping Mouse** (p. 173) is difficult to distinguish by appearance alone, but it occurs in regions west of this species' range. *Peromyscus* **mice** (pp. 176–82) have much shorter tails.

Pacific Jumping Mouse
Zapus trinotatus

Total length: 8¹/₄–9⁷/₈ in.
Tail length: 4¹/₄–6 in.
Weight: ³/₄–1 oz.

Like other jumping mice, the Pacific Jumping Mouse is a long-term hibernator—adults sleep from October until April. Before entering hibernation, jumping mice accumulate fat in their bodies to sustain them during their long dormancy. All of these mice emerge from hibernation at the same time; the stimulus is the rise in soil temperatures around their winter nests.

Jumping mice jump by pushing off with the hindfeet and landing on their forefeet. When trying to escape a threat, they can leap well over a yard almost straight up. Their long tails are critical for balance when jumping, and they may be drummed against the ground in alarm.

DESCRIPTION: Down the back from the nose to the rump is a dark brown dorsal stripe flecked heavily with black. The sides are ochraceous to golden in color, and the undersides are creamy white. The dorsal hair is short and rough. The forelegs are short, and the hindlegs and feet are extremely long. The thin, bicolored, scaly tail is equal to or longer than the length of the body, and it is sparsely haired without a white tip. The ears are dark with light edges, and the whiskers are abundant.

HABITAT: These mice favor areas where plant cover is dense, such as streamsides, thickets, moist fields and some woodlands. They appear to be especially common where skunk cabbage grows. In mountains they range from valley floors to above treeline in wet sedge meadows.

FOOD: Underground fungi, grass seeds, berries and tender vegetation are staples. In spring many insects and other invertebrates are eaten.

DEN: The hibernation nest, made of finely shredded vegetation, is 1–2 ft. underground in a burrow that is 3¹/₂–10 ft. long. The burrow entrance is plugged solidly before hibernation. The breeding nest is typically built among interwoven, broad-leaved grasses or in sphagnum moss in a depression.

YOUNG: These mice emerge from hibernation in late spring. Breeding takes place within a week after the female emerges. Following a gestation of 18 to 23 days, four to eight naked, hairless, blind young are born. The young nurse for a month and grow slowly; nevertheless, they must reach a critical weight and size if they are to survive hibernation. Females have one or two litters per year.

SIMILAR SPECIES: The **Western Jumping Mouse** (p. 172) is usually less distinctly tricolored and is found in areas east of this species. *Peromyscus* **mice** (pp. 176–82) have much shorter tails.

RANGE: This jumping mouse is found from extreme southwestern B.C. (not including Vancouver Island) through Washington and Oregon to north-coastal California.

Western Harvest Mouse
Reithrodontomys megalotis

Total Length: 4¹/₄–6 in.
Tail Length: 2³/₈–3¹/₈ in.
Weight: ⁵/₁₆–¹/₂ oz.

Probably the smallest mouse in California, the Western Harvest Mouse is most active during the two hours after sunset, but its activity may continue almost until dawn, particularly on dark, moonless nights. It often uses vole runways through thick grass to reach foraging areas, and it is named for its habit of collecting grass cuttings in mounds along trail networks. The Western Harvest Mouse does not store food in any great quantities, though, which is understandable for an animal that usually lives for less than a year.

DESCRIPTION: This mouse closely resembles the House Mouse (p. 191)—it is small and slim, with a small head and pointed nose, and it has a conspicuous, long, sparsely haired tail and large, naked ears. The bicolored tail is grayish above and lighter below. The upperparts are brownish, and the underparts are grayish white or sometimes pale cinnamon. Harvest mice are the only mice in this region to have a longitudinal groove on each incisor.

RANGE: This mouse ranges from extreme southern Alberta and British Columbia south nearly to the Yucatan peninsula of Mexico. It does not inhabit rough mountain regions.

HABITAT: Harvest mice occur in both arid and moist places—grasslands, sagebrush, weedy waste areas, fence lines and even cattail-choked marsh edges—as long as there is abundant overhead cover.

FOOD: The Western Harvest Mouse eats lots of green vegetation in spring and early summer, and at those times of year its runways may sport piles of grass cuttings. During most of the year, however, seeds and insects dominate the diet.

DEN: This native mouse builds its ball-shaped nest, which is about 3 in. in diameter, either on the ground or low in shrubs or weeds. The nest is made of dry grasses and is lined with soft material, such as cattail fluff. One nest may house several mice and have multiple entrances.

YOUNG: Reproduction occurs in the warmer months or all year if conditions are favorable. The average litter of four is born after a 23- to 24-day gestation. Hair is visible by five days; the eyes open after 10 to 12 days; and at 19 days the young are weaned. A female becomes sexually mature at four to five months.

SIMILAR SPECIES: The very similar **Salt-marsh Harvest Mouse** (p. 175) is found only in salt-marshes of the San Francisco Bay area. The **House Mouse** (p. 191) is generally larger and has a hairless tail. The **Deer Mouse** (p. 178) has much whiter undersides.

Salt-marsh Harvest Mouse
Reithrodontomys raviventris

Total Length: 4⅝–6⅞ in.
Tail Length: 2¼–3¾ in.
Weight: 5/16–7/16 oz.

The Salt-marsh Harvest Mouse is one of the smallest of the 28 or so threatened and endangered mammal species (including marine mammals) in California. This harvest mouse is associated with glassworts or pickleweed, which are common around San Francisco. Conversion and disruption of natural marsh habitat clearly threatens the survival of this highly localized species. The filling of marshes, the invasion of non-native marsh species (both plants and animals), sewage effluent and industrial discharge are serious hazards to the salt-marsh ecosystem and the unique species that live within it.

DESCRIPTION: This mouse closely resembles the Western Harvest Mouse (p. 174), except that the tail is thicker near the base and is either one color or only slightly bicolored. Over the back the fur is mainly dark brown, and the undersides are tawny or somewhat cinnamon in color. Its tail is long and sparsely haired, and it has large, naked ears. Harvest mice are the only mice in this region to have a longitudinal groove on each incisor.

HABITAT: The Salt-marsh Harvest Mouse has a small and fragmented habitat in the bay area. About 80 percent of the historic marshes in the region have been destroyed. Unfortunately, waterfowl management in the marshes has been shown to be incompatible with the survival of this species.

FOOD: This mouse feeds primarily on the seeds of grasses and other plants in its marshy home. Because of its adaptations to a salty environment, this species is able to drink seawater.

DEN: The Salt-marsh Harvest Mouse builds a grassy nest off the ground in bush or shrub, usually inside either a clump of vegetation or an old bird's nest. The inside of the nest is lined with cattail fluff, down or soft, fine grass.

YOUNG: Reproduction occurs from March through late October. The average litter of four is born after a little more than three weeks. The young are altricial, and development is probably similar to that of the Western Harvest Mouse.

SIMILAR SPECIES: The very similar **Western Harvest Mouse** (p. 174) is found throughout the entire state. The **House Mouse** (p. 191) is generally larger and has a hairless tail. The **Deer Mouse** (p. 178) has much whiter undersides.

RANGE: This species is confined to the tidal and non-tidal salt-marshes of the San Francisco Bay system (San Francisco, San Pablo and Suisun Bays).

Cactus Mouse
Peromyscus eremicus

Total length: 6¹/₄–8⁵/₈ in.
Tail length: 3¹/₄–5 in.
Weight: ⁵/₈–1³/₈ oz.

HABITAT: The Cactus Mouse generally inhabits arid areas such as deserts with yucca and cactus stands and rocky outcroppings.

FOOD: These mice may climb to forage, and they feed mainly on the seeds of desert plants, the fruits and flowers of mesquite and hackberry, green vegetation and insects.

One of the major features distinguishing the Cactus Mouse from the very similar Deer Mouse (p. 178) is its long tail. The tail is usually 55 percent or more of the total length, and it is sparsely furred. Cactus Mice are well suited to the dry environment of southern California, but they will become inactive in their nests during serious food or water shortages. In some seasons, they can be difficult to locate, unless they are in or near a riparian area where they will remain active.

DESCRIPTION: The Cactus Mouse is yellowish orange or cinnamon above and bright white below. The large ears are nearly hairless and extend well above the fur on the head and the black eyes protrude. The tail is pinkish brown and indistinctly bicolored, darker above and lighter below. The feet and heels are pink and nearly hairless.

DEN: Nests are located in clumps of cactus, among rocks or in the burrows of other small mammals. The nest is a sphere of grass and fine dry vegetation about 4 in. across.

YOUNG: The breeding season extends from February to June, though reproductive activity probably correlates with the growth of plants and insects following rain, and mating has been known to occur in the fall. Following a gestation of about 21 days, two to three young are born. The pink, naked, blind young weigh about ¹/₁₆ oz. at birth and are weaned about three to four weeks later. In suitable conditions the female may mate again immediately after giving birth so the weanlings are evicted from the nest to make room for the new litter.

SIMILAR SPECIES: The **Deer Mouse** (p. 178) has a shorter tail, the **California Mouse** (p. 177) has a well-furred tail, the **Pinyon Mouse** (p. 182) is typically grayer in color, the **Canyon Mouse** (p. 180) has a slight tuft on its tail and the **Brush Mouse** (p. 181) has a distinctly bicolored tail.

RANGE: The Cactus Mouse is found in southern California, southern Nevada and southwestern Utah, ranging south through much of Arizona, southern New Mexico and southwestern Texas.

California Mouse
Peromyscus californicus

Total Length: 8⁵/₈–11 in.
Tail Length: 4⁵/₈–6¹/₈ in.
Weight: 1¹/₈–1⁷/₈ oz.

This large *Peromyscus* mouse shows very unusual parental behavior. Most mice separate after mating, and the female is left alone to raise the young. California Mice, however, have strong pair bonds between the male and female and they raise their young together. Studies have even shown that the extra heat from the male causes the young to grow faster than young of single female litters. The paired male and female share the job of defending and maintaining their nest. These mice are semi-arboreal, and unable to dig burrows in the ground. Able only to enlarge existing cracks or holes in wood, they must make their nest in natural tree cavities or share a nest with a woodrat (*Neotoma*) species, hence their alternate common name, the Parasitic Mouse.

ALSO CALLED: Parasitic Mouse.

DESCRIPTION: This yellow or gray mouse is the largest *Peromyscus* mouse in North America. A buffy or gray spot is often on the breast, and the back may be flecked with black. Its undersides are usually white, as are its feet. The tail may be slightly bicolored: dark on top and light underneath.

HABITAT: California Mice are found in a variety of habitats, such as forests, ravines, chaparral and brushy areas.

DEN: Large ground or tree nests, made by a woodrat, such as the Dusky-footed Woodrat (p. 190), are often inhabited by these mice. The two species may live together in the same nest, but they maintain separate living chambers. Nest materials are dry twigs, grasses and other vegetation.

FOOD: These mice feed on a variety of foods, such as seeds, fruits, flowers, insects and other arthropods. They appear to be especially fond of seeds from the California Bay.

YOUNG: In one year, a female can have several litters. The most common litter size is two young, born after a gestation of 35 to 45 days. This species is unusual in forming long-term pair bonds and raising young together.

SIMILAR SPECIES: All other species in this genus are smaller. The **woodrats** (pp. 186–90), which live with these mice, are much larger.

RANGE: These mice are found in southeastern and coastal California.

Deer Mouse

Peromyscus maniculatus

Upon first seeing a Deer Mouse, many people are surprised by how cute this little animal is. The large, protruding, coal black eyes give it a justifiably inquisitive look, while its dainty nose and long whiskers continually twitch, sensing the changing odors in the wind.

Wherever there is groundcover, from thick grass to deadfall, Deer Mice scurry about with great liveliness. These small mice are omnipresent over much of their range, and they may well be one of the most numerous mammals in California. When you walk through forested wilderness areas, they are in your company, even if their presence remains hidden.

Deer Mice most frequently forage along the ground, but they are known to climb trees and shrubs to reach food. During winter in areas of snow cover, Deer Mice are the most common of the small rodents to travel above the snow. In doing so, however, they are vulnerable to nighttime predators. The tiny skulls of these rodents are among the most common remains in the regurgitated pellets of owls, a testament to their importance in the food web.

The Deer Mouse, which is named for the similarity of its coloring to that of the White-tailed Deer, commonly occupies farm buildings, garages and storage sheds, often alongside the House Mouse (p. 191). In a few high-profile cases, people have died from exposure to the *Hanta* virus, which is associated with the feces and urine of the Deer Mouse. The virus can become airborne, so if you find Deer Mouse droppings, it is best to wear a mask and spray the area with water and bleach before attempting to remove the animal's waste.

DESCRIPTION: Every Deer Mouse has protruding, black, lustrous eyes, large ears, a pointed nose, long whiskers and a sharply bicolored tail, with a dark top and light underside. In contrast to these constant characteristics, the color of the adult's upperparts is quite variable: yellowish buff, tawny brown, grayish brown or blackish brown. The upperparts, however, are always sharply distinct from the bright white undersides and feet. A juvenile has uniformly gray upperparts.

HABITAT: These ubiquitous mice occupy a variety of habitats, including grasslands, mossy depressions, brushy areas, tundra and heavily wooded regions. Another habitat these little mice greatly favor is human-made buildings—our warm, food-laden homes are palatial residences to Deer Mice.

RANGE: The Deer Mouse is the most widespread mouse in North America. Its range extends from Labrador almost to Alaska and south through most of North America to south-central Mexico.

Total Length: 5¹/₂–8³/₄ in.
Tail Length: 2¹/₈–4⁷/₈ in.
Weight: ³/₈–⁷/₈ oz.

FOOD: Deer Mice horde food, and their caches can be almost anywhere, such as hollow logs, tree cavities, burrows or abandoned birds' nests. Their main foods include seeds or fruits from grasses, chokecherries, buckwheat and other plants. They also eat insects, nestling birds and eggs.

DEN: As the habitat of this mouse changes, so does its den type: in meadows it nests in a small burrow or makes a grassy nest on raised ground; in wooded areas it makes a nest in a hollow log or under debris. Nests can also be made in rock crevices and certainly in human structures.

YOUNG: Breeding in California occurs from April to December, and gestation lasts for 21 to 24 days. The helpless young number one to nine (usually four or five) and weigh about ¹/₁₆ oz.

at birth. They open their eyes between days 12 and 17, and about four days after that, they venture out of the nest. At three to five weeks the young are completely weaned and are soon on their own. A female is sexually mature in about 35 days; a male is in about 45 days.

SIMILAR SPECIES: The **House Mouse** (p. 191) and the **Western Harvest Mouse** (p. 174) lack the distinct bright white belly and sharply bicolored tail. The **Canyon Mouse** (p. 180) has a longer tail, as do **jumping mice** (pp. 172–73). The **Northern Grasshopper Mouse** (p. 183) is larger and more robust.

DID YOU KNOW?

Adult Deer Mice displaced a mile from where they were trapped were generally able to return to their home burrows within a day. Perhaps they range so widely in their travels that they recognized where they were and simply scampered home.

Canyon Mouse
Peromyscus crinitus

Total Length: 6³/₈–7¹/₂ in.
Tail Length: 3¹/₈–4⁵/₈ in.
Weight: ³/₈–³/₄ oz.

This interesting mouse is named for the dry, rocky habitats in which it lives. The Canyon Mouse often lives on buttes and mesas devoid of vegetation, and it therefore has a particularly effective metabolism for life in arid regions. It rarely drinks—it can survive on the water metabolized from its food—and in situations of extreme aridity and heat it rests in torpor until conditions improve. Canyon Mouse bones dating to the 13th century were found to the east and southeast of its present range, which may indicate that conditions were drier there at that time.

DESCRIPTION: The Canyon Mouse has very large, sparsely furred ears. Its thinly haired tail is longer than the head and body (at least 55 percent of the total length), distinctively bicolored and somewhat tufted at the tip. The undersides and feet are white. The upperparts are brown, and the division between the darker back and white underside is sharp.

HABITAT: Bare rock seems to be a habitat requirement of the Canyon Mouse. It is found in deserts or rocky canyons where stands of black brush, saltbush, bunchgrass and sagebrush grow. It can be found up to about 6000 ft. elevation.

FOOD: These mice have a diverse, omnivorous diet that changes seasonally between seeds and other vegetation and insects. These mice do not need to drink; they metabolize water from insects and green vegetation.

DEN: Nests are located in protected areas such as burrows, among rocks, in logs or in old buildings.

YOUNG: Typically, the Canyon Mouse has two litters a year. Breeding occurs in early spring and early fall, and the average litter size is one to five young.

SIMILAR SPECIES: The **Pinyon Mouse** (p. 182) is larger and has longer ears and hindfeet. The **Deer Mouse** (p. 178) tends to have a shorter tail. Habitat and range are often the best indicators of a mouse's identity.

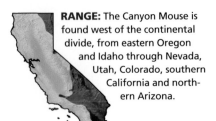

RANGE: The Canyon Mouse is found west of the continental divide, from eastern Oregon and Idaho through Nevada, Utah, Colorado, southern California and northern Arizona.

Brush Mouse

Peromyscus boylii

Total Length: 7¹/₈–9³/₈ in.

Tail Length: 3⁵/₈–4³/₄ in.

Weight: ³/₄–1¹/₄ oz.

Brush Mice take a slightly different approach to evading danger. Rather than taking to the undergrowth like most other frightened mice, they earn their name by running up into shrubs. Brush Mice are not master arborealists in the league of tree squirrels, but nevertheless their attempts at climbing often result in separating them from their threats. The long tail thrashes back and forth, counterbalancing the animal like a tightrope walker with a balance pole. These mice commonly occur throughout much of California, in evergreen oak communities with lots of underbrush. Areas without underbrush are ill-suited to this mouse and are occupied by other types of mice, such as the Pinyon Mouse (p. 182).

DESCRIPTION: This small to medium-sized mouse has a brown back and a sharply demarcated white belly. The feet are white, the ears are large and the long tail (more than 55 percent of the total length) is bicolored. A rather indistinct tuft is on the tail tip.

HABITAT: The Brush Mouse can be found in rocky and arid areas, particularly where there is some oak, juniper or pinyon vegetation.

FOOD: Brush Mice have been known to eat a wide variety of food items, many of them depending on the season. Seeds of conifers, berries and insects are common items, while the fruit of cactus is also consumed. It commonly forages in shrubs and bushes.

DEN: Nests are located in burrows, among rocks, in logs or buildings or in other protected areas.

YOUNG: Although it is capable of reproducing every month of the year under ideal situations, there are likely only two litters a year. Breeding likely takes place between April and May and then again in September and October. Litters contain one to five (usually three) young.

SIMILAR SPECIES: The **Deer Mouse** (p. 178) has a tail that is shorter than the length of the head and body. The **Pinyon Mouse** (p. 182) has longer ears. The **Canyon Mouse** (p. 180) has shorter ears.

RANGE: The Brush Mouse is a western animal that ranges from Oregon, Idaho and Wyoming south through northern Mexico.

Pinyon Mouse
Peromyscus truei

Total Length: 6³/₄–9¹/₈ in.
Tail Length: 3–4⁷/₈ in.
Weight: ⁵/₈–1¹/₈ oz.

Through much of California, the Pinyon Mouse can be found living in arid and semi-arid environments. As its name suggests, this mouse is associated with pinyon pines and junipers, and it nearly always lives in rocky outcroppings where these plants are abundant. Pinyon Mice are well adapted to heat and aridity, and during the hottest part of the day they rest inside their cool, sheltered nests. These mice do not hibernate, but they may enter torpor in response to severe aridity. Even when this mouse is not active, it can be detected by pinyon and juniper seed husks tossed in loose piles, which tell the story of this mouse's food preferences.

DESCRIPTION: The dorsal color is variable and can be lead-colored, brownish, cinnamon or rich tawny, and it is separated sharply from the white to creamy white underparts. The thin tail (about 50 percent of the total length) is distinctly hairy and bicolored dark above and white below. The ears are longer than the hindfeet and sparsely haired, the eyes are large and protruding, the nose is pointed and the whiskers are long. The feet are white.

HABITAT: The Pinyon Mouse is an inhabitant of arid foothill lowlands, and it is seldom found above 7000 ft. It seems restricted to areas of pinyon and juniper, particularly where rocky slopes dominate.

FOOD: During arid months, much of the diet consists of insects and spiders. Year-round foods include seeds and nuts, particularly cones from pines and junipers.

DEN: Nests are located among rocks, in logs and hollow trunks, in buildings or in other protected areas.

YOUNG: The Pinyon Mouse has several litters between April and September, each consisting of three to six altricial young.

SIMILAR SPECIES: The **Canyon Mouse** (p. 180) has smaller ears and a relatively larger tail (55 percent of its length). The **Brush Mouse** (p. 181) and the **Cactus Mouse** (p. 176) have smaller ears, and the **California Mouse** (p. 177) is larger.

RANGE: The Pinyon Mouse ranges from central Oregon to Colorado and south through Mexico.

Northern Grasshopper Mouse
Onychomys leucogaster

Total Length: 5¹/₈–7¹/₂ in.
Tail Length: 1¹/₈–2³/₈ in.
Weight: ⁷/₈–1⁷/₈ oz.

The bulldog of the mice in this region, the Northern Grasshopper Mouse is found only in dry sage-brush areas of northeastern California. This mouse has a fierce disposition toward both prey and non-prey species, and it frequently usurps the home of another small mammal, eating it and modifying the burrows for its own needs. In contrast to its attitude toward other species, the Northern Grasshopper Mouse seems to make a devoted parent; both the male and female care for the young, bringing food to the nest until their offspring become self-sufficient.

DESCRIPTION: Although the dorsal color of this species is variable through-out its range, here in California the Northern Grasshopper Mouse tends to be rich brown. The undersides are bright white. The short tail—it is less than 50 percent of the total length—is thick, sharply bicolored (darker above, white below) and has a white tip. This mouse appears to be stocky for its size. The rumpled appearance of the fur and the odor that grasshopper mice tend to develop is reduced by sand bathing.

HABITAT: This mouse occurs in dry, open habitats with sandy or gravelly soils, especially sagebrush flats.

FOOD: The diet changes seasonally but consists mainly of insects, seeds and veg-etation. Insects (and other arthropods) include grasshoppers, crickets, beetles, scorpions, spiders, moths and butterflies. It can even overpower and kill mice and birds up to three times its own weight.

DEN: Nests are typically found in a bur-row, either dug by the mouse itself or "stolen" from another burrowing mam-mal and refurbished. The burrow system of grasshopper mice is complex, with many different burrows for different purposes such as caching, nesting or defecating.

YOUNG: Breeding occurs between Feb-ruary to September, and females have two or three litters of three or four young each. Gestation is typically 32 to 38 days. The young weigh ¹/₁₆–¹/₈ oz. and are naked and blind at birth.

SIMILAR SPECIES: The **Southern Grass-hopper Mouse** (p. 184) is very similar but has a different range and longer tail. The **Deer Mouse** (p. 178) has a similar coloration but is smaller and has a thinner, longer tail.

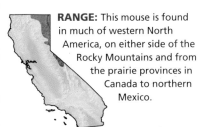

RANGE: This mouse is found in much of western North America, on either side of the Rocky Mountains and from the prairie provinces in Canada to northern Mexico.

Southern Grasshopper Mouse
Onychomys torridus

Total Length: 4⁵/₈–6³/₈ in.

Tail Length: 1¹/₄–2⁵/₈ in.

Weight: ³/₄–1 oz.

Like its more northerly counterpart, see p. 183, the Southern Grasshopper Mouse is a burly resident of arid areas. The large form of this mouse befits its predatory nature. Studies indicate it has characteristics normally associated with carnivores: it exhibits social bonds and elaborate courtship, and it has long claws, enhanced jaw muscles and teeth suitable for shearing animal matter. Unlike other mice, it even "howls." Its howl is within human hearing and can carry far in dry air.

ALSO CALLED: Scorpion Mouse.

DESCRIPTION: The dorsal color is variable, but in California this species is mainly light brown or cinnamon, and the entire belly is white. The nose is pointed, the dark, lustrous eyes protrude noticeably, and the ears are large. The tail—slightly more than 50 percent of the total length—is thick, sharply bicolored (darker above, white below) and has a white tip. The thick legs, broad feet and broad shoulders of this mouse give an impression of burliness.

HABITAT: This mouse occurs in desert and sandy brushlands, especially with mesquite and yucca.

FOOD: The diet changes seasonally, but the bulk of the foods eaten include seeds of grasses, vegetation and a variety of insects. This fierce mouse even eats scorpions (as its alternate common name suggests); to do so, it immobilizes the dangerous tail and bites off the stinger. It can even overpower and kill mice and birds up to three times its own weight.

DEN: Burrow systems are complex, with several burrows each serving a different purpose. Nest burrows are usually located about 6 in. below the surface. The entrance is plugged by day, which helps retain moisture.

YOUNG: Breeding occurs between May and July. Gestation is 30 to 37 days. A litter usually contains three or four young, which weigh ¹/₁₆–¹/₈ oz. and are naked and blind at birth. Females have two or three litters a year.

SIMILAR SPECIES: The **Northern Grasshopper Mouse** (p. 183) is very similar but has a different range and a shorter tail. The **Deer Mouse** (p. 178) has a similar coloration but lacks the burly proportions and has a thinner, longer tail.

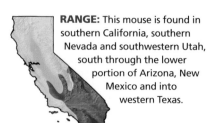

RANGE: This mouse is found in southern California, southern Nevada and southwestern Utah, south through the lower portion of Arizona, New Mexico and into western Texas.

Hispid Cotton Rat
Sigmodon hispidus

Total Length: 8³/₄–14³/₈ in.

Tail Length: 3¹/₈–6¹/₂ in.

Weight: 3⁷/₈–8 oz.

Like most other small mammals, the Hispid Cotton Rat is an important prey species within its range. Fortunately, the heavy predation by avian and terrestrial predators is balanced by this species' high fecundity—one of the highest of all mammalian species. Populations of Hispid Cotton Rats fluctuate quite dramatically depending on the season. Typically, these cotton rats are most abundant in the summer months.

DESCRIPTION: The Hispid Cotton Rat has a grizzled grayish brown coat, with somewhat lighter gray undersides. Some individuals may have numerous black flecks over the back. Coat color may be regionally variable depending on soil color. The tail is less than half of the total length and is coarsely ringed and sparsely haired.

HABITAT: This cotton rat tends to occupy grassy areas with suitable cover, such as overgrown clearings and croplands. Cover is necessary to avoid avian predators. In California, this cotton rat tends to prefer the margins of watercourses.

FOOD: Primarily vegetarian, the Hispid Cotton Rat feeds on green vegetation. Seasonally, it may consume some insect matter. Like many other small mammals, this cotton rat meets its water requirements from the water in its food. Food is not stored in the burrow. In agricultural areas this rodent can cause damage to sugar cane and sweet potatoes.

DEN: Normally, a house of grass and dry vegetation is constructed aboveground and beneath suitable cover such as a shrub. Sometimes the den will be in a shallow burrow. The house or burrow contains a nest of dry grasses woven together, and distinct, well-worn trails lead to the house. In cold regions, the nests are woven quite tightly for insulation. In very warm regions, the nest is loosely constructed and may be just cup-shaped rather than a hollow ball.

YOUNG: In California, this cotton rat mates year-round, and females usually have several litters per year. Gestation is 27 days and litter size can range from 1 to 15 young. Young are weaned at 12 days and adult size is reached in 100 days.

SIMILAR SPECIES: The **Arizona Cotton Rat** (*S. arizonae*) is very similar, although it averages larger and has a smaller range in California.

RANGE: This cotton rat is found throughout the southeastern states. A small, isolated population inhabits extreme southern California and neighboring Arizona.

Bushy-tailed Woodrat
Neotoma cinerea

While most people have heard of "packrats," few people know that this nickname applies to woodrats. The Bushy-tailed Woodrat is a fine example of a packrat—it is widely known for its habit of collecting all manner of objects and trinkets into a heap. This animal is also sometimes called a "trade rat," because it is nearly always carrying something in its teeth, only to drop that item to pick up something else instead. Thus, camping gear, false teeth, tools or jewelry may disappear from a campsite, with a stick, bone or pinecone kindly left in its place.

Bushy-tailed Woodrats tend to nest in rocky areas, and because their nests are large and messy, woodrat homes are easier to find than the residents. The places in which woodrats can build their nests are limited, and rival males fight fiercely over their houses. Female woodrats are likely attracted to males that have secure nests, and several females may be found nesting with a single male.

The Bushy-tailed Woodrat may have proportionally the longest whiskers of any rodent in the region. Extending well over the width of the animal's body on either side, a woodrat's whiskers serve it well as it feels its way around in the darkness of caves, mines and the night. Woodrats are most active after dark, so a late-night prowl with flashlight in hand may catch the reflective glare of woodrat eyes as the animals investigate their territories.

DESCRIPTION: The back is gray, pale pinkish or grizzled brown. The belly is white. The long, soft, dense, buffy fur overlies a short, soft underfur. The long, bushy, almost squirrel-like tail is gray above and white below. There are distinct juvenile and sub-adult pelages: a juvenile's back is gray, and it has short tail hairs; a sub-adult has brown hues in its back, and its tail has long guard hairs. A tawny adult pelage is developed in fall. All woodrats have large, protruding, black eyes, big, fur-covered ears and long, abundant whiskers.

HABITAT: This woodrat's domain usually includes rocks and shrubs or abandoned buildings, mine shafts or caves. It has a greater elevational range than other woodrats, extending from grasslands to the alpine.

FOOD: Leaves of shrubs are probably the most important component of the diet, but conifer needles and seeds, juniper berries, mushrooms, fruits, grasses, rootstocks and bulbs are all eaten or stored

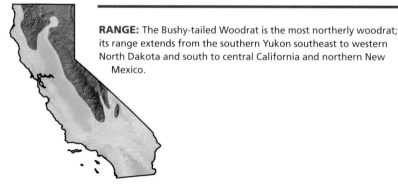

RANGE: The Bushy-tailed Woodrat is the most northerly woodrat; its range extends from the southern Yukon southeast to western North Dakota and south to central California and northern New Mexico.

Total Length: 11–18 in.
Tail Length: 4³/₄–8³/₄ in.
Weight: 2³/₄–18 oz.

for later consumption. To provide adequate winter supplies, a woodrat gathers and stores about 2 gal. of food. One woodrat may make several caches.

DEN: Large numbers of sticks, plus a large variety of bark, dung and other materials, are piled near the nest site. There are often no inner passages or chambers in this accumulation. Instead, a lined, ball- or cup-shaped nest is built of fibrous material and is situated nearby, usually more than 11 ft. above the ground, either in a narrow crevice, in the fork of a tree, on a shelf or sometimes in a stove in an abandoned cabin.

YOUNG: Mating usually takes place between March and June. Following a 27- to 32-day gestation period, three or four helpless young are born. They are ⁷/₁₆–⁵/₈ oz. at birth and their growth is rapid. Special teeth help them hold on to their mother's nipples almost continuously. Their incisors erupt at 12 to 15 days, and their eyes open on day 14 or 15. They first leave the nest at about 22 days, and they are weaned at 26 to 30 days. The young reach sexual maturity the spring following their birth. Some females bear two litters in a season.

SIMILAR SPECIES: The **Desert** (p. 189), **White-throated** (p. 188) and **Dusky-footed** (p. 190) **woodrats** all lack the bushy tail. The **Norway Rat** (p. 192) is a similar size, but does not have a bushy tail and tends to live near human activity. The **American Pika** (p. 286) has no visible tail, and its muzzle is shorter.

DID YOU KNOW?

When a very old woodrat nest in an old cabin near a mountain hotel was torn apart some years ago, a collection of silverware dating back to the earliest days of the hotel was found.

White-throated Woodrat
Neotoma albigula

Total Length: 11–16 in.
Tail Length: 3–7¼ in.
Weight: 4¾–7 oz.

The White-throated Woodrat is not a common inhabitant of California, but it may be found in south-eastern parts of the state. This rodent prefers arid conditions; brushy plains and deserts suit its needs best. This woodrat is skilled at running uninjured over cacti. Woodrats are inquisitive and alert-looking animals that, when encountered, often share a brief stare with a naturalist before they turn and retreat to safety.

DESCRIPTION: The back is mainly brown or grayish, and the belly is white or light gray. The tail is lightly haired and colored the same as the body. The ears are moderately long, and the snout is pointed, with abundant, long whiskers. A patch of all-white hair is at its throat.

RANGE: This woodrat is found in southern Colorado and Utah, most of Arizona and New Mexico into Texas and Mexico. Small numbers are found in southeastern California.

HABITAT: A variety of arid habitats suit this woodrat, such as rocky terrain, scrub-lands, deserts and sagebrush flats. Pinyon-juniper regions and mesquite–prickly pear regions are favored.

FOOD: Cactus fruit appears to make up much of the diet. Other foods include juniper and pinyon fruits, yucca and some vegetation.

DEN: The nest is hidden with cactus spines and small twigs, and it is usually at the base of a cactus or in a rocky crevice. Rarely does this woodrat use an underground chamber.

YOUNG: Reproduction takes place from January to July. Females have not been recorded to have multiple litters in one year. Their development is similar to that of other woodrats, with the young becoming sexually mature the spring after their birth.

SIMILAR SPECIES: The **Bushy-tailed Woodrat** (p. 186) has a distinctly bushier tail. The **Desert Woodrat** (p. 189) lacks the white throat spot and the **Dusky-footed Woodrat** (p. 190) has dusky hindfeet.

Desert Woodrat
Neotoma lepida

Total Length: 8⁷/₈–15 in.
Tail Length: 3³/₄–7³/₈ in.
Weight: 3⁷/₈–4³/₄ oz.

Small and forceful, the Desert Woodrat is famous for its dominating presence in the deserts and other arid regions of the southwestern U.S. Among the great variety of nocturnal desert rodents, these woodrats are the dominant species. In arid regions in much of lower California, Desert Woodrats build their homes inside or in burrows underneath prickly pear cacti. When the dry season begins and drought negatively affects most animals, each woodrat staunchly defends its own cactus, permitting no other rodent to share in this valuable water source. The Desert Woodrat is quite at home in the cactus; it runs freely and uninjured over the dangerous spines that repel most other animals.

DESCRIPTION: Desert Woodrats are mainly buff, gray or sooty colored above and light gray to white underneath. Their tails are sparsely furred and sharply bicolored: sooty gray above and buff below. Their hindfeet are white, but all the hairs over the body—even white ones—are gray at the base.

HABITAT: These woodrats are found in arid regions of many types: deserts, juniper-pinyon areas or sagebrush flats, but they are seldom found far from prickly pear cacti.

DEN: Primarily associated with *Opuntia* cacti, the woodrat lives in burrows at the base of or, less frequently, inside the cactus. Their nests look like ramshackle arrangements of twigs, cactus spines, vegetation and other odds and ends.

FOOD: Their diet is composed of cactus pulp and fruits as well as nuts, seeds, fruits and bark of other plants.

YOUNG: Mating occurs in early spring. After a gestation period of about one month, a litter of three or four altricial young is born. The young mature quickly, and by day 15 their eyes are open.

SIMILAR SPECIES: The **Dusky-footed Woodrat** (p. 190) is larger, and its feet and ankles are dusky colored; the **Bushy-tailed Woodrat** (p. 186) has a well-furred, bushy tail; and the **White-throated Woodrat** (p. 188) has a distinct white throat.

RANGE: This woodrat is found in southeastern Oregon, southwestern Idaho, Nevada, southern California, much of Utah and the northwest corner of Arizona.

Dusky-footed Woodrat
Neotoma fuscipes

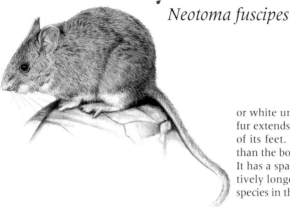

Total Length: 13–19 in.
Tail Length: 6¼–8⅞ in.
Weight: 8¼–9⅜ oz.

or white underneath. Its gray or dusky fur extends over its ankles and the tops of its feet. The head is usually grayer than the body, sometimes a sooty color. It has a sparsely furred tail that is relatively longer than most other *Neotoma* species in the region.

These semi-arboreal rodents are accomplished gatherers and homemakers. They build nests either on the ground or in a tree, sometimes as high as 50 ft. off the ground. Nest building is time consuming, and the home is never finished. Woodrats are famed for their preoccupation with caching objects and trinkets. Usually food is carried away to special chambers in their twiggy nest, but sometimes shiny bits of metal, an old fork, a piece of plastic or anything of "value" to the sensibilities of the woodrat are also cached away. The nests are often occupied by more than one woodrat and usually to several other animal species as well. Small mammals, frogs, beetles and other invertebrates are commonly found inside the home of a Dusky-footed Woodrat.

DESCRIPTION: This woodrat is grayish or buff brown on its back and pale gray

HABITAT: Favoring areas with lots of sticks and twigs, these woodrats are found mainly in hardwood forests and in dense shrublands throughout much of the state.

DEN: These woodrats make large, heaped piles of sticks, bark, plants and miscellaneous objects on the ground or in a well-supported fork of a tree. Inside is a maze of passageways and chambers for caching or sleeping. Usually one female, and sometimes two, occupy the nest, and although the individuals may change, a nest may be used and improved for many generations.

FOOD: Their diet consists largely of green vegetation, with seeds, fruits, nuts and fungi being consumed in small amounts.

YOUNG: Mating can occur from early spring to late fall, with females having only one litter per year. Gestation is about 33 days, and litter size is two to four altricial young. Outside the mating season a male lives separately in a small nest.

SIMILAR SPECIES: The larger **Bushy-tailed Woodrat** (p. 186) has a flattened and bushy tail; the **White-throated Woodrat** (p. 188) has a distinct white throat; and the smaller **Desert Woodrat** (p. 189) has white hindfeet.

RANGE: These woodrats are found along the west coast from Oregon through California.

House Mouse
Mus musculus

Total Length: 5–7³/₄ in.
Tail Length: 2¹/₂–4 in.
Weight: ¹/₂–⁷/₈ oz.

Thanks to its habit of catching rides with humans, first aboard ships and now in train cars, trucks and containers, the House Mouse is now found in most countries of the world. In fact, the House Mouse's dispersal closely mirrors the agricultural development of our species. As humans began growing crops on the great sweeping plains of middle Asia, this mouse, native to that region, began profiting from our storage of surplus grains and our concurrent switch from a nomadic to a relatively sedentary lifestyle. Within the small span of a few hundred human generations, farmed grains began to find their way into Europe and Africa for trade. Along with these grain shipments, stowaway House Mice were spread to every corner of the globe.

DESCRIPTION: The back is yellowish brown, gray or nearly black, the sides may have a slight yellow wash, and the underparts are light gray. The head is small, and the nose is pointed and surrounded by abundant whiskers. There are large, almost hairless ears above the protruding black eyes. The long, hairless, tapered tail is gray and slightly lighter below than above. The brownish feet tend to be whitish at the tips.

HABITAT: This introduced mouse inhabits homes, outbuildings, barns, granaries, haystacks and trash piles. Wilderness cabins occupied only in summer are far more apt to be invaded by Deer Mice than by House Mice.

FOOD: Seeds, stems and leaves constitute the bulk of the diet, but insects, carrion and human food, including meat and milk, are eagerly consumed.

DEN: The nest is constructed of shredded paper and rags, vegetation and sometimes fur combined into a 4-in. ball beneath a board, inside a wall, in a pile of rags or in a haystack.

YOUNG: If abundant resources are available, breeding may occur throughout the year. Gestation is about three weeks, resulting in a litter of four to eight helpless young. They are weaned at 16 to 17 days. At six to eight weeks, the young become sexually mature.

SIMILAR SPECIES: The **Western Harvest Mouse** (p. 174) has a clearly bicolored tail and a distinct longitudinal groove on the front of each upper incisor tooth. The **Deer Mouse** (p. 178) has a bright white belly and distinctively bicolored tail.

RANGE: The House Mouse is widespread in North America, inhabiting nearly every city, hamlet or farm from the Atlantic to the Pacific and north to the tundra.

Norway Rat
Rattus norvegicus

Total Length: 13–18 in.
Tail Length: 4³/₄–8³/₄ in.
Weight: 7–17 oz.

While it is said that absence makes the heart grow fonder, it's a sure bet that no one would miss rats. Even a naturalist has trouble defending this species. The mountain regions of California are largely inhospitable to Norway Rats, but otherwise, they are found statewide. Everywhere Norway Rats occur, they are subject to public scorn and intense pest-control measures.

Norway Rats were introduced to North America in about 1775, and they have established colonies in most cities and towns south of the boreal forest. These great pests feed on a wide variety of stored grain, garbage and carrion, gnaw holes in walls and contaminate stored hay with urine and feces. They have also been linked to the transfer of diseases to both livestock and humans.

More than any other animal, the Norway Rat is viewed with disgust by most people. As one of the world's most studied and manipulated animals, however, much of our biomedical and physiological knowledge can be attributed to experiments involving these animals—a rather significant contribution for a hated pest.

ALSO CALLED: Brown Rat.

DESCRIPTION: The back is a grizzled brown, reddish brown or black. The paler belly is grayish to yellowish white. The long, round, tapered tail is darker above and lighter below. It is sparsely haired and scaly. The prominent ears are covered with short, fine hairs. Occasionally, someone releases an albino, white or piebald Norway Rat that had been kept in captivity.

HABITAT: Norway Rats nearly always live in proximity to human habitation. Where they are found away from humans, they prefer thickly vegetated regions with abundant cover. Abandoned buildings in the wilderness are more frequently occupied by Bushy-tailed Woodrats than by Norway Rats.

RANGE: The Norway Rat is concentrated in cities, towns and farms throughout coastal North America, southern Canada and most of the U.S.

FOOD: This rat eats a wide variety of grains, insects, garbage and carrion. It may even kill young chickens, ducks, piglets and lambs. Green legume fruits are also popular items, and some shoots and grasses are consumed. Birdseed in feeders seems to be a favorite.

DEN: A cavity scratched beneath a fallen board or a space beneath an abandoned building may hold a bulky nest of grasses, leaves and often paper or chewed rags. Although Norway Rats are able to, they seldom dig long burrows.

YOUNG: After a gestation of 21 to 22 days, 6 to 22 pink, blind babies are born. The eyes open after 10 days. The young are sexually mature in about three months. In Washington and Oregon, Norway Rats seem to breed mainly in the warmer months of the year, but in some cities they may breed year-round.

SIMILAR SPECIES: The **Bushy-tailed Woodrat** (p. 186) has a white belly, and its tail is covered with long, bushy hair. The **Common Muskrat** (p. 204) is larger and has a laterally compressed tail.

DID YOU KNOW?

Some historians attribute the end of the Black Death epidemics in Europe to the southward invasion of the Norway Rat and its displacement of the less aggressive Black Rat, which was much more apt to inhabit human homes.

Black Rat
Rattus rattus

Total Length: 13–18 in.
Tail Length: 6¼–10 in.
Weight: 4½–12 oz.

Although the Black Rat may well appear as black, the most dominant color in California is a yellowish brown, slightly flecked with black. Otherwise, it is very similar in appearance to the Norway Rat, although generally slimmer with a tail that is longer than the head and body. The Black Rat is apt to live amongst humans, especially in warm attics. This rat is even less inclined to live in mountain areas than the Norway Rat; it is rarely found above 2600 ft.

ALSO CALLED: Roof Rat, Tree Rat.

Western Red-backed Vole
Clethrionomys californicus

Total Length: 5¹/₂–6⁵/₈ in.
Tail Length: 1³/₄–2¹/₄ in.
Weight: ⁵/₈–1¹/₈ oz.

While many voles leave runways on the forest floor from routine foraging expeditions, the Western Red-backed Vole follows no set foraging route and is unlikely to leave the telltale trails. To further disguise its whereabouts, this vole rarely runs out in the open. Using the cover of leaf litter, logs, rocks and thick vegetation, this vole remains safely out of sight from all but the most perceptive of predators. Forest-dwelling hawks, Coyotes, weasels and owls are among the species that prey upon the Western Red-backed Vole. Like other voles, it does not hibernate. Instead, it remains active, and in areas of snow it makes burrows below the snow but above the ground.

DESCRIPTION: This vole is dark chestnut brown with reddish highlights, often mixed with black above. The sides lighten considerably, and the undersides are buffy gray in color. The tail is slightly bicolored and is about half the length of the head and body.

HABITAT: A vole of deep forests, the Western Red-backed Vole favors dense woodlands with abundant fallen logs and debris.

DEN: Nests are made using lichens and other dry and soft bits of vegetation such as grass or moss. These voles do not dig their own burrows; instead, they use the burrows of other small mammals. Nests are either in the burrow or on the ground surface under a log or in a rock crevice.

FOOD: These voles primarily eat green vegetation, but some seeds or fruit may also be consumed.

YOUNG: Mating occurs from March to October, allowing for multiple litters. Gestation is about 18 days, and litter size is two to four altricial young.

SIMILAR SPECIES: The **Southern Red-backed Vole** (*C. gapperi*) is a close relative, but its range is north and east of this vole and it is much redder in color. The **Red Tree Vole** (*Arborimus longicaudus*) has a visibly longer tail. The **White-footed Vole** (p. 195) does not have any reddish coloration.

RANGE: This vole is found south of the Columbia River, continuing southward into northern California.

White-footed Vole
Arborimus albipes

Total Length: 6³/₈–7¹/₂ in.
Tail Length: 2⁵/₈–2⁷/₈ in.
Weight: ⁵/₈–1 oz.

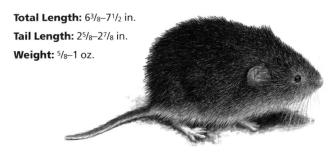

This secretive and rare vole is sometimes considered a member of the genus *Phenacomys*. It lives only along the coastal region of Oregon and northern California. Although its range hugs the coastline, this vole favors alder and dense forests along freshwater streams. In both California and Oregon, it is considered a sensitive species that may become an endangered species. There are no reliable population estimates for this vole, but it is rarely seen or caught. Its major predators include weasels, owls, minks, spotted skunks and domestic cats. Our household cats are efficient hunters and can very seriously threaten populations of indigenous animals.

DESCRIPTION: This fairly large vole is rich brownish gray in color, with lighter gray or brown undersides. The sparsely haired tail is sharply bicolored: it has a dusky stripe on top and a wider, whitish stripe below. It has small eyes and large, nearly naked ears.

HABITAT: These voles prefer moist, dense deciduous forests close to freshwater streams. Old logs and other debris make suitable cover for these elusive rodents.

DEN: In a well-covered area, such as underneath a log or a dense shrub, this vole builds small ground nests. Nest material is dry grasses and other soft plant material.

FOOD: These voles consume large quantities of leaves and smaller amounts of roots, ferns, grasses and aquatic plants. There are no records of this vole feeding on fungi, seeds, fruits or animal matter.

YOUNG: Reproduction is known to occur from April to July, but the breeding season may be longer than this in ideal conditions. Litter size is two to four young, but little else is known about the reproduction of these voles.

SIMILAR SPECIES: This vole is outwardly similar to the **Long-tailed Vole** (p. 201) and the **Western Red-backed Vole** (p. 194). The Long-tailed Vole is usually larger, and the Western Red-backed Vole often has red highlights or a red streak over its back.

RANGE: White-footed Voles occur along the coast of Oregon and into northern California.

Sonoma Tree Vole
Arborimus pomo

Total Length: 6¼–6⅞ in.

Tail Length: 2½–3 in.

Weight: ⅝–¾ oz.

Ｈigh up in the humid old-growth forests of California, Sonoma Tree Voles are protected from heavy precipitation and winds. These voles are closely associated with Douglas-fir, and in these large trees they build their nests. One nest may be used by several generations, and each vole inhabiting it builds it up more. An active nest is conspicuous, because it has green needles, fresh cut branchlets and resin ducts scattered over the top. In mature coniferous forests, Spotted Owls are the main predators of these voles. The greatest threat to this rare vole, however, is logging and deforestation of old-growth forests. Extensive logging fragments their habitat to such a great extent that populations become irrevocably isolated or disappear entirely.

DESCRIPTION: This tree vole is reddish brown on its back, with rusty highlights on its otherwise light gray undersides. Its furry tail is greater than half the length of the head and body and colored dusky brown on top and paler below. It has small, nearly naked ears.

RANGE: This vole is confined to the coniferous forests of north-coastal California.

HABITAT: A tree-loving microtine, this vole favors dense coniferous forests. The preferred tree is Douglas-fir because it provides the vole with food as well.

DEN: In a tree, from 5–115 ft. off the ground, this vole constructs a large round nest (as much as 3 ft. in diameter). The nest material is mainly twigs and needles, with fecal pellets and resin ducts (removed from needles eaten as food) used to secure the inside and cement the nest to the tree.

FOOD: The Sonoma Tree Vole feeds almost exclusively on needles from Douglas-fir trees. Where this tree is uncommon, they will consume needles of other conifer species. They eat young needles whole, and with mature needles they first bite off the resin ducts to use in their nests. Sometimes they consume the inner bark of young twigs.

YOUNG: Mating appears to occur throughout the year, and females may have multiple litters. Because of delayed implantation, the gestation period may be 27 to 48 days. The average litter size is two young. The young are altricial, and nurse until they are three weeks old. After three weeks, their eyes open, and they begin feeding on foliage and rapidly gain weight.

SIMILAR SPECIES: The **White-footed Vole** (p. 195) has a thinner, sparsely haired tail. The **Western Red-backed Vole** (p. 194) is not as red as this vole and it lives on the ground.

Western Heather Vole
Phenacomys intermedius

Total Length: 4¹/₄–6¹/₄ in.

Tail Length: 1–1⁵/₈ in.

Weight: ⁷/₈–1³/₄ oz.

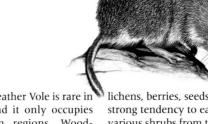

The Western Heather Vole is rare in California, and it only occupies high-elevation regions. Woodlands and alpine areas near Lake Tahoe and Mount Shasta are good places to find this vole.

The common name refers to the heather plants that are common habitat components of the high-elevation areas this vole favors. As well, it may feed on the inner bark of these heathers. It consumes a high percentage of bark seasonally, and (like other voles) it has a caecum with modified, ³/₈-in. villi that assist in digesting this fibrous and lignin-rich food.

DESCRIPTION: This vole has a short, thin, strongly bicolored tail that is slate gray above, sometimes with a few white hairs, and white below. The tops of the feet are silvery gray, and the belly hairs have light tips, giving the entire undersurface a light gray hue. Various dorsal colors are seen, but the most common is a grizzled buffy gray or brown. The ears are rounded, and scarcely extend above the fur. There is tawny or orangish hair inside the front of the ear.

HABITAT: This vole seems to prefer open areas in a variety of habitats in the mountains, including alpine tundra and coniferous forest.

FOOD: The Western Heather Vole feeds primarily on green vegetation, grasses, lichens, berries, seeds and fungi. It has a strong tendency to eat the inner bark of various shrubs from the heather family.

DEN: The summer nest is made in a burrow up to 8 in. deep, and it is lined with fine dry grass and lichens. In winter, the nest is built on the ground in a snow-covered runway.

YOUNG: Mating occurs between April and August. Following a gestation of about three weeks, one to eight (usually four or five) pink, helpless young are born. They nurse almost continuously, and their growth is rapid. By two weeks, they are well furred and have opened their eyes. This vole becomes sexually mature after two to three months, but a young male does not breed in his first year.

SIMILAR SPECIES: The **Long-tailed Vole** (p. 201) has a longer tail. The **Western Red-backed Vole** (p. 194) is reddish over its back.

RANGE: The Western Heather Vole occurs from northwestern British Columbia south through the western mountains to central California and northern New Mexico.

Montane Vole
Microtus montanus

Total Length: 5¼–7¼ in.
Tail Length: 1¼–2¼ in.
Weight: ½–1¾ oz.

In northeastern parts of California, the Montane Vole is a common resident of valleys, montane regions and some grasslands. This great abundance means that if you see a vole in this part of the state, there is a good chance it is a Montane Vole. More importantly, the high numbers of this vole indicate its ecological importance. This numerous vole is a steady food supply for larger creatures such as owls, raptors, weasels, Coyotes and more. At its highest densities, the Montane Vole is reported to reach numbers of more than 2500 an acre, though its populations cycle and numbers usually peak well below 500 an acre.

DESCRIPTION: The Montane Vole is a small, thickset mammal with short ears largely hidden in the fur and dark protruding eyes. The back is brown to black. The belly is a light gray. The head is rounded, and the snout is blunt. Most of each limb is hidden in the body's fur and skin, giving the animal a short-legged appearance. The tail is relatively long, bicolored and sparsely covered with hair.

HABITAT: This vole is found in mountain meadows, valleys and some arid sagebrush communities.

FOOD: Green shoots form the majority of the diet when they are available. At other times of the year, seeds or even bark may be eaten.

DEN: This vole commonly makes its nest in short burrows, under logs or at the base of shrubs. In areas of snow, this vole's nest is under the snow but above the ground.

YOUNG: Montane Voles may have several litters in a year, usually between spring and fall. Gestation is about 21 days, after which six to eight young are born.

SIMILAR SPECIES: Other voles may not be readily distinguishable. The **Townsend's Vole** (p. 200) is larger. The **Long-tailed Vole** (p. 201) has a longer tail, and the **Sagebrush Vole** (p. 203) has a shorter tail.

RANGE: The Montane Vole occurs from southern British Columbia to Montana and south to New Mexico and California.

California Vole

Microtus californicus

Total Length: 6¼–8⅜ in.
Tail Length: 1½–2⅝ in.
Weight: 1½–3½ oz.

While walking through grassy areas and open woodlands in much of California, stop to look at the ground around you. If there are numerous runways in the surface debris that resemble miniature bobsled routes, an excess of cut grass or vegetation and small holes in the soil, you may be in the territory of a California Vole. The ability of this creature to so significantly alter the appearance of its home ground is quite prodigious, considering its size. If you're lucky, following one of the runways may lead you to a food source or a nest.

This vole can be extremely common—up to 200 individuals per acre. In non-cultivated areas this density is sustainable, but in orchards, vineyards and cropland (especially alfalfa), it may reach pest proportions.

DESCRIPTION: This vole is a grizzled brown color above, often flecked with black, and lighter gray below. The tail is long and distinctly bicolored, brownish above and paler below. It has pale brown or grayish feet and inconspicuous furred ears.

HABITAT: These voles are comfortable over a large range of elevations in a variety of habitats, including dry, grassy slopes, salt or freshwater marshes and moist meadows.

DEN: Similar to the majority of voles, the California Vole digs burrows. Nests are made of grass and moss, and they are either found in a small burrow chamber or under surface cover such as a log or rock.

FOOD: This vole eats a variety of vegetation: in winter it feeds mainly on roots and tubers; in summer it dines on grasses, seeds and leaves.

YOUNG: Breeding occurs throughout the year, but it ceases in periods of drought. Gestation is 21 days, and females may have multiple litters in a year, with one to nine young that are blind and nearly hairless at birth. Their growth is fast and at two weeks their eyes are open and weaning follows.

SIMILAR SPECIES: This vole differs from most other *Microtus* voles by having a visibly shorter tail and pale feet. The **Creeping Vole** (p. 202) has a short tail, but it inhabits a different range.

RANGE: Common throughout its range, this vole occurs in southwestern Oregon and throughout most of California.

Townsend's Vole

Microtus townsendii

Total length: 6⁵/₈–9 in.
Tail length: 2–2³/₄ in.
Weight: 1⁵/₈–4 oz.

The Townsend's Vole is one of largest voles in North America. As with many vole species, populations periodically explode and then abruptly crash, but the mechanism that triggers these fluctuations is unknown.

Runways are used by generations of voles and may be up to 2 in. deep. In these well-used networks, the intersections often serve as latrines. In extreme cases, the pile of droppings may be 7 in. long by 3 in. wide and may create a ramp 5 in. high—an obstacle the voles simply scurry over as they travel the runways.

DESCRIPTION: This large, dark brown vole has broad ears that extend noticeably above the fur. It has a long, blackish-brown tail and similarly colored feet with brown claws. The protruding black eyes measure more than ³/₁₆ in. in diameter.

RANGE: The Townsend's Vole occurs in southern British Columbia, south through western Washington and Oregon into northern California.

HABITAT: These voles occur in moist fields, sedge meadows and sometimes in boggy areas. Occasionally, they can be found even in subalpine and alpine meadows.

FOOD: Townsend's Voles prefer tender marsh and grassland vegetation. They may also consume the bark of shrubs, some stems and the roots of conifers and starchy roots.

DEN: During rainy seasons, nests are placed on or above the soil surface, often on hummocks. During dry periods subterranean burrow systems and underground nests are maintained. The nests are made of dry grasses.

YOUNG: Breeding occurs from early February until October. Following a gestation of 21 to 24 days, one to nine young are born in the grassy nest. They are weaned and leave the nest at 15 to 17 days. Young females born early will mate and bear litters in their first summer. Males mature later.

SIMILAR SPECIES: The **Montane Vole** (p. 198) and the **Creeping Vole** (p. 202) are smaller. The **California Vole** (p. 199) has a shorter tail. The **Long-tailed Vole** (p. 201) has a longer tail that is not uniformly dark.

Long-tailed Vole
Microtus longicaudus

Total Length: 6³/₄–9 in.
Tail Length: 2¹/₄–2⁷/₈ in.
Weight: 1¹/₄–2 oz.

Long-tailed Voles inhabit much of northern California, but in a patchy distribution pattern. These voles were more widespread in California during the Pleistocene, when cooler climatic conditions prevailed. Poorly adapted to hot and dry conditions, they can no longer thrive everywhere they used to. In parts of their range north of California they may be found at lower elevations, but in this state, Long-tailed Voles are confined to the mountains and equally cool, moist places.

DESCRIPTION: The upperparts are variously colored, ranging from grizzled grayish to dark gray brown, but the black tips on the guard hairs may give this vole a dark appearance. The sides are paler than the back, and the undersides are paler still. The tail of this vole is more than one-third of the total length (about 2³/₈ in. long) and indistinctly bicolored. The upsides of the feet are gray.

HABITAT: This vole lives in a variety of habitats, including grassy areas, mountain slopes, mixed forests, alpine tundra and among alders or willows in the vicinity of water.

FOOD: Summer foods consist of green leaves, grasses and berries. In winter, this vole eats the bark of heathers, willows and trees.

DEN: The simple burrows made by this vole under logs or rocks are often poorly developed. The nest chamber is lined with fine, dry grass, moss or leaves. In areas of snow, the nests are subnivean (above the ground but below the snow).

YOUNG: Mating is presumed to occur from May to October, with the females often having two litters of two to eight (usually four to six) young a year. Gestation is about three weeks. The young are helpless at birth, but at about two weeks old, their eyes open, they are weaned, and they leave the nest. Some young females have their first litter when they are only six weeks old.

SIMILAR SPECIES: The **Townsend's Vole** (p. 200) has a blackish, mildly bicolored tail. Other *Microtus* species in the region have shorter tails.

RANGE: This vole ranges south from eastern Alaska and the Yukon along the Rocky Mountains to New Mexico and Arizona. Its range extends west to the Pacific as far south as California.

Creeping Vole
Microtus oregoni

Total length: 4³/₄–6 in.
Tail length: 1³/₁₆–1⁵/₈ in.
Weight: ¹/₂–⁷/₈ oz.

Years of walking through prime Creeping Vole habitat will, on very rare occasions, produce encounters with this secretive animal. "Creeping" probably refers to this vole's preference for underground burrows and runways. This kind of concealment means seeing one in the wild is very unlikely. The Creeping Vole is also the smallest vole in its range, making it that much more difficult to spot.

DESCRIPTION: This small, slender vole appears to have very plush fur because the guard hairs are about as long as the underfur. A Creeping Vole is dull or sooty brown above and gray below. Its feet and tail are dark gray. The eyes and ears are small.

HABITAT: Openings in moist coniferous forests at sea level or in montane forests are preferred habitat for this species. Its burrows are found in friable woodland soils and mossy bogs. It also inhabits brushland beside cultivated fields.

FOOD: The Creeping Vole eats a wide variety of plant stems and roots. Potatoes and fallen apples are favorites when available. When this vole uses mole tunnels to feed in people's gardens, the guiltless mole gets blamed for the pilfering.

DEN: The nest is a mass of grasses or fine vegetation located just beneath a log or rotten stump. Numerous tunnels just below the soil surface extend out from the nest. Most of the time this vole lives a subterranean existence, and it often uses the burrows of the Coast Mole (p. 320).

YOUNG: Spring and summer are the peak mating times (though this species may breed throughout the year), and after a gestation of 23 to 24 days, one to five naked, pink, blind young are born. A female may have up to five litters in a summer, but three are more common. The young are weaned at 13 days and disperse. The females are sexually mature at 22 days and males at 42 days.

RANGE: The Creeping Vole is a species of the Pacific Northwest, ranging from southwestern British Columbia to northern California.

SIMILAR SPECIES: Other local voles are larger; the **Long-tailed Vole** (p. 201) and the **Townsend's Vole** (p. 200) have longer tails.

Sagebrush Vole
Lemmiscus curtatus

Total Length: 4¼–5½ in.

Tail Length: 1¹/₁₆–1⅛ in.

Weight: ¾–1⅜ oz.

diet of green material and feed on seeds, roots and the inner bark of shrubs.

The unusual Sagebrush Vole is unlike other voles in the region. While most voles live in moist or wet areas, this vole prefers arid or semi-arid canyon and brushland habitat. Rodents that live in such dry habitats usually adapt to a diet heavy in insects, but the Sagebrush Vole remains a strict vegetarian, feeding solely on green vegetation and seeds. This vole is also colonial; colony members excavate burrows close to one another, and up to 30 burrow entrances can be found in a cluster. Colony numbers vary greatly because of yearly population fluctuations.

DESCRIPTION: This small, stout vole has short ears and legs and long, lax hair. It is a very pale ashy gray in color, with buffy tinges around the ears and nose. The undersides are silvery. The tail is shorter than the hindfoot, and it is dark above and light below.

HABITAT: In keeping with its name, the Sagebrush Vole thrives in arid grassland regions, sagebrush flats and dry canyons.

FOOD: The spring and summer diet include a variety of plant material, especially the new green shoots of grasses and leaves of forbs. In fall and winter, they may switch from their preferred

DEN: A shallow but extensive system of burrows leads to a grass-lined nest chamber. Colonies vary greatly in size and density, but burrow entrances in a colony number from 8 to 30. Colonies are often located under debris such as dead sagebrush or wood.

YOUNG: Peak mating occurs between April and September, but the species probably breeds all year long. After a gestation period of about 25 days, a litter of 1 to 13 helpless young is born. The young grow rapidly, and they are weaned and out of the nest within three weeks.

SIMILAR SPECIES: Long-tailed (p. 201), **Townsend's** (p. 200) and **Montane** (p. 198) **voles** all have tails that are longer than 1 in. and greater than the length of the hindfoot.

RANGE: The range skirts western Montana and northern Idaho, extends from southern Alberta to North Dakota, to northern Colorado, southwest to Nevada and California, and north to central Washington.

Common Muskrat

Ondatra zibethicus

The Common Muskrat is not a "mini-beaver," nor is it a close relative of that large rodent; rather, it is a highly specialized aquatic vole that shares many features with the American Beaver (p. 206) as a result of their similar habitats. Like a beaver, a muskrat can close its lips behind its large orange incisors so it can chew underwater without getting water or mud in its mouth. Its eyes are placed high on its head, and a muskrat can often be seen swimming with its head and sometimes its tail above water. The Common Muskrat dives with ease; it can remain submerged for over 15 minutes and can swim the length of a football field before surfacing.

Although muskrats are found naturally in California, their abundance today—especially in the Sacramento–San Joaquin Valley—is because of introductions. Muskrats are strongly associated with water, and individuals rarely leave their pond once they are established. When a young, recently weaned muskrat becomes independent and leaves the nest, it disperses from its birth pond to establish its own territory. These dispersing muskrats may be seen traveling over land, a tragic requirement for many— their numbers can be tallied all too easily on seasonal roadkill surveys.

Muskrats lead busy lives. They are continually gnawing cattails and bulrushes, whether eating the tender shoots or gathering the coarse vegetation for home building. Muskrat homes rise above shallow waters throughout the region, and they are of tremendous importance not only to these aquatic rodents, but also to geese and ducks, which make use of muskrat homes as nesting platforms.

Both sexes have perianal scent glands that enlarge and produce a distinctly musk-like discharge during the breeding season. Although this scent is by no means unique to the Common Muskrat, its potency is sufficiently notable to have influenced this animal's common name. An earlier name for this species was "musquash," from the Algonquin, Cree and Natick, but the source is believed to be the Abenaki name *moskuas*. Through the association with musk the name changed to "muskrat."

DESCRIPTION: The coat generally consists of long, shiny, tawny to nearly black guard hairs overlying a brownish-gray undercoat. The flanks and sides are lighter than the back. The underparts are gray, with some tawny guard hairs. The long tail is black, nearly hairless, scaly and laterally compressed with a

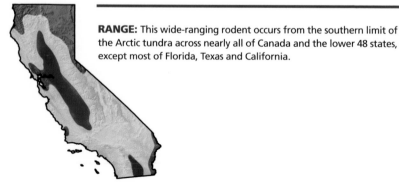

RANGE: This wide-ranging rodent occurs from the southern limit of the Arctic tundra across nearly all of Canada and the lower 48 states, except most of Florida, Texas and California.

Total Length: 1½–2 ft.
Tail Length: 7¾–11 in.
Weight: 1¾–3½ lb.

dorsal and ventral keel. The legs are short. The hindfeet are large and partially webbed and have an outer fringe of stiff hairs. The tops of the feet are covered with short, dark gray hair. The claws are long and strong.

HABITAT: Muskrats occupy sloughs, lakes, marshes and streams that have cattails, rushes and open water. Often they can be found in human habitats, such as irrigation ditches. They are not present in high mountains.

FOOD: The summer diet includes a variety of emergent herbaceous plants. Cattails, rushes, sedges, irises, water lilies and pondweeds are staples, but a few frogs, turtles, mussels, snails, crayfish and an occasional fish may be eaten. In winter, muskrats feed on submerged vegetation.

DEN: Muskrat houses are built entirely of herbaceous vegetation, without the branches or mud of beaver lodges. The dome-shaped piles of cattails and rushes have an underwater entrance. Muskrats may also dig bank burrows, which are 15–50 ft. long and have entrances that are below the usual water level.

YOUNG: Breeding takes place in spring and summer in northern parts of California, but in the southern part of the state mating occurs year-round. Each female produces two or three litters a year. Gestation lasts 25 to 30 days, after which six to seven young are born. The eyes open at 14 to 16 days, the young are weaned at three to four weeks and they are independent at one month. Both males and females are sexually mature the spring after their birth.

SIMILAR SPECIES: The **American Beaver** (p. 206) is larger and has a broad, flat tail, and typically only its head is visible above water when it swims. The **Norway Rat** (p. 192) is smaller and has a round tail. The **Mountain Beaver** (p. 270) has a very short tail.

DID YOU KNOW?

Muskrats are highly regarded by native peoples. In one story, it was Muskrat who brought some mud from the bottom of the flooded world to the water's surface. This mud was spread over a turtle's back, thus creating all the dry land we now know.

American Beaver

Castor canadensis

The American Beaver is truly a great North American mammal. Its much-valued pelt motivated some of the earliest explorers, and even today the beaver serves as an international symbol for wild places. Quite surprising to many Americans, foreign tourists often hold out great hopes of seeing these aquatic specialists during their visits. Fortunately, the American Beaver can be regularly encountered in wet areas throughout most of northern California, where its engineering marvels can be studied in awe-inspiring detail.

One of the few mammals that significantly alters its habitat to suit its needs, the beaver often sets back ecological succession and brings about changes in vegetation and animal life. Nothing seems to bother a beaver like the sound of running water, and this busy rodent builds dams of branches, mud and vegetation to slow the flow of water. The dam is a mechanism for survival that evolved in parts of North America where winter is severe. The deep pools that the beaver's dams create allow it to remain active beneath the ice in winter, at a cost of vast amounts of labor—a single beaver may cut down hundreds of trees each year to ensure its survival in regions with long winters.

Beavers live in groups that generally consist of a pair of mated adults, their yearlings and a set of young kits. This family group generally occupies a tightly monitored habitat that consists of several dams, terrestrial runways and a lodge. In most cases, the lodge is a complex structure of branches and mud. Some beavers, especially adult male beavers, tunnel into the banks of rivers, lakes or ponds for their den sites. In areas where trees do not commonly grow or currents are swift, females may also occupy bank dens.

Although the American Beaver is not a fast mover, it more than compensates with its immense strength. It is not unusual for this solidly built rodent to handle and drag—with its jaws—a 20-lb. piece of wood. The beaver's flat, scaly tail, for which it is so well known, increases an animal's stability when it is cutting a tree, and when slapped on the water or ground, communicates alarm.

Beavers are well adapted to their aquatic lifestyles. They have valves that allow them to close their ears and nostrils when they are submerged, and clear membranes slide over the eyes. Because the lips form a seal behind the incisors, beavers can chew while they are submerged without having water and mud enter the mouth. In addition

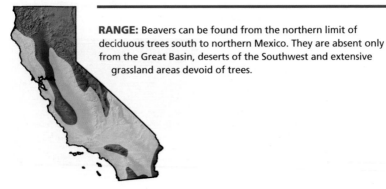

RANGE: Beavers can be found from the northern limit of deciduous trees south to northern Mexico. They are absent only from the Great Basin, deserts of the Southwest and extensive grassland areas devoid of trees.

Total Length: 3–4 ft.
Tail Length: 11–21 in.
Weight: 35–66 lb.

to their waterproof fur, beavers have a thin layer of fat to protect them from cold waters, and the oily secretion they continually groom into their coats keeps their skin dry.

The American Beaver is an impressive and industrious animal that shapes the physical settings of many wilderness areas. Although most tree cutting and dam building occurs at dusk or at night, you may see beavers during the day—sometimes working, but usually sunning themselves.

DESCRIPTION: The chunky, dark brown American Beaver is the second-largest rodent in the world, taking a backseat only to the South American Capybara. It has a broad, flat, scaly tail, short legs, a short neck and a broad head with short ears and massive, protruding, orange-faced incisors. The underparts are paler than the back and lack the reddish-brown hue. The nail on the second toe (and sometimes also the first) of each webbed hindfoot is split, allowing it to be used as a comb in grooming the fur. The forefeet are not webbed.

HABITAT: Beavers occupy freshwater environments wherever there is suitable woody vegetation. They are sometimes even found feeding on dwarf willows above treeline.

FOOD: Bark and cambium, particularly that of aspen, willow, alder and birch, is favored, but aquatic pond vegetation is eaten in summer. Beavers sometimes come ashore to eat grains or grasses.

DEN: Beaver lodges are cone-shaped piles of mud and sticks. Beavers construct a great mound of material first, and then chew an underwater access tunnel into the center and hollow out a den. The lodge is typically located away

DID YOU KNOW?

Beavers are not bothered by lice or ticks, but there is a tiny, flat beetle that lives only in a beaver's fur and nowhere else. This beetle feeds on beaver dandruff, and its meanderings probably tickle sometimes, because beavers often scratch themselves when they are out of water.

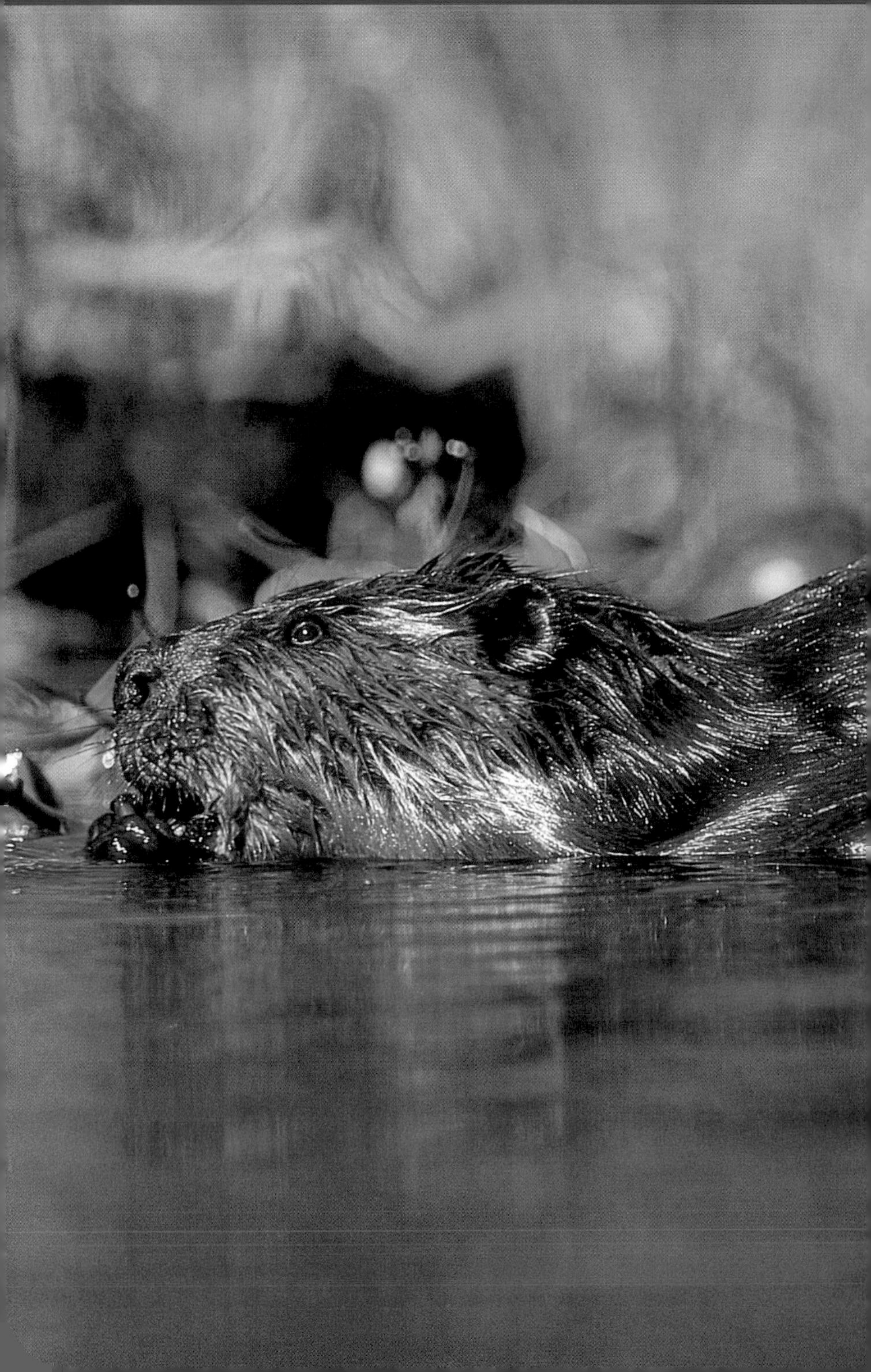

foreprint

walking trail

from shore in still water; in flowing water it is generally on a bank. Access to the lodge is from about 3½ ft. below the water's surface. A low shelf near the two or three plunge holes in the den allows much of the water to drain from the beavers before they enter the den chamber. Beavers often pile more sticks and mud on the outside of the lodge each year, and shreds of bark accumulate on the den floor. Adult males generally do not live in the lodge but dig bank burrows across the water from the lodge entrance. These burrows, the entrances to which are below water, may be as long as 160 ft., but most are much shorter.

YOUNG: Most mating takes place in February, but occasionally as much as two months later. After a gestation of 106–110 days, a litter of usually four kits is born. A second litter may be born in some years. At birth, the 12–23-oz. kits are fully furred, their incisors are erupted and their eyes are nearly open. The kits begin to gnaw before they are one month old, and weaning takes place at two to three months. Beavers become sexually mature when they are about two years old, at which time they often disperse from the colony.

Common Muskrat

SIMILAR SPECIES: The **Common Muskrat** (p. 204) is much smaller, and its long tail is laterally compressed rather than paddle-shaped. The **Northern River Otter** (p. 110) has a long, round, tapered, fur-covered tail, a streamlined body and a small head.

Great Basin Pocket Mouse
Perognathus parvus

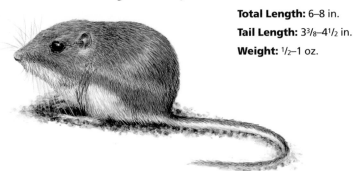

Total Length: 6–8 in.
Tail Length: $3^3/_8$–$4^1/_2$ in.
Weight: $^1/_2$–1 oz.

Whereas some wild mammals literally come to your back door, others require a visit to their special place of residence. The Great Basin Pocket Mouse is among the latter—it is a specialized rodent that lives only in northern and eastern regions of California. Residents of arid, sparsely vegetated flatlands, pocket mice are fond of dust baths: they roll and dig in sandy areas and then brush their fur with both their forefeet and hindlimbs. Like other pocket mice, they even invert their cheek pouches to clean them against the sand. The subspecies *P. p. xanthonotus*, found in Kern county, was once considered a separate species, the Yellow-eared Pocket Mouse.

DESCRIPTION: The back is a glossy, yellowish buff, with many black-tipped hairs overlaying the fur and giving a peppered appearance. A narrow, buffy line separates the back color from the uniform white or buffy-white underparts and feet. The tail is generally more than half the animal's total length, and it is darker above and lighter below. The hindfoot is $^7/_8$–1 in. long.

HABITAT: These pocket mice live in sandy soils in semi-arid and arid areas.

FOOD: Cheatgrass seeds form the bulk of the diet, but this mouse also eats grain and seedlings of winter wheat, and, especially in spring, considerable numbers of insects.

DEN: Burrows are shallow and form a network of storage, refuge burrows and a nest chamber with a small, grassy nest. The tunnel entrances are often plugged with soil by day.

YOUNG: Mating occurs in spring and early summer. About four to six helpless young are born after a gestation of 21 to 28 days. The young are weaned at 25 days, when they weigh about $^1/_4$ oz.

SIMILAR SPECIES: The **Little Pocket Mouse** (p. 212) has a pale brown tail. The **Long-tailed Pocket Mouse** (p. 214) has a strongly crested and tufted tail. Other pocket mice can often be distinguished by range.

RANGE: The Great Basin Pocket Mouse is found in semi-desert areas of the interior of British Columbia, south to California, Nevada and northern Arizona and east as far as southwestern Wyoming.

White-eared Pocket Mouse
Perognathus alticola

Total Length: 6³/₈–7¹/₈ in.
Tail Length: 2⁷/₈–3³/₄ in.
Weight: about 1 oz.

The rarest of all pocket mice, the White-eared Pocket Mouse lives only in a few scattered locations of southern California. It was once found in both the Tehachapi Mountains and the San Bernardino Mountains, but specimens have not been recorded in the latter location since 1938. Very little is known about this species, although it probably has similar habits to others of its kind, particularly the very similar Great Basin Pocket Mouse (p. 210).

DESCRIPTION: This large pocket mouse is brown or grayish over its back, with light or white undersides. The tail base is the same color as the back, changing to dark gray or black near the tip. The underside of the tail is white. Relative to the body size, this pocket mouse has a shorter tail than others that share its range. It is unique in having a hindfoot greater than ³/₄ in. long.

HABITAT: The White-eared Pocket Mouse appears to favor grassland and arid shrubland communities. Dominant plant species include Russian thistle and sagebrush. Some individuals have been found in areas of open pine forests.

DEN: Like others of its kind, this species makes a burrow underground. Inside the burrow is a small chamber with a nest made of fine dry grass. White-eared Pocket Mice become dormant in very hot and very cold weather.

FOOD: This species is not well studied, but it probably feeds on seeds, green vegetation and insects.

YOUNG: Mating peaks in late spring and summer, and gestation is 21 to 28 days. The average litter size is five, although litters as large as eight are possible. The young are probably weaned in about three weeks.

SIMILAR SPECIES: Neither the **San Joaquin Pocket Mouse** (p. 213) or the **Little Pocket Mouse** (p. 212) have such long and dark hairs at the tips of their tails. The **California Pocket Mouse** (p. 218) has spine-like hairs on its back and sides.

RANGE: This species is found only in the Tehachapi Mountains along the western Mojave Desert and possibly the San Bernardino Mountains as well.

Little Pocket Mouse
Perognathus longimembris

Total Length: 4¹/₄–6 in.
Tail Length: 2¹/₈–3³/₈ in.
Weight: about ¹/₄ oz.

Small and abundant, these pocket mice are nocturnal denizens of arid areas in the western states. At their peak population density, these mice can number up to 400 individuals per acre. High densities like this one has can quickly diminish the available food sources, but this little mouse has mechanisms to cope with food scarcity. If hunger persists for more than 24 hours, the mouse slips into dormancy for a few days, thus conserving energy. Throughout their range in central and southern California, these mice experience either a dry or cold season during which food is unavailable. To outlast such seasons, they remain dormant in their burrows.

DESCRIPTION: This pocket mouse has soft fur that is usually grayish yellow in color, although color varies regionally as soil color changes. The fur may be flecked with black hairs above, and the undersides may be brownish to nearly white. They have two external cheek pouches for carrying food or nesting material. At the base of their ears are two conspicuous white patches of fur. The tail, longer than the length of the head and body, is pale brown.

HABITAT: This pocket mouse lives in sandy or gravelly soils of deserts, brushy areas, rocky outcroppings and rolling terrain.

DEN: Pocket mice excavate burrows with chambers for sleeping, nesting and food storage. The burrow openings are marked with piles of dirt, but usually the entrance is plugged.

FOOD: When foraging, the pocket mouse eats fresh green vegetation such as forbs and grass. The food that it carries back to the burrow for storage consists mainly of non-perishable seeds.

YOUNG: This species mates from spring through to fall, and females may have two litters per season. Gestation lasts 22 or 23 days, and litter size is one to six young.

SIMILAR SPECIES: The more widespread **Great Basin Pocket Mouse** (p. 210) is larger and has a slightly two-toned tail. The **San Joaquin Pocket Mouse** (p. 213) is nearly indistinguishable, but it is found only in the San Joaquin Valley. Other pocket mice are often best differentiated by range.

RANGE: The Little Pocket Mouse is found from southeastern Oregon through most of Nevada, the western edge of Utah and central and southern California.

San Joaquin Pocket Mouse
Perognathus inornatus

Total Length: 5–6³/₈ in.
Tail Length: 2¹/₂–3¹/₈ in.
Weight: ³/₈–⁵/₈ oz.

A well-known behavior of the San Joaquin Pocket Mouse is sandbathing. In its grassland or desert habitat, this pocket mouse spends a part of each day rubbing its sides and belly in the sand. To begin, it rapidly scratches the sand with its forepaws to create a good rubbing bed in which to stretch out. The mouse lies down and performs a series of stretches and bends, alternating from one side to the other and then to the belly. The sand and rubbing may feel good, but more importantly, the fur is cleaned and any parasites are removed from it.

DESCRIPTION: This species has soft fur that is usually orangish buff in color, although color varies regionally as soil color changes. Their undersides may be pale buff or nearly white. They have two external cheek pouches for carrying food or nesting material. At the base of their ears may be two whitish patches of fur. The tail, longer than the length of the head and body, is pale brown and slightly tufted.

HABITAT: These pocket mice live in grassy or weedy areas on open fine soils and rolling terrain.

DEN: This pocket mouse excavates a burrow with separate chambers for sleeping, nesting and food storage. The burrow openings are marked with piles of dirt, but usually the entrance is plugged.

FOOD: Primary foods include green vegetation such as grasses and forbs, which are consumed immediately, and seeds, which may be stored for later. A considerable number of insects are also eaten.

YOUNG: Mating occurs from March through to July, and most females have two litters per season. Gestation lasts 22 or 23 days, and litter size is four to six young.

SIMILAR SPECIES: The **Little Pocket Mouse** (p. 212) is nearly indistinguishable, but it does not occur in the San Joaquin Valley. The more widespread **Great Basin Pocket Mouse** (p. 210) is larger and has a slightly two-toned tail.

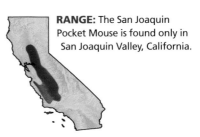

RANGE: The San Joaquin Pocket Mouse is found only in San Joaquin Valley, California.

Long-tailed Pocket Mouse
Chaetodipus formosus

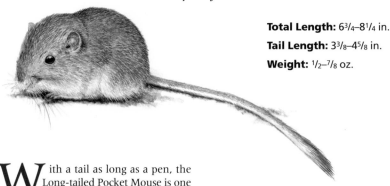

Total Length: 6³/₄–8¹/₄ in.
Tail Length: 3³/₈–4⁵/₈ in.
Weight: ¹/₂–⁷/₈ oz.

With a tail as long as a pen, the Long-tailed Pocket Mouse is one of the easier pocket mice to identify. It lives in desert areas and is active mainly at night. This mouse is a fair-weather friend, and when temperatures become too high or too low, it enters a torpid state safe inside its burrow. In winter it may hibernate, but true dormancy is regionally variable. When this pocket mouse forages for food, it stuffs its external cheek pouches with non-perishable seeds that it will store near or inside its burrow. If it finds insect larvae or cutworms, it eats them immediately to benefit from the water they contain.

DESCRIPTION: This softly furred animal is mainly gray or brown above, and whitish or slightly yellowish below. The tail is mildly bicolored, grayish above and whitish below, and over the last third is a dark-colored crest of tufted hairs. It has long ears and long hindfeet that lack fur on the sole.

RANGE: These pocket mice are found mainly in Nevada, eastern California, western Utah and just into northern Arizona.

HABITAT: This species inhabits rocky or gravelly soils along slopes and ridges of deserts and canyons.

DEN: These pocket mice dig shallow, simple burrows into sandy soils. The burrow can be easily identified by the pile of dirt at the entrance. When this species becomes torpid, it remains hidden inside its burrow with the entrance plugged.

FOOD: Presumably, this pocket mouse feeds mainly on seeds and some vegetation like others of its genus. All pocket mice consume soft-bodied insects, such as cutworms and other larvae.

YOUNG: These pocket mice mate between early spring and late summer, and some females may have two litters during this time. Litter size averages five young that are altricial at birth, but they grow rapidly.

SIMILAR SPECIES: The tail of a **Great Basin Pocket Mouse** (p. 210) is weakly crested and tufted. The **Little** (p. 212) and **San Joaquin** (p. 213) **pocket mice** have partially furred soles on their hindfeet and are usually lighter in color. Range is often a good tool to differentiate pocket mice species.

Bailey's Pocket Mouse
Chaetodipus baileyi

Total Length: 7⁷/₈–9 in.
Tail Length: 4¹/₄–5³/₈ in.
Weight: ⁷/₈–1³/₈ oz.

Although many of its habits are similar to those of other pocket mice and other desert-dwelling rodents, the Bailey's Pocket Mouse has a couple of unique traits. Usually a very wary nighttime forager, this pocket mouse will be more courageous when there is no moon, and therefore less likelihood of being seen by a predator. Nevertheless, if an owl should see this pocket mouse and attempt to strike, the mouse has such good ears that it can hear the owl as it swoops down. To avoid being caught, the pocket mouse makes a last-second leap into the air—an evasive tactic that is successful as much as 90 percent of the time.

DESCRIPTION: This large pocket mouse is mainly brownish or gray overall, with light brown or yellowish flecks throughout its coat. The undersides are mainly whitish, and the strongly crested tail is similarly bicolored. It lacks the distinct rump spines that can be found on several other *Chaetodipus* species, but it has distinct black hairs that resemble spines.

HABITAT: This species thrives in desert conditions, especially in transition areas from sandy flats to rocky outcroppings. It is usually found in areas of shrub cover.

DEN: This nocturnal rodent makes a burrow that has a chamber for the small, grassy nest. Although it is active most of the year, it may remain dormant in its burrow during periods of extreme heat. Other parts of the burrow are used to store food.

FOOD: Bailey's Pocket Mouse feeds on seeds of grasses and forbs, green vegetation and a variety of insects. It can eat jojoba (*Simmondsia chinensis*) seeds, which are toxic to most other species. Like many desert species, it is able to survive on the water in its food and does not need to drink.

YOUNG: Reproductive cycles coincide with seasonal rainy months. Gestation is from two to three weeks, after which a litter of about three to five young is born.

SIMILAR SPECIES: Other pocket mice in the same range are smaller; the **Sonoran Desert Pocket Mouse** (p. 216) is more yellowish than gray overall.

RANGE: This species is found in southern California and Arizona, and extreme southwestern New Mexico, extending into the desert regions of Mexico.

Sonoran Desert Pocket Mouse
Chaetodipus pencillatus

Total Length: 6³/₈–8¹/₂ in.
Tail Length: 3¹/₄–4¹/₂ in.
Weight: ¹/₂–³/₄ oz.

True to its name, the Sonoran Desert Pocket Mouse is extremely well adapted to life in arid climates. Like many other desert animals, this species has no need to drink, because it can metabolize all the water it needs from the food it eats. Although some creatures that have this ability will eat water-rich vegetables in captivity, this desert-hardened species never does. Another characteristic of this pocket mouse is its ability tolerate cool night-time temperatures. Even while other desert creatures retire on very cool nights, this species can stay out foraging. Only very cold weather will force it into a light torpor in its burrow.

DESCRIPTION: This medium-sized pocket mouse is yellowish brown to yellowish gray over its back, and its undersides are white. Some long, black hairs are found flecked throughout the coat.

Its long tail is similarly bicolored and crested and tufted. The tuft on the tail is dusky colored.

HABITAT: As can be expected, this species occupies desert regions, but not where rocky soils predominate. It seems to be associated with shrubs such as saltbrush and mesquite.

DEN: This pocket mouse makes a burrow where it nests and stores food. In one chamber, a baseball-sized grassy nest can be found.

FOOD: Seeds are the dominant food, such as from grasses, forbs and nearby shrubs. It appears to feed on fairly large seeds. Small amounts of insect larvae and green vegetation are also consumed.

YOUNG: Peak breeding occurs in April and May, although if conditions are good mating can take place anywhere from February to September. After a gestation of about 23 days, a litter of two to eight young is born.

SIMILAR SPECIES: Both the **Long-tailed Pocket Mouse** (p. 214) and the **Bailey's Pocket Mouse** (p. 215) lack the yellowish color in their coats. The other *Chaetodipus* species have spines on their rumps.

RANGE: This pocket mouse is found in southern California, southern Nevada, Arizona, southern New Mexico and southward into Mexico.

San Diego Pocket Mouse
Chaetodipus fallax

Total Length: 6⁷/₈–7⁷/₈ in.

Tail Length: 3¹/₂–4⁵/₈ in.

Weight: about ⁵/₈ oz.

The San Diego Pocket Mouse is found in arid regions around San Diego and neighboring regions. In its preferred dry habitats, this nocturnal creature seeks out areas of light shrub cover. Pocket mice are vulnerable to many nighttime predators, including owls, snakes, Bobcats, Coyotes and foxes. Light shrub cover is essential to help conceal pocket mice as they go about their nightly foraging. Despite being somewhat hidden, all pocket mice are important prey species in arid habitats.

DESCRIPTION: The large San Diego Pocket Mouse is mainly brown over its back with whitish undersides, separated by a band of yellow or buffy fur. This pocket mouse has bristles or spines over its rump and hips; those on its rump are blackish, and those on its hips are whitish. Its tail is strongly crested and bicolored, dark like its back above, and whitish below. This pocket mouse has ears that are less than ³/₈ in long.

HABITAT: This rodent prefers regions of sagebrush, yucca, mixed chaparral, pinyon-juniper, and coastal shrub. At night, this pocket mouse forages for seeds under the shrubs and grasses.

DEN: Like other desert rodents, the San Diego Pocket Mouse makes burrows in sandy soil. One chamber houses a small nest of dry grasses and other vegetation. Other passages are used for food storage.

FOOD: These pocket mice are primarily seed eaters. They rely heavily on the seeds from grasses for much of the year, and some forbs and shrubs when available. Like other pocket mice, it probably feeds on green vegetation and insects and their larvae when available.

YOUNG: Although reproduction can occur throughout the year if conditions are favorable, the peak appears to be from March to May, and sometimes again in autumn. The gestation is about 25 days, and the litter size is usually two to four young.

SIMILAR SPECIES: The **California Pocket Mouse** (p. 218) is very similar, but its ears are longer than ³/₈ in. The **Spiny Pocket Mouse** (p. 219) is paler and lacks the yellowish band on its sides. Other pocket mice species in the region lack spines.

RANGE: This pocket mouse is found in southern California and Baja Mexico.

California Pocket Mouse
Chaetodipus californicus

Total Length: 7¹/₂–9¹/₄ in.

Tail Length: 4–5⁵/₈ in.

Weight: about ³/₄ oz.

Unlike their cousins, the kangaroo mice, pocket mice are not agile jumpers. The California Pocket Mouse has a long tail that aids in balance, but its hindfeet are not long enough nor strong enough to produce long jumps. Along coastal regions in California, this species is the most common pocket mouse. The climate in the range of this mouse is normally fair, but at times of inclement weather these mice hole up in their burrows in a torpid state. Lack of food or water also causes this state of torpor. There is no true hibernation for this species because it is mainly active throughout the year.

DESCRIPTION: This pocket mouse is mainly dark brown or gray, with distinctive spine-like bristles on its rump. Its sides are a lighter brown color, and the line between the darker brown back is distinct. The tail has a prominent tuft on the tip, and it is bicolored brownish above and whitish below. This pocket mouse has ears that are longer than ³/₈ in., with long hairs directly in front of each one.

HABITAT: This species inhabits sage and scrubby areas and chaparral slopes.

DEN: Like others of its kind, the California Pocket Mouse digs simple burrows into sandy soils. The entrance is often marked with a spoil pile, but the opening is usually plugged during the day. Although the burrow is not complex, there is a separate chamber for sleeping.

FOOD: Very little is known about the details of this species' habits, but presumably it feeds on seeds like other pocket mice. Green vegetation and insects are also eagerly consumed.

YOUNG: There is usually only one litter per year born sometime between April and June. In favorable conditions, a female might have a second litter. Litter size varies from two to five altricial young.

SIMILAR SPECIES: The **San Diego Pocket Mouse** (p. 217) is very similar, but its ears are shorter than ³/₈ in. The **Spiny Pocket Mouse** (p. 219) is paler and lacks the yellowish band on its sides. Other pocket mice species in the region lack spines.

RANGE: This species occurs in central and southwestern California.

Spiny Pocket Mouse

Chaetodipus spinatus

Total Length: 6¹/₂–8⁷/₈ in.

Tail Length: 3¹/₂–5 in.

Weight: ³/₈–⁵/₈ oz.

The distinct Spiny Pocket Mouse has numerous bristles or spine-like hairs over its rump and sides, sometimes extending as far forward as the shoulders. The spines are more pronounced in this species than for any other in the California region. Across the border into Arizona is the counterpart of this species, the Rock Pocket Mouse. The two are virtually identical and have similar habitats, but the Colorado River separates these two species and nowhere do their ranges overlap. Although the presence of the Spiny Pocket Mouse has been well documented, the species is surprisingly under-studied.

DESCRIPTION: This species is mainly light dusky gray or yellowish brown above and whitish underneath. The strongly crested tail is only faintly bicolored. Over its rump and sides are distinct white spines, many of which have brown tips. Its ears are quite small; they are less than ³/₈ in. This species has rough fur overall.

HABITAT: Like others of this genus, the Spiny Pocket Mouse thrives in arid environments. It is usually found where cover is available. Typical cover plants include tamarisk, mesquite, sagebrush and some desert succulents.

DEN: Little information has been gathered about the details of this species, but presumably its habits are similar to others of its kind. Pocket mice excavate burrows with one chamber for a small, baseball-sized grassy nest and a few separate passages for food storage.

FOOD: Most likely this pocket mouse feeds on the seeds of nearby grasses, forbs and shrubs. Like other pocket mice, small amounts of green vegetation and invertebrates are probably eaten as well.

YOUNG: Few studies have been done on this species, but it appears that litter size is around four, and gestation is probably like that of other pocket mice, roughly 23 to 28 days.

SIMILAR SPECIES: The **California Pocket Mouse** (p. 218) and the **San Diego Pocket Mouse** (p. 217) also have spines, but they both have a buffy or yellowish band separating their darker backs from their lighter undersides. All other pocket mice in California lack spines.

RANGE: This desert-loving rodent is found in southern California, southern Arizona and into Baja Mexico.

Dark Kangaroo Mouse
Microdipodops megacephalus

Total Length: 5⁷/₈–7 in.
Tail Length: 2⁵/₈–4 in.
Weight: ³/₈–⁵/₈ oz.

Walking primarily on its hindfeet rather than on all four, the Dark Kangaroo Mouse shares characteristics of both kangaroo rats and pocket mice. Its tail is not tufted like a kangaroo rat's tail, but it is nearly as long. The large hindfeet of kangaroo mice are specialized for hopping, like the kangaroo rats, but their body size is small, like a pocket mouse. The Dark Kangaroo Mouse is one of two members of this genus in California. Both species are similar in appearance and are specialists that live only in arid sagebrush deserts of the Great Basin. If you find yourself in the habitat of a kangaroo mouse and you surprise one close to its nest, your presence may aggravate it and cause it to stand on its hindlegs to staunchly defend its territory.

DESCRIPTION: The Dark Kangaroo Mouse is blackish or gray above. The fur below is nearly white, sometimes sooty in appearance because the base of each hair is gray. Their tails are black-tipped but not tufted; the widest part of the tail is the middle and it tapers at either end. Research indicates that fat is stored in the tail. Their incisors are not grooved.

HABITAT: These mice are found in sagebrush flats and scrubby areas and places of loose sands and coarse gravelly soils. In some areas they are common.

DEN: Kangaroo mice excavate a burrow for sleeping and storage of food. The burrows are quite simple, ranging between 2–4 ft. in length.

FOOD: The main food source is seeds, especially those from Desert Star (*Mentzelia* sp.) and some green vegetation. Other plant seeds are also consumed, as well as insects. Non-perishable foods are stored in the burrow.

YOUNG: These kangaroo mice mate throughout spring and summer, but most females bear their litter between May to June. Litter size varies from two to seven young.

RANGE: These mice range from southeast Oregon through most of Nevada and western Utah, as well as extreme eastern parts of California.

SIMILAR SPECIES: The **Pale Kangaroo Mouse** (p. 221) is lighter overall, and its hairs are white at the base. **Kangaroo rats** (pp. 222–33) are similar but larger, often with white patches on their faces and necks. **Pocket mice** (pp. 210–19) are usually smaller and more uniformly colored. Neither have tails that are widest in the middle, like kangaroo mice.

Pale Kangaroo Mouse
Microdipodops pallidus

Total Length: 5⁷/₈–6⁷/₈ in.
Tail Length: 2⁷/₈–3⁷/₈ in.
Weight: ³/₈–⁵/₈ oz.

The two species of kangaroo mice here in California are very similar and therefore hard to tell apart. Nevertheless, identifying a specimen as a member of the *Microdipodops* genus is easy and worthwhile. The Pale Kangaroo Mouse, and its browner counterpart, the Dark Kangaroo Mouse (p. 220), are unique among the mammals of North America. Their most distinguishing feature is a tail with fatty tissue that is widest in the middle. This characteristic is otherwise only seen in certain small desert mammals of Africa and Australia. Here in California, the Pale Kangaroo Mouse can be locally common in suitable habitat of Mono and Inyo counties.

DESCRIPTION: This kangaroo mouse is cinnamon pinkish in color, without flecking in the fur. The undersides are white. The tail is the same color as the back, but not tufted or dark at the tip; the widest part of the tail is the middle and it tapers at either end. The incisors are not grooved.

HABITAT: These mice are common in sagebrush flats, especially areas of very fine sand. They do require some brushy cover.

DEN: Kangaroo mice live in burrows that they excavated themselves. During the day the burrow is plugged. Burrows are quite simple, between 2–4 ft. in length, and they lack any specialized chambers.

FOOD: The main food source for these mice is the seeds of desert grasses and forbs. Other plant seeds are consumed to a smaller extent, as well as insects. This kangaroo mouse probably stores food in its burrow.

YOUNG: These kangaroo mice mate from spring to autumn, but most females bear their litter in May or June. Litter size varies from two to seven young.

SIMILAR SPECIES: The **Dark Kangaroo Mouse** (p. 220) is darker overall, and its hairs are dark at the base. **Kangaroo rats** (pp. 222–33) are similar but larger, often with white patches on their faces and necks, and **pocket mice** (pp. 210–19) are usually smaller and more uniformly colored. Neither have tails that are widest in the middle, like kangaroo mice.

RANGE: The Pale Kangaroo Mouse is found in speckled populations through Nevada and slightly into eastern California.

Ord's Kangaroo Rat
Dipodomys ordii

Total Length: 9–11 in.
Tail Length: 5½–6¼ in.
Weight: 1½–3⅜ oz.

This nocturnal desert rodent is best seen on dark, moonless and overcast nights. If you shine a flashlight across sandy, scrubby areas, this sand-dweller might be revealed. Its motion is distinctive: it hops like a kangaroo and does not use its forelimbs for locomotion. By day, a kangaroo rat retires to its sand burrow and plugs the door.

Much of a kangaroo rat's food is taken from the sand; it forages slowly, sifting out seeds with its sharp foreclaws. Seeds that are to be eaten immediately are first husked, but those to be stored are left intact. The kangaroo rat transports the food to its burrow in spacious external cheek pouches.

DESCRIPTION: The back is yellowish buff, with a few black hairs down the center, the sides are buff, and the belly is white. There is a white spot above the eye and behind the brownish-black ear. A black patch marks the base of the whiskers. A diagonal, white line runs across the hip. The extremely long hindfeet have five toes and are white on top and brownish black on their hairy soles. The long tail is tufted and has a dark stripe on both the dorsal surface and the ventral surface.

HABITAT: This kangaroo rat occupies sandy, grassland and sagebrush semi-desert sites, and even some disturbed areas.

FOOD: Seeds make up more than three-quarters of the year-round diet. Insects, and their larvae, account for one-fifth of the diet in spring.

DEN: Burrows are usually located in the sides of sand dunes, dry eroded channels or road slopes, and they are about 3 in. in diameter. The tunnels branch frequently, with some branches used for food storage and at least one as a nesting chamber.

YOUNG: Breeding occurs in early to mid-spring, and sometimes again in mid-summer. After a 29- to 30-day gestation period, a litter of usually three to five young is born in a nest built just beforehand.

SIMILAR SPECIES: The lower incisors of the **Chisel-toothed Kangaroo Rat** (p. 223) are broad and have flat edges, like a chisel. **The California Kangaroo Rat** (p. 229) is larger and darker, and has only four toes on its hindfeet; it has a prominent white tuft on the tip of its tail.

RANGE: This rodent occurs from southeastern Alberta and southwestern Saskatchewan south through the Great Plains and western Texas into Mexico, and from eastern Oregon south through the Great Basin and Arizona.

Chisel-toothed Kangaroo Rat
Dipodomys microps

Total Length: 9⁵/₈–12 in.
Tail Length: 5¹/₄–6⁷/₈ in.
Weight: 1⁷/₈–2⁵/₈ oz.

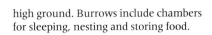

This mainly nocturnal kangaroo rat is unique among the genus *Dipodomys*. It is the only one that has broad, flat-edged lower incisors. All the others have awl-like lower incisors. As useful as this characteristic is to mammalogists, it might not be very useful for field identification. A Chisel-toothed Kangaroo Rat in the wild is not going to open its mouth to you for easy viewing. When you are in kangaroo rat country during the spring mating season, listen closely in the evening. If you are lucky, you will hear the male drumming his feet on the ground in an attempt to draw the female out of her burrow.

DESCRIPTION: This kangaroo rat is tawny or dusky colored above with whitish undersides. It has five toes on the hindfoot. Light spots are found above each eye and behind the ears. The tail has a wide dark stripe on the dorsal surface and the ventral surface. The white stripe in between is narrower than either of the two dark stripes. The lower incisors are broad and flat across the top, unlike any other kangaroo rat. The fur of the cheek pouches is gray.

HABITAT: This kangaroo rat is common in open pinyon/juniper woodlands and scrubby areas such as sagebrush or shadscale flats.

DEN: The Chisel-toothed Kangaroo Rat makes burrows in soft banks or other high ground. Burrows include chambers for sleeping, nesting and storing food.

FOOD: Seeds are a major food item, but when available, this rodent feeds on green vegetation. The chisel-like teeth of this kangaroo rat are used to scrape off the salty epidermis of favored leaves, allowing this rodent access to the nutrients without the difficulty of a high-salt intake.

YOUNG: Mating occurs in February or March, and after a gestation of just over a month, one to four young are born. Females usually have just one litter per year.

SIMILAR SPECIES: No other member of the genus has flat lower incisors or gray fur on its cheek pouches. The **California Kangaroo Rat** (p. 229) has only four toes on its hindfeet, is larger and darker and has a white tuft at the tip of the tail.

RANGE: This species is found from southeastern Oregon throughout much of Nevada, northwestern Utah, southern California, and extreme northwest Arizona.

Panamint Kangaroo Rat
Dipodomys panamintinus

Total Length: 11–13 in.
Tail Length: 6¹/₈–8 in.
Weight: about 2¹/₂ oz.

Noted by mammalogists for its belligerent nature, the Panamint Kangaroo Rat seems to be at the top of the pecking order in areas where more than one species of kangaroo rat occur. The subordinate position of other kangaroo rats prevents competition for food and burrow sites. Even between themselves, Panamint Kangaroo Rats can be so aggressive that encounters between individuals can result in fatal fights. This aggression forces the members of a population to be well spaced throughout their range. Such low densities mean the habitat is not fully utilized by the Panamint Kangaroo Rats alone, thus leaving food and space enough for other kangaroo rats.

DESCRIPTION: This tricolored kangaroo rat is brownish or gray above, cinnamon colored on its sides, and whitish below. It has light cheek patches, a white eyebrow and a white spot at the base of each ear. The tail is almost 60 percent of the total length, and it is strongly crested with dark hairs at the tip. The top and bottom of the tail have dusky stripes, while the sides of the tail are whitish. It has five toes on its hindfeet.

HABITAT: This medium-sized kangaroo rat lives in arid scrubby areas. Associated plants include Joshua trees, juniper and creosote bushes.

DEN: Under a bush or tree where sand accumulates into a mound, this kangaroo rat makes its burrow. Sometimes the burrow may be a simple hole in the mound, or it may be a system of many tunnels and entrances.

FOOD: In summer, these animals feed on new grass shoots and green vegetation. Later in the year they feed more on seeds and juniper cones.

YOUNG: Mating occurs from February to May, and females probably have only one litter per year. Gestation is 29 days, and average litter size is three or four young. The young require 10 days before they have fur and 17 or 18 days before their eyes open. Until they reach maturity, the young are paler than the adults.

SIMILAR SPECIES: The **Merriam's Kangaroo Rat** (p. 231) is similar, but has only four toes on the hindfoot. The **Ord's Kangaroo Rat** (p. 222) is smaller and darker, and has a shorter tail. The **Heermann's Kangaroo Rat** (p. 228) has a longer tail with little or no crest.

RANGE: This kangaroo rat is found in extreme western and southern Nevada and in scattered areas of central and southern California.

Stephen's Kangaroo Rat
Dipodomys stephensi

Total Length: 11–12 in.
Tail Length: 6½–7⅛ in.
Weight: about 1¾ oz.

Found only in California, this medium-sized kangaroo rat is thought to be declining in numbers. Fortunately, a small population in the Ramona Valley was recently discovered, and a few populations in protected reserves are being monitored. Like other kangaroo rats, the Stephen's Kangaroo Rat is nocturnal, and ferociously solitary. When in contact with another member of the same species, it will fight furiously until one animal withdraws. Only during the mating season is there a measure of tolerance for the company of another kangaroo rat.

DESCRIPTION: This kangaroo rat is mainly a sandy brown color with flecks of dark gray over its back. The undersides are white, as are the tops of the feet. A white spot appears above each eye and at the base of each ear. The tail is strongly crested and looks grizzled because many of the dark hairs have white bases. The tail is dark on the tip, light on the sides and dark below. The base of the whiskers and top of the nose is dark brown. The hindfeet have dusky soles and five toes.

HABITAT: Stephen's Kangaroo Rats are found in arid regions, such as sagebrush flats and sparse annual grasslands.

DEN: Although this rodent may excavate its own burrow, it often refurbishes an abandoned pocket gopher burrow. Burrows can be quite complex, with several passages and a distinct nest chamber.

FOOD: This granivore feeds mainly on annual grasses and some forbs and the seeds of these plants.

YOUNG: The peak mating period is spring to late summer, and in years of high rainfall some females may have two litters. After a gestation of about 25 days a litter of two or three young is born.

SIMILAR SPECIES: The **Agile Kangaroo Rat** (p. 227) has darker soles on the hindfeet and a whiter tail tuft. The **Panamint Kangaroo Rat** (p. 224) has larger ears.

RANGE: This species is found only in southern California in Riverside and San Diego counties. No one knows if this species can still be found in San Bernardino County.

Narrow-faced Kangaroo Rat
Dipodomys venustus

Total Length: 12–13 in.
Tail Length: 6⁷/₈–8 in.
Weight: about 3 oz.

As its name says, this kangaroo rat really does have a narrow face. This field mark can actually help you identify it amidst the numerous other kangaroo rats in California. The alternate name for this species is the Santa Cruz Kangaroo Rat, so look for information in other texts under both names. Its specific epithet, *venustus*, is the Latin word for "charming" or "elegant"—perhaps in reference to its shapely face. While most kangaroo rats live in arid and harsh landscapes, this one inhabits humid coastal regions with dense green vegetation. In this mild and humid climate, the Narrow-faced Kangaroo Rat thrives and has a seemingly easier life than those that inhabit the deserts.

ALSO CALLED: Santa Cruz Kangaroo Rat.

DESCRIPTION: This medium-sized kangaroo rat is richly colored, with a dark grayish or brown back, ochraceous sides and white underparts. Its ankles, sides of the heels, tail stripes, nose and ears are nearly black. The sides of its long tail are nearly white, and the base (at the rump) is black. It has five toes on its hindfeet.

HABITAT: This species favors the coastal regions of central California. The climate of this region is moderated by the ocean and experiences frequent bouts of fog. Like many rodents, this animal benefits from human activity and makes its home in agricultural regions.

DEN: These rodents construct simple burrows that have two entrances, several passages and separate nesting and food-caching chambers. Often there are simple escape burrows in the vicinity.

FOOD: Normally, this kangaroo rat feeds on the seeds of forbs, and when available, it eats oats, barley and rye. It does not readily feed on green vegetation or roots.

YOUNG: Mating occurs in spring and summer, with some females having two litters. Little is known about the young, but litter size is two to four.

SIMILAR SPECIES: In Northern California, this species overlaps with **Heermann's Kangaroo Rat** (p. 228), which has shorter ears and a wider face. Other kangaroo rats in the vicinity have four toes on their hindfeet.

RANGE: The Narrow-faced Kangaroo Rat is found only in Monterey and Santa Cruz areas of western California.

Agile Kangaroo Rat
Dipodomys agilis

Total Length: 11–13 in.

Tail Length: 6¹/₂–8 in.

Weight: about 1¹/₂–2⁵/₈ oz.

Unlike many other kangaroo rats, the Agile Kangaroo Rat does not favor arid desert habitats. This species is commonly found in woodland and chaparral communities. Still, life there is no easier than desert life. When rodent numbers are high, other seed-eaters may compete for the same seeds that this kangaroo rat feeds on. Worse yet, a variety of predators regularly prey on kangaroo rats, and Coyotes—one of their primary predators—will even den within or near an area of high kangaroo rat density. The status of the subspecies *D. a. simulans* (the Dulzura Kangaroo Rat) is very controversial; some zoologists believe it is a separate species.

ALSO CALLED: Pacific Kangaroo Rat.

DESCRIPTION: This medium-sized kangaroo rat is very dark brown over its back, with pure white undersides. The hindfeet have five toes each, and their tops are white and their soles are dark. The tail is strongly crested and tufted at the end, and the white stripe along each side of the tail is very distinct. The fur of the forearms, cheeks and behind the eyes and ears is pale or nearly white. At the base of the whiskers is a brownish patch of fur.

HABITAT: This kangaroo mouse prefers areas of sandy or fine gravelly soils in chaparral, brush or open woodlands.

DEN: Burrows are excavated in loose soils, and within the burrow is a nest chamber and passages for storing food.

FOOD: Seeds compose the majority of the diet, including those of grasses, forbs and even shrubs and trees. Acorns have been found in the burrows of several individuals. Some green vegetation, flowers and insects are also consumed.

YOUNG: Young are born in the nest chamber after a gestation of about 30 days. Breeding occurs mainly from spring to late summer, and the litters usually contain two to four young.

SIMILAR SPECIES: The **Heermann's Kangaroo Rat** (p. 228) is nearly identical, but it is usually lighter in color on the back. The bottom dark tail stripe on the **Panamint Kangaroo Rat** (p. 224) tapers to an indistinct point at the tip.

RANGE: The Agile Kangaroo Rat is found only in southern California in the South Coast Ranges.

227

Heermann's Kangaroo Rat
Dipodomys heermanni

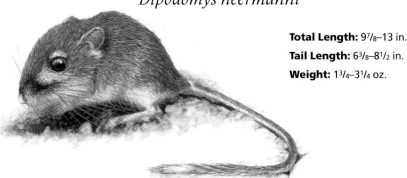

Total Length: 9^7/$_8$–13 in.
Tail Length: 6^3/$_8$–8^1/$_2$ in.
Weight: 1^3/$_4$–3^1/$_4$ oz.

Unlike most other kangaroo rats, pocket mice and kangaroo mice, Heermann's Kangaroo Rats are unable to supply all of their water requirements from their metabolism of seeds and other food alone. Heermann's Kangaroo Rats need to drink from rain puddles or dew to maintain their water balance. There are several subspecies, and one of them, the Morro Bay Kangaroo Rat, is listed as endangered by the federal government. It was last known to inhabit one small privately owned area in San Luis Obispo County. Habitat destruction is the primary cause, and the probability of a full recovery is slim.

DESCRIPTION: This kangaroo rat has long, silky fur that is mainly brown over the back and nearly white underneath. Its tail is dusky on the top and bottom, and white on the sides. The tail has a dark-colored crest and a distinct white tip. The ears are nearly black. It has five toes on the hind feet.

HABITAT: This kangaroo rat lives in a variety of habitats, ranging from rolling hills to woodlands and foothills.

DEN: Heermann's Kangaroo Rat mainly uses the burrows from other rodents such as ground squirrels. It may dig new portions on the burrow and, once excavated, the dusty soil is used for dust-bathing.

FOOD: Typical for the genus, this rodent eats the seeds of many plants and grasses. More so than other kangaroo rats, this one may eat large amounts of green vegetation.

YOUNG: The peak of the mating season is in April, but mating activity occurs from February to October. Females may have more than one litter of two to five young. The young grow quickly, and they open their eyes and are weaned at about 17 days old.

SIMILAR SPECIES: The **Narrow-faced Kangaroo Rat** (p. 226) has an obviously narrower face and a longer tail. The **Giant Kangaroo Rat** (p. 230) is larger. The **Big-eared Kangaroo Rat** (*D. elephantinus*) has larger ears.

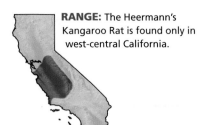

RANGE: The Heermann's Kangaroo Rat is found only in west-central California.

California Kangaroo Rat
Dipodomys californicus

Total Length: 10–13 in.
Tail Length: 6–8¹/₂ in.
Weight: about 1³/₄ oz.

As is true for many small mammals, climate plays a significant role in regulating the population sizes of kangaroo rats. California Kangaroo Rats, for example, appear to suffer greater losses from wet weather in severe winters than by the natural predation of foxes, Coyotes and owls. Entire populations can be decimated in one bad winter. Despite this sensitivity to weather extremes, California Kangaroo Rats can cope very well with milder weather fluctuations in the summer. They are active even on nights with light rain, and only stay inside during storms. After rainstorms, these hardy creatures diligently carry out the blobs of mud that accumulated in their burrows.

DESCRIPTION: This medium-sized kangaroo rat is dark gray above and nearly white below. It has four toes on the hindfoot, and its tail is strongly white-tipped. The long tail has distinct white bands on each side, and a dark band on the top and bottom. The white bands taper to a point before the tuft on the end. It has four toes on its hindfeet.

HABITAT: This species lives primarily in desert regions, but sometimes in scrubby areas or chaparral. It favors well-drained soils to burrow in.

DEN: The burrows of this rodent are typical of the genus, often having several tunnels, a nest chamber, a sleeping chamber, a food store, and a number of escape passageways.

FOOD: This kangaroo rat feeds mainly on seeds and berries. In spring and summer, it feeds significantly on green vegetation.

YOUNG: Although mating usually occurs from February to April, the breeding season extends through to September. Females may have more than one litter per year, averaging two to four young per litter. Gestation is about one month.

SIMILAR SPECIES: The **Chisel-toothed Kangaroo Rat** (p. 223) is smaller and lighter in color, and the tuft on the tail of an **Ord's Kangaroo Rat** (p. 222) is not white. **Heermann's Kangaroo Rat** (p. 228) has five toes on the hindfoot.

RANGE: This species is found from south-central Oregon into northern California.

Giant Kangaroo Rat
Dipodomys ingens

Total Length: 12–14 in.
Tail Length: 6¹/₄–7³/₄ in.
Weight: 3¹/₂–6³/₄ oz.

As its name suggests, this species is the largest of all the kangaroo rats. The Giant Kangaroo Rat inhabits the arid southwestern edge of the San Joaquin Valley. Unlike others in this genus, this kangaroo rat makes very elaborate burrows and has a complex method of storing seeds. The Giant Kangaroo Rat makes pits at the surface where it piles fresh seeds. After the seeds have dried in the open pit, it then covers the pit with soil. A few weeks later, it removes the seeds and stores them in the passages of its underground burrow. The covered pits around the territory of a Giant Kangaroo Rat can be very large and numerous—the volume of seeds in one pit can measure ¹/₂–14 gal., and one particularly avid individual made more then 800 pits around its home burrow.

DESCRIPTION: This large kangaroo rat has the typical coloration seen in this genus. It is dusky to cinnamon brown above, with somewhat lighter sides and white undersides. The relatively short tail is brown along the top and bottom and white on the sides. The tip of the tail is dusky colored and mildly tufted. The white facial markings are somewhat muted when compared to others in this genus.

HABITAT: Arid flatlands and grassy areas are the primary habitat for this species. It does not seem to require much cover around its territory.

DEN: An elaborate burrow system is excavated. There are many entrances, passages and chambers. Chambers are used for food storage and for the grassy nest.

FOOD: Seeds are the primary food for this species, but when available it also consumes green vegetation and insects.

YOUNG: The mating season is early spring to late summer, and a litter of three to six young is born after a gestation of about 32 days. Females may have two litters per season.

SIMILAR SPECIES: The large **Desert Kangaroo Rat** (p. 233) has only four toes on the hindfoot. Other *Dipodomys* species are smaller, and many have different ranges.

RANGE: The Giant Kangaroo Rat is found only in southern California along the southwestern edge of the San Joaquin Valley.

Merriam's Kangaroo Rat
Dipodomys merriami

Total Length: 7³/₄–11 in.
Tail Length: 4⁷/₈–7 in.
Weight: 1³/₈–1⁷/₈ oz.

Like other kangaroo rats, Merriam's Kangaroo Rats are solitary and strongly territorial. The breeding season is the only time when these desert rodents endure the company of one another in a relatively peaceful manner. Males and females may even mate with more than one partner before returning to the seclusion of their home burrow. Kangaroo rats are mainly nocturnal, and they are only out foraging for brief periods in the early part of the night; they spend most of their time inside their burrows.

DESCRIPTION: This small kangaroo rat is tawny brown above and white below. It has a black mark at the base of the whiskers and a white mark above each eye and below each ear. Its long tail has a thin, brown stripe on the top and bottom, and a wider white stripe on each side. The tip of the tail is distinctly tufted and dusky brown. Each hindfoot has four toes.

HABITAT: Merriam's Kangaroo Rats live in a variety of different soils, from sandy to rocky, in a variety of different habitats. Main habitats include sagebrush flats and creosote scrublands.

DEN: Burrows are simple and shallow; a typical burrow entrance is marked by a small mound at the base of a shrub. Passages and chambers are used for food storage, and one chamber houses a small nest of dry grass and other fine materials.

FOOD: Like others of its kind, this kangaroo rat will feed mainly on seeds from shrubs and grasses. At times, it consumes green vegetation and insects.

YOUNG: The reproductive period is from late January to August. Young are born in the nest after a gestation of about 29 days. Females probably have two litters per year, and a litter contains two to five young.

SIMILAR SPECIES: The **Fresno Kangaroo Rat** (p. 232) is very similar, but it inhabits a different range. Other kangaroo rats with four toes are larger and usually have white-tufted tails.

RANGE: It is found in southeastern California, southern Nevada and extreme southwestern Utah and south through much of Arizona, southern New Mexico, western Texas and into Mexico.

Fresno Kangaroo Rat
Dipodomys nitratoides

Total Length: 8¹/₄–10 in.
Tail Length: 4³/₄–6 in.
Weight: about 1¹/₂ oz.

The smallest of the kangaroo rats, the Fresno Kangaroo Rat is found only in California. Three subspecies occur here in the San Joaquin Valley and surrounding areas, all of which declined through habitat loss in the region. Heavy rainfall can also cause a decline in the numbers of this arid-environment rodent, because too much moisture will cause its stored seeds to sprout or mold. Like most other species in this genus, the Fresno Kangaroo Rat does not require free water to drink—it can metabolize all the water it needs from the food it eats. Moreover, this kangaroo rat does not even like to get wet. If water soaks its fur it will quickly roll in dust or sand until its fur is dry.

DESCRIPTION: This species is one of the smallest kangaroo rats. It is mainly tawny to dusky colored above, and white below. A black patch marks the base of the whiskers, and pale buff fur is seen around the eyes and in front of the ears. The tail has a brown band along both the top and bottom, and a white band down each side. The two white bands taper out before the end of the tail. The tail has a dusky-colored tuft. Each hindfoot has four toes.

HABITAT: Fresno Kangaroo Rats prefer areas of arid, alkaline flats. Vegetation in these areas includes grasses and some shrubs, such as saltbrush and sagebrush.

DEN: Shallow burrows are excavated in friable soils, and they tend to have several passages and chambers. Pits dug along the walls of the burrow are used to store seeds, and one chamber of the burrow houses the grassy nest.

FOOD: Foraging for seeds of grasses and forbs occurs at night. Some green vegetation is consumed when available, and insects and their larvae are probably eaten occasionally as well.

YOUNG: Mating probably occurs throughout the year, but certainly from December to September. Females may have two litters per year, and each litter contains one to three young.

SIMILAR SPECIES: The **Merriam's Kangaroo Rat** (p. 231) is very similar, but it inhabits a different range. Other kangaroo rats with four toes are larger and usually have white-tufted tails.

RANGE: The Fresno Kangaroo Rat is found only in the San Joaquin Valley in central California.

Desert Kangaroo Rat
Dipodomys deserti

Total Length: 12–15 in.
Tail Length: 7¹/₈–8¹/₂ in.
Weight: 2³/₄–4⁷/₈ oz.

Inhabiting some of the most arid environments in California, the large Desert Kangaroo Rat is the king of desert rodents. When other rodents such as pocket mice and other kangaroo rats share the same habitat, the Desert Kangaroo Rat is the dominant species. It is highly specialized for arid environments: it requires no free drinking water (it can meet all its water requirements from the foods it consumes) and it can burrow into and live comfortably in the sands that make up most of its environment.

DESCRIPTION: The Desert Kangaroo Rat is one of the largest members of this genus. It is a tawny brown color above, and white below. The tail is only indistinctly banded; the top band is dusky colored and blends into the nearly white side bands, and the bottom band is much paler then the top band. The tail is crested, tufted and white-tipped. The facial marks are relatively indistinct.

HABITAT: True to its name, the Desert Kangaroo Rat occupies some of the most arid environments in California. Sandy areas and dunes within its range are always occupied, as well as some creosote and shad-scale scrub areas.

DEN: Complex burrows are excavated in sandy areas, but not in dunes that shift. Many passes are intertwined and lead to food storage chambers. One chamber is for the small nest made of dry grasses and other fine material such as animal hair.

FOOD: The main foods include seeds and leaves of desert forbs. In winter and spring green vegetation makes up a large portion of the diet.

YOUNG: The breeding season is primarily from late February to June. After a gestation of about 30 days, three to five young are born. Females may have two litters in a year. The young are weaned within four weeks.

SIMILAR SPECIES: The large **Giant Kangaroo Rat** (p. 230) has five toes on the hindfoot. Other *Dipodomys* species are smaller, and many have different ranges.

RANGE: This desert rodent is found only in western and southern Nevada, southeastern California, western Arizona and into Mexico.

Northern Pocket Gopher
Thomomys talpoides

Total Length: 7 1/2–10 in.
Tail Length: 1 5/8–3 in.
Weight: 2 5/8–7 3/8 oz.

The Northern Pocket Gopher is one of nature's rototillers. This ground-dwelling rodent continually tunnels through dark, rich soils, and one individual is capable of turning over 16 tons of soil every year. Evidence of pocket gopher workings is commonplace on the land, in the form of freshly churned earth neatly piled in crescent-shaped mounds with the burrow entrance (usually plugged with soil) near the center of the crescent. In many agricultural areas, the Northern Pocket Gopher is the most controlled "nuisance" mammal because of its mounds, which can damage machinery and cover vegetation.

DESCRIPTION: This squat, bullet-headed rodent has visible incisors, long foreclaws and a thick, nearly hairless tail. A row of stiff hairs surrounds the naked soles of the forefeet. The upperparts, which are slightly darker than the underparts, often match the soil color—individuals may be black, dark gray, brown or even light gray.

HABITAT: This adaptable animal avoids only dense forests, wet or waterlogged, fine-textured soils, very shallow rocky soils or areas exposed to strong winter freezing of the soil.

FOOD: Succulent underground plant parts are the staple diet, but in summer, pocket gophers emerge from their burrows at night to collect green vegetation.

DEN: The elaborate burrow system may be two-tiered, with the upper level used for foraging and as a latrine, and the lower level (more permanent) used for food storage and nesting. Only a single gopher occupies a burrow system, except during the breeding season, when a male may share a female's burrow for a time.

YOUNG: Breeding occurs once a year, in April or May. Following a 19- to 20-day gestation, three to six young are born in a grass-lined nest. Weaning takes place at about 40 days.

SIMILAR SPECIES: Pocket gophers are all very similar; the **Botta's Pocket Gopher** (p. 237) often has more white under the chin, and the **Mountain Pocket Gopher** (p. 236) has pointed ears. The **Townsend's Pocket Gopher** (p. 238) is larger.

RANGE: This species occupies most of the northern Great Plains and most of the central Rockies south to northern Arizona and New Mexico. It occurs as far east as western Minnesota and as far west as western Oregon.

Western Pocket Gopher
Thomomys mazama

Total length: 7¼–9⅜ in.
Tail length: 2⅛–3⅛
Weight: 1⅞–3⅜ oz.

Despite being perfectly adapted to subterranean existence, the Western Pocket Gopher is one of the only members of this genus to regularly come aboveground. Usually emerging in nighttime hours or on warm, overcast days, this pocket gopher may be seen feeding on grasses or forbs. It reaches up and bends the vegetation down to get at the tender buds or seeds. Like most other rodents, pocket gophers have enamel only on the front parts of their constantly growing incisors. As the rodent gnaws, the back of the tooth is worn away quickly while the enameled front layer does not. This uneven wear produces a very sharp edge on the teeth.

DESCRIPTION: This richly colored pocket gopher can be reddish brown, gray, plain brown or nearly black. The color of an individual is dependent on the color of the soil in which it lives. Their ears are distinctly pointed, and large patches of dark fur are directly behind the base of each ear.

HABITAT: This pocket gopher is found in a variety of habitats, from flat grasslands to low mountain regions.

FOOD: Western Pocket Gophers feed on green herbaceous vegetation but have a preference for grasses, false dandelions and lupines. When these gophers feed from underground, they eat roots and tubers and pull plants into their burrows from underneath.

DEN: These pocket gophers make two types of burrows: a shallow burrow that is used for feeding on surface and sub-surface plants, as well as a deeper burrow used for food storage and a den chamber.

YOUNG: Mating occurs from March to June, and each litter contains three to five young. Females have one or two litters per year, and gestation is about 28 days.

SIMILAR SPECIES: The **Townsend's Pocket Gopher** (p. 238) is much larger. All pocket gophers can be very difficult to distinguish, but the range is often a good indicator.

RANGE: The Western Pocket Gopher occurs in the western third of Washington, much of western Oregon and into northern California.

Mountain Pocket Gopher
Thomomys monticola

Total Length: 6⁵/₈–11 in.
Tail Length: 1⁵/₈–3³/₄ in.
Weight: 2¹/₂–3¹/₈ oz.

The Mountain Pocket Gopher, like other members of the genus, has unique adaptations for subterranean life. It has powerful digging claws for excavating burrows, a stout body, short ears, small eyes and a short neck. Even its fur is special—it can lay either forward or backward, allowing the gopher to move in any direction in its cramped burrow. Pocket gophers dig lateral burrows with slanting entrances, and as the dirt piles up in the passage behind them they turn around and bulldoze the dirt out to the surface using their suitably stubby heads.

DESCRIPTION: Mountain Pocket Gophers are tawny to rufous brown in color, with pale buffy or golden undersides. Their ears are pointed, not rounded, and there are dark patches at the rear base of each ear. Their stout noses are darker than the rest of their face.

RANGE: The Mountain Pocket Gopher occurs in northeastern California and slightly into eastern Nevada.

HABITAT: This ground dweller prefers open areas amidst coniferous forests.

DEN: These gophers dig deep lateral burrows, for sleeping and storing food, and shallow burrows for foraging routes. Once the burrow has been excavated, they plug the entrance from the inside to maintain the right temperature and moisture content inside.

FOOD: Like other gophers, they feed on roots, bulbs, shoots and some green vegetation. Much of what they collect is transported in their external cheek pockets to a storage chamber in their burrow.

YOUNG: Presumably their reproduction is similar to other pocket gophers. Mating occurs in spring and summer, and litter size probably averages three or four young. The young are altricial and require several weeks to develop. At two months they disperse, and at three months they are sexually mature.

SIMILAR SPECIES: The **Northern Pocket Gopher** (p. 234) and the **Botta's Pocket Gopher** (p. 237) have rounded ears; range can help to identify this species.

Botta's Pocket Gopher
Thomomys bottae

Total Length: 6⁵/₈–11 in.
Tail Length: 1⁵/₈–3³/₄ in.
Weight: 2¹/₂–8⁷/₈ oz.

Most people have mixed feelings about pocket gophers. In natural areas, pocket gophers are an important component of the ecosystem. Annually, these animals turn up large volumes of soil, which aerates the ground, cycles the soil nutrients and improves water absorption. Studies have shown that where pocket gophers live in normal numbers, some plants grow better, and others, such as dandelions (which are a favorite pocket gopher food) are less abundant. Gopher mounds can interfere with agricultural machinery, however, and the gophers may compete with livestock for vegetation.

DESCRIPTION: Botta's Pocket Gophers are dark or grayish brown above and slightly paler below. Their tails are sparsely furred and are tawny or gray in color. Their ears are rounded and inconspicuous.

HABITAT: These pocket gophers live in a variety of habitats and soil types, from deserts to mountain meadows and from sandy to clay soils.

DEN: Like other pocket gophers, the Botta's spends most of its life underground. It digs nest chambers, special waste tunnels, deep lateral tunnels (for dens and food storage) and shallow tunnels (for foraging routes).

FOOD: Pocket gophers feed on vegetation of all sorts, especially the roots and tubers they encounter while burrowing and the shoots they pull down into their burrows. They also consume some aerial plant parts, such as leaves, seeds and fruit.

YOUNG: Botta's Pocket Gophers may have several litters in one season. In ideal habitats, they may breed throughout the year. Litters average six young each, and the gestation period is 18 or 19 days.

SIMILAR SPECIES: All pocket gophers can be very difficult to distinguish, but the range is often a good indicator. The **Northern Pocket Gopher** (p. 234) has less white under the chin, and the **Mountain Pocket Gopher** (p. 236) has pointed ears.

RANGE: The Botta's Pocket Gopher is found from southwestern Oregon through California into Baja and western Mexico and east to Colorado, western Texas and north-central Mexico.

Townsend's Pocket Gopher
Thomomys townsendii

Total Length: 9–13 in.
Tail Length: $2^1/_4$–$4^3/_8$ in.
Weight: $4^1/_2$–13 oz.

As exceptional fossorial rodents, all pocket gophers have special adaptations for life underground. The incisors of a pocket gopher remain outside the lips even when the mouth is closed. This characteristic allows the gopher to eat food underground or dig through the earth without getting soil particles in its mouth. Another unusual characteristic of gophers is the external cheek pouches that are used to carry food and nesting material. Daily grooming involves cleaning the fur-lined cheek pouches. Oddly, the cheek pouches can be turned inside-out to make grooming easier. Special muscles in the cheek maintain the pouches and pull them back inside after the grooming is finished.

DESCRIPTION: These large gophers are slaty black or sooty gray above (usually the same color as the soils in which they live) and slightly paler below. Their tails are sparsely furred and are grayish in color. Their ears are rounded and have dark spots to the rear.

HABITAT: These pocket gophers live in areas of deep soil, such as river valleys and old lake beds.

DEN: As with others of the genus, these gophers spend most of their life underground. They sleep in special nest chambers, and they have special tunnels for wastes. Deep lateral tunnels are for dens and food storage, while shallow tunnels are foraging routes.

FOOD: These gophers feed on vegetation of all sorts, especially roots, tubers and shoots protruding into their burrows. They also consume some aerial plant parts, such as leaves, seeds and fruit.

YOUNG: Townsend's Pocket Gophers may have two or more litters in one season. In ideal habitats, they may breed throughout the year. Litter size ranges from 3 to 10 young, and gestation is 18 or 19 days.

SIMILAR SPECIES: All pocket gophers can be very difficult to distinguish, but the range is often a good indicator. The **Western Pocket Gopher** (p. 235) and **Northern Pocket Gopher** (p. 234) are much smaller.

RANGE: The Townsend's Pocket Gopher is found scattered throughout Idaho, western Montana, southeastern Oregon, northern Nevada and northeastern California.

Alpine Chipmunk
Tamias alpinus

Total Length: 6¹/₂–8 in.
Tail Length: 2¹/₂–3³/₈ in.
Weight: 1–1³/₄ oz.

Pale and tiny creatures, Alpine Chipmunks are at home in the high regions of the Sierra Nevada. Perhaps because of their extreme alpine habitat, Alpine Chipmunks put on a layer of fat before entering hibernation. This behavior greatly increases their chances of survival, as does having stored food in their den.

When these chipmunks are not feeding or storing food, they often spend a warm afternoon sunbathing on rocks. They are very sensitive to high temperatures, however, and if the sun gets too warm they retire to their nests. Chipmunks are comfortable only in fair weather, because too much heat distresses them and they cannot tolerate cold temperatures. If the day were stormy or even too windy, Alpine Chipmunks would rather stay warm in their dens than go outside.

DESCRIPTION: This species is a small chipmunk with a yellowish-gray coat, often with an orange tone on the undersides, the tail and the face. Its stripes are clear and lightly contrasting, and the tail is black-edged and black-tipped.

HABITAT: Alpine Chipmunks inhabit shale areas, rocky slopes and subalpine forests of mountain regions.

DEN: These chipmunks build their nests in crevices of rocks or in or under hollow logs. They may also use simple burrows. The design includes a nest chamber, sometimes a separate food chamber and an escape entrance.

FOOD: Alpine Chipmunks feed primarily on seeds and alpine plants, but they savor fungi and berries whenever possible.

YOUNG: Hibernation occurs from fall to spring, and adults emerge in April and mate by May or June. Young are born in early summer, and grow rapidly for about five weeks. By week six, the youngsters have full-color coats and have almost achieved adult size.

SIMILAR SPECIES: The **Least Chipmunk** (p. 240) has a longer tail, cast with yellow rather than orange. The numerous chipmunks of California are very difficult to tell apart, but range can help.

RANGE: This Chipmunk is found only in the Sierra Nevada Mountains of California.

Least Chipmunk
Tamias minimus

Total Length: 7–9¹/₂ in.
Tail Length: 3–4¹/₄ in.
Weight: 1¹/₄–2¹/₂ oz.

Like most chipmunks, the Least Chipmunk is very common within its range and can be seen by anyone willing to invest the time and effort in a search. In California this chipmunk is a shrub-steppe species, and it is especially common near campgrounds. In some areas it can be the most commonly seen chipmunk species.

The coat of this chipmunk changes seasonally; in summer its coat is new and bright, and in winter its coat is duller, as if it rolled in the dust to mute its colors.

DESCRIPTION: Like all chipmunks, this tiny chipmunk has three dark and two light stripes on its face, and five dark and four light stripes on its body. The central dark stripe runs from the head to the base of the tail, but the other dark stripes end at the hips. The overall color is grayer and paler than other chipmunks, and the underside of the tail is yellower. The tail is quite long—more than 40 percent of the total length, and it is usually held erect when the chipmunk runs.

HABITAT: This chipmunk is common in sagebrush flats and arid grasslands.

FOOD: The bulk of the diet consists of conifer seeds, nuts, some berries and insects. It is common for chipmunks to eat eggs, fledgling birds, young mice or even carrion. Chipmunks have internal cheek pouches in which they carry food to their caches.

DEN: Least Chipmunks generally den in underground burrows with concealed entrances, but some individuals live in wood and rock cavities aboveground.

YOUNG: Breeding occurs about two weeks after chipmunks emerge from hibernation in spring. After about a one-month gestation, a litter of two to seven (usually four to six) helpless young is born in a grass-lined nest chamber, usually in April. The young develop rapidly, and the mother may later transfer them to a tree cavity or tree nest.

SIMILAR SPECIES: The slightly larger **Yellow-pine Chipmunk** (p. 241) tends to have brighter colors. The **Alpine Chipmunk** (p. 239) has a shorter, more orangish tail. The numerous chipmunks of California are very difficult to tell apart, but range can help.

RANGE: The range spreads from the central Yukon to western Quebec, from Washington to northern California, from North Dakota to southern New Mexico, and east to just west of Lake Michigan and north of Lake Huron.

Yellow-pine Chipmunk
Tamias amoenus

Total Length: 7³/₄–9¹/₂ in.

Tail Length: 3¹/₄–4¹/₄ in.

Weight: 1⁵/₈–3 oz.

The sound of scurrying among fallen leaves, a flash of movement and sharp, high-pitched "chips" will direct your attention to the fidgety behavior of a Yellow-pine Chipmunk. Using fallen logs as runways and the leaf litter as its pantry, this busy animal inhabits much of northeastern California. The word "chipmunk" is thought to be derived from the Algonquian word for "head first," which is the manner in which a chipmunk descends a tree, but contrary to cartoon-inspired myths, chipmunks spend very little time in high trees. They prefer the ground, where they bury food and dig golf ball–sized entrance holes to their networks of underground tunnels.

DESCRIPTION: This chipmunk is brightly colored, from tawny to pinkish cinnamon. Three dark and two light stripes are on the face, and five dark and four light stripes are on the back. The light stripes are white or grayish. The dark stripes are nearly black, and the central three extend all the way to the rump. The sides of the body and the underside of the tail are ochreous. The female tends to be larger than the male.

HABITAT: The Yellow-pine Chipmunk inhabits a wide variety of areas, including open coniferous forests, sagebrush flats, rocky outcroppings and pastures with small shrubs. It may be seen at ranches or farms well away from mountains or forests, attracted there by livestock feed.

FOOD: This chipmunk loves to dine on ripe berries, nuts, seeds, grasses, mushrooms and even insects and some other animals. It may be an important predator on eggs and nestling birds during the nesting season.

DEN: The Yellow-pine Chipmunk usually lives in a burrow that has a concealed entrance. It can sometimes be found in a tree cavity, but it seldom builds a tree nest.

YOUNG: The young are born in May or June, after spring mating and about one month of gestation. Usually five or six young are born in a grass-lined chamber in the burrow. They are blind and hairless at birth, but their growth is rapid, and they are usually weaned in about six weeks.

SIMILAR SPECIES: The **Least Chipmunk** (p. 240) may have duller colors. The **Long-eared Chipmunk** (p. 248) is more reddish overall but has less distinct stripes.

RANGE: This mountain chipmunk occurs in British Columbia, extreme western Alberta and the northwestern U.S., south to central California.

Yellow-cheeked Chipmunk
Tamias ochrogenys

Total Length: 9¹⁄₈–12 in.
Tail Length: 3³⁄₄–5¹⁄₈ in.
Weight: 2¹⁄₈–4¹⁄₄ oz.

For a chipmunk enthusiast, spotting a Yellow-cheeked Chipmunk is quite an achievement. This elusive chipmunk lives deep in the forests of north-coastal California, where it is more often heard than seen. Like a ventriloquist, its metallic chatter can be heard clearly amidst the trees, but the source cannot be pinpointed.

This stripy beast is the largest chipmunk in California. With its streamlined body, it is a fluid and agile climber. Whether resting or feeding, a chipmunk always keeps an eye out for danger. A nearby danger sends it scurrying to safety. As it scampers away, a frightened chipmunk calls out a series of *chik, chik, chik* sounds to warn any nearby chipmunks of the lurking danger.

DESCRIPTION: This chipmunk is large, with a very dark dorsal stripe that is more prominent than the other dark stripes. The outer two pale stripes are clearer and more prominent than the inner two pale stripes. The tail is fairly thin and not bushy. There are distinct pale patches behind each ear.

HABITAT: This chipmunk is common in coastal redwood forests. The climate here is so humid and mild that the chipmunk does not hibernate.

DEN: This large chipmunk lives either in simple burrows or in a tree cavity. Some chipmunks may build nests low in a tree, but whether this species does is uncertain.

FOOD: Yellow-cheeked Chipmunks eat a wide range of seeds, nuts, berries and mushrooms. Non-perishable food is stored in their burrows for winter.

YOUNG: Mating occurs in spring, and young are born from May to June. The litter size is two to six young that are altricial and grow quickly. Chipmunks have unusual longevity and may live from five to eight years in the wild.

SIMILAR SPECIES: The other large chipmunks, **Allen's** (p. 243), **Merriam's** (p. 246) and **Siskiyou** (p. 244) all have different ranges. Other chipmunks are smaller.

RANGE: This large chipmunk is found only in coastal forested regions of northern California.

Allen's Chipmunk
Tamias senex

Total Length: 9–10 in.

Tail Length: 3³/₄–4³/₈ in.

Weight: 2³/₈–3⁷/₈ oz.

Of all the chipmunks, the Allen's Chipmunk has an inordinate fondness for eating fungi. Little craters where a fungus or truffle was dug up can be found throughout areas inhabited by this chipmunk. Humid forests and lush, brushy areas are the favored habitats of the Allen's Chipmunk. A good clue to confirm the identity of this chipmunk in such areas is its call: different from every other species, the Allen's Chipmunk calls out three to five metallic barks, followed by a single chirped note. Habitat, vocalizations, and the holes it makes in the ground are the best ways to identify the Allen's Chipmunk. It has highly variable pelage that changes both seasonally and regionally.

ALSO CALLED: Shadow Chipmunk.

DESCRIPTION: This species is a large, grayish chipmunk with indistinct stripes. Only its dark dorsal stripe is conspicuous. It has white spots behind each ear, and its tail is a pale tawny color with light edges.

HABITAT: Allen's Chipmunks prefer humid white fir and red fir forests and lush, brushy areas. In California, they are especially associated with riparian areas.

DEN: Like other chipmunks, the Allen's Chipmunk usually excavates simple burrows. The design includes a nest chamber, sometimes a separate food chamber and an escape entrance. It may also build its nests in log crevices.

FOOD: These chipmunks feed primarily on seeds, mushrooms and other fungus (especially truffles) and some insects, but generally on less vegetation than other chipmunks.

YOUNG: The mating season lasts for one month, starting in April. A litter of three to five young is born sometime in late spring. The young are pink and blind at birth, but within four to five weeks they resemble little adults.

SIMILAR SPECIES: The **Yellow-cheeked Chipmunk** (p. 242)—which is hard to distinguish visually—does not sound a chirped note after a series of metallic barks, and it has a different range.

RANGE: This chipmunk has a thin range in central Oregon, moving south and east into California and slightly into northwestern and north-central Nevada.

Siskiyou Chipmunk
Tamias siskiyou

Total Length: 8⅝–11 in.

Tail Length: 3⅝–5 in.

Weight: 1¾–4 oz.

This chipmunk is a member of a closely related group of four chipmunk species. The Siskiyou, Townsend's (*T. townsendii*), Yellow-cheeked (p. 242), and Allen's (p. 243) chipmunks were at one time considered the same species. All four have similar outward appearances and are the largest of the western chipmunks.

Like most chipmunks, Siskiyou Chipmunks prefer solitary lifestyles. Social interactions between these chipmunks are rare and short-lived. In spring, males are energetic and looking for receptive females. Courtship involves playful games of tag where two or even three chipmunks dart through the underbrush. As is true in the courtship of many mammal species, a certain level of propriety is necessary if mating between the chipmunks is to occur. Ill-mannered males that act inappropriately once in the burrow may end up getting walloped and tossed out by the slightly larger females.

RANGE: Siskiyou Chipmunks are found only in western and coastal areas of northern California and southern Oregon.

DESCRIPTION: This chipmunk is large, with wide, nearly black dorsal stripes. The ears are slightly bicolored: tawny in front, gray in back. The bushy tail is dark on top, red below and fringed with white-tipped hairs.

HABITAT: These chipmunks live in brushy areas and open forests of coastal regions.

DEN: Siskiyou Chipmunks usually live in simple burrows, but they may take up residence in a tree cavity or hollow log.

FOOD: These chipmunks eat a variety of foods, including seeds, nuts, fruits, some vegetation and adult and larval insects.

YOUNG: After mating in early spring, gestation lasts for 30 or 31 days. The female has a litter of three to five pups. The young are pink and blind at birth. After just five weeks, the young are almost full grown and have full-color coats.

SIMILAR SPECIES: The slightly larger **Yellow-cheeked Chipmunk** (p. 242) is difficult to distinguish, but it inhabits regions south of the Siskiyou. The **Sonoma Chipmunk** (p. 245) is smaller and has darker hindfeet. The numerous chipmunks of California are very difficult to tell apart, but range can help.

Sonoma Chipmunk
Tamias sonomae

Total Length: 8⅝–11 in.
Tail Length: 3⅝–5 in.
Weight: 1¾–3¾ oz.

These large chipmunks live in northwestern California where several other chipmunk species also dwell. When many species of chipmunks occupy the same range, they frequently develop differences between their calls, which allows each chipmunk to identify members of its own species. The call of Sonoma Chipmunks is slower and lower in pitch than the calls of other chipmunks. Their coats are tinged dark brown, and the pale stripes appear slightly yellow. Their outer pair of dark stripes are often indistinct, a trait common among chipmunks of this region.

Sonoma Chipmunks spend great lengths of time stretched out on logs or the tops of bushes, where they partake of warm sunbeams and a view of their surroundings. When they are not basking, they are eagerly searching for food and stuffing their larders.

DESCRIPTION: This species is a large, brown chipmunk. The outermost pair of dark stripes is indistinct, and the dark facial stripes show no black in them. Dark spots are between the ear and eye, and the tail is reddish, becoming paler at the base.

HABITAT: Sonoma Chipmunks inhabit brushy and open areas of coniferous forests, as well as some arid chaparral regions.

DEN: These chipmunks may build nests in several types of dwellings, including simple burrows, hollow logs or tree crevices.

FOOD: Like most chipmunks, Sonoma Chipmunks will eat a variety of foods, such as conifer cones, seeds, insects and fungi.

YOUNG: In early spring, mating occurs. After a gestation period of about 30 days, four or five babies are born. Females give birth in the same den in which they hibernate, but they may move the babies elsewhere as conditions improve. After five weeks of care, the young have striped coats like their mother and are almost as big.

SIMILAR SPECIES: The **Siskiyou Chipmunk** (p. 244) is larger and has paler hindfeet. Other northern Californian species are larger. The numerous chipmunks of California are very difficult to tell apart, but range can help.

RANGE: Sonoma Chipmunks are found in mountain regions of northern California.

Merriam's Chipmunk
Tamias merriami

Total Length: 8¼–11 in.
Tail Length: 3½–5½ in.
Weight: 2½–4 oz.

front and behind the eyes. The tail is long and edged with fine white hairs.

These chipmunks share many characteristics with other western chipmunks, making proper identification in the wild a difficult task. A good clue to help identification is that the overall coloration of Merriam's Chipmunks is blurry and lacks intensity, as if they took a dunk in a mud puddle.

Unwitting forest helpers, chipmunks are vital components of a forest ecosystem: the extensive burrows they dig aerate the soil and bring up earth from below; their feeding habits help keep in check many weed and insect species that are prone to population outbursts; their forgotten seed caches germinate, augmenting seed dispersal for forest plants; and they are an essential prey species for many forest carnivores.

DESCRIPTION: This chipmunk has indistinct stripes, white undersides and an overall dull grayish-brown appearance. There are small dark spots directly in

HABITAT: These chipmunks inhabit a variety of habitats, including rocky areas, brushlands and low-elevation coniferous forests.

DEN: These chipmunks may build nests in several types of dwellings, including simple burrows, hollow logs or tree crevices. Like most other chipmunks, they hibernate in winter, but this dormancy is interrupted frequently to eat.

FOOD: Food is abundant for these chipmunks in their low mountain homes, and their favorite meals include pinyon pine nuts, acorns, flowers and fruits.

YOUNG: In early spring, mating occurs, and by late April, a litter of three to six young is born. The young are hairless and blind at birth. Within 30 days, the young are able to run and play outside the den.

SIMILAR SPECIES: Long-eared Chipmunks (p. 248) have a distinct white patch behind each ear. **California Chipmunks** (p. 247) also have indistinct stripes, but are somewhat redder. **Yellow-cheeked Chipmunks** (p. 242) inhabit more northerly regions. Other chipmunks in the same range have distinct stripes. The numerous chipmunks of California are very difficult to tell apart, but range can help.

RANGE: This chipmunk is found in central and southern California, with low numbers in northern California.

California Chipmunk
Tamias obscurus

Total Length: 8¹⁄₄–9³⁄₈ in.
Tail Length: 3⁵⁄₈–4 in.
Weight: 2–3¹⁄₈ oz.

Several chipmunk species have peculiar behavioral characteristics that help to distinguish them from other species. California Chipmunks are selective about where they sit when they call. They typically call when sitting on the tops of bushes. The repertoire of these chipmunks is highly varied, including sharp barks, chirps, chiks, and chuck-a-chucks. Certain types of calls serve as warnings for nearby chipmunks and are used when a predator is spotted. Some calls are more sociable and serve to encourage neighboring chipmunks to join in a conversation. The *chuck* sound causes other chipmunks close by to be quiet and alert.

DESCRIPTION: This medium-sized chipmunk has brownish facial stripes and a nearly black eye stripe. The stripes down its back are indistinct, and the dark stripes are reddish and the pale stripes are grayish. The outer two pale stripes are paler than the inner two. The top of head is pale gray.

HABITAT: This chipmunk lives in mixed chaparral and coniferous forests, especially areas with rocky outcroppings.

DEN: Typically, the California Chipmunk makes burrows in the ground. Burrows are quite elaborate and have a distinct nest chamber.

FOOD: Primary foods include seeds, nuts and berries. Some items are eaten immediately while others are stored for later. Various food caches, which differ in size and the type of food they contain, can be found both outside and inside the burrow. Using primarily their sense of smell, chipmunks later return to their caches and dig up the goods.

YOUNG: Breeding occurs as early as January, and after a one-month gestation, a litter of usually four to six young is born. The young are born blind and hairless. They grow rapidly, and they are usually weaned in less than six weeks.

SIMILAR SPECIES: Merriam's Chipmunk (p. 246) also has indistinct stripes, but with dark stripes that are less reddish than the California Chipmunk. The numerous chipmunks of California are very difficult to tell apart, but range can help.

RANGE: California Chipmunks are found in a few areas of southern California and into Mexico.

Long-eared Chipmunk
Tamias quadrimaculatus

Total Length: 7⁷/₈–10 in.

Tail Length: 1³/₈–1¹/₂ in.

Weight: 2¹/₂–3¹/₂ oz.

DESCRIPTION: This medium to large chipmunk has a reddish tinge to its bright colors, and there is little contrast between light and dark stripes. The tail is reddish and edged with white. Mature Long-eared Chipmunks have, behind each ear, prominent patches of white that are much larger than the patches occurring on other species.

The presence of Long-eared Chipmunks in the Sierra Nevada of northeastern California is obvious by torn apart conifer cones and tiny craters in the ground. These Chipmunks have a predilection for eating fungi and frequently dig up tasty mushrooms and truffles in addition to their regular diet of seeds and nuts. Caterpillars, beetle larva and termites often occur on their menu as well.

Long-eared Chipmunks must eat the fresh grubs and fungi while they can. When they retire for hibernation in late November, they must rely on their larder of stored seeds and nuts. These rodents are light hibernators, and they wake every few days to eat a good meal and rid the body of wastes. On particularly nice winter days, a few chipmunks may venture out of their burrows before starting the next period of hibernation.

HABITAT: These chipmunks prefer open brushy areas and coniferous forests of the Sierra Nevada Mountains.

DEN: These chipmunks may build nests in several types of dwellings, including simple burrows, hollow logs or tree crevices.

FOOD: Long-eared Chipmunks eat fungi, truffles, seeds, nuts, insects and other invertebrates. In some seasons, they may eat nothing but fungi.

YOUNG: Mating occurs in spring, after hibernation. Following a gestation period of about 31 days, a litter of two to six young is born. Like all other chipmunks, Long-eared Chipmunks start life looking a bit like pink gummy bears, but within five weeks they transform into fully striped young adults.

RANGE: These chipmunks occur in the Sierra Nevada of northeastern California and extreme western Nevada.

SIMILAR SPECIES: The **Yellow-pine Chipmunk** (p. 241) is less reddish overall but has more distinct stripes. The **Panamint Chipmunk** (p. 250) is smaller, has shorter ears and lacks the white spot behind each ear.

Lodgepole Chipmunk
Tamias speciosus

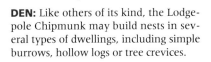

Total Length: 7³/₄–9¹/₂ in.
Tail Length: 2⁵/₈–4¹/₂ in.
Weight: 1³/₄–2¹/₈ oz.

As their name suggests, Lodgepole Chipmunks are associated with lodgepole pine and red fir forests in the mountains of eastern and central California. Much of this range is shared with Merriam's Chipmunks (p. 246), which are the low-elevation counterparts to Lodgepole Chipmunks. Separation of chipmunk species by habitat preference or elevation is necessary for each species to thrive. Unlike many other mammals, chipmunks are not strongly territorial regarding their home ranges. Tensions only rise when food stores or food sources are in danger of pilferage by other chipmunks. Lodgepole Chipmunks and Merriam's Chipmunks have specialized niches that allow them to occupy the same geographic range.

DESCRIPTION: This medium-sized chipmunk has distinct stripes but with little contrast between the light and dark ones. The outermost dark stripes may be nonexistent, and the facial stripes are indistinct. The ears are dark in front and light behind, and dark spots are in front and behind the eyes. The tail has dark ring near the tip.

HABITAT: These chipmunks are found in lodgepole pine and red fir forests of California, often in areas with manzanita.

DEN: Like others of its kind, the Lodgepole Chipmunk may build nests in several types of dwellings, including simple burrows, hollow logs or tree crevices.

FOOD: This chipmunk feeds primarily on seeds, nuts, insects and fungi. Insects and fungi may form a larger part of its diet than for other chipmunks.

YOUNG: Mating occurs in May or June—a few weeks after emergence from hibernation—and about one month later a litter of three to six young is born. The young are blind and hairless, but in four to five weeks, they have full-color coats and are nearly adult size.

SIMILAR SPECIES: The top of the **Uinta Chipmunk's** (p. 251) head is gray. The **Panamint Chipmunk** (p. 250) is smaller.

RANGE: Lodgepole Chipmunks are found in east and central California.

Panamint Chipmunk
Tamias panamintinus

Total Length: 7¹/₂–8⁵/₈ in.
Tail Length: 3¹/₈–4 in.
Weight: 1¹/₂–2¹/₄ oz.

Panamint Chipmunks spend much of the year awake and gathering food. They can be seen outside their burrows almost year-round if the weather is mild. During periods of inclement weather these chipmunks enter a state of dormancy in their burrows. Their hibernation state usually does not last for more than a week at a time.

As with other squirrels, courtship and mating occur as soon as the adults have emerged from their winter dens. Newborn chipmunks have extraordinary growth rates, which puts considerable stress on the mother. An attentive parent, she ensures they are well fed and nurtured.

DESCRIPTION: This chipmunk tends to have a reddish appearance. Whereas other chipmunks have two brown or two black stripes through the face, this chipmunk has a black stripe above its eyes and one brown stripe below its eyes. On its back, the outer dark stripes are indistinct or nonexistent. The top of its head is gray, and its ears are tawny.

HABITAT: Panamint Chipmunks thrive among boulders and on rocky outcroppings or cliffs in areas of pinyon pine and juniper forests.

DEN: The burrow is usually located at the base of a tree or stump, or in a crevice among rocks. The burrow is not very complex, and one passage leads to a chamber filled with a nest of shredded vegetation. Less frequently, some individuals may build spherical nests in trees, but most prefer burrows or rock crevices.

FOOD: The primary foods for this species include seeds, fruits, willow catkins, insects, some mushrooms and lichens. Carrion is consumed when available.

YOUNG: Mating occurs in spring. Females have an unusually long gestation of about 36 days, after which three to seven babies are born. The young are independent by August.

SIMILAR SPECIES: The Long-eared Chipmunk (p. 248) is larger and has larger ears and a white spot behind each ear. The **Lodgepole Chipmunk** (p. 249) is larger. The **Uinta Chipmunk** (p. 251) has more distinct stripes on its back. The numerous chipmunks of California are very difficult to tell apart, but the range can help.

RANGE: Panamint Chipmunks are found only in southwestern Nevada and south-central California.

Uinta Chipmunk
Tamias umbrinus

Total Length: 7³/₄–9¹/₂ in.
Tail Length: 2⁷/₈–4¹/₂ in.
Weight: 2–3 oz.

Uinta Chipmunks must be constantly alert for predators lurking around them. Threats can come from the sky, the ground, or even below them. Many raptors take a large toll on chipmunk populations, as do foxes, Bobcats, and snakes. Perhaps the most effective predators of chipmunks are the weasels. Weasels are voracious carnivores that chase chipmunks until they are exhausted. Because weasels are small and streamlined, they can sneak up on chipmunks from rock crevices or chase them into their burrows. Despite the relentless predation on chipmunks, some chipmunks have been known to live five to seven years in the wild, an unusually long time for a small rodent.

DESCRIPTION: This medium-sized chipmunk has an overall grayish color. The top of its head, neck and back are gray, the sides and shoulders are brownish and its undersides are nearly white. The stripes on its back are dark and distinct. Its tail is black tipped and white edged.

HABITAT: The primary habitat for this species includes coniferous, hardwood and mixed-wood forests.

DEN: This species is one of the most arboreal of the chipmunks. It often builds its nest in a tree cavity or an old log. Many individuals use burrows at the base of a tree. The nest chamber is about the size of a cantaloupe, and the nest is made of dry grasses and other fine material.

FOOD: Seeds comprise the majority of the diet, especially those from montane trees and shrubs. Pinyon pine nuts are relished. Some vegetation, mushrooms and insects are also consumed.

YOUNG: Mating commonly takes place in spring, and in late June or early July—after a gestation of about one month—a litter of four to six young is born. The young develop quickly and are weaned by mid-August.

SIMILAR SPECIES: The **Lodgepole Chipmunk** (p. 249) has a brown forehead. The **Panamint Chipmunk** (p. 250) has less distinct stripes on its back. The numerous chipmunks of California are very difficult to tell apart, but the range can help.

RANGE: This chipmunk has a patchy distribution, including west-central California, Nevada, north-central Arizona, Utah, north-central Colorado and Wyoming.

Yellow-bellied Marmot
Marmota flaviventris

True to its name, the Yellow-bellied Marmot has distinct yellowish or burnt orange undersides. When this marmot is curious about or watchful of something, it often sits back on its hindlegs in an upright position that displays its delightfully bright belly.

Yellow-bellied Marmots have a fairly lackadaisical routine: they sleep late in the morning, eat heartily for breakfast and then snooze dreamily in the shade for the afternoon. Counting hibernation and nighttime sleep, Yellow-bellied Marmots spend about 80 percent of their lives in their burrows. They like their dens to be kept clean, and when they emerge from hibernation they throw out their used bedding and replace it with fresh grass and leaves. Throughout summer, they continue to keep their bedding clean and their burrows free of debris.

Colonies of Yellow-bellied Marmots have a strict social order, and whenever members of a colony are eating or wrestling with their family members, at least one marmot plays watchdog. This sentinel is responsible for warning the others if danger approaches. The alarm call is a loud chirp, which varies in duration and intensity depending on the nature of the threat: short, steady notes probably translate as "Heads up, pay attention"; loud, shrill notes convey the message "Into your burrows, now!" Different urgent warnings are reserved for immediate dangers, such as a circling eagle or an approaching fox.

In some areas of California, marmot population sizes seem to be regulated by the availability of suitable hibernation sites. The dominant male of a colony evicts younger males as they become sexually mature, and these banished marmots appear to suffer especially high overwinter mortalities.

ALSO CALLED: Rockchuck.

DESCRIPTION: The back is tawny or yellow brown, grizzled by the light tips of the guard hairs. The feet and legs are blackish brown. The head has whitish-gray patches across the top of the nose, from below the ear to the shoulder and from the nose and chin toward the throat, which leaves a darker brown patch surrounding the ear, eye and upper cheek on each side of the face. The ears are short and rounded. The whiskers are dark and prominent. The dark, grizzled, bushy tail is often arched behind the animal and flagged from side to side. The bright buffy yellow belly, sides of the neck, upper jaw and hips are responsible for the common name.

RANGE: Yellow-bellied Marmots are found from central British Columbia and extreme southern Alberta south into central California and northern New Mexico.

Length: 19–26 in.
Tail Length: 5–7½ in.
Weight: 3½–8 lb.

HABITAT: Large rocks, either in the form of talus or outcrops, are a necessity, which accounts for this animal's alternate name "rockchuck." The Yellow-bellied Marmot may be found in valley bottoms, high deserts or alpine tundra, but never in dense forests. In California it occurs mainly at high elevations, semi-open areas and arid grasslands with abundant broken rock or stone piles.

FOOD: Abundant herbaceous or grassy vegetation must be available within a short distance of the den. Like many sciurids, this marmot occasionally feeds on road-killed carrion and other animal matter when available.

DEN: Each adult maintains its own burrow, with individuals of the highest social status nearest the colony center. A burrow is typically 8–14 in. in diameter. It slants down for 20–39 in. and then extends another 10–15 ft. to end beneath or among large rocks in a bulky nest lined with grass.

YOUNG: Three to eight young are born in a litter in June after a 30-day gestation. Naked and blind at birth, they first emerge from the burrow at three to four weeks of age. Well-fed females become sexually mature before their first birthdays. Males and females born at higher elevations usually do not get to breed until they are at least two years old.

SIMILAR SPECIES: The Yellow-bellied Marmot is the largest squirrel in the region. The **Mountain Beaver** (p. 270) has a short tail and is brown overall. **Ground squirrels** (pp. 256–62) are smaller and have less bushy tails.

> ### DID YOU KNOW?
>
> Yellow-bellied Marmots frequently bask in the morning sun, probably to warm up. At about midday they retire to their cool burrows, but in late afternoon they reemerge to feed. They seem to have poor control of their body temperature: in summer it may range from 34° C to 40° C.

White-tailed Antelope Squirrel
Ammospermophilus leucurus

Total Length: 7⅝–9⅜ in.
Tail Length: 2⅛–3⅜ in.
Weight: 3–5½ oz.

White-tailed Antelope Squirrels live in large aggregations where each adult maintains at least one burrow and a strict social order is established among the males. In the northern parts of their range, outside California, White-tailed Antelope Squirrels may hibernate for about two months, though as a whole the genus is non-hibernating. Their special adaptations are for surviving hot desert environments, rather than cold winter conditions. To survive the heat of the desert, antelope squirrels press their bellies to the dirt in shaded areas to quickly draw heat out of their bodies. When they are too hot, they may also climb into shady shrubs to catch a cooling breeze or retire to their burrows.

RANGE: This squirrel is found from southeastern Oregon and southwestern Idaho to southern California, and in a patchy distribution eastward to western Colorado and northwestern New Mexico.

DESCRIPTION: These antelope squirrels have a distinct pale band down each side. In summer, they have tawny coats, and in winter, their coats are cast with gray. The undersides are pale, and the tail is white underneath.

HABITAT: The most widespread *Ammospermophilus* species, the White-tailed Antelope Squirrel inhabits deserts, valley bottoms, gravelly washes, sagebrush plateaus, creosote flats and foothills.

DEN: White-tailed Antelope Squirrels make simple burrows that have no mounds of dirt at the entrance. Inside the burrow is a chamber used for sleeping and raising young.

FOOD: These squirrels eat green vegetation, seeds, insects and other invertebrates and some vertebrate matter.

YOUNG: Mating occurs anywhere from February to June, and the litter size is 5 to 14 young. As the young mature, they spar and wrestle to determine dominance.

SIMILAR SPECIES: Nelson's Antelope Squirrel (p. 255) lives in a different area, is larger and lighter in color, and its tail is not as white underneath. **Golden-mantled Ground Squirrels** (p. 262) have dark stripes bordering their pale side stripe and live in a different habitat.

Nelson's Antelope Squirrel
Ammospermophilus nelsoni

Total Length: 9–11 in.
Tail Length: 2⅝–3⅛ in.
Weight: about 5½ oz.

A threatened species, the Nelson's Antelope Squirrel is the rarest member of the genus. Populations have declined mainly due to habitat loss and population fragmentation. Now, the sizable populations in western Kern County and on the Carrizo and Elkhorn plains are closely monitored. Reintroductions from these areas may proceed to repopulate this species in parts of California where it has disappeared.

California Ground Squirrels (p. 259) often live among antelope squirrels and share the same food sources, but very little competition exists between these species because the ground squirrels spend five to eight months of the year dormant—from November to February the scarce food sources are eaten solely by Nelson's Antelope Squirrels.

ALSO CALLED: San Joaquin Antelope Squirrel.

DESCRIPTION: Adult squirrels have a yellowish-tawny body with pinkish-orange highlights behind the fore and hindlegs. A prominent white stripe runs down each side, and the tail is whitish underneath.

HABITAT: These ground dwellers inhabit rolling desert country, sandy washes and shrubby flats. Dominant plant species include salt bush, ephedra, bladder pod, goldenbush, snakeweed and Mormon tea.

DEN: These desert specialists excavate burrows in loamy or alluvial soils. Small colonies of 6 to 10 individuals live in these elaborate burrows. Several passages end in nest chambers.

FOOD: Nelson's Antelope Squirrels feed mainly on insects, seeds, vegetation, cactus pulp and cactus fruits.

YOUNG: Adults mate in either late winter or early spring. Females bear only one litter per year, after about 26 days of gestation. The young number from 6 to 11, and they are totally helpless at birth. Their growth rates are remarkable, and within six weeks the youngsters are nearly indistinguishable from the adults.

SIMILAR SPECIES: The **White-tailed Antelope Squirrel** (p. 254) lives in a different area and is smaller and darker in color, and its tail is pure white underneath. **Golden-mantled Ground Squirrels** (p. 262) have dark stripes bordering their pale side stripe and live in a different habitat.

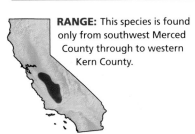

RANGE: This species is found only from southwest Merced County through to western Kern County.

Piute Ground Squirrel
Spermophilus mollis

Total Length: 6⅝–11 in.
Tail Length: 1¼–2⅞ in.
Weight: 4½–12 oz.

In the past, the Piute Ground Squirrel was considered a subspecies of the Townsend's Ground Squirrel (*S. townsendii*). Studies have shown that there is no hybridization between these species, and they differ genetically from each other, even though they are nearly identical in appearance. The Piute Ground Squirrel estivates and hibernates, starting in July and lasting at least until the end of January. Before July, individuals must fatten themselves sufficiently to survive dormancy. Ground squirrels eat large quantities of food in both spring and early summer, but the weight gain occurs primarily in summer. This is attributable to a fast metabolism in spring, which creates high energy for activity, and a low metabolism in summer, which allows for weight gain.

ALSO CALLED: Great Basin Ground Squirrel.

RANGE: It is found in two disjunct populations: a smaller one in central Washington and a larger one from southeastern Oregon and central Idaho, to extreme northeastern California, well into Nevada and western Utah.

DESCRIPTION: These ground squirrels are small and typically pale smoky gray above, sometimes with a pinkish tinge. Their undersides are pale, and the short tail is fringed with white and is reddish underneath. Often their faces have a reddish tinge as well.

HABITAT: These ground squirrels occur in desert and semi-arid communities, especially areas dominated by sagebrush or greasewood.

DEN: These ground squirrels form colonies of up to 30 adults per hectare. The burrow system includes multiple entrances that are distinguishable by piled-up dirt around the hole.

FOOD: This ground squirrel has a diet similar to others of its kind; it feeds mainly on vegetation, insects and carrion.

YOUNG: Females have one litter per year, after mating in early spring. In March, the litter is born and has 6 to 10 young. The young are altricial, and require their mother's milk for at least three weeks.

SIMILAR SPECIES: The **Belding's Ground Squirrel** (p. 257) has a brown streak down its back. The **California Ground Squirrel** (p. 259) has a V-shaped pattern on its upper back.

Belding's Ground Squirrel
Spermophilus beldingi

Total Length: 9–12 in.
Tail Length: 1³/₄–3 in.
Weight: 8–12 oz.

Belding's Ground Squirrels, and their relatives that also estivate, have the longest dormancy of any North American mammal. They enter estivation in August, and this state continues on to become hibernation. Waking finally in mid- to late March, these squirrels can spend as much as two-thirds of the year dormant. Similar to all other squirrels, the males emerge from their winter burrows first and females follow two weeks later. About five days after the females emerge they are receptive to mating. The males, ready since they emerged three weeks earlier, battle fiercely for the females. The fighting is intense, because the females are receptive for a mere three to six hours.

DESCRIPTION: Richly colored squirrels, Belding's Ground Squirrels have a slight pinkish tone. Down their backs, these squirrels have a broad, chestnut brown stripe. The tops of their heads and the undersides of their tails are a cinnamon-pink color, as are their forelegs and chin.

HABITAT: The squirrels inhabit sub-alpine meadows and grassy areas such as farmland, mowed areas and golf courses.

DEN: These semi-colonial squirrels make simple, long burrows ending in nest chambers. Although many individuals share the same vicinity, the burrows are not connected.

FOOD: A diet of grains, green vegetation, seeds, insects and small vertebrates allow these ground squirrels to at least double their weight before they enter dormancy.

YOUNG: Mating occurs immediately after emergence from hibernation, and after a gestation of about 22 days, a litter of three to eight young is born.

SIMILAR SPECIES: The **California Ground Squirrel** (p. 259) has a V-shaped pattern on its upper back. The **Piute Ground Squirrel** (p. 256) lacks the chestnut brown stripe down its back.

RANGE: These ground squirrels are found in central and eastern Oregon, southwestern Idaho, central Nevada and northeastern California.

Rock Squirrel

Spermophilus variegatus

Total Length: 17–21 in.
Tail Length: 6³/₈–10 in.
Weight: 21–28 oz.

talus slopes. It is sometimes encountered along brushy streamsides.

With its long, bushy tail, the Rock Squirrel resembles a tree squirrel and, more so than other ground squirrels, it is an agile climber that often seeks out berries and seeds in trees and shrubs. It may even make a maternal nest in a hollow tree. The Rock Squirrel also goes against the ground squirrel norm by only having a short, intermittent hibernation period. Much to a naturalist's surprise, it is not uncommon to see a Rock Squirrel abroad in December.

DESCRIPTION: The back is grayish to blackish gray and often appears mottled. The shoulder area is darker than the rump. The sides and upper surfaces of the feet are brownish. The belly is a light grayish brown. The bushy tail is rarely as long as the body.

HABITAT: True to its name, this squirrel inhabits rocky areas, primarily on low cliffs, canyon walls, boulder piles and

FOOD: Seeds and fruits seem to be the staple component of the diet, but the Rock Squirrel also consumes insects, other invertebrates, young birds, eggs and carrion.

DEN: Rock Squirrels form colonies that have a distinct social order. Females make their burrows in the center of the colony territory, while one dominant and a few subordinate males burrow on the outskirts. The burrows are often dug underneath large boulders, which provide excellent protection against predators. The entrances are located in rock crevices, and the burrows may be up to 11 yd. long. The burrow ends in a spherical nest chamber that is filled with insulating grass. Some food may be stored in the burrow.

YOUNG: A litter contains three to nine young, which weigh about ¹/₄ oz. at birth. Unlike other ground squirrels, Rock Squirrels may have two litters a year, one in May or June and another in August or September.

SIMILAR SPECIES: No other large, bushy-tailed ground squirrel is found in the same range. The similar **California Ground Squirrel** (p. 259) has a different range. The much smaller **Round-tailed Ground Squirrel** (p. 261) has a long, round tail that is not bushy.

RANGE: The Rock Squirrel is found from northern Colorado west to southeastern California and south into Mexico through Arizona and western Texas.

California Ground Squirrel
Spermophilus beecheyi

Total length: 14–20 in.
Tail length: 5³/₄–8⁷/₈ in.
Weight: 10–26 oz.

This impressive, sturdy ground squirrel is a daring creature that easily climbs 20 ft. up cottonwood trees to feed on the tasty catkins. This behavior, as well as its large size and long, bushy tail may cause someone to mistakenly identify the California Ground Squirrel as a tree squirrel. These ground squirrels seem antisocial in comparison to most other ground dwellers: they either live alone or in informal colonies. When in colonies, each member avoids the living space of the others.

ALSO CALLED: Gray Digger, Douglas's Ground Squirrel.

DESCRIPTION: This large ground squirrel is mainly brown in color with light-colored dapples over the back. A good diagnostic feature is the V-shaped pattern of light fur that begins at the nape of their neck and runs over each shoulder to their sides. This light-colored "V" encloses an area of much darker brown fur. They also have long, conspicuously bushy tails that are edged with white.

HABITAT: These ground dwellers favor open areas such as pastures, rocky outcroppings and rolling hills. Overall, they are not too particular about where they live; in some regions they inhabit sparsely wooded hillsides.

FOOD: This squirrel is certainly not choosy about what it eats; it consumes the seeds, stems, leaves, roots and fruits of most plants, as well as regularly eating insects and small vertebrates.

DEN: The burrows excavated by these ground squirrels range from 5–200 ft. long and 3–6 in. wide. Adults form loose colonies. The prime location for a burrow is under a log, a boulder or a tree.

YOUNG: Soon after emerging from hibernation, mating occurs. Gestation lasts for almost one month, and the litter size is usually five to eight young. At just eight weeks old, the young resemble the adults and are beginning to burrow for themselves. In some parts of their range, the young of the season may not hibernate, remaining active all year to feed and mature.

SIMILAR SPECIES: The similar **Rock Squirrel** (p. 258) has a different range. No other ground squirrels in California have such bushy tails.

RANGE: The California Ground Squirrel is found in south-central Washington, western Oregon, most of California and west-central Nevada.

Mohave Ground Squirrel
Spermophilus mohavensis

Total Length: 8⅝–9 in.
Tail Length: 2¼–2⅞ in.
Weight: 3–4⅝ oz.

These small desert specialists are at home in the arid Mohave Desert of California. To survive in this harsh climate, these little ground squirrels must hibernate almost eight months of the year, from August to March. Food is scarce during these months, and these squirrels are unable to compete for what few morsels are available. The food available is eaten by White-tailed Antelope Squirrels, which also live in the desert and do not hibernate.

Like other ground squirrels, they adopt an upright, bowling pin–type stance outside their burrows. In this position, they have a good view of their surroundings and can easily locate approaching predators. If danger is sensed, a short, high-pitched *peep* is given as a warning. The sound sends other ground squirrels in the area scurrying to the safety of their burrows. Their main predators are badgers, hawks, foxes and Coyotes.

RANGE: As its name suggests, this ground squirrel is found only in the Mohave Desert of southern California.

DESCRIPTION: Mohave Ground Squirrels have white bellies and gray coats with a slight pink glow. Their tails are thin and colored cinnamon on top and white underneath. When they are running, they hold their tails over their backs to expose this white color and reflect away the sun's harsh rays.

HABITAT: Brushy flats and deserts are the main habitat for this species.

FOOD: Mohave Ground Squirrels feed mainly on green vegetation, seeds, beans and insects. A general feeder, they will even feed on carrion when available.

DEN: These mainly solitary ground squirrels excavate burrows in such a way that the entrances are well hidden. As they dig, they scatter the dirt away from the hole, preventing a mound from forming. Without a mound to indicate the entranceway, the burrow is hard to see.

YOUNG: This species mates soon after emergence from hibernation. The litter size is four to nine young, and gestation is probably about 30 days. The young are altricial, but they grow quickly.

SIMILAR SPECIES: The **Round-tailed Ground Squirrel** (p. 261) has a longer, round, cinnamon-colored tail.

Round-tailed Ground Squirrel
Spermophilus tereticaudus

Total Length: 8–11 in.
Tail Length: 2³/₈–4³/₈ in.
Weight: 5–6¹/₂ oz.

Round-tailed Ground Squirrels excavate their burrows in the dry, sandy earth of southern California. During hot afternoons, they either retire to their cool dens or they climb into scrubby bushes to avoid the burning sand. Although they are excellent diggers, these squirrels often use burrows excavated by other animals, such as pocket gophers or kangaroo rats. When Round-tailed Ground Squirrels are startled, they run for cover by diving into *any* burrow. Regardless of what may be at home, they would rather take their chances with another burrowing animal than a badger, hawk, Coyote, fox, or Bobcat.

Most Round-tailed Ground Squirrels put on enough fat to survive three months of hibernation, lasting from late October to the end of January. Some of the squirrels living in the southern regions may not hibernate at all.

DESCRIPTION: True to their names, Round-tailed Ground Squirrels have long, round-tipped tails. Their tails are thin, like other ground squirrels, with gray on top and cinnamon tones below. These squirrels have no patterns or unique markings in their coats to help identification. Their fur is mainly cinnamon colored or tawny gray. Some of the longer hairs down their sides may be tipped with yellow or light gray, lending a slight sheen to their coats.

HABITAT: The primary habitat is desert regions and scrub flatlands.

FOOD: These ground squirrels feed primarily on seeds, green vegetation, cactus pulp and grasshoppers.

DEN: Burrows are excavated at the base of a small shrub. Sometimes this ground squirrel uses an abandoned burrow from another desert rodent. Typically there is no dirt pile at the entrance. One passage leads to a small nest chamber.

YOUNG: In spring these squirrels mate, and by mid-May the females bear their young, after about 27 days of gestation. The litter size for these squirrels is 1 to 12; the number depends entirely on the abundance of water and vegetation.

SIMILAR SPECIES: The **Mohave Ground Squirrel** (p. 260) is difficult to distinguish, but its shorter tail has white underneath and its body has pinkish highlights. The **Rock Squirrel** (p. 258) is much larger and has a bushy tail.

RANGE: This ground squirrel is found in southern California, southern Nevada, southwestern Arizona and into Mexico.

Golden-mantled Ground Squirrel
Spermophilus lateralis

Total Length: 11–13 in.
Tail Length: 3³/₄–4³/₄ in.
Weight: 6–12 oz.

buffy-white eye ring is broken near the ear. Two black stripes on either side of a white stripe run along each side from the top of the shoulder to near the top of the hip. The back is grizzled gray. The belly and feet are pinkish buff to creamy white. The top of the tail is blackish, bordered with cinnamon buff. The lower surface of the tail is cinnamon buff in the center.

This charming ground squirrel wins the attention of many campers and hikers in wilderness areas. Unfortunately, it is frequently the victim of mistaken identity. Misled by the long white and black side stripes, onlookers often call this small ground squirrel a chipmunk.

Although Golden-mantled Ground Squirrels are common around campsites and picnic areas and they frequently mooch handouts from visitors, feeding them (or any other wildlife) is illegal in national parks. Human handouts often lead to extreme obesity in animals. Visitors are encouraged to satisfy their interest with close observations and photography.

DESCRIPTION: The head and front of the shoulders are a rich chestnut. The

HABITAT: This squirrel inhabits montane and subalpine forests wherever rocky outcroppings or talus slopes provide adequate cover.

FOOD: Green vegetation, seeds, fruits, fungus, insects and carrion make up the majority of the diet.

DEN: Burrows are typically found beneath a log or rock. Two or more entrances are common, and the main passage ends in a nest chamber. Blind tunnels serve as food storage sites.

YOUNG: Breeding follows soon after the female emerges from hibernation in spring. After a gestation of 27 to 28 days, four to six naked, blind pups are born between mid-May and early July.

SIMILAR SPECIES: Similar-looking **Chipmunks** (pp. 239–51) are much smaller, and their stripes extend through the face. **Antelope squirrels** (pp. 254–55) lack the dark stripes bordering the light side stripe and live in different habitats. No other ground squirrel in California has stripes.

RANGE: This rock-dwelling squirrel's range is restricted to the Rocky Mountains, southern Cascades and Sierra Nevada.

Eastern Gray Squirrel
Sciurus carolinensis

Total Length: 17–20 in.
Tail Length: 8¹/₄–9³/₄ in.
Weight: 14–25 oz.

In many cities and surrounding areas of California, people can watch the sinuous movements of this large, introduced tree squirrel. This species is quite similar to the native Western Gray Squirrel. Although it is called a "gray" squirrel, black and albino forms may occur.

DESCRIPTION: In California, this large tree squirrel is mainly gray with yellow or ochraceous highlights on the sides, and a nearly pure white belly. The bushy tail is flattened top to bottom. Some individuals and even certain populations may be black.

HABITAT: These squirrels prefer mature deciduous or mixed forests, with lots of nut-bearing trees.

FOOD: These nut-lovers feed mainly on the seeds of acorn, maple, ash and elm. In spring and summer, they also eat buds, flowers, leaves and occasionally animal matter, such as eggs or nestling birds.

DEN: Eastern Gray Squirrels den in trees year-round. They build either drays (spherical leaf and twig nests) or they use natural tree cavities or woodpecker holes.

YOUNG: Breeding occurs from December to February, rarely in July or August. Most females have only one litter a year. Gestation is 40 to 45 days, after which a litter of one to eight helpless young is born. The eyes open at 32 to 40 days, and weaning occurs about three weeks later.

SIMILAR SPECIES: The **Western Gray Squirrel** (p. 264) is very similar, but lacks the yellowish or ochraceous highlights. The **Eastern Fox Squirrel** (*S. niger*) which can be seen in numerous cities and nearby nut orchards, has rusty or yellowish highlights on the face, underside, forelegs and tail. The **Douglas's Squirrel** (p. 266) is smaller and browner.

Eastern Fox Squirrel

RANGE: This squirrel's native range encompasses all of the eastern U.S. and parts of Canada to southern Manitoba in the north and eastern Texas in the south.

Western Gray Squirrel
Sciurus griseus

This large tree squirrel is a common resident of the humid deciduous forests throughout the West Coast. Intermingling tree branches are like highways to these squirrels, allowing them to cover great distances without ever touching the ground. Their nests are at least 20 ft. off the ground, and often near the tops of tall trees. Such heights effectively remove them from the reach of many carnivores. In winter, they ignore their leafy nests that are too easily visible in the leafless branches, and take up lodging in a tree cavity instead. Tree cavities tend to be warmer as well as more secret, and thereby help this non-hibernating squirrel during cold snaps. Like all squirrels, they prefer mild days and will not leave their nests during stormy, windy or cold weather.

When searching for food, Western Gray Squirrels travel in trees and on the ground, and much of what they collect is stashed away for future use. They make their caches in forked tree branches, under fallen logs or buried in the ground. When they forget about a food cache, the seeds may germinate and help replenish the plants on which they feed.

Western Gray Squirrels are extremely curious and adept problem-solvers. If traps are set to catch one, the squirrel investigates the trap and fiddles with it, rather than entering and getting caught. Squirrel traps are often found empty and over-turned. Many gray squirrels learn to pilfer the nuts from the trigger mechanism of a trap without getting caught.

ALSO CALLED: California Gray Squirrel, Columbian Gray Squirrel, Silver Gray Squirrel.

DESCRIPTION: This large tree squirrel is mainly gray above and speckled with many white-tipped hairs. The undersides are white or nearly white, and the backs of the ears are reddish or tawny in color. Its bushy tail is colored at the edges with bands of gray, white and black. Unlike the two introduced large tree squirrels, the Eastern Fox Squirrel and the Eastern Gray Squirrel (p. 263), this species almost completely lacks rusty or yellowish hairs in its coat (other than its ears).

HABITAT: This squirrel is abundant in woodland areas, especially oak woods. It is found from sea level to low elevations in the Sierra Nevada Mountains. The only places it avoids are dry, treeless deserts and high mountain areas.

FOOD: These squirrels feed heavily on nuts, such as acorns, hazelnuts and

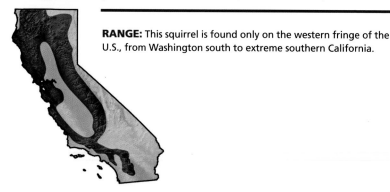

RANGE: This squirrel is found only on the western fringe of the U.S., from Washington south to extreme southern California.

Total length: 18–25 in.
Tail length: 9¹/₂–12 in.
Weight: 18–34 oz.

almonds, conifer cones, seeds and berries. Sometimes, they consume bark, buds, sap, fungi and insects. A common sight is a squirrel gnawing on bone or antler, from which it gets many essential minerals. These squirrels' predilection for eating nuts can make them serious pests in nut orchards. In some areas of California, Western Gray Squirrels dine almost exclusively on truffles.

DEN: Gray squirrels are adept at making large, spherical leaf and twig nests high up in a tree. The spherical nests, called "drays," can measure more than 2 ft. in diameter. In winter, they do not hibernate, but may move their residence to a tree cavity and wait out excessively cold days.

YOUNG: Mating can occur as early as November in the southern part of the range, but usually mating occurs in early spring. Litters of three to five young are born anywhere from February to June. The young are altricial, looking like pink gummy bears at birth, and they are completely dependent on their mother for the first few weeks. Females usually have one litter per year, but in favorable conditions two litters is not uncommon.

SIMILAR SPECIES: The **Eastern Fox Squirrel** (p. 263) and **Eastern Gray Squirrel** (p. 263) both have more red or yellow in their coats. The **Douglas's Squirrel** (p. 266) is smaller and much browner in color.

DID YOU KNOW?

If you are out in the forest during the day and you hear a hoarse barking sound, it's not the sound of a dog following you—it's the call of the Western Gray Squirrel.

Douglas's Squirrel
Tamiasciurus douglasii

Few squirrels have earned such a reputation for playfulness and agility as the Douglas's Squirrel. This squirrel is a well-known forest inhabitant that often has a saucy regard for its human neighbors. Like a one-man band, the Douglas's Squirrel firmly scolds all intruders with shrill chatters, clucks and sputters, falsettos, tail flicking and feet stamping. Even when it is undisturbed, this chatterbox often chirps as it goes about its daily routine. A Douglas's Squirrel is delightful but difficult to watch, because it is very active and, by comparison, we are too slow and awkward along the forest floor.

Living almost exclusively in coniferous forests, these squirrels leap easily from limb to limb as they search for food. Douglas's Squirrels have a seemingly insatiable appetite for conifer cones. Running along conifer branches, they nip the cones free and let them fall to the ground. On a busy day, these squirrels bombard the forest floor with cones for much of the morning—one particularly fast squirrel cut 537 sequoia cones in 30 minutes. When enough cones are cut, the squirrel eagerly transfers them to large cone caches beside tree stumps or under fallen logs.

Because the Douglas's Squirrel does not hibernate, it needs to store massive amounts of food in caches. These food caches, which in extreme cases can reach the size of a garage, are the secret to the Douglas's Squirrel's success. Much of its efforts throughout the growing season are concentrated on filling these larders, and biologists speculate that the squirrel's characteristically antagonistic disposition is a result of having to continually protect its food stores.

By early spring, Douglas's Squirrels are ready to mate. Their courtship involves daredevil leaps through the trees and high-speed chases over the forest floor. The young venture out from the nest by July or August. They are playful and frequently challenge nuts or mushrooms to a bout of aggressive mock combat.

ALSO CALLED: Chickaree.

DESCRIPTION: In summer the eye ring, feet and underparts are pumpkin orange, and the back and head are grizzled olive brown. The ear tufts are black, as are the flank stripes that separate the brown back and orange underside. The bushy tail is dark reddish in color. The winter coat is more grizzled and gray, and the tail may have long, white hairs flecked throughout. The whiskers are black.

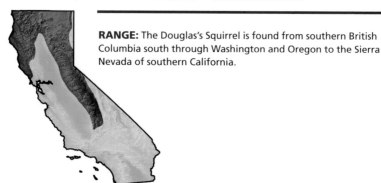

RANGE: The Douglas's Squirrel is found from southern British Columbia south through Washington and Oregon to the Sierra Nevada of southern California.

Total length: 11–14 in.

Tail length: 3⅞–6⅛ in.

Weight: 5¼–11 oz.

HABITAT: The coniferous coastal rainforest and Cascade and Sierra Nevada forests are home to this species, though it sometimes ventures out into logged areas. The Douglas's Squirrel may inhabit cities where suitable numbers of trees are present.

FOOD: This squirrel feeds mainly on fir, pine, spruce and hemlock seeds and green cones, but it also consumes maple samaras, alder catkins, other seeds and nuts, berries and mushrooms. When this squirrel feeds, it typically carries cones to a particular spot in a tree, eats out the seeds and discards the scales and cores. The result is a large pile on the forest floor beneath the tree that is called a midden. Like other squirrels, animal matter is eaten when available.

DEN: The nest is typically in a hollow tree, but the squirrel may construct a dray (leaf and twig nest) high in a conifer, often using an abandoned hawk's or crow's nest as a foundation.

YOUNG: Following mating in early April, two to eight (usually four) young are born after a gestation of 35 days. The eyes open at four to five weeks, and the young are weaned when they are seven to eight weeks old. After weaning, the young then have to establish their own territories. Juveniles are sexually mature following their first winter.

SIMILAR SPECIES: The **Western Gray Squirrel** (p. 264), **Eastern Gray Squirrel** (p. 263) and **Eastern Fox Squirrel** (p. 263) are all much larger. The **Northern Flying Squirrel** (p. 268) is a similar size, but it is a sooty pewter color and has distinct glide membranes.

Northern Flying Squirrel
Glaucomys sabrinus

Like drifting leaves, Northern Flying Squirrels seem to float from tree to tree in forests throughout much of northern California. These arboreal performers are one of two species of flying squirrels in North America that are capable of distance gliding.

Although it is not capable of true flapping flight—bats are the only mammals to have mastered it—a flying squirrel's aerial travels are no less impressive, with extreme glides of up to 110 yards. Enabling the squirrels to "fly" are its glide membranes—cape-like, furred skin extending down the length of the body from the forelegs to the hindlegs.

Before a glide, a squirrel identifies a target and maneuvers into the launch position: a head-down, tail-up orientation along the tree trunk. Then, using its strong hindlegs, the squirrel propels itself into the air with its legs extended. Once airborne, it resembles a flying paper towel that can make rapid side-to-side maneuvers and tight downward spirals. Such control is accomplished by making minor adjustments to the orientation of the wrists and forelegs. On the ground and in trees, flying squirrels hop or leap, but the skin folds prevent them from running. They are also unable to swim.

The call of the Northern Flying Squirrel is a loud *chuck chuck chuck*, which increases in pitch to a shrill falsetto when the animal is disturbed. Like other tree squirrels, the Northern Flying Squirrel does not hibernate. On very cold days, however, groups of 5 to 10 individuals can be found huddled in a nest to keep warm.

DESCRIPTION: Flying squirrels have a unique web or fold of skin that extends laterally to the level of the ankles and wrists to become the abbreviated "wings" with which the squirrel glides. They have large, dark, shiny eyes. The back is light brown, with hints of gray from the lead-colored hair bases. The feet are gray on top. The underparts are light gray to cinnamon precisely to the edge of the gliding membrane and edge of the tail. The tail appears flattened because of long hairs that extend only to the sides; this feather-shaped tail adds to the buoyancy of the "flight" and helps the tail function as the rudder and elevators do on a plane.

HABITAT: Coniferous mountain forests are prime flying squirrel habitat, but these animals are sometimes found in deciduous forests as well.

FOOD: The bulk of the diet consists of lichens and fungi, but flying squirrels also

RANGE: This flying squirrel occurs in eastern Alaska and across most of Canada in appropriate habitats. Its range extends south through the western mountains to California and Utah, around the Great Lakes and through the Appalachians.

Total Length: 9³/₄–15 in.

Tail Length: 4¹/₄–7 in.

Weight: 2⁵/₈–6¹/₂ oz.

eat buds, berries, some seeds, a few arthropods, bird eggs and nestlings and the protein-rich, pollen-filled male cones of conifers. They cache cones and nuts.

DEN: Nests in tree cavities are lined with lichen and grass. Leaf nests, called "drays," are located in a tree fork close to the trunk. Twigs and strips of bark are used on the outside, with progressively finer materials used inside until the center consists of grasses and lichens. If the dray is for winter use, it is additionally insulated to a diameter of 16 in.

YOUNG: Mating takes place between late March and the end of May. After a six-week gestation, typically two to four young are born. They weigh about ³/₁₆ oz. at birth. The eyes open after about 52 days. Ten days later they first leave the nest, and they are weaned when

they are about 65 days old. Young squirrels first glide at three months, but it takes them another month to become skilled. Flying squirrels are not sexually mature until after their second winter.

SIMILAR SPECIES: No other mammal in the region has the distinctive flight membranes of a flying squirrel. The **Douglas's Squirrel** (p. 266) is browner overall and is generally active during the day.

DID YOU KNOW?

Northern Flying Squirrels are often just as common in an area as the well-known tree squirrels, but they are nocturnal and therefore rarely seen. Flying squirrels routinely visit bird feeders at night; they value the seeds as much as sparrows and finches do.

Mountain Beaver

Aplodontia rufa

From an evolutionary standpoint, the Mountain Beaver is considered to be the oldest living rodent. Unlike other rodents, the Mountain Beaver depends on the availability of ferns in its environment. Although ferns are toxic to most other rodents, they are the primary food for this creature, hinting at its ancient origin.

The Mountain Beaver's cheek teeth are also unlike those of most other rodents: they have a single central lobe of dentine surrounded by a ridge of enamel. Other rodents have teeth that show complex folding with a proliferation of enamel. When digging a burrow, a Mountain Beaver may come across stones and lumps of clay 3–4 in. across. It keeps these stones in its burrow and occasionally gnaws upon them to sharpen its teeth. These "Mountain Beaver baseballs" are also used to block the entrances of vacated burrows.

Mountain Beavers can climb sapling trees as high as 13 ft., allowing them to eat the tender shoots. They can also swim for short distances. When foraging, they collect leafy branches and other vegetation and carry the spoils to their burrows. There they sit on their short tails, grasp the vegetation in their forepaws and use their semi-opposable thumbs.

Like a lagomorph, this rodent reingests its soft fecal pellets, allowing better absorption of nutrients the second time through the action of bacteria. Hard fecal pellets, the result of the reingested soft pellets, are seized with the incisors and thrown into a burrow latrine.

ALSO CALLED: Sewellel, Boomer, Aplodontia.

DESCRIPTION: At first glance, the Mountain Beaver looks similar to a muskrat or giant pocket gopher, except that it has a very short, well-furred tail. Its stocky body is covered with coarse, reddish-brown or grayish-brown fur. It has light grayish-brown or tawny undersides. The short, strong limbs each have five toes, and the forelimbs are equipped with long, laterally compressed, cream-colored claws. The soles of the feet are naked to the heel. There is a light spot below each of the short, round ears, and the white whiskers are abundant.

HABITAT: The Mountain Beaver occupies wooded areas from near sea level to treeline. It favors early seral vegetative stages with an abundance of shrubs, forbs and young trees. The highest densities of these animals appear to be in deciduous

RANGE: The Mountain Beaver is a western North American species that ranges from the Nicola Valley in British Columbia to southeast of San Francisco near the Nevada-California border in the Sierra Nevada.

Total length: 1–1$\frac{1}{2}$ ft.
Tail length: $\frac{3}{4}$–2 in.
Weight: $\frac{5}{8}$–3 lb.

forests of mountain parks; few occupy dense, old coniferous forests.

FOOD: These animals consume a wide variety of plants, but sword fern and bracken fern form the bulk of the diet during all seasons. Bracken fern is poisonous to most herbivores, but the Mountain Beaver is unharmed by it. In October, when the protein content of red alder leaves is highest, up to three-quarters of a male's diet may be composed of these leaves. The Mountain Beaver may also feed on seedlings and the cambium of saplings.

DEN: The Mountain Beaver constructs an extensive burrow system consisting of tunnels 5–7 in. high by 6–10 in. wide radiating out from nest chambers. Numerous burrows penetrate to the surface, but only a few have dirt piles around the opening. The nest chambers, about 1 ft. in diameter, contain dried leaves and grasses trampled into a flat pad. Generally, the nest is 1–5 ft. beneath the surface, but burrows may penetrate up to 10 ft. below ground. Pockets in the walls of some larger burrows may contain roots, stems and leaves. Sometimes tent-like structures of sticks, leaves and succulent vegetation are found over burrow entrances.

YOUNG: After a gestation of 28 to 30 days, the young are born in March or April in the subterranean nest. Each of the one to four altricial young weighs about $\frac{7}{8}$ oz. Their eyes open at 45 to 54 days, and they then begin to eat vegetation and grow exponentially. Neither sex becomes sexually mature until the second winter.

SIMILAR SPECIES: The **Yellow-bellied Marmot** (p. 252) has a longer, bushy tail and distinct orangish coloration. The **Common Muskrat** (p. 204) has a long, naked, scaly tail and is always associated with water.

DID YOU KNOW?

In cold regions, the Mountain Beaver is rarely seen in winter, but it does not hibernate. It stays underground, awake in its warm, moist den where it feeds on stored vegetation.

RABBITS, HARES & PIKAS

These rodent-like mammals are often called lagomorphs after the scientific name of the order, Lagomorpha, which means "hare-shaped." Rabbits, hares and pikas share the characteristic chisel-like upper incisors of rodents, and taxonomists once grouped lagomorphs and rodents together. Unlike rodents, however, lagomorphs have a second tiny pair of upper incisors. Casual observers never see these peg-like teeth, which lie immediately behind the first upper incisor pair.

Lagomorphs are strict vegetarians, but they have relatively inefficient, non-ruminant stomachs that have trouble digesting such a diet. To make the most of their meals, they defecate pellets of soft, green, partially digested material that they then reingest to obtain maximum nutrition. Bacteria that enter the food in the intestines contribute to better digestion and absorption of nutrients the second time around.

**White-tailed Jackrabbit
Summer Coat**

**White-tailed Jackrabbit
Winter Coat**

Rabbit & Hare Family (Leporidae)

Rabbits and hares are characterized by their long, upright ears, long jumping hindlegs and short, cottony tails. These timid animals are primarily nocturnal. Rabbits build a maternity nest for their young, which are blind, naked and altricial at birth. Hares (and some rabbits) spend most of the day resting in shallow depressions, called "forms." Unlike rabbits, hares are precocial at birth, meaning they are born fully furred with open eyes, and soon after birth they begin to feed on vegetation.

Desert Cottontail

Pika Family (Ochotonidae)

American Pika

Pikas are the most rodent-like lagomorphs, and with their short, rounded ears and squat bodies, they look similar to small guinea pigs. Their front and rear limbs are about the same length, so pikas do not hop like rabbits and hares. They scurry and make small bounds through the rocks and talus of their home territories. Pikas are most active during the day, and they are often seen in rocky alpine areas.

Pygmy Rabbit
Brachylagus idahoensis

Total Length: 10–12 in.
Tail Length: 1³/₁₆–1¹/₄ in.
Weight: 10–15 oz.

A small, white spot is on the side of each nostril. The small tail is entirely gray.

Unlike all other native rabbits, the Pygmy Rabbit excavates its own burrow in the hard soil of sagebrush flats. This rabbit is considered a keystone species for this habitat type, meaning that it is unable to thrive anywhere else, and many other species in the habitat depend on its presence. This rabbit's burrows become home to many species of invertebrates and some vertebrates, and the rabbit itself is reliable prey for predators in the sagebrush community. When you are walking through waist-high sagebrush within this rabbit's range, you might stir up the occasional Pygmy Rabbit that will dart quickly away from you.

DESCRIPTION: This rabbit is tiny and colored tawny or cinnamon. Sometimes the coat is dark gray to nearly black.

HABITAT: The Pygmy Rabbit is always found in association with dense stands of sage or rabbitbrush. It favors desert or semi-desert conditions, wherever it can find earth soft enough for digging.

FOOD: The bitter leaves of the sagebrush make up the bulk of the diet. When available, grasses and other succulent vegetation are eaten.

DEN: This small rabbit digs burrows that are about 3 in. in diameter. There are at least two entrances, usually beneath large, dense sagebrush plants. A shallow trench typically radiates out from each entrance, and the rabbit often crouches in the trench so only its ears and eyes are visible.

YOUNG: Pygmy Rabbits mate in spring or early summer. After a gestation of 27 to 30 days, a litter of six naked, blind young are born between March and early August.

SIMILAR SPECIES: The Pygmy Rabbit is so small that it could only be mistaken as a juvenile of a different species of rabbit. The only rabbit occupying the same range is the **Mountain Cottontail** (p. 276), but it is larger and paler and has longer ears.

RANGE: The Pygmy Rabbit is primarily a Great Basin animal that ranges between the Rocky Mountains and the Cascade Mountains in Montana, Idaho, Utah, Nevada, California and Oregon.

Brush Rabbit

Sylvilagus bachmani

Total Length: 11–15 in.
Tail Length: 3/4–1 5/8 in.
Weight: 1–2 lb.

The Brush Rabbits of the Pacific coast are good examples of Allen's Rule, which states that animals of the same species in warmer regions tend to have longer appendages and larger external features. Brush Rabbits living in the hot areas of lower California have much longer ears than those living in northern California and Oregon. Allen's Rule suggests this elongation is a method of cooling, because the ears are thin and contain many blood vessels. Another explanation, however, is that sound travels poorly in hot, dry air, so larger ears may also be an adaptation for better hearing.

DESCRIPTION: This small rabbit ranges in color from tawny brown to reddish brown, and it is often flecked throughout with dark gray base hairs. The undersides are lighter than the back, but are not white. In winter, the coat color is slightly lighter than the summer coat. The whiskers are black, and the ears are just over 2 in. long. Their rounded tails are mainly white.

HABITAT: True to their name, the Brush Rabbits favor open to heavy brush cover and shrubby areas.

DEN: These rabbits sleep in forms and raise young in fur-lined forms. When the mother leaves her nesting form, she covers it with a layer of grass.

FOOD: Throughout the summer, Brush Rabbits feed on grasses, clover and berries. In winter or in periods of drought, woody vegetation is eaten.

YOUNG: These rabbits can have up to five litters per year, from February to August. Gestation is 27–30 days, and litter size averages three or four young.

SIMILAR SPECIES: The **Desert Cottontail** (p.278) occupies part of the same range, but it is smaller and has shorter ears and a gray tail.

RANGE: This rabbit can be found in western Oregon and down the West Coast to Baja California.

Mountain Cottontail
Sylvilagus nuttallii

During the early evening, Mountain Cottontails emerge from their daytime hideouts to graze on succulent vegetation. If you are a patient observer, you may see them as they daintily nip at grasses, always just a short leap from dense bushes or a rocky shelter.

The prime habitat for Mountain Cottontails is neither fully wooded areas nor completely open flats. They require good protective cover to hide from predators, but in areas where foliage is too dense they are handicapped in their ability to detect an approaching predator. They are preyed upon heavily by Bobcats, Coyotes, owls and hawks.

Mountain Cottontails spend most of their days sitting quietly in dug-out depressions, called "forms," beneath impenetrable vegetation or under boards, rocks, abandoned machinery or buildings. These mid-sized herbivores have small home ranges that rarely exceed the size of a baseball field. Heavy rains greatly diminish cottontail activity, restricting them to their hideouts for the duration of the storm. Mountain Cottontails do not hibernate during winter, but their activity is somewhat reduced, and in regions of snow they follow regular trails that are easy to locate.

The scientific name of the Mountain Cottontail refers to Thomas Nuttall, an explorer in the early 1800s. Although Nuttall was primarily a botanist, he made significant contributions to all fields of natural history. He was also renowned for his absent-mindedness and misadventures. During his journey across the continent to the Pacific Ocean on the Wyeth expedition in 1834, he got lost on many occasions. This misguided explorer, however, identified many new species of plants and animals despite his frequent gaffes along the way.

ALSO CALLED: Nuttall's Cottontail.

DESCRIPTION: This rabbit has dark, grizzled, yellowish-gray upperparts and whitish underparts year-round. The tail is blackish above and white below. A rusty-orange patch is on the nape of the neck, and the front and back edges of the ears are white. The ears are usually held erect when the rabbit runs.

HABITAT: A major habitat requirement is cover, whether it is brush, rocky outcroppings or buildings. These rabbits like edge situations where trees meet meadows or where brushy areas meet agricultural land.

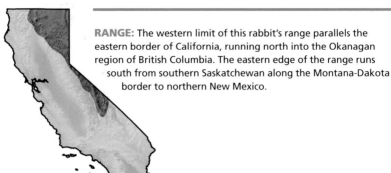

RANGE: The western limit of this rabbit's range parallels the eastern border of California, running north into the Okanagan region of British Columbia. The eastern edge of the range runs south from southern Saskatchewan along the Montana-Dakota border to northern New Mexico.

Total Length: 13–16 in.
Tail Length: 1¼–2½ in.
Weight: 1½–2¼ lb.

FOOD: Grasses and forbs are the primary foods, but in many areas these cottontails feed heavily on sagebrush and juniper berries.

DEN: Mountain Cottontails live in shallow burrows and rock crevices, and often they rest in forms beneath dense vegetation. The young are born in a nest that is dug out by the female and lined with grass and fur. The doe arrives at the nest and lies over the top while the young nurse. The nest is essentially invisible, and a casual observer would never suspect that the female was nursing, or that a nest of babies lay beneath her.

YOUNG: Breeding begins in April, and after a 28- to 30-day gestation, a litter of one to eight (usually four or five) young is born. The female is in estrus and breeds within hours of giving birth, so there can be two or more litters a season. The young are born blind, hairless and with their eyes closed. They grow quickly and are weaned just before the birth of the subsequent litter.

SIMILAR SPECIES: The **Desert Cottontail** (p. 278) has sparsely haired ears, and it lacks the rusty-orange patch on the nape of the neck. Both the **Snowshoe Hare** (p. 280) and the **White-tailed Jackrabbit** (p. 284) are larger and become white in winter. The **Pygmy Rabbit** (p. 274) is smaller and darker and has smaller ears. The **European Rabbit** (p. 285) is usually larger and may have a multicolored coat.

DID YOU KNOW?

Rabbits and hares depend on intestinal bacteria to break down the cellulose in their diets. Because the bacterial products reenter the gut beyond the site of absorption, rabbits eat their pellets to run the material through the digestive tract a second time.

Desert Cottontail
Sylvilagus audubonii

Old age is unknown to the Desert Cottontail. As an animal that lives near the bottom of the food web, each turn in life holds extreme risk. This cottontail produces high numbers of offspring to counter the high rates of predation. At the age of two, healthy females can have up to four litters in the season—a necessity, because few, if any, reach the age of three.

During summer, Desert Cottontails are most active between sunset and sunrise. Foraging in low light conditions probably gives the rabbits some measure of protection against predators. In winter, the rabbits reverse their habits and become more active during the day. When pursued, they tend to dodge and zig-zag at high speeds until they finally reach shelter.

Desert Cottontails are quite unlike most other kinds of rabbits, which tend to rest during the day in worn beds. Instead, Desert Cottontails use the abandoned burrows of ground squirrels, prairie-dogs and even badgers as sites to hole-up during the day or during inclement weather. Despite their affinity for underground resting sites, these rabbits have been known to climb up into fallen and leaning trees to better view their surroundings.

Although these characteristics were largely unknown when this rabbit was initially described, the tribute of its scientific name to John James Audubon is most appropriate. Audubon is primarily known as an expert on birds, but he also made significant contributions to some of the first descriptive treatments of American mammals. Audubon, like the Desert Cottontail, was an independent spirit and did things his own way, including climbing up trees to get a better look at the world.

DESCRIPTION: The Desert Cottontail is a rusty grayish brown above. The sides are paler than the back and may have a yellowish wash. The throat and upper forelegs are rusty. The belly is white. The tail is dark above and white below. Its ears have sparse hairs on the inside.

HABITAT: This rabbit favors sagebrush-covered slopes, especially those with fractured rock outcrops and brushy streamside areas.

FOOD: This rabbit eats succulent tips of grasses, forbs and some sagebrush. It eats more brushy material in winter.

DEN: This cottontail may shelter in prairie-dog burrows, among shattered rocks, beneath buildings or in scrap lumber piles, but the young are often

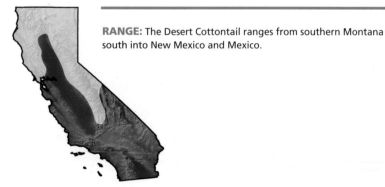

RANGE: The Desert Cottontail ranges from southern Montana south into New Mexico and Mexico.

Total Length: 15–18 in.
Tail Length: 1½–2⅜ in.
Weight: 2–2½ lb.

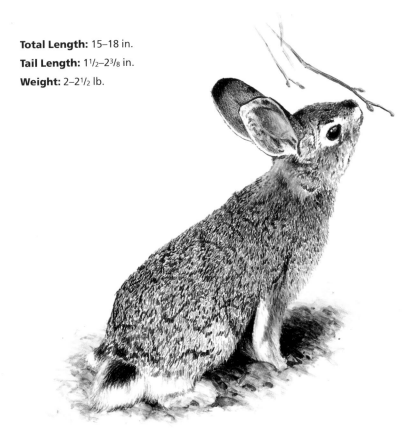

born into a pear-shaped nest dug by the mother and lined with grass and fur.

YOUNG: After a 28- to 30-day gestation period, the first litter is born in May. Two to four litters in a season are possible because the female mates again within hours of giving birth. The blind, naked young grow rapidly. Their eyes open in 10 days, and the young leave the nest when they are just two weeks old. The newly emerged young are attractive with their large eyes, long ears and tiny, "powder-puff" tails. Unfortunately for them, night-hunting owls consider them a tasty meal. Spring-born females may have a litter during their first summer, but they are not full grown until they are six to nine months old.

SIMILAR SPECIES: The **Mountain Cottontail** (p. 276) has hairier ears with white edges and a rusty-orange patch on the nape of the neck. The **Pygmy Rabbit** (p. 274) is much smaller. The **Snowshoe Hare** (p. 280) turns white in winter.

DID YOU KNOW?

Unlike other rabbits, the Desert Cottontail has special adaptations for life in arid environments. In particular, its kidneys are designed to retain more water and concentrate salts to reduce water loss in the urine.

Snowshoe Hare
Lepus americanus

The Snowshoe Hare is able to withstand the most unforgiving aspects of mountain wilderness because it possesses several fascinating adaptations for winter. As its name implies, the Snowshoe Hare has very large, furry hindfeet and can easily walk on areas of soft snow, whereas other animals sink into the powder. This ability is a tremendous advantage for an animal that is preyed upon by so many different species of carnivores.

It is well known that populations of hares fluctuate in close correlation with predator cycles, but few people realize that other species are involved in the cycle. Recent studies have shown that as hares increase in numbers, they overgraze willow and alder in their habitat. These plants are their major source of food during the winter months. In response to overgrazing, willow and alder shoots produce a distasteful and toxic substance that is related to turpentine. This substance protects the plants and initiates starvation in the hares. As the hares decline, so do the predators. Once the plants recover their growth after a season or two, their shoots become edible again and the hare population increases.

In response to shortening day lengths at the onset of winter, Snowshoe Hares in most of their range start molting into their white winter camouflage, whether snow falls or not. The hares have no control over the timing of this transformation, and if the year's first snowfall is late, some individuals will lose their usual concealment, becoming visible from great distances—to naturalists and predators alike—as bright white balls in a brown world. The hares seem to be aware of this predicament, and they often seek out any small patch of snow on which to squat. In some areas, these hares do not turn white in winter, an adaptation to the lack of significant snowfall.

DESCRIPTION: The summer coat is rusty brown above, with the crown of the head darker and less reddish than the back. The nape of the neck and top of the tail are grayish brown, and the ear tips are black. The chin, belly and lower surface of the tail are white. Adults have white feet; juveniles have dark feet. In winter (in areas where the hares turn color), the terminal portion of nearly all the body hair becomes white, but the hair bases and underfur are lead gray to brownish. The ear tips remain black.

HABITAT: Snowshoe Hares may be found throughout most of the Cascades

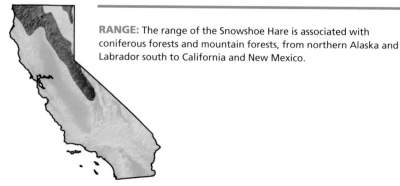

RANGE: The range of the Snowshoe Hare is associated with coniferous forests and mountain forests, from northern Alaska and Labrador south to California and New Mexico.

Total Length: 15–21 in.
Tail Length: 1⁷/₈–2¹/₈ in.
Weight: 2¹/₄–3¹/₄ lb.

and Sierra Nevada, almost anywhere there is forest or dense shrub. Despite their name, they may even live in areas lacking winter snow.

FOOD: In summer, a wide variety of grasses, forbs and brush may be consumed. In winter, mostly the buds, twigs and bark of willow and alder are eaten. Hares occasionally eat carrion.

DEN: Snowshoe Hares do not keep a customary den, but they sometimes enter hollow logs or the burrows of other animals, or run beneath buildings.

YOUNG: Breeding activity can occur from mid-February to July. After a gestation of 35 to 37 days, one to seven (usually three or four) young are born under cover, but often not in an established form or nest. The female breeds again within hours of the birth, and she may have as many as three litters in a season. The young hares are precocial and can hop within a day; they feed on grassy vegetation within 10 days. In five months, they are fully grown.

SIMILAR SPECIES: The larger **White-tailed Jackrabbit** (p. 284) has longer ears and a slightly longer tail, and its winter underfur is creamy white. The larger **Black-tailed Jackrabbit** (p. 282) has longer ears, and it does not turn white in winter. The **cottontails** (p. 276–79) are generally smaller and do not turn white in winter.

DID YOU KNOW?

When alarmed, this hare may drum its hindfeet on the ground, a characteristic that might have given rise to the character "Thumper" in Disney's *Bambi*.

Black-tailed Jackrabbit
Lepus californicus

Despite having a partially black tail, this hare's most prominent feature is its ears. Black-tipped ears that extend far above this hare's head are a characteristic that, more than any other, identifies this open-country mammal. In fact, when fully opened, the ears may account for about 19 percent of the hare's total body surface. The three hares of California demonstrate a relationship between the size of their ears and the latitude in which they live (on a North American scale): the Black-tailed Jackrabbit, the most southerly hare, has the longest ears; the White-tailed Jackrabbit has intermediate ears; and the most northerly Snowshoe Hare has the shortest ears. Huge ears, such as those of the Black-tailed Jackrabbit, help cool this hare, which occupies hot, arid areas. At the other extreme, the Snowshoe Hare's smaller ears prevent precious energy from escaping during cold winters. Ear size may also contribute to hearing ability—sound moves better through cold air than it does through warm air. Hares that live in warmer climates have evolved larger ears; perhaps they are better equipped for hearing approaching predators.

Coyotes are the major predators of the Black-tailed Jackrabbit, and in some areas the density of Coyotes correlates with Black-tailed Jackrabbit numbers. In turn, the Black-tailed Jackrabbit densities are directly proportional to summer precipitation.

During the day Black-tailed Jackrabbits lie quietly in a form scraped out beneath a sagebrush bush or beside some other type of cover. These hares lie quietly and motionless, depending upon their camouflage for protection. With the approach of a predator, however, jackrabbits rocket from their shelter and quickly attain speeds of up to 35 m.p.h. They attempt to elude danger by changing direction abruptly and using leaps up to 6 ft. high and 20 ft. long.

DESCRIPTION: This gray to grayish-brown hare has extremely large, long, black-tipped ears. The belly is white to buffy white. A black mid-dorsal stripe on the tail runs up onto the back. These hares never turn white in winter, and there is only one annual molt.

HABITAT: The Black-tailed Jackrabbit occupies nearly all habitats within its range except high mountain forests. It prefers valley bottoms or irrigated fields in intermontane valleys, and it can be found on barren ridges devoid of trees.

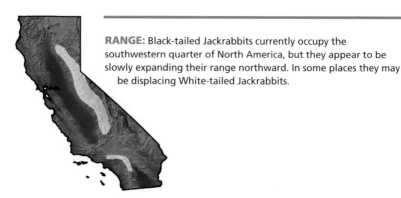

RANGE: Black-tailed Jackrabbits currently occupy the southwestern quarter of North America, but they appear to be slowly expanding their range northward. In some places they may be displacing White-tailed Jackrabbits.

Total Length: 20–24 in.

Tail Length: 2³/₄–3³/₄ in.

Weight: 5–10 lb.

FOOD: These jackrabbits feed on a wide variety of both herbaceous and woody vegetation, with a larger proportion of shrubby material being consumed in winter. Studies have revealed that 30 Black-tailed Jackrabbits eat about as much as a cow. They may have peculiar eating habits: one plant may be eaten in its entirety, while neighboring plants of the same species are ignored.

DEN: There is no den, but the hare spends most of the day crouched in a form it scratches out of the ground.

YOUNG: After a gestation of 41 to 47 days, a litter of one to eight (usually two to four) young is born. The newborns are fully furred and have their eyes open. Instead of staying in a common nest, they are distributed more than 300 ft. apart, and the female nurses each one separately throughout the night. The young are weaned at six to seven weeks. At 10 weeks they are 90 percent of their adult size. Within hours after birth, the female

becomes attractive to a male, but she flees at his approach. A vigorous chase ensues that may cover a few miles. Ultimately, the male seizes the female by the nape of her neck and mates with her. Adult females may have up to four litters in a season, and young females from early litters may mature fast enough to have their own litters late in the season.

SIMILAR SPECIES: The **White-tailed Jackrabbit** (p. 284) has slightly shorter ears, turns white in winter and has a grayish upper surface on its tail. The **Snowshoe Hare** (p. 280) has shorter ears and turns white in winter.

DID YOU KNOW?

The name "jackrabbit" is a shortened (and more refined) version of "jackass rabbit." These mammals were so-named in recognition of their large, donkey-like ears.

White-tailed Jackrabbit
Lepus townsendii

Total Length: 21–25 in.
Tail Length: 2³/₄–4¹/₄ in.
Weight: 6¹/₂–12 lb.

The White-tailed Jackrabbit is a lean sprinter and the largest hare in California, but it can only be found in northeastern parts of the state. A creature of open country, the White-tailed Jackrabbit may be encountered either by day as it bursts from a hiding place with ears erect and tail extended, bounding out of danger with ease, or at night in the flash of car headlights.

Like most herbivores, the White-tailed Jackrabbit is drawn to salt, which, unfortunately, is found in great abundance on roads. Its need for salt, together with this rabbit's preference for traveling on solid surfaces, results in high numbers of roadway deaths each year.

ALSO CALLED: Prairie Hare.

DESCRIPTION: In summer, the upperparts of this large hare are light grayish brown and the belly is nearly white. By mid-November, the entire coat is white, except for the grayish forehead and muzzle and black ear tips. It has a fairly long, white tail that sometimes bears a grayish band on the upper surface.

HABITAT: This hare prefers open areas. It will enter open woodlands to seek shelter in winter, but it avoids forested areas.

FOOD: Grasses and forbs make up most of the rabbit's diet.

DEN: There is no true den, but a shallow form beside a rock or beneath sagebrush serves as a daytime shelter. In winter, jackrabbits may dig depressions or short burrows as shelters in regions of snow.

YOUNG: One to nine (usually three or four) young are born in a form after a 40-day gestation. The fully furred newborns have open eyes and soon disperse, meeting their mother to nurse only once or twice a day. By two weeks old they eat some vegetation; at five to six weeks they are weaned, often just before the birth of the next litter.

SIMILAR SPECIES: The more widespread **Black-tailed Jackrabbit** (p. 282) has longer ears and does not turn white in winter. In winter, the **Snowshoe Hare** (p. 280) has lead gray, not creamy white, hair bases. The **cottontails** (pp. 276–79) are much smaller with shorter legs.

RANGE: The White-tailed Jackrabbit seems to be expanding its range northward. It is currently found from eastern Washington east to southern Manitoba and south to east-central California and eastern Kansas.

European Rabbit
Oryctolagus cuniculus

Total length: 18–24 in.
Tail length: 2⁵/₈–3¹/₂ in.
Weight: 3–5 lb.

Symbolically, rabbits are associated with reproduction, hence the phrase "breeds like a rabbit." For Easter celebrations, rabbits are popular images that represent new life, renewal and fertility.

Because European Rabbits have high reproductive rates and are highly adaptable, they thrive almost everywhere they have been introduced. The Hudson's Bay Company, as well as many settlers, raised European Rabbits and introduced them into the wild in several western states. The idea was to populate common hunting areas with a rapidly reproducing game rabbit larger than the cottontail.

ALSO CALLED: Belgian Hare, Domestic Rabbit, San Juan Rabbit.

DESCRIPTION: This rabbit's coloration is highly variable, in an array of grays and browns as well as black and white. Some individuals have multicolored coats, owing to their ancestry as a favorite pet animal that was bred for color variation.

HABITAT: This Old World rabbit generally avoids heavily wooded areas in favor of open fields, brushy areas and parkland.

FOOD: European Rabbits feed on short grasses and leafy herbaceous plants. When such plants are not available, they will consume any available vegetation. These rabbits threaten both native plant species and the animals that depend on them.

DEN: Although these rabbits may be found singly, they often live in large colonies and dig extensive burrows. Nests are made of grass and other soft fibers and are built in special chambers of the burrow system.

YOUNG: Each year a female European Rabbit can have as many as six litters, with up to 12 young in each litter. The young are altricial, but they grow rapidly. Predation on juvenile rabbits is high.

SIMILAR SPECIES: Cottontail rabbits (pp. 276–79) are usually smaller than the European Rabbit, and **hares** have distinctly longer ears. Any rabbit with unusual coloration is a European Rabbit.

RANGE: These rabbits occur in scattered populations in much of the U.S. and parts of Canada. Some are the result of escaped pets.

American Pika
Ochotona princeps

Inhabiting an intricate landscape of boulders high in the mountains, the American Pika is often regarded as one of the cutest animals in the alpine wilderness. This relative of the rabbit scurries among the rocks of a talus slope as it makes its way between feeding areas and shelter. When it returns from gathering food, an American Pika carries vegetation clippings crossways in its mouth—a bundle sometimes half as large as the pika itself. Large piles of clippings are accumulated on or under the rocks in a pika's territory and will feed the pika during winter.

Pikas are extremely vocal animals that are often heard before they are seen. The proper pronunciation of their name is *pee-ka,* which mimics their high-pitched voices: they emit bleats reminiscent of a tricycle horn whenever they see something out of the ordinary. These sounds are often the best clues of their presence, because pikas are difficult to distinguish in their boulder-strewn habitat; when a pika is momentarily glimpsed from afar, one is never quite sure whether it is a genuine sighting or just a pika-sized rock. To the patient naturalist intent on pika observations, however, viewing can be intimate and rewarding, because these animals often permit a close approach. When you see a pika escape into a crevice beneath the rocks, sit quietly and wait—soon it will come out again, seemingly oblivious to your unobtrusive presence.

In winter, pikas dig snow tunnels as far as 100 yd. out from their rock shelters to collect and eat plants. The talus slopes that are their homes often receive great quantities of snow, which helps insulate the animals from the mountain winters. Rarely venturing into the chill of the open air, pikas tend to remain beneath the snow, feeding upon the grass they so meticulously gathered and dried earlier in the year.

DESCRIPTION: This gray to tawny-colored, chunky, soft-looking mammal has large, rounded ears and beady black eyes. The whiskers are long. There is no external tail. The front and rear legs are nearly equal in length, so pikas scamper or make four-footed leaps.

HABITAT: Pikas generally occupy talus slopes in the mountains, although they have occasionally been spotted among the jumbled logs swept down by avalanches.

FOOD: The pika diet includes a wide variety of plants that are found in the vicinity of this animal's rocky shelter.

RANGE: Pikas occur from the mountains of west-central Alberta and southern British Columbia south to California, Utah and northern New Mexico.

Total Length: 6³/₈–8¹/₂ in.

Tail Length: There is no visible tail.

Weight: 4¹/₄–6¹/₄ oz.

Broad-leaved plants, grasses and sedges are all clipped and consumed.

DEN: Pikas build grass-lined nests, in which the young are born, beneath the rocks of their home.

YOUNG: Mating occurs in spring, and after a 30-day gestation, a litter of two to five (usually three) young is born. The newborns are furry, weigh ¹/₄–⁵/₁₆ oz. and have closed eyes, which open after 10 days. The young are weaned when they are 30 days old and two-thirds grown. Pikas are sexually mature after the first winter. There is sometimes a second summer breeding period.

SIMILAR SPECIES: The only other gray mammal of comparable size that might occupy the same rocky slopes as the American Pika is the **Bushy-tailed Woodrat** (p. 186), but this woodrat has a long, bushy tail.

DID YOU KNOW?

Pikas have high-frequency calls that "bounce" readily, so although they are often heard, they can be difficult to locate. This characteristic is advantageous to a pika because it can warn other pikas about a potential predator without revealing its whereabouts.

BATS

Only three groups of vertebrates have achieved self-powered flight: bats, birds and the now-extinct reptilian pterosaurs. In an evolutionary sense, bats are a very successful group of mammals. Worldwide, about 20 percent of all mammalian species are bats, and they are second only to rodents in both diversity of species and number of individuals. Unfortunately, across North America, populations of several bat species appear to be declining, and some have been placed on rare and endangered species lists.

Unlike the feathered wing of a bird, a bat's wing consists of double layers of skin stretched across the modified bones of the fingers and back to the legs. On the hand, only the thumb is free. A small bone, the calcar, juts backward from the foot to help support the tail membrane, which stretches between the tail and each leg. The calcar is said to be keeled when there is a small projection of skin from its side.

Bats generate lift by pushing their wings against the air's resistance, so they tend to have large wing surface areas for their body size. This method of flight is less efficient than the airfoil lift provided by bird or airplane wings, but it allows bats to fly slower and gives them more maneuverability. Slower flight is a real advantage when trying to catch insects or when hovering in front of a flower.

All bats have good vision, but their nocturnal habits have led to an increased dependence on their sense of hearing—most people are acquainted with the ability of many bat species to navigate or capture prey in the dark using echolocation. The tragus, a slender lobe that projects from the inner base of many bats' ears, is thought to help in determining an echo's direction.

No other mammals in California are as misunderstood as bats. They are thought to be mysterious creatures of the night, souls of the dead and blind, rabid creatures that commonly become tangled in people's hair. In truth, bats are extremely beneficial creatures whose considerable collective hunger for night-flying insects results in fewer agricultural pests.

Big Free-tailed Bat

Free-tailed Bat Family (Molossidae)

The free-tailed bats are so named because they have tails that extend beyond the edge of the membrane that stretches between their hindlegs. Most free-tailed bats occur in warm tropical parts of the world, but four species are recorded in California. Free-tailed bats are sometimes called mastiff bats, because their snub noses and wrinkled faces resemble those of mastiff dogs.

Evening Bat Family (Vespertilionidae)

The majority of the bats that occur in California belong to the evening bat family. True to their name, most members of this family are active in the evening, and often again before dawn, when they typically feed on flying insects. A few species migrate to warmer regions for winter, but most hibernate in caves or abandoned buildings and mines.

Spotted Bat

New World Leaf-nosed Bat Family (Phyllostomidae)

The aptly named leaf-nosed bats have an unusual, leaf-like projection on the tip of their snouts that is frequently referred to as the "noseleaf." Members of this family vary greatly in form and behavior. Some are specialists of feeding on fruits, while others may specialize in feeding on pollen, insects or nectar. Two species of leaf-nosed bats occur in California.

California Leaf-nosed Bat

Brazilian Free-tailed Bat
Tadarida brasiliensis

Total Length: 3½–4½ in.
Tail Length: 1¼–1¾ in.
Forearm: 1½–1¾ in.
Weight: ⁵/₁₆–⁷/₁₆ oz.

More than other bats, Brazilian Free-tailed Bats display the massiveness of their populations as they vacate their roosts for the moth-laden night skies. In the Carlsbad Caverns of New Mexico, for instance, the collective wingbeats of millions of free-tailed bats leaving their daytime roosts sound like the roar of a whitewater river, and the rising column can be seen at great distances. Colonies in California do not reach the tremendous numbers that are seen elsewhere, but they are still fairly common and often assemble in large numbers. In California, these bats are nonmigratory and hibernate in small colonies for the winter.

ALSO CALLED: Guano Bat.

DESCRIPTION: This bat is the smallest free-tailed bat and it is dark brown to grayish on the back and lighter on the underside. The ears are separated at the base. The upper lip is wrinkled. There is very little membrane connecting the hindlegs and tail, thus the name "free-tailed."

HABITAT: In northern areas of their range in western U.S., these bats are mostly found in pinyon-juniper woodlands.

FOOD: These bats forage primarily on such night-flying insects as beetles, ants and especially moths.

DEN: Individuals are known to roost in buildings, crevices, tunnels, mines and caves in California. Large populations can carpet the walls and ceilings of caves and mines, and nursery colonies can have as many as 1500 pups per square foot.

YOUNG: Females ovulate for a short period of time in March, and mating is spread out over a five-week overlapping period. One or two young are born in June. At birth, the young are two-thirds the length of their mothers; within three weeks they equal her in mass.

RANGE: The small Brazilian Free-tailed Bat is one of the most wide-ranging mammals in North and South America. In North America, it occurs from Oregon to North Carolina and south through Mexico.

SIMILAR SPECIES: The **Pocketed Free-tailed Bat** (p. 291) has ears that are joined at the base. The other free-tailed bats in California are larger.

Pocketed Free-tailed Bat
Nyctinomops femorosaccus

Total Length: 3⁷/₈–4⁵/₈ in.
Tail Length: 1¹/₈–1⁵/₈ in.
Forearm: 1⁴/₅ in.
Weight: ¹/₈–⁵/₈ oz.

This small free-tailed bat is a rapid flyer that emerges a couple of hours after sunset. Given that it prefers to forage in the dark, it is rare to see one. However, this species is quite vocal, and its clicks and chirps can be heard by humans (many other bats use sounds that are beyond our hearing range). As it drops into flight from its roost, it emits a very loud and high-pitched call. The name "Pocketed" refers to a small pocket or fold of the skin membrane in the vicinity of its knee.

DESCRIPTION: This bat is the second smallest free-tailed bat. It is mainly dark gray or brown above and below. Sometimes reddish highlights are over the back, and often the undersides are slightly paler than the back. The hairs all have light or nearly white bases. Its tail is free for about half of its overall length. There are deep vertical grooves along its upper lip, and its large ears are joined at the base at the top of its head.

HABITAT: This bat is specialized for arid environments and does well in the southern desert areas of California. Nevertheless, it does require drinking water, especially in dry seasons, and it stays in the vicinity of water that has a large enough surface for it to drink from on the wing.

FOOD: Insects, especially moths, but also bees, flies, true bugs and beetles, make up the diet.

DEN: This bat lives in small colonies of up to 100 individuals. Colonies can be located in a cave, rock crevice or human-made structure.

YOUNG: In early July, a single young is born. Gestation for this species is not known. Females have only one off-spring per year. By mid- to late August the young are flying, but weaning may not occur until as late as September.

SIMILAR SPECIES: The **Brazilian Free-tailed Bat** (p. 290) has ears that are not joined at the base. The other free-tailed bats in California are larger.

RANGE: This bat is found in southern California and southern Arizona and into Mexico. Two disjunct populations are known, in the Big Bend region of Texas and in southeastern New Mexico.

Big Free-tailed Bat
Nyctinomops macrotis

Total Length: 5¹/₈–5⁵/₈ in.
Tail Length: 1³/₄–2¹/₈ in.
Forearm: 2¹/₄–2¹/₂ in.
Weight: 1¹/₄–1¹/₂ oz.

The Big Free-tailed Bat is a giant among Californian bats, but even at that, it is little larger than a sparrow. The size of this bat's wings is what gives it the illusion of being larger. Unlike birds, bats have large heads (with teeth), solid bones, heavy limbs and fleshy tails, all of which add to the total body weight and necessitate relatively large wings to get the bats into flight. The large wings also enable bats to fly at slower speeds and with far more maneuverability than birds—a great advantage when catching slow-flying insects.

DESCRIPTION: This large bat has a wingspan of about 18 in. Its fur is reddish brown to black, but the base of each hair is white. Most of the tail length (about 1 in.) is free of the membrane joining the hindlegs. The ears are jointed at the base, and they are long enough to extend beyond the nose if they were pushed forward. The upper lip has deep vertical wrinkles.

HABITAT: These bats are most common in rocky areas, particularly cliffs and crevices.

FOOD: Like many nocturnal bats, they feed primarily on moths, but they will opportunistically take whatever other edible insects can be caught.

DEN: Roost sites are often in rock crevices, cliffs and caves, but they have also been found in buildings and hollow trees.

YOUNG: Only a single young is born each year, in late spring or early summer. Females separate themselves from the males into a maternal colony to give birth and for the duration of nursing.

SIMILAR SPECIES: The large **Western Mastiff Bat** (p. 293) has very large but truncate ears, and it lacks the deep wrinkles on its upper lip. The **Brazilian Free-tailed Bat** (p. 290) and **Pocketed Free-tailed Bat** (p. 291) are both smaller.

RANGE: This free-tailed bat occurs from Utah and Colorado south to southeastern California, southern Texas and Mexico.

Western Mastiff Bat
Eumops perotis

Total Length: 5¹/₂–7¹/₄ in.

Tail Length: 1³/₈–3¹/₈ in.

Forearm: 3 in.

Weight: about 2¹/₄ oz.

The unusual Western Mastiff Bat is a definite rule breaker in the free-tailed bat family. Despite being one of the mastiff bats, it does not have the heavily wrinkled muzzle that is typical of others in this family. As well, there is not a well-defined reproductive period for this species, and young can be born anywhere from April to August—even November in exceptional cases. Both sexes are found in the same roosts, unlike other species that have separate maternal colonies for females and young. Lastly, the feeding behavior of this bat is quite unique. It will feed for as long as 6¹/₂ hours at night, and it seems to be a finicky eater. Using its smooth, flexible lips, it prefers to pluck wings, heads and legs off its insect prey and consume only their tender abdomens.

DESCRIPTION: This bat is the largest bat in North America, and yet it is still a fair bit smaller than a robin. Its fur is short and sparse, and it is mainly grayish brown overall. The hairs are whitish at the base. Its large ears appear very bonnet-like and are joined at the base at the top of the head. Its upper lips lack the deep wrinkles seen on other members of this family.

HABITAT: This bat is at home in arid regions that have suitable rocky sites and cliff sites for roosting. It may occur in some semi-arid open woodlands.

FOOD: The primary insect prey is, surprisingly, bees and wasps, with moths coming in a close second. Other large insects such as cicadas, dragonflies and grasshoppers are also eaten

DEN: Western Mastiff Bats roost in rock crevices along cliffs, and they require a sizable drop from their roost in order to achieve flight.

YOUNG: Ovulation in the females is quite variable, but mating peaks in spring. Females each have one young, and gestation is estimated at 80 to 90 days.

SIMILAR SPECIES: The large **Big Free-tailed Bat** (p. 292) has large ears that protrude well past the nose if laid forward and deep vertical wrinkles on its upper lip. The **Brazilian Free-tailed Bat** (p. 290) and **Pocketed Free-tailed Bat** (p. 291) are both smaller.

RANGE: This mastiff bat is found in southern California, extreme southern Nevada, southern Arizona, extreme southwestern New Mexico, the Big Bend region of Texas, and into Mexico.

Fringed Bat
Myotis thysanodes

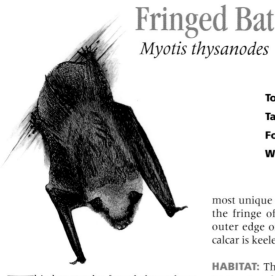

Total Length: 3³/₈–3³/₄ in.
Tail Length: 1¹/₂–1³/₄ in.
Forearm: 1⁵/₈–1³/₄ in.
Weight: ³/₁₆–⁵/₁₆ oz.

This bat can be found throughout California. Of the myotis bats, a small number belong to a group called the long-eared myotis bats, all of which have long ears and prefer high-elevation forests. The Fringed Bat is part of this group, but it has shorter ears and is found at lower elevations than the others. A conspicuous fringe of stiff hairs along the outer edge of the membrane between the hindlegs and tail is a characteristic that usually distinguishes this bat from others, although it is a useless field mark when the bat is in flight.

DESCRIPTION: This large bat, with a wingspan of up to 12 in., typically has pale brown fur that is darker on the back than on the undersides. The black-ish ears are long and would extend well past the nose if pushed forward. The most unique characteristic of this bat is the fringe of small, stiff hairs on the outer edge of the tail membrane. The calcar is keeled.

HABITAT: This bat is most frequently encountered in woodlands or grass-lands near water sources. It occurs mainly at mid-elevations, but on the coast it ventures into low-elevation forests, and there are occasional reports of high-elevation forays.

FOOD: Moths, flies, beetles, lacewings and crickets are commonly eaten by these bats. The presence of flightless insects in their diet has led to the speculation that these bats may glean some insects from foliage.

DEN: These bats roost in caves, mines and buildings. Up to several hundred Fringed Bats will cluster in maternal roosts in summer.

YOUNG: One or rarely two young are born in June or early July. The young bats reach adult size by three weeks, at which time they are capable of limited flight. Maternal colonies contain only females and the young of the year.

SIMILAR SPECIES: All the mouse-eared bats (*Myotis* spp.) are generally indistinguishable as they fly in dim light. It requires precise measurements and careful attention to detail to identify the species.

RANGE: The Fringed Bat is found from southern British Columbia through the western states and into Mexico.

Long-eared Bat
Myotis evotis

Total Length: 3¹/₄–4¹/₄ in.
Tail Length: 1³/₈–1⁷/₈ in.
Forearm: 1¹/₂–1⁵/₈ in.
Weight: ¹/₈–⁵/₁₆ oz.

The nightly dramatic bat sagas taking place in summer skies are largely unknown to humans. In apparent silence, the bats of California navigate and locate prey by producing ultrasonic pulses (up to five times higher in pitch than our ears can detect) and listening for the echoes of these sounds as they bounce off objects. In North America, bats are mainly insectivorous, and the aptly named Long-eared Bat appears to be well equipped for insect hunting.

DESCRIPTION: The wingspan of this medium-sized bat is about 11 in. The upperparts are light brown to buffy yellow. The undersides are lighter. Its black, naked ears are ³/₄–1 in. long. The tragus is long and narrow. Its wings are mainly naked, and only the lower fifth of the tail membrane is furred. The calcar is keeled.

HABITAT: This bat occurs in forested areas with old-growth features, adjacent to rocky outcrops or open habitats. It occasionally occupies buildings, mines and caves.

FOOD: Feeding peaks at dusk and just before dawn. Moths, flies and beetles are the primary prey.

DEN: Both sexes of this mainly solitary bat hibernate in caves and mines in winter. In spring, groups of up to 30 females gather in nursery colonies in tree cavities, under loose bark, in old buildings, under bridges or in loose roof shingles. Males typically roost in caves and mines in summer.

YOUNG: Mating takes place in fall, before hibernation begins, but fertilization is delayed until spring. In June or early July, after a gestation of about 40 days, a female bears one young. Twins are uncommon. The young mature quickly and are able to fly on their own in four weeks.

SIMILAR SPECIES: All the mouse-eared bats (*Myotis* spp.) are generally indistinguishable as they fly in dim light. It requires precise measurements and careful attention to detail to identify the species.

RANGE: The Long-eared Bat is found from southern British Columbia east to southern Saskatchewan and south to northwestern New Mexico and Baja California.

California Bat
Myotis californicus

Total Length: 3–3³/₄ in.
Tail Length: 1¹/₄–1⁵/₈ in.
Forearm: 1¹/₄–1³/₈ in.
Weight: ¹/₈–³/₁₆ oz.

HABITAT: This bat can be found roosting in rock crevices, mines and buildings and under bridges and loose tree bark. It forages mainly over forested areas, shrub-steppe areas and arid grasslands.

California Bats emerge shortly after sunset, and for a few minutes in the remaining twilight, they can be followed as they fly erratically through the sky. As if surfing on invisible waves in the air, fluttering California Bats rise and dive at variable speeds in the pursuit of unseen prey. These activities appear random, but they are actually deliberate and purposeful.

FOOD: During the night, California Bats forage opportunistically in areas such as cliffs or poplar groves that attract night-flying insects, or over water for emerging adult caddisflies and mayflies. Additionally, they can be observed in tree canopies feeding on moths, beetles and flies. Generally, they fly 6–10 ft. above the ground or water when foraging.

DESCRIPTION: This small, yellowish brown bat has a wing span of about 9 in. The foot is tiny, and it has a keeled calcar. Its ears and face are much darker than the rest of the body.

DEN: California Bats are not too selective of their roosts, and they have been found in rock crevices, mine shafts, tree cavities, buildings and bridges.

RANGE: The California Bat, truly a western bat, is found in coastal regions from southern Alaska south to California and Mexico. It ranges east into Montana, Colorado, New Mexico and Texas.

YOUNG: These bats mate in fall, and a single young is born in May or June. By mid- to late July the young are able to fly. Weaning occurs later.

SIMILAR SPECIES: All the mouse-eared bats (*Myotis* spp.) are generally indistinguishable as they fly in dim light. Precise measurements and careful attention to detail are required to identify the species.

Western Small-footed Bat
Myotis ciliolabrum

Total Length: 3–3¹/₂ in.
Tail Length: 1³/₁₆–1³/₄ in.
Forearm: 1¹/₈–1³/₈ in.
Weight: ¹/₈–¹/₄ oz.

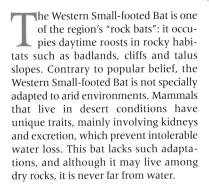

The Western Small-footed Bat is one of the region's "rock bats": it occupies daytime roosts in rocky habitats such as badlands, cliffs and talus slopes. Contrary to popular belief, the Western Small-footed Bat is not specially adapted to arid environments. Mammals that live in desert conditions have unique traits, mainly involving kidneys and excretion, which prevent intolerable water loss. This bat lacks such adaptations, and although it may live among dry rocks, it is never far from water.

DESCRIPTION: The glossy fur of this attractive bat is yellowish brown to gray or even coppery brown above, and its undersides are almost white. The flight membranes and ears are black, and the tail membrane is dark brown. Its wingspan is 8–10 in., and some fur may be found on both the undersurface of the wing and the upper surface of the tail membrane. Across its face, from ear to ear, is a dark brown or black "mask." True to its name, this bat has small feet, relative to others in this family. The calcar is strongly keeled.

HABITAT: The Western Small-footed Bat prefers rocky or grassland regions, especially riverbanks, ridges and outcroppings with abundant rocks for roosting. It is sometimes found in rocky areas of pine forests.

FOOD: Like most bats in California, the Western Small-footed Bat primarily eats flying insects, including moths, flies, bugs and beetles.

DEN: In summer, this bat roosts in trees, under loose bark, in buildings or in rock crevices. It hibernates in caves or mines in winter, from November to March. Nursery colonies occur in bank crevices, under bridges or under the shingles of old buildings.

YOUNG: In small nursery colonies, one young per female is born from late May to early June. Twins are more common for this species than for most others. By mid-August the young are flying.

SIMILAR SPECIES: In dim light, you cannot see the Western Small-footed Bat's "mask"; precise measurements and careful attention to detail are required to identify the species.

RANGE: The Western Small-footed Bat is found from southern British Columbia east to southwestern Saskatchewan and south through most of the western U.S. and well into Mexico.

Little Brown Bat

Myotis lucifugus

Total Length: 2³/₈–4 in.

Tail Length: 1–2¹/₈ in.

Forearm: 1³/₈–1⁵/₈ in.

Weight: ³/₁₆–⁵/₁₆ oz.

On nearly every warm, calm summer night, the skies of California are filled with marvelously complex screams and shrills. Unfortunately for people interested in the world of bats, these magnificent vocalizations occur at frequencies higher than our ears can detect. One of the most common of these nighttime screamers, and quite likely the first bat most people will encounter, is the Little Brown Bat.

DESCRIPTION: This bat's coloration ranges from light to dark brown on the back, with somewhat paler undersides. The tips of the hairs are glossy, giving this bat a coppery appearance. The wing and tail membranes are mainly unfurred, although fur may appear around the edges. The calcar of this bat is long and un-keeled. The tragus, which is nearly straight, is half the length of the ear. The wingspan is 8³/₄–11 in.

HABITAT: At home almost anywhere, you may find Little Brown Bats in buildings, attics, roof crevices and loose bark on trees or under bridges. Wherever these bats are roosting, waterbodies are sure to be nearby. They need a place to drink and a large supply of insects for their nightly foraging.

FOOD: Little Brown Bats feed exclusively on night-flying insects. Foraging for insects can last for up to five hours. Later, the bats take a rest in night roosts (a different place from their day roosts). Another short feeding period occurs just prior to dawn, before the bat returns to its day roost.

DEN: These bats may roost alone, in small groups or in colonies of more than 1000 individuals. A loose shingle, an open attic or a hollow tree are all suitable roosts for a Little Brown Bat. In winter, the bats hibernate in large numbers in caves and old mines.

YOUNG: Mating occurs either in late fall or in the hibernation colonies. Fertilization of the egg is delayed until the female ovulates in spring, and by June, pregnant females form nursery colonies in a protected location. In late June or early July, one young is born to a female after about 50 to 60 days of gestation. The young are blind and hairless, but their development is rapid and their eyes open in about three days. After one month, the young are on their own. The longest recorded life span for this species is 31 years.

SIMILAR SPECIES: All mouse-eared bats (*Myotis* spp.) are generally indistinguishable as they fly in dim light. It requires precise measurements and careful attention to identify the species.

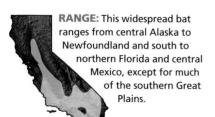

RANGE: This widespread bat ranges from central Alaska to Newfoundland and south to northern Florida and central Mexico, except for much of the southern Great Plains.

Cave Bat
Myotis velifer

Total Length: 3¹/₂–4¹/₂ in.
Tail Length: 1⁵/₈–1⁷/₈ in.
Forearm: 1²/₃ in.
Weight: ¹/₄–³/₈ oz.

The not-so-appropriate common name for this species would seem to imply an exclusive preference for cave dwelling. Alas, like other bats, the Cave Bat does roost in mines, under bridges and even in old buildings. One of the larger *Myotis* species, this bat has a strong, even flight, distinctly less erratic than others of its kind. This characteristic probably has advantages on windy nights—a swift wind is enough to halt the foraging activity of many bat species.

DESCRIPTION: This large *Myotis* bat has a variable body color, but here in California most range from dark brown to nearly black. The fur is not glossy, but the base of the hairs is quite light. A bare spot may be on the middle of the back. Unlike other bats, its facial color may be paler than the fur. The ears reach the tip of the nose when laid forward.

HABITAT: This bat lives in arid regions, such as desert scrublands and sagebrush country. Desert riparian areas are also inhabited.

FOOD: The majority of insects consumed by this bat include moths and beetles, but other night-flying insects are probably eaten when encountered.

DEN: The Cave Bat roosts in caves, mines, under bridges and in buildings. In winter, large colonies are found in caves. Colonies commonly number around 5000, and in Kansas, nursery colonies have been estimated at up to 20,000 individuals.

YOUNG: Young are born in large nursery colonies. Mating occurs in fall, but because of delayed fertilization, the single young is not born until late spring, after a gestation of about 60 to 70 days.

SIMILAR SPECIES: All the mouse-eared bats (*Myotis* spp.) are generally indistinguishable as they fly in dim light. It requires precise measurements and careful attention to detail to identify the species.

RANGE: The Cave Bat is found in Mexico and the southern states from southeastern California through Arizona and southern New Mexico, and from Texas north to Kansas.

Yuma Bat
Myotis yumanensis

Total Length: 3–3⁵⁄₈ in.
Tail Length: 1¹⁄₄–1³⁄₄ in.
Forearm: 1¹⁄₄–1¹⁄₂ in.
Weight: ¹⁄₈–³⁄₁₆ oz.

Like most bats, Yuma Bats spend much of the summer days hanging comfortably in warm roosts, shifting slightly as temperatures rise and fall. They rest, relax and snuggle against one another until the moon rises and draws them outside. With nightfall, Yuma Bats fly out over the nearest wetland, snapping up rising insects in the cool, calm night air. Often their stomachs are full within 15 minutes, and their foraging is finished for the night. They then return to their night roost, where they digest the evening meal before foraging again just before dawn.

DESCRIPTION: This medium-sized bat has brown to black fur on the back, with somewhat lighter undersides. The ears are long enough to extend to the nose when pushed forward. The tragus is blunt and only about half the length of the ear. The wingspan is about 9 in. The calcar is not keeled.

HABITAT: This bat tends to occur in grasslands or shrub areas throughout California, particularly in areas close to water; it usually forages over lakes and streams. It is common in wooded canyon bottoms.

FOOD: Much of the Yuma Bat's diet consists of emerging adult caddisflies, mayflies and midges. These insects have larval forms that develop underwater.

DEN: Yuma Bats typically roost and form their maternal colonies in buildings, trees and caves and under south-facing siding and shingles. These structures must be within foraging distance of a source of water.

YOUNG: As in many types of bats, mating occurs during fall, with the sperm stored within the female until fertilization in spring. A single young is usually born in June or July.

SIMILAR SPECIES: All the mouse-eared bats (*Myotis* spp.) are generally indistinguishable as they fly in dim light. It requires precise measurements and careful attention to detail to identify the species.

RANGE: The Yuma Bat is found from west-central British Columbia south to California and Mexico and east to Colorado and western Texas; it is largely absent from the Great Basin.

Long-legged Bat
Myotis volans

Total Length: 3³/₈–4 in.
Tail Length: 1³/₈–2¹/₈ in.
Forearm: 1³/₈–1³/₄ in.
Weight: ³/₁₆–³/₈ oz.

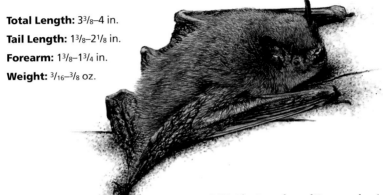

The leg bones of this uncommon bat are responsible for its common name. Unfortunately, the Long-legged Bat's leg bones are only fractionally longer than those of the very similar Western Small-footed Bat (p. 297), so they are not a good distinguishing characteristic in the field. Noticeable differences do occur, however, in habitat selection. The Long-legged Bat lives in or near coniferous forests, especially in the vicinity of water.

DESCRIPTION: Although this bat is the heaviest of the "little brown bats," it is heavier by an almost imperceptible amount. The wingspan is 10–11 in. The fur can be uniformly light brown to reddish to dark chocolate brown, but it is mainly dark brown. A well-defined keel is on the calcar. The underwing is usually furred out to a line connecting the elbow and knee.

HABITAT: This bat lives primarily in coniferous forests that are near waterbodies. It may forage along the sides of mountain lakes.

FOOD: The diet is composed primarily of moths, flies, true bugs and beetles.

DEN: The Long-legged Bat spends winter hibernating in caves or mines. In summer, it roosts in trees, buildings or rock crevices. Nursery colonies are located in bank crevices, under bridges or under south-facing shingles on old buildings.

YOUNG: Mating occurs in fall. Fertilization is delayed until spring, and the young are born in July or August, in large nursery colonies. One young per female is born. The young mature quickly, flying on their own in about four weeks. The longest recorded life span for this species is 21 years.

SIMILAR SPECIES: All the mouse-eared bats (*Myotis* spp.) are generally indistinguishable as they fly in dim light. It requires precise measurements, careful attention to detail and a technical key to identify the species.

RANGE: The Long-legged Bat ranges from northwestern British Columbia southeast to western North Dakota and south through most of the western U.S.

Southern Yellow Bat
Lasiurus ega

Total Length: 4¹/₄–5¹/₈ in.
Tail Length: 1⁵/₈–2¹/₄ in.
Forearm: 1⁵/₈ in.
Weight: ¹/₄–³/₄ oz.

This bat species has been subject to much controversy over whether it is actually one, two or three species. In California, the subspecies *L. e. xanthinus* has often been proposed as a separate species, the Western Yellow Bat. The structural differences between these subspecies are extremely minor, and, for now, biologists accept them as one species.

ALSO CALLED: Western Yellow Bat, Southwestern Yellow Bat.

DESCRIPTION: This bat has a small body with yellowish or tawny-colored fur. There are black or gray flecks throughout

RANGE: This bat is found from southern California east to extreme southwestern New Mexico and extreme southern Texas, continuing south through Mexico.

the coat. The fur extends onto the wing membrane along the forearm, and about halfway onto the tail membrane on the dorsal side. It has large, pointed ears that reach the tip of the nose when laid forward.

HABITAT: This yellow bat occupies various habitats, including low-elevation woodlands, open arid regions and tropical forests. It seems to favor roosting in palm trees, and expanding palm plantations may increase the numbers of these bats.

FOOD: A preference for hard-bodied insects such as beetles has been noted, but this bat probably feeds on a variety of insects relative to the habitat it is in.

DEN: Rarely more than one bat will roost in a single palm tree. Other roosts include a variety of different tree species and thatch rooftops. Records in California are from spring, summer and fall; this species' whereabouts in winter are unknown.

YOUNG: The majority of females give birth in June. *Lasiurus* females have four nipples, and one to four young per female is possible. On average, a female has two young.

SIMILAR SPECIES: The **Western Red Bat** (p. 303) is more red than yellow, and the **Hoary Bat** (p. 304) has a grizzled gray appearance.

Western Red Bat
Lasiurus blossevillii

Considering that most other bats in California have brownish fur, the Western Red Bat stands out and should be easy to recognize. Unfortunately, this bat is not common, and the chances of seeing one are slim. It is widespread but sparsely distributed in California, and in cold areas it may migrate to warmer regions during winter. Additionally, the Western Red Bat begins foraging as late as two hours after sunset, at a time when it is too dark to recognize its reddish hue.

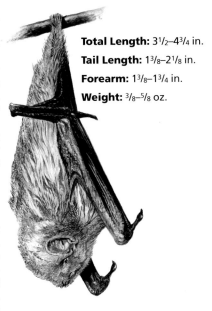

Total Length: 3¹/₂–4³/₄ in.
Tail Length: 1³/₈–2¹/₈ in.
Forearm: 1³/₈–1³/₄ in.
Weight: ³/₈–⁵/₈ oz.

ALSO CALLED: Desert Red Bat.

DESCRIPTION: The orange or reddish fur is up to ¹/₂–³/₄ in. long over the back, face, throat and around the ears. Males tend to be brighter than females, and some individuals may have a slightly frosted appearance. The wingspan is 11–13 in. The top of the membrane between the hindlimbs is densely furred on the anterior portion. The short, rounded, pale ears are almost hairless inside. *Lasiurus* bats are unique in having four mammae; all other bats here have two.

HABITAT: This bat seems to prefer edge situations and patchy mosaic habitats. Any mix of grasslands, shrubs, forests, riparian areas and cropland are suitable. It does not inhabit desert areas.

FOOD: When it forages near farmlands, the Western Red Bat may feed heavily on agricultural pests. It primarily eats moths, plant hoppers, flies and beetles, and it may sometimes alight on vegetation to pick off insects. The peak feeding period is well after dusk.

DEN: In summer, these solitary bats roost in foliage, which provides shade. The space beneath the roost must be free of obstacles to allow the bats to drop into flight.

YOUNG: Mating takes place in August and September, but ovulation and fertilization are delayed until spring. Gestation appears to be 80 to 90 days, and one to four young are born in June. They are thought to be able to fly when three or four weeks old and are weaned at five or six weeks.

SIMILAR SPECIES: The **Southern Yellow Bat** (p. 302) is more yellow than red, and the **Hoary Bat** (p. 304) has a grizzled gray appearance.

RANGE: The Western Red Bat ranges from South America north to extreme southern British Columbia.

Hoary Bat

Lasiurus cinereus

The Hoary Bat is one of the largest bats in California, with a wingspan of about 16 in., but it weighs less than the smallest chipmunk. It flies later into the night than most bats in the region, and once the last of the daylight has disappeared, the Hoary Bat courses low over wetlands, lakes and rivers in conifer country. It may not be as acrobatic in its foraging flights as the smaller *Myotis* bats, but no one who has ever witnessed a Hoary Bat in flight could fail to be impressed by its aerial accomplishments.

The large size of the Hoary Bat is often enough to identify it, but the light wrist spots, which are sometimes visible, confirm the identification. Many of the Hoary Bat's long hairs have brown bases and white tips, giving the animal a frosted appearance and its common name. Though attractive, this coloration makes the Hoary Bat very difficult to notice when it roosts in a tree—it looks very similar to dried leaves and lichens.

Hoary Bats, as well as other tree-dwelling bats, have been the focus of scientific study to determine the importance of old roost trees in their habitat. These bats have complex requirements: while old trees may well be important, water quality and the availability of hatching insects in wetlands may be equally significant.

The few records from the northern mountains of Canada suggest that female Hoary Bats may migrate quite far north. The males, it is thought, migrate only as far as the northern U.S., where they likely court and mate with the females. While the males may remain at these sites for summer, some impregnated females seem to push farther north, where the young are born.

DESCRIPTION: The large Hoary Bat has light brown to grayish fur, and the white hair tips give it a heavily frosted appearance. Its throat and shoulders are buffy yellow or toffee colored. Its wingspan is 15–16 in. The ears are short, rounded and furred, but the edges of the ears are naked and black. The tragus is blunt and triangular. The upper surfaces of the feet and tail membrane are completely furred. The calcar is modestly keeled. Like other *Lasiurus* bats, the Hoary Bat has four mammae.

HABITAT: The Hoary Bat is often found near open grassy areas in coniferous and deciduous forests or near lakes.

FOOD: The diet consists mainly of moths, plant hoppers, flies and beetles, including many agricultural pests when this bat forages near farmlands.

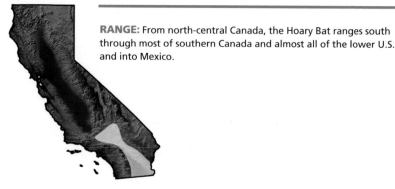

RANGE: From north-central Canada, the Hoary Bat ranges south through most of southern Canada and almost all of the lower U.S. and into Mexico.

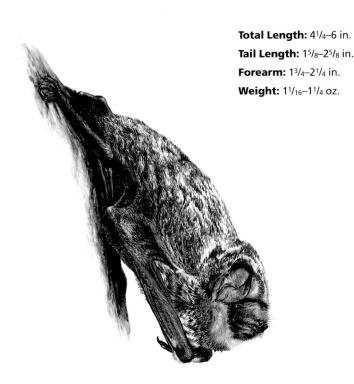

Total Length: 4¼–6 in.
Tail Length: 1⅝–2⅝ in.
Forearm: 1¾–2¼ in.
Weight: 1¹/₁₆–1¼ oz.

Feeding activity does not peak until well after dusk.

DEN: This migratory bat may stay in parts of California year-round, while in other regions it may migrate farther north or south depending on the season. During summer, it roosts alone in the shade of foliage, with an open space beneath the roost so that it can drop into flight. When migrating, these bats have been known to travel in large flocks.

YOUNG: Hoary Bats mate in fall, but the young are not born until late May or June because fertilization is delayed until the female ovulates in spring. Gestation lasts about 90 days, and a female, which has four mammae, usually bears two young. She places the first young on her back while she delivers the next. Before they are able to fly, young bats roost in trees and nurse between their mother's nighttime foraging flights.

SIMILAR SPECIES: The **Western Red Bat** (p. 303) is reddish rather than hoary gray, and the **Southern Yellow Bat** (p. 302) is yellowish. The **Big Brown Bat** (p. 309) is almost as large but does not have a frosted appearance.

DID YOU KNOW?

The Hoary Bat is the most widespread species of bat in North America, and it is the only terrestrial mammal native to the Hawaiian Islands.

Western Pipistrelle
Pipistrellus hesperus

In grasslands and shrub-steppe communities throughout California, Western Pipistrelles may be the first bat many people see; they begin foraging in the evening while there is still sunlight, and in the morning they feed well after dawn. They forage throughout summer to develop a layer of fat. In northern regions, the pipistrelles may migrate southward, and in some areas they hibernate. Whichever method the bats use during winter—hibernating or migrating—they require the fat layer for sustenance.

Like other bats, Western Pipistrelles are very clean. After foraging each night, they spend as much as 30 minutes grooming their fur and cleaning out debris or bugs that have accumulated. They use their tongues wherever they can reach, and otherwise, like a cat, they moisten their hindfeet to clean the remaining areas. Special attention is given to cleaning the ears. As bats are dependent on their hearing to "see" the world through echolocation, a dirty ear would be intolerable. All bats have good eyesight too, but as nighttime fliers, hearing is more useful.

The flight of the Western Pipistrelle is weak and erratic. Its slow flight is advantageous to it when enthusiastic naturalists are attempting to net one.

Once it detects the net, it has enough time to turn in the air and avoid being caught. Being a weak flyer, however, means it cannot cover great distances for food, shelter or water. Another downfall of its feeble flight is that a swift breeze nearly halts its foraging, and strong winds force it back to its roost.

DESCRIPTION: The Western Pipistrelle is the smallest bat in the U.S. Its wingspan is only $7^{1}/_{2}$–$8^{1}/_{2}$ in. It is uniformly colored above, usually tawny yellow, grayish or even reddish brown and whitish below. The wings, interfemoral membrane, ears, nose and feet are almost black, and it has a short, club-shaped tragus and a keeled calcar. The contrast of its dark face and light fur gives the appearance that it is wearing a mask.

HABITAT: Western Pipistrelles are most common in arid regions with rocky or scrubby areas. Sometimes found close to cities, they are usually the first bat out in the evening and may even be seen in broad daylight. One great threat to these miniature bats is desiccation. Some anomalous populations of Western Pipistrelles live in arid regions where no other bat species occurs—far from suitable roosting sites, such as cliffs, rocky

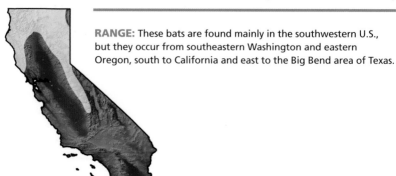

RANGE: These bats are found mainly in the southwestern U.S., but they occur from southeastern Washington and eastern Oregon, south to California and east to the Big Bend area of Texas.

Total Length: $2^{3}/_{8}$–$3^{3}/_{8}$ in.
Tail Length: 1–$1^{1}/_{4}$ in.
Forearm: 1–$1^{1}/_{4}$ in.
Weight: 0.1–0.2 oz.

outcroppings, buildings or caves. They cannot fly the distance between their locality and the nearest shelter. As they are unable to survive arid climates for long without shelter, one hypothesis suggests they may roost in ground burrows of desert rodents. This idea has not been substantiated, but it may account for these unusually remote populations. In just four instances, individual bats were found underneath surface rocks in these desert areas.

FOOD: Western Pipistrelles feed on tiny insects such as flies, some beetles, leafhoppers and plant hoppers. Because of the small size of this bat, large insects are inedible.

DEN: When roosting or hibernating, these bats can be found in caves, mines, crevices and old buildings. Some bats in northern areas migrate southward instead of hibernation. Maternity colonies are found in crevices of rocky cliffs or in sheltered nooks of old buildings.

YOUNG: In June, females give birth to two young, usually in protected maternity colonies. These maternity colonies are not more than about 12 females, and sometimes a female may roost alone to bear her young. The young require their mother's care for several weeks until they are mature. Females that are lactating are at great risk of dehydration, and they can be seen any hour of the night at watering holes nearby their roost.

SIMILAR SPECIES: The combination of small size, pale fur and black ears, face and wing membranes makes this bat distinctive. Most *Myotis* **bats** (pp. 294–301) are larger and have a much longer tragus.

DID YOU KNOW?

The erratic and jerky flights of the pipistrelle bats in Europe brought about the common name for bats as "flittermouse" (*fledermaus* in German).

Silver-haired Bat
Lasionycteris noctivagans

Total Length: 3⅝–4¼ in.
Tail Length: 1⅜–2 in.
Forearm: 1½–1¾ in.
Weight: ¼–⅝ oz.

DESCRIPTION: The fur is nearly black, with long, white-tipped hairs on the back giving it a frosty appearance. The naked ears and tragus are short, rounded and black. The wingspan is 11–12 in. A light covering of fur may be seen over the entire surface of the tail membrane.

The handsome Silver-haired Bat flies slowly and leisurely during twilight hours in much of northern California. Twilight actually happens twice in a 24-hour period: once after sunset (vesperal twilight) and again before sunrise (auroral twilight). The feeding forays of bats also happen twice a day. Silver-haired Bats usually fly fairly low to the ground, and they don't seem to be disturbed by the presence of an inquisitive human. If you chance to find one, either at night or in very early morning, you may be able to watch it for some time as it dips and flops about the twilight sky catching insects. Listen closely as well, you may hear the subtle *wicka-wicka-wicka* of its leathery wings.

HABITAT: Forests are the primary habitat, but this bat can easily adapt to parks, cities and farmlands.

FOOD: This bat feeds mainly on moths and flies, and it forages over standing water or in open areas near water.

DEN: The summer roosts are usually in tree cavities, under loose bark or in old buildings. In winter these bats may hibernate in caves, mines or old buildings. Females form nursery colonies in protected areas, such as tree cavities, narrow crevices or old buildings.

YOUNG: Breeding takes place in fall or during a break in hibernation, but fertilization is delayed until the female ovulates in spring. In early summer, after a gestation of about two months, one or two young are born to each female.

RANGE: This bat is found along the southeastern coast of Alaska, across the southern half of Canada and through most of the U.S., but it is absent from the Gulf Coast, southern California, Nevada and southwestern Arizona.

SIMILAR SPECIES: The Silver-haired Bat's white-tipped black hairs are unique among the bats of the region. The **Big Brown Bat** (p. 309) has mainly brown, glossy fur. The **Hoary Bat** (p. 304) does not have black fur.

Big Brown Bat
Eptesicus fuscus

Total Length: 3⅝–5½ in.
Tail Length: ⅞–2⅜ in.
Forearm: 1⅝–2⅛ in.
Weight: 7/16–1 oz.

The Big Brown Bat is not overly abundant anywhere, but its habit of roosting and occasionally hibernating in houses and other human structures makes it a more commonly encountered bat. It is also a bat that may be seen on warm winter nights, because it occasionally takes such opportunities to change hibernation sites. The relative frequency of Big Brown Bat sightings doesn't save this species from the anonymity that plagues most bats, however, because the "big" in its name is relative—this sparrow-sized bat still looks awfully small against a dark night sky.

DESCRIPTION: This big bat is mainly brown, with lighter undersides, and its fur appears glossy or oily. On average, a female is larger than a male. The face, ears and flight membranes are black and mainly unfurred. The blunt tragus is about half as long as the ear. The calcar is usually keeled.

HABITAT: This large bat easily adapts to parks, cities, farmlands and buildings. In the wild, it typically inhabits forests.

FOOD: A fast flier, the Big Brown Bat feeds mainly on beetles and plant hoppers, rarely moths or flies. Near farmlands, it feeds heavily on agricultural pests. Foraging usually occurs at heights of no more than 30 ft., and the two peak feeding periods are at dusk and just before dawn.

DEN: In summer, this bat usually roosts in tree cavities, under loose bark or in buildings. It spends winter hibernating in caves, mines or old buildings. Nursery colonies are found in protected areas, such as tree cavities, large crevices or old buildings.

YOUNG: These bats breed in fall or during a wakeful period in winter, but fertilization is delayed until the female ovulates in spring. A female gives birth to one or two young in early summer, after about a two-month gestation. As in most bats, the female has two mammae. This bat is quite long lived; one individual was known to be 19 years old.

SIMILAR SPECIES: The Big Brown Bat is not easy to distinguish from the other large bats, but the **Hoary Bat** (p. 304) has frosted brown or gray fur, and the **Silver-haired Bat** (p. 308) has frosted black fur. The *Myotis* **bats** (pp. 294–301) are smaller.

RANGE: This bat occurs from the southern tier of the Canadian provinces southward through most of the U.S.

Spotted Bat
Euderma maculatum

Total Length: 4¹/₄–4³/₄ in.
Tail Length: 1³/₄–2 in.
Forearm: 1⁷/₈–2 in.
Weight: ¹/₂ oz.

The Spotted Bat is an exhibitionist among a guild of committed conformists. One glance at a Spotted Bat instantly reveals that this is no ordinary bat. The long, pink ears and the three huge, white polka dots that adorn its otherwise black back are sufficiently distinctive for this bat to stand out in a crowd, but its flare is not restricted to visual appeal. While feeding, the Spotted Bat gives loud, high-pitched, metallic squeaks that are easily heard by humans. Because most bats vocalize beyond our hearing, it is unusually pleasing to listen to the aerial drama of the rare Spotted Bat.

DESCRIPTION: The back is primarily black. A large, white spot is on each shoulder, another is on the rump and sometimes light-colored hairs are behind the neck. The belly is whitish. The long, pinkish to light tan ears project forward in flight but are folded back when the bat roosts. The wingspan is about 12 in.

HABITAT: These bats are found in highland ponderosa pine regions in early summer. In August they descend to lower-elevation deserts.

FOOD: Spotted Bats appear to be a specialized predator on noctuid moths, a large and diverse family of night-flying insects. Beetles also make up a portion of the diet.

DEN: In summer, Spotted Bats are known to roost primarily in rock cracks and crevices on cliffs and in caves.

YOUNG: Usually one young is born in early summer. Even at a young age the ears are large, but the white spots on the back are absent on newborns.

SIMILAR SPECIES: The exceptionally large ears and large, white spots make Spotted Bats distinctive among bats. The **Townsend's Big-eared Bat** (p. 312) also has large ears, but it lacks the black and white markings.

RANGE: This bat occurs from southern British Columbia, southern Idaho and southern Montana through to Arizona and New Mexico.

Pallid Bat
Antrozous pallidus

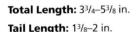

Total Length: $3^3/_4$–$5^3/_8$ in.
Tail Length: $1^3/_8$–2 in.
Forearm: $1^7/_8$–$2^3/_8$ in.
Weight: $9/_{16}$–$1^1/_4$ oz.

It might seem absurd that after millions of years of flight specialization, bats would be found foraging on the ground, but such is the case with Pallid Bats. These bats are still committed fliers, but they frequently land to take insects, other invertebrates and small vertebrates from the ground and from vegetation.

While bats have few predators in the night skies, on the ground they are vulnerable to many threats. The light dorsal color of the Pallid Bat might be a protective adaptation that helps it blend in with the pale sands of its typical desert habitat.

DESCRIPTION: The back is light yellow. The underparts are pale cream or almost white. Individual hairs are always darker at the tip than at the base, which is opposite to the coloration seen on most other bats. The broad, tan ears are extremely long, and if pushed forward, they may extend past the muzzle. The median edge of the ears is not folded. The wingspan is about 15 in.

HABITAT: The Pallid Bat is typically associated with rocky outcrops near open, dry areas, but occasionally it is found in evergreen forests.

FOOD: Insects are the main food, but some small vertebrates, such as lizards, have also been reported. The bat may incidentally eat some fruits and seeds.

DEN: Pallid Bats gather in night roosts following foraging. These sites are generally in caves, overhangs or buildings. Their day roosts are nearby, typically in buildings or rock crevices.

YOUNG: These bats mate from October through December and occasionally into February. The sperm is stored in the female's reproductive tract until ovulation in spring. Young are born in May and June, and twins are common.

SIMILAR SPECIES: The **Townsend's Big-eared Bat** (p. 312) is brown and smaller than the Pallid Bat, has more prominent lumps on its nose and has larger ears that are joined at the base.

RANGE: The Pallid Bat ranges west of the Rockies from British Columbia to Baja California, into Utah, Colorado and western Texas, and south to central Mexico.

Townsend's Big-eared Bat
Corynorhinus townsendii

Few animals have ears to match the unusual Townsend's Big-eared Bat. In fact, the ears of this bat can be more than one-third the length of its body. If an elephant had the same proportions, a fully grown African elephant (at up to 25 ft. including the trunk) would have ears nearly 9 ft. long—dimensions approaching that of the famous Walt Disney character, Dumbo.

As humans, we tend to perceive the world primarily through our eyes, but the world can be explored just as effectively through other senses. Bats hold unquestionable supremacy in the aerial world of sound. Typically, the sounds that are produced by bats range between 20 kHz and 100 kHz. Most musical notes are at about 0.5 kHz, which demonstrates that bat call frequencies can be as much as 200 times higher than our ears can detect. Most bats echolocate at different frequencies, so a person equipped with a bat detector—these things actually exist—can identify the species of a bat from its ultrasonic nighttime calls. If you have good high-frequency hearing, and only on a quiet night, you might hear the clicking sounds of bats in the air above you without the aid of equipment.

As well as catching flying insects directly in their mouths, bats also use the membranes of their wings and tail almost like a baseball glove. They deftly catch the insects and then pass them up toward the mouth. Typically, Townsend's Big-eared Bats forage in the evening twilight. Only pregnant females forage again in the morning twilight, and when these females are lactating, they may venture out for a third feeding foray as well.

DESCRIPTION: This medium-sized brown bat's most noticeable features are its large, membranous ears, which can measure up to $1^1/_2$ in. The ears are joined across the forehead at their bases. The median ear edges are double, and a prominent network of blood vessels are visible in the extended ears. At rest, the ears are curled and folded, almost resembling Bighorn Sheep horns. There is a set of conspicuous facial glands between the eye and nostril on each side of the snout. The belly is a lighter shade of brown than the back. This bat's wingspan is about 12 in.

HABITAT: This bat is found in open areas near coniferous forests and in arid areas.

FOOD: Townsend's Big-eared Bats emerge quite late in the evening, so they are seldom observed while feeding.

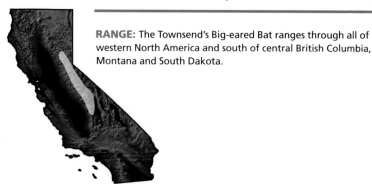

RANGE: The Townsend's Big-eared Bat ranges through all of western North America and south of central British Columbia, Montana and South Dakota.

Total Length: 3½–4½ in.
Tail Length: 1¼–2½ in.
Forearm: 1⅝–1⅞ in.
Weight: ¼–⅜ oz.

They forage along forest edges and are not thought of as gleaners. They catch mainly small moths in the air but also readily take beetles and flies.

DEN: Maternity colonies are found in warm areas of caves and abandoned mines. These colonies are not as large as in other species, and clusters of over 100 females and young are uncommon. Males in summer tend to be solitary. During winter hibernation, Townsend's Big-eared Bats tend to move deep into caves where temperatures are constant.

YOUNG: Mating occurs following ritualized courtship behavior in October and November. A single pup that is a quarter of its mother's weight at birth is born between May and July. The maximum recorded life span for this species is 16 years.

SIMILAR SPECIES: Because of its huge ears, this species can only possibly be confused with the **Pallid Bat** (p. 311), which is larger and paler and has smaller ears that are not joined at the base. The **Spotted Bat** (p. 310) also has huge ears, but its large, white spots make it unmistakable.

DID YOU KNOW?

Despite derogatory references to bats as "flying rats," they are actually more closely related to primates than they are to mice and other rodents.

California Leaf-nosed Bat
Macrotus californicus

Total Length: 3¹/₄–3⁵/₈ in.
Tail Length: 1¹/₄–1⁵/₈ in.
Forearm: 1⁷/₈–2¹/₈ in.
Weight: ⁷/₁₆–³/₄ oz.

This unusual bat is a resident of southern California, and it is the most northerly representative of the Phyllostomidae family. This species neither hibernates nor migrates, and it has special roosting techniques to survive the cool winter months. Whereas in summer these bats will roost singly or in small groups, in winter they roost in large colonies deep inside caves. Often the caves selected are geothermally heated, so this natural heat plus the heat of their bodies keeps the colony at a comfortable temperature. Only during their 1¹/₂- to 2¹/₂-hour foraging trips are they subject to uncomfortable temperatures.

DESCRIPTION: The California Leaf-nosed Bat is mainly light grayish brown above and paler below. The hairs of its coat have light bases. Its flight membranes and ears are nearly black. It has large ears and a simple triangular noseleaf.

HABITAT: Although it possesses no special adaptations for arid environments, this bat inhabits desert and scrub areas. It changes roosting sites as necessary to raise or cool its body temperature.

FOOD: This bats depends on its eyesight more than other bats. It gleans resting diurnal insects, like butterflies, off foliage, using its eyesight. Echolocation is used in total darkness. A variety of night-flying insects and diurnal insects are eaten.

DEN: Summer roosts, where one to a couple hundred bats can be found, are located in a cave, mine or old building. Winter roosts are deep in caves where temperature and humidity are constant and there is little air movement.

YOUNG: Females have one young per year, usually sometime from May to July. Maternal colonies of a few hundred females form in a region of a cave separate from the males.

SIMILAR SPECIES: The **Mexican Long-tongued Bat** (p. 315) has a much longer nose and tiny ears.

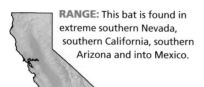

RANGE: This bat is found in extreme southern Nevada, southern California, southern Arizona and into Mexico.

Mexican Long-tongued Bat
Choeronycteris mexicana

Mexican Long-tongued Bats are found in southern California and are the only pollen and nectar specialists in the state. They are not year-round residents here—by November or December the bats have left for regions farther south, and they return in spring. They are primarily found only during warm months when plenty of flowers are in bloom. Their long nose and long tongue are adaptations for feeding on nectar from a wide variety of night-blooming flowers. Their feeding activity makes them important pollinators for several plant species. They have broad wings that enable slow flight, and they even have the ability to hover—though not as well as the famed hummingbirds.

Total Length: 2¹/₈–3¹/₈ in.

Tail Length: ¹/₄–³/₈ in.

Forearm: 1²/₃–2⁴/₅ in.

Weight: ³/₈–⁵/₈ oz.

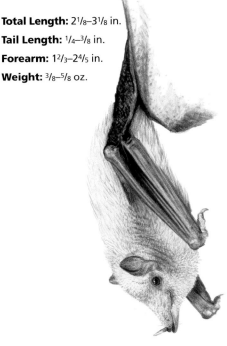

DESCRIPTION: This leaf-nosed bat is brown or dusky gray above and slightly paler below. Because this bat is not dependent on echolocation to find its food, it ears are much reduced. It has a very tiny tail and a small noseleaf.

HABITAT: This species is home in a variety of habitats, including urban areas with abundant flowers and fruit trees. The wild habitats include montane woodlands, riparian areas, tropical forests, arid scrubland and deserts with dominant succulents.

FOOD: Almost three-quarters of the diet is nectar, and about one-quarter is pollen. Fruits are eaten occasionally, and insects are eaten very rarely.

DEN: Roosting sites include caves, mines, culverts, buildings and rock crevices in cliffs. This bat has been known to share roosting sites with the California Leaf-nosed Bat (p. 314) and Townsend's Big-eared Bat (p. 312).

YOUNG: Pregnant females have been found from spring through to late summer, but the peak for births appears to be in June. Females have one young per season. The mothers carry their young with them while foraging.

SIMILAR SPECIES: The **California Leaf-nosed Bat** (p. 314) has a much shorter nose and very large ears.

RANGE: This species is found from southwestern California east to extreme southwestern New Mexico and south into Mexico.

INSECTIVORES & OPOSSUMS

This grouping, unlike the others in this book, actually encompasses two separate orders of mammals: shrews and moles belong to the insectivore order; opossums belong to the marsupial order. Although insectivores and opossums differ in many ways, they are united in their position as evolutionarily the oldest mammals in California.

Mole Family (Talpidae)

Moles are some of the most subterranean mammals. They spend the majority of their lives underground, and they have special adaptations that make this possible. They look a bit like large, rotund shrews, except their tails are proportionately shorter and their forelimbs are highly modified. The rotund appearance results from lack of a visible neck—the head merges smoothly with the body. This stream-lined shape makes moving in underground tunnels much easier. The hands appear enormous, with long claws, and they are turned outward like paddles, enabling moles to almost "swim" through soil. Their fur is lax, meaning it can lay forward or backward, enabling the mole to move forward or backward in tunnels easily. Their eyesight is poor, as might be inferred from their tiny eyes, but their hearing is superb. Their most important sensory organ is the snout, which is flexible and usually hairless.

Moles consume up to twice their weight in food daily, and although earthworms are their primary food, they also consume great numbers of pest insect larvae.

Broad-footed Mole

Shrew Family (Soricidae)

Shrews first appeared in the times of the Cretaceous dinosaurs, and biologists consider the modern members to be most similar to the earliest placental mammals. Many people mistake shrews for very small mice. Shrews do not have a rodent's prominent incisors, however, and they have tiny ears and long, slender, pointed snouts with many tiny teeth behind their incisors. Also, all North American shrews have teeth with chestnut-colored points.

Because they are so small, shrews lose heat rapidly to their surroundings, and their metabolisms surpass those of all other mammals. These tiny mammalian furnaces use energy at such a high rate that they may eat three times their own weight in invertebrate and vertebrate food each day. Some shrews have a neurotoxic venom in their saliva that enables them to subdue amphibians and mice that outweigh them. In turn, shrews are eaten by owls, hawks, foxes, Coyotes and weasels.

Water Shrew

Shrews do not hibernate, but their periods of intense food-searching activity, which last 30 to perhaps 45 minutes, are interspersed with hour-long energy-conserving periods of deep sleep, during which the body temperature drops.

Of the shrews of California, only the Marsh Shrew and Water Shrew are reasonably easy to identify visually, provided you can get a long enough look at them. The other species must be distinguished from one another on the basis of tooth and skull characteristics, distribution and to some extent habitat, although in many cases the ranges overlap.

Opossum Family (Didelphidae)

Virginia Opossum

The Virginia Opossum is the only marsupial in North America north of Mexico. Marsupials get their name from the marsupium, or pouch, in which newborns of most species are typically carried. Because they have a simple yolk-sac placenta, marsupials bear extremely premature young that range from honeybee to bumblebee size at birth. Once in the marsupium, the young attach to a nipple and continue the rest of their development outside the uterus. There is also a difference in dentition between placental mammals and marsupials: early placental mammals typically have four premolars and three molars, while early marsupials have three premolars and four molars. Most of the world's marsupials live in Australia and New Zealand, with some in South and Central America.

American Shrew Mole
Neurotrichus gibbsii

Total Length: 4–5 in.
Tail Length: 1¹/₄–1⁵/₈ in.
Weight: ¹/₄–³/₈ oz.

By its name alone, we can assume that this creature is more shrew-like than other moles found in this region. If you stumble across an American Shrew Mole in northwestern California, you may think you have found a shrew because it has small forelimbs, it spends some time aboveground and it has a long, sparsely haired tail.

The American Shrew Mole is the least subterranean mole in California. It is intermittently active throughout the day, pushing its way through leaf litter and decaying vegetation instead of digging tunnels like other moles. As a shrew mole forages, it moves slowly and cautiously beneath the leafy debris. It can even move its forelimbs beneath the body and run with an agility impossible for other moles.

DESCRIPTION: This small, shrew-like mole is nearly black with a relatively long, hairy tail, tiny eyes, ear pinnae no more than ¹/₄ in. long and large, scaly feet. The claws are long, but not flattened and broad as in other moles. The shrew mole may be blind; a pigmented layer of skin is over the anterior surface of the lens.

HABITAT: American Shrew Moles prefer to live where there is abundant leaf litter, dead vegetation and rotting logs near streams, ravines or forested hillsides.

FOOD: Earthworms and sowbugs make up more than half of the shrew mole's diet. A wide assortment of other invertebrates and some vegetation are also eaten.

DEN: Commonly, shallow burrows are enlarged into chambers 3–5 in. in diameter. Nests in these chambers are made of dry leaves. Nests and all burrows are not built more than 12 in. below the surface.

YOUNG: Most mating occurs from March to May, but some individuals may breed as early as February or as late as September. Litter size varies from one to six extremely tiny young, about ¹/₃₂ oz. Females may have multiple litters in one season.

SIMILAR SPECIES: Other mole species (pp. 319–21) have flattened claws and enormous forefeet. The **Marsh Shrew** (p. 330) and **Water Shrew** (p. 329) have longer, well-haired tails. Other **shrews** (pp. 322–33) are smaller and do not have modified forelimbs.

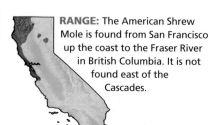

RANGE: The American Shrew Mole is found from San Francisco up the coast to the Fraser River in British Columbia. It is not found east of the Cascades.

Townsend's Mole

Scapanus townsendii

Total Length: 7³/₄–9¹/₄ in.
Tail Length: 1¹/₄–2 in.
Weight: 2¹/₄–6 oz.

The stocky Townsend's Mole—the largest mole in North America—literally swims through the soil using its powerfully muscled forelimbs equipped with shovel-like claws. Spoil from building burrows is thrust vertically to the surface from below, and the resulting hemispherical mound of dirt is the proverbial "molehill." During its foraging at night, this mole may venture into lawns, leaving a disfiguring series of soil mounds on the surface. The moles are beneficial to soil aeration, turnover, water absorption and pest control.

DESCRIPTION: This mole's rotund body is covered with short, black, velvety fur. The snout is long, the neck is short, the hindfeet are small and the tail is short and almost naked. The forefeet are enormously enlarged and cannot be rotated beneath the body; the claws are flattened and heavy. The tiny eyes lie beneath the skin and are probably useless. The nostrils at the end of the naked snout are crescent-shaped and point up.

HABITAT: Townsend's Moles prefer loose soil or cultivated fields, but they also occupy open brushlands in valley bottoms.

FOOD: Earthworms, insects of all stages and other invertebrates make up most of the diet, but some vegetation is also consumed.

DEN: This mole digs shallow surface tunnels where most feeding occurs, as well as deeper tunnels with a nest chamber up to 8 in. in diameter. The two-layered nest consists of coarse green grass with an inner layer of fine dry grass, moss and leaves. Tunnels radiate out from the nest chamber to other parts of the burrow system.

YOUNG: Mating occurs in February with a single litter of one to four born in late March. The hairless altricial young weigh about ³/₁₆ oz. at birth. At about 30 days they are fully furred and weaned, and they leave the maternal burrows in May and June. They are sexually mature after their first winter.

SIMILAR SPECIES: The **Coast Mole** (p. 320) is smaller, always less than 8 in. long. The **Broad-footed Mole** (p. 321) has a relatively hairier tail.

RANGE: These moles are found west of the Cascades from the U.S.-Canada border near Huntingdon, British Columbia, south to northern California.

Coast Mole
Scapanus orarius

Total Length: 5³/₄–6⁷/₈ in.
Tail Length: 1–1⁵/₈ in.
Weight: 2–3 oz.

The mammalian equivalent to backhoes and bulldozers, moles toil about underground and bring subsurface soil to the surface. The surface deposits are known as "molehills," and a typical molehill of a Coast Mole is about 7 in. high. Between October and March, when the soil is moist and most digging occurs, one mole may push up 200 to 400 hills. Their activity aerates the soil, encourages water absorption and circulates nutrients.

DESCRIPTION: In winter, the upperparts of the Coast Mole are dark mouse gray, sometimes with a silvery sheen. In summer, the fur often has a brownish tinge. The tail is pinkish and sparsely haired. The nose tip is naked and pink. Tiny, functionless eyes are beneath the skin. The feet are hairless, and the forefeet are enlarged and turned outward.

HABITAT: This mole inhabits a variety of soil types in meadows, deciduous woodlands, brush and even some coniferous forests if the soil is not too acidic.

FOOD: Earthworms make up more than three-fourths of the diet. Other invertebrates and some vegetation are also eaten.

DEN: The tunnels are 2 in. in diameter and may be 3–36 in. beneath the surface. Chambers 4 in. or greater in diameter are expanded at regular intervals. Breeding nests about 8 in. in diameter are located about 6 in. beneath the surface. The nest is lined with coarse grass and has several connecting tunnels.

YOUNG: A single litter of two to five is born each year in late March or early April following breeding in February.

SIMILAR SPECIES: The **Townsend's Mole** (p. 319) is larger and more rotund. The **Broad-footed Mole** (p. 321) has a relatively hairier tail.

RANGE: The Coast Mole is found from extreme southwestern British Columbia, down the coast into northern California and from northwestern Oregon slightly into Idaho.

Broad-footed Mole

Scapanus latimanus

Total Length: 5¼–7½ in.
Tail Length: ⅞–1¾ in.
Weight: about 2 oz.

Like all moles, the Broad-footed Mole is well suited to subterranean life—it terminates at one end with a supersensitive snout, and at the other end with an equally sensitive tail. Its unique fur is velvety to prevent soil from sticking to it and is capable of lying both forwards and backwards over the body. With its sensitive tail and snout and its two-way fur, the mole is ideally suited for moving forward or backward in its tunnel. The mole is unable to put its forefeet palm down against the ground; so well designed for "swimming" through the soil are these feet that they permanently stick out sideways, much like paddles with claws.

DESCRIPTION: The Broad-footed Mole is shiny gray with coppery highlights and with slightly lighter undersides. The tail is short and has sparse, silvery fur. The eyes of a mole are greatly reduced in size and are essentially useless. The front feet of this mole are very close to the head, and give the appearance that the mole has no neck.

HABITAT: These moles live in the soft, moist soils of a variety of habitats, from valleys to mountain meadows.

DEN: Moles spend most of their lives in their burrows. Special chambers are used for sleeping and raising young.

FOOD: These moles primarily feed on earthworms, although other invertebrates such as snails, slugs and insects and some vegetation may also be consumed.

YOUNG: Mating occurs from February to late March, and a litter of two to six young are born in a grass-lined burrow chamber in April or May. The young are altricial and require several weeks of growth to reach full size.

SIMILAR SPECIES: Both the **Townsend's Mole** (p. 319) and **Coast Mole** (p. 320) are much larger and have less hairy tails, and the **American Shrew Mole** (p. 318) is much smaller.

RANGE: These moles occur from south-central Oregon throughout most of California.

Mt. Lyell Shrew
Sorex lyelli

Total Length: 3⁷/₈–4 in.
Tail Length: 1³/₈–1⁵/₈ in.
Weight: ¹/₁₄–¹/₈ oz.

The Mt. Lyell Shrew may be well be the least-studied shrew in California. It is found only at elevations above 6500 ft. in the central Sierra Nevada, but few are ever seen alive as they seldom live longer than one year. If you see one at all, it is most likely a dead one in spring; starvation and predation in late winter claims many. It is believed that this species evolved from an isolated population of the Masked Shrew (*S. cinereus*) that inhabited this region during the last ice age. As no information on this species' life history exists, the information below is derived from *S. cinereus*.

DESCRIPTION: These small shrews have brown backs, lighter brown sides and gray underparts. The winter coat is paler, and the fur is short and velvety. It has a long, flexible snout, tiny eyes, small feet and a faintly bicolored tail, which is dark above and light below.

RANGE: The Mt. Lyell Shrew is found only in the mountains of Tuolumne and Mono Counties of California.

HABITAT: The Mt. Lyell Shrew favors montane forests and willow stands within grassy areas. It is found at elevations higher than 6500 ft.

FOOD: Insects probably account for the bulk of the diet, but this shrew may also eat significant numbers of other invertebrates such as slugs and snails. Most shrews will eat carrion when they encounter it.

DEN: Like other shrews, the nest is probably located under logs, in debris, between rocks or in burrows. Nests are typically about 2–4 in. in diameter and look like a woven grass ball. The nest does not have a central cavity; the shrew simply burrows to the inside.

YOUNG: The reproductive cycle for this species is unknown. Gestation is probably less than 20 days. Litter size for shrews in general averages about four to six young. The young are born naked, toothless and blind. Their growth is rapid: eyes and ears open in just over two weeks, and the young are weaned by three weeks.

SIMILAR SPECIES: Most shrews look very similar. Without a specimen and a technical key, it is almost impossible to identify a shrew reliably.

Preble's Shrew
Sorex preblei

Total Length: 3³/₈–3³/₄ in.
Tail Length: 1³/₈ in.
Weight: ¹/₁₆–¹/₈ oz.

The very small and rare Preble's Shrew competes with the Mt. Lyell Shrew as being the rarest and least studied shrew species in the state. It is known only from a handful of sites in the Cascades, and researchers are not even sure if their range is continuous or scattered and patchy. Because most long-tailed shrews (genus *Sorex*) are very similar, it can be assumed that the Preble's Shrew behaves much like other shrews. The areas where this shrew occurs are commonly inhabited by Yellow-pine Chipmunks, Western Harvest Mice, Deer Mice and an assortment of voles and other shrews as well.

DESCRIPTION: The Preble's Shrew has a brownish-gray back that grades to lighter colors on the sides and underside. If you raise the upper lip on the side of the snout, four single pointed teeth are to be seen behind the large, lobed first incisor. The third of these unicuspid teeth is not smaller than the fourth.

HABITAT: This tiny shrew seems to prefer dry sagebrush desert environments or grasslands with rocky areas. In California, they have been found in fir and pine forests.

FOOD: The Preble's Shrew is thought to eat mostly invertebrates, such as beetles, crickets, wasps, caterpillars and spiders.

DEN: The den is often found in soft soil, among rocks or under woody debris. The nest chamber is exceedingly small, and the entrance to the burrow is small and indistinct.

YOUNG: Little is known about this shrew's reproduction, but it is probably similar to other shrews. Mating likely occurs from April through July, with females having multiple litters a year.

SIMILAR SPECIES: Range and habitat can help identify shrew species. Differences between most shrews are slight, and identification in the field is nearly impossible without a technical key and the animal in hand.

RANGE: Preble's Shrews are found in extreme southeastern Washington, south through eastern Oregon into California and Nevada and east into Idaho, Montana and as far south as Colorado.

Vagrant Shrew
Sorex vagrans

Total Length: 3³/₈–4³/₄ in.
Tail Length: 1³/₈–1⁵/₈ in.
Weight: ³/₁₆–¹/₄ oz.

The Vagrant Shrew and the Montane Shrew (p. 326) may be the most difficult mammals in California to distinguish from one another. Even experts have trouble telling whether the two tiny, medial tines on the upper incisors are located near the upper limit of the dark tooth pigment (Vagrant Shrew) or within the pigmented part of the incisor (Montane Shrew). Naturally, live shrews would never submit to such scrutiny, but luckily it is an issue only where the two ranges overlap.

ALSO CALLED: Wandering Shrew.

DESCRIPTION: This shrew is pale brown on the back and sides in summer. In winter, it is slightly darker over the back. The undersides vary from silvery gray to buffy brown. The tail is bicolored: whitish below, pale brown above.

HABITAT: The Vagrant Shrew favors forested regions that have water nearby. Sometimes it occurs in moister habitats, such as the edges of mountain brooks with willow banks.

FOOD: This shrew eats a variety of adult and larval insects, earthworms, spiders, snails, slugs, carrion and even some vegetation.

DEN: The spherical, grassy nest is usually built in decayed logs. It lacks a central cavity.

YOUNG: Mating begins in March, and litters of two to nine young are born between early April and mid-August. Females likely have more than one litter a year. The young are helpless at birth, and they must feed heavily from their mother to complete their rapid growth. Their eyes and ears open in about two weeks, and they are weaned soon thereafter.

SIMILAR SPECIES: Range and habitat can help identify shrew species. Differences between most shrews are slight, and identification in the field is nearly impossible without a technical key and the animal in hand.

RANGE: The Vagrant Shrew's range extends from western Montana, Wyoming and Colorado west to the Pacific Coast and north into British Columbia and extreme southwestern Alberta.

Fog Shrew
Sorex sonomae

Total Length: 4¹/₈–7¹/₈ in.
Tail Length: 1³/₈–3³/₈ in.
Weight: ³/₁₆–¹/₂ oz.

When naming a new species, the common name is often chosen to reflect certain qualities of the animal, its range or its habitat. Such is the case for the Fog Shrew. This large, brown shrew is found along the Oregon and California coastline, specifically in the active fog belt. Recent studies have revealed some information about this uncommon species, but it is much less studied then most other shrew species. Observations of its grooming behavior show that it is meticulous about keeping clean. It cleans its face with moistened forefeet, much like a cat does.

ALSO CALLED: Sonoma Shrew.

DESCRIPTION: This large shrew is predominantly brown, with undersides darker than the back. Some individuals may be grayer than others. The long tail is the same color as the body. Its teeth can help distinguish it because the tine is lacking on the first upper incisor.

HABITAT: These shrews primarily inhabit moist forested areas, marshes or areas of dense cover near muddy streams. Alder, maple, hemlock and red cedar are common in the overstory of this shrew's preferred habitat.

FOOD: Like other shrews, the Fog Shrew feeds on invertebrates such as insect larva and adults, slugs, snails and earthworms.

DEN: Fog Shrews probably build spherical nests like other *Sorex* species. These nests are usually in a sheltered area such as in a decayed log or under a dense shrub. A spherical nest is a simple bundle of grass without a central cavity.

YOUNG: Very little is known about the reproductive behavior of the Fog Shrew. It probably has a gestation similar to other shrews, less than 20 days, and it likely mates and bears young in spring and summer. The litter size is two to six young.

SIMILAR SPECIES: Most shrews are impossible to identify without a specimen and a mammal key.

RANGE: The Fog Shrew is found in moist coastal forests, from southwestern Oregon through northwestern California.

Montane Shrew
Sorex monticolus

Total Length: 3³/₈–5 in.
Tail Length: 1³/₈–2 in.
Weight: ³/₁₆–¹/₄ oz.

The successful Montane Shrew is one of the most widespread members of its genus. It can be found from Alaska and the Yukon south to Mexico, in a variety of different habitats. As much at home on coastal islands as high mountaintops, this shrew is more of a generalist than other shrews. It is not even finicky about what it eats. Where Montane Shrews coexist with other *Sorex* species, these generalists are usually the most numerous.

ALSO CALLED: Dusky Shrew.

DESCRIPTION: This mid-sized shrew has a pale brown back and sides in summer. Its back is slightly darker in winter. The undersides are silvery gray to buffy brown. The bicolored tail is whitish below and the same color as the back above.

RANGE: The Montane Shrew is found from Alaska southeast to Manitoba, south along the Rocky Mountains to Mexico and through the western states to California.

HABITAT: The Montane Shrew can be found in moist alpine meadows and wet sedge meadows, among willows alongside mountain brooks and in damp coniferous forests with nearby bogs.

FOOD: This shrew eats a variety of adult and larval insects, earthworms, spiders, snails, slugs, carrion and even some vegetation.

DEN: Montane Shrews usually build their spherical nests in decayed logs. The nest is a simple bundle of grass without a central cavity.

YOUNG: Mating occurs from March to August, during which time a female likely has more than one litter of two to nine young. The young are helpless at birth, and they must nurse heavily from their mother to complete their rapid growth. The eyes and ears open in about two weeks, and they are weaned soon afterward.

SIMILAR SPECIES: The differences between most shrews are slight, and identification in the field is nearly impossible without a technical key and the animal in hand.

Ornate Shrew

Sorex ornatus

Total Length: 3³/₈–4¹/₄ in.
Tail Length: 1¹/₈–1³/₄ in.
Weight: about ³/₁₆ oz.

This species lives in very different habitat types here in California. Some populations live in upland forested regions, while others live in inland marshy areas. Still more live in coastal salt-marsh areas, where they exhibit a phenomenon called "salt-marsh melanism," a tendency of animals living in salt-marsh areas to be much darker than those living elsewhere. The Ornate Shrews living in salt marshes around San Francisco are nearly black. In upland regions of California these shrews are mainly brown or gray. In response to having an average life span of only 12 to 18 months, the life cycle of these shrews is very compact. Within their few months of life they molt twice, have one or two litters and adults even show distinct tooth wear from their voracious eating habits. Alas, despite their common name, there is nothing particularly flashy about this species, and they are just as difficult to distinguish in the field as any other shrew species.

DESCRIPTION: Although its name suggests a flamboyant appearance, this shrew is an inconspicuous grayish-brown color. Its undersides are somewhat paler. Adults in salt-marsh areas are nearly black. Their short, hairy tail is brown above and below.

HABITAT: This species lives in a variety of habitats, including salt marshes in coastal regions, inland freshwater marshlands and upland open woodlands. Open pine forests are also suitable.

FOOD: Like others of its kind, this species feeds on insects, their larvae and other invertebrates. It probably scavenges carrion when available.

DEN: Small, grassy nests are built in a protected area such as in a rock crevice, inside a hollow log or under thick vegetation.

YOUNG: The peak reproductive period appears to be March and April, and gestation is 21 days. The litter size is about five young, and they grow rapidly.

SIMILAR SPECIES: This shrew is small, but differences between most shrews are slight. Identification in the field is nearly impossible without a technical key and the animal in hand.

RANGE: The Ornate Shrew is found in southwestern California, Santa Catalina Island and into Baja, Mexico.

Inyo Shrew
Sorex tenellus

Total Length: 3³/₈–4 in.
Tail Length: 1³/₈–1⁵/₈ in.
Weight: about ¹/₈ oz.

Very little work has been done on the elusive Inyo Shrew. This species has only been found in a handful of localities. Perhaps researchers may find them elsewhere, but there are very few successful methods of trapping this species. Specific data on the life history of this species is sparse, and much of the information is inference based on its nearest relatives. In fact, the Ornate Shrew (p. 327) and the Dwarf Shrew (*S. nanus*) are so closely related that many scientists believe them to be the same species. Despite their close association, it is generally accepted to treat them as separate species until further research has been conducted.

DESCRIPTION: This small shrew is mainly a dull gray color, with lighter, sometimes buffy undersides. The summer coat is slightly richer in color than the winter coat. Its tail is grayish brown and slightly darker above than below.

RANGE: Inyo Shrews are known to occur in southwestern Nevada and Mono and Inyo Counties in California. They have also been recorded in Lassen National Park.

HABITAT: Shady, relatively moist microhabitats within the mountains of the arid Great Basin region are the primary habitat for this species. It has always been found above 7500 ft.

FOOD: Very little research has been conducted on this species, but it probably feeds on the same foods that other shrew species feed on. Likely foods include insects, insect larvae, other invertebrates and maybe even carrion.

DEN: Nothing has been substantiated, but Inyo Shrews probably make small, grassy nests under the protective cover of a rock, log or thick shrub.

YOUNG: Presumably the Inyo Shrew has a reproductive cycle similar to that of the Ornate Shrew. Young born in the nest will grow rapidly, and when they emerge from the nest they are only slightly smaller than the adults but otherwise almost indistinguishable. Gestation is probably about three weeks, and the litter size is likely the average for shrews, about five young.

SIMILAR SPECIES: This shrew is very small. Differences between most shrews are slight, and identification in the field is nearly impossible without a technical key and the animal in hand.

Water Shrew
Sorex palustris

Total Length: 5¹/₂–6³/₄ in.
Tail Length: 2³/₈–3³/₈ in.
Weight: ⁵/₁₆–¹¹/₁₆ oz.

As everyone would agree, most of the shrews in California have few distinguishing characteristics. Water Shrews, however, are an exception in the region's shrewdom—these finger-sized heavyweights are so unusual in their habits that they deserve celebrity status.

DESCRIPTION: This species and the Marsh Shrew (p. 330) are the largest shrews west of the Great Plains. The Water Shrew has a velvety black back and contrasting light brown or silver underparts. The third and fourth toes of the hindfeet are slightly webbed, and a stiff fringe of hairs around the hindfeet aid in swimming. Males tend to be somewhat larger than females.

HABITAT: This shrew can be found alongside flowing streams that have undercut, root-entwined banks, in sphagnum moss on the shores of lakes and sometimes in nearly dry stream-beds or alpine regions.

FOOD: Aquatic insects, spiders, snails, other invertebrates and small fish form the bulk of the diet. With true shrew frenzy, these scrappy water lovers may even attack fish half as large as themselves.

DEN: This shrew dens in a shallow burrow in a root-entwined bank, in a sphagnum moss shoreline or even in the wood debris of a beaver lodge. The nest is a spherical mound of dry vegetation, such as twigs, leaves and sedges, and is about 4 in. in diameter.

YOUNG: Water Shrews breed from February until late summer, and females have multiple litters each year. Females born early in the year usually have their first litter in that same year. Litters vary in size from five to eight young, and, as with other shrews, the young grow rapidly and are on their own in a few weeks.

SIMILAR SPECIES: The **Marsh Shrew** (p. 330) is slightly larger, and it has a limited range. Other, smaller shrews lack the velvety black fur of the Water Shrew.

RANGE: This shrew ranges from Alaska to Labrador and south along the Cascades and Sierra Nevada to California, along the Rocky Mountains to New Mexico and along the Appalachians almost to Georgia.

Marsh Shrew
Sorex bendirii

Total Length: 5³/₄–6⁷/₈ in.
Tail Length: 2³/₈–3¹/₈ in.
Weight: about ¹/₂ oz.

Little is known about this fascinating species. It captures much of its food in water and, like the Water Shrew and a few small rodents, it can even run across the surface a short distance before diving under. Beneath the water it appears silvery because of air trapped in the fur. This trapped air makes the Marsh Shrew so buoyant that, when it ceases swimming, it quickly pops to the surface like a cork.

The Marsh Shrew immobilizes its prey by a rapid series of bites and these "frozen" creatures may be stored for a few hours. During rainy winter months, this shrew may move over half a mile from the nearest waterbody.

ALSO CALLED: Pacific Water Shrew.

DESCRIPTION: This large shrew has almost uniform velvety blackish or blackish-brown fur in winter; in summer the pelage is somewhat browner. The tail is dark above and below. The nose is pointed, and the hindfeet are fringed with stiff hairs that help in swimming.

HABITAT: These shrews inhabit marshy areas along slow-moving streams and other wetlands.

FOOD: Both aquatic and terrestrial invertebrates are avidly devoured. Insects of all stages are eaten.

DEN: The nest is a ball of dry grasses, often beneath the loose bark of a fallen tree or within a rotted log or stump.

YOUNG: The typical litter size is four to seven, and the young are born in a bulky nest of grass. Virtually nothing is known of gestation or how long it takes the young to be independent. Sexual maturity probably follows independence because maximum life span does not exceed 1¹/₂ years.

SIMILAR SPECIES: The **Water Shrew** (p. 329) is about the same size but has silvery undersides and a bicolored tail. The **Trowbridge's Shrew** (p. 331) is much less than half the weight of the Marsh Shrew.

RANGE: From extreme southwestern British Columbia, this species follows the area west of the Cascade Mountains south as far as San Francisco, California.

Trowbridge's Shrew
Sorex trowbridgii

Total Length: 4¹/₄–5¹/₄ in.
Tail Length: 1⁷/₈–2³/₈ in.
Weight: about ¹/₄ oz.

The Trowbridge's Shrew tends to collect and store seeds, a behavior not reported in other North American shrews. Because its diet is diverse, it has an advantage over Vagrant Shrews and Montane Shrews where the ranges overlap.

Trowbridge's Shrews are active both day and night, but their periods of activity are short, followed by periods of quiescence. These shrews probably all die before they are 1¹/₂ years old, but during late summer their populations peak because of the early summer births.

DESCRIPTION: This velvety, dark gray shrew has undersides nearly as dark as the back. In summer, the body color is slightly brownish. The tail is sharply bicolored, dark above and light below; the tail of a young animal is hairy but tends to become less so in older individuals. The ears are nearly hidden in the hair, and vibrissae are long and abundant. The feet are whitish to light tan.

HABITAT: Throughout its range, this shrew frequents mature forests with abundant ground litter. Generally, it appears to prefer dry ground beneath Douglas-fir, but when other shrews are absent, it occupies ravines, swampy woods and areas where deep grass borders salmonberry thickets.

FOOD: The diet is primarily small insects, spiders, centipedes, snails, slugs, earthworms and flatworms, but these shrews also often eat Douglas-fir seeds and seeds of other plants. They occasionally even eat subterranean fungi.

DEN: This shrew's nest has not been described, but it is likely similar to that of other shrews.

YOUNG: Ordinarily three to six young are born in spring and early summer. During this time, adult females are continually pregnant.

SIMILAR SPECIES: Within its range the **Marsh Shrew** (p. 330) is the only other species with dark undersides, but it is much larger and heavier with far fewer vibrissae.

RANGE: Trowbridge's Shrews are found from southwestern British Columbia along the coast into central California.

Merriam's Shrew
Sorex merriami

Total Length: 3³/₈–4¹/₄ in.
Tail Length: 1¹/₄–1⁵/₈ in.
Weight: ¹/₈–¹/₄ oz.

Remains of Merriam's Shrews were found in pottery jars during archeological investigations at Mesa Verde National Park in Colorado. The researchers concluded that the animals were collected intentionally by the Native American inhabitants. Although there is no full explanation to this unusual discovery, it seems unlikely that the shrews were to be eaten, because they are exceedingly small and smelly. The smell of Merriam's Shrews is particularly bad, and their noxious odor may have protected stored food from pilfering by rodents.

DESCRIPTION: This small shrew has grayish or brownish-gray upperparts and whitish underparts and feet. In winter it is brighter in appearance. The tail, although sparsely furred, is bicolored.

The males have very large flank glands. If you lift the upper lip and view the four unicuspid teeth behind the upper incisor, the unicuspid teeth appear to be crowded together. The second one is the largest, and the third is larger than the fourth.

HABITAT: This shrew inhabits sagebrush flats, deserts, semi-deserts and sometimes dry grasslands. It seems to favor drier habitats than those occupied by other *Sorex* species.

FOOD: The Merriam's Shrew is thought to eat mostly insects, including beetles, crickets, wasps and caterpillars. Spiders are likely another seasonally common food source.

DEN: These shrews make typical shrew nests, often under logs or in soft soil.

YOUNG: Mating occurs from April through July, with females having multiple litters of typically four to seven young in a year.

SIMILAR SPECIES: Without a technical key and the animal in hand, it can be impossible to identify which shrew you are looking at, but range and habitat should narrow the choices.

RANGE: The Merriam's Shrew has been found from Washington State to North Dakota south to New Mexico and Arizona in appropriate habitat.

Desert Shrew
Notiosorex crawfordi

Total Length: 3–3⅝ in.
Tail Length: ⅞–1¼ in.
Weight: 1/16–⅛ oz.

Like all shrews, the Desert Shrew is strictly territorial, and it will resolutely defend its home range against all that enter it. This aggressive tendency often makes the courting season a bit confusing. Influenced by contradictory urges to both kill and to mate, this shrew is fastidious in its mate selection. It is thought that the large flank glands of the Desert Shrew serve an important and fragrant purpose during this selection process.

True to its name, the Desert Shrew inhabits arid environments. Like many other small mammals of the desert, it does not need to drink fresh water. Instead, its urinary system is designed to maximize water retention, and it metabolizes enough water from the food it eats.

DESCRIPTION: The Desert Shrew is a gray or brownish shrew with light gray undersides. Unlike other shrews, its ears are conspicuous. The flank glands are larger than those of any other North American shrew. Unlike other shrews, its teeth pigmentation is orange, not burgundy.

HABITAT: This shrew lives in arid environments, such as deserts or sagebrush flats, especially in areas of prickly pear cactus. Other associated vegetation includes agave, assorted cacti and dwarf shrubs.

FOOD: Desert Shrews feed mainly on insects and other invertebrates. Usually only the soft parts are consumed.

DEN: Very little is known about the habits of this shrew, but it is frequently found inside woodrat nests or in clumped vegetation at the base of a cactus or shrub.

YOUNG: This shrew probably breeds through spring and summer, and perhaps into fall. Litters are suspected to number three to five young.

SIMILAR SPECIES: Although most shrews are difficult to identify visually, the Desert Shrew is unique because of the orange pigmentation on its teeth.

RANGE: These shrews are found from southern California east to Arkansas and south into Mexico.

Virginia Opossum
Didelphis virginiana

Among the mammals of North America, the Virginia Opossum is unique because of its prehensile tail, maternal pouch, opposable "big toe" and habit of faking death. Famed by its portrayals in children's literature, the opossum is widely known but poorly understood. Few people realize that this animal is a marsupial, and that it is more closely related to the kangaroos and koalas of Australia and to other marsupials of Central and South America than to any other mammal native to the U.S. or Canada.

Thanks to the many children's stories, we conjure up images of opossums hanging in trees by their tails. This behavior is not nearly as common as literature suggests. An opossum's tail is prehensile and strong, but it is unlikely to be used in such a manner unless the animal has slipped or is reaching for something.

The phrase "playing 'possum" is derived from the feigned death scene that is put on by a frightened opossum. If a Virginia Opossum cannot scare away an intruder with fervent hissing and screeching, it rolls over, dangles its legs, closes its eyes, lolls its tongue out and drools. Possibly, this death pose is so startling that the opossum will be left alone.

If you do much driving through the Virginia Opossum's range, it should not be long before you encounter one. Unfortunately, opossums are frequent victims of roadway collisions. They are slow-moving animals that forage at night and find the bounty of road-killed insects and other animals hard to resist. With an abundance of food, opossums may become very fat. They draw upon their reserves in winter in colder parts of their range, but much of California is still too cold or dry for these creatures, with their naked ears and tails.

DESCRIPTION: This opossum is a cat-sized, gray mammal with a white face, long, pointed nose and long tail. Its ears are black, slightly rounded and nearly hairless. Its tail is rounded, scaly and prehensile. The legs, the base of the tail and patches around the eyes are black. Its overall appearance is grizzled from the mix of white, black and gray hairs. No other U.S. mammal resembles this opossum, and it is the only terrestrial mammal in the U.S. or Canada to have 50 teeth in all.

HABITAT: Moist woodlands or brushy areas near watercourses seem to be favored, but given a warm enough climate and access to permanent water,

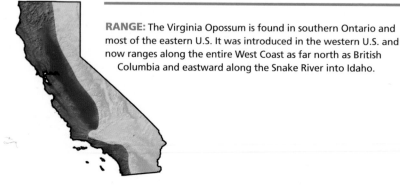

RANGE: The Virginia Opossum is found in southern Ontario and most of the eastern U.S. It was introduced in the western U.S. and now ranges along the entire West Coast as far north as British Columbia and eastward along the Snake River into Idaho.

Total Length: 27–33 in.
Tail Length: 12–14 in.
Weight: 2$\frac{1}{2}$–3$\frac{1}{2}$ lb.

Virginia Opossums may be found almost anywhere, including cities.

FOOD: A full description of the opossum diet would include almost everything organic. These omnivores eat invertebrates, insects, small mammals, birds, grain, berries and other fruits, grass and carrion.

DEN: By day, opossums hide in burrows dug by other mammals, in hollow trees or logs, under buildings or in rock piles. In colder parts of the region, they may remain holed up in a den for days during cold weather, but they do not hibernate.

YOUNG: Up to 25 young may be born in a litter after a gestation of 12 to 13 days. The young must crawl into the pouch and attach to one of the 9 to 17 nipples if they are to survive. After about three months in the pouch, an average of eight to nine young emerge, weighing about 5$\frac{1}{2}$ oz. each. Females mature sexually when they are six months to a year old.

SIMILAR SPECIES: No other mammal shares the combination of characteristics seen in the opossum. Its young, newly emerged from the pouch, might be mistaken for **rats** (pp. 192–93), but rats do not have naked, black ears.

DID YOU KNOW?

At about the size of a honeybee at birth, a Virginia Opossum begins life as one of the smallest baby mammals in North America.

Introduced Species

California has become home to a large number of non-native species. Some of the established non-native species were intentionally released here, while others were accidental introductions. Elsewhere in North America, harsh winters prevent the establishment and spread of non-native species, but the mild climate of most of California is suitable for many exotic species. They often become significant problems both environmentally and economically. Some introduced species can thrive so well that they out-compete and exclude native mammals from their habitats. In some cases, introduced species may prey so heavily on native animals and plants that the native species become threatened or endangered. Established non-native species may also become serious agricultural pests. In the past, certain exotic animals have been intentionally introduced as game species and even as control measures for other introduced species, but such releases are invariably ill-conceived and ill-fated. Preventing the establishment of exotic species is an issue of special concern for many organizations and government departments.

The following is a list of introduced species that do not have a full entry this book.

FERAL DOG (*Canis familiaris*)

Pet dogs that have been lost or abandoned often survive and reproduce, resulting in wild populations of these canids. Feral dogs can be nuisances and often prey heavily on native animals.

FERAL CAT (*Felis catus*)

Pet cats can also become feral. Felines are exceptional hunters, and their skills at birding can decimate entire populations of native birds. As well as birds, feral cats feed on amphibians, reptiles, small mammals and even invertebrates.

FERAL BURRO (*Equus asinus*)

Feral burros likely derive from lost and escaped working burros over the last 150 years. Both feral burro and feral horse (p. 52) populations are monitored in California, and these animals are often confined in reserves.

BURCHELL'S ZEBRA (*Equus burchelli*)

Introduced at Hearst Ranch (p. 21), this zebra was a special attraction for more than 10 years. Small numbers of Burchell's Zebra are naturalized and are still seen along Highway 1 near San Simeon.

AXIS DEER (*Axis axis*)

Introduced from India, Axis Deer were released in small numbers from the San Francisco Zoo in the 1940s, and their numbers have increased. Their populations are monitored in the state, and restricted hunting is permitted.

SAMBAR DEER (*Cervus unicolor*)

Another member of the Hearst Ranch landed immigrants, the Sambar Deer exists in small numbers in the vicinity of the ranch, and the population may be growing. This small deer is native to India and Southeast Asia.

FALLOW DEER (*Dama dama*)

The Fallow Deer has a long history of introductions as an ornamental and game species around the world but is native to southern Turkey. A small population was kept at Hearst Ranch, and individuals may have been introduced from elsewhere as well.

FERAL CATTLE (*Bos taurus*)

Hardly glamorous renegades, feral cattle do occur as individuals escaped and lost from domestic stock. Cattle are unmistakable, but only truly feral cattle will lack tattoos and brands.

BARBARY SHEEP
(*Ammotragus lervia*)

Native to only North Africa, the Barbary Sheep has a distinct presence in several southern states. Once featured at the Hearst Ranch Zoo, this species now has a sizable population in California. Although the Department of Fish and Wildlife considers it a non-game species, limited hunting occurs.

FERAL SHEEP (*Ovis aries*)

In the southern states and in Central and South America, domestic sheep routinely become feral. As heavy grazers, they may cause damage to native plants. Feral sheep are not regulated in California.

BLACKBUCK (*Antilope cervicarpa*)

A resident of the Hearst Ranch, the Blackbuck drew much excitement from visitors for its striking colors and twisted horns. The Blackbuck is native to India and was once the most abundant ungulate there.

FERAL GOAT (*Capra hircus*)

Feral goats exist in favorable climates wherever domestic goats are found. They can cause enormous damage to plant species and their habitats. Feral goats on islands have been known to damage the terrain extensively and cause drastic declines of both the native plants that they feed on and the native animals that they out-compete.

HIMALAYAN TAHR
(*Hemitragus jemlahicus*)

Native to the Himalayas, this goat-like bovid was featured at the Hearst Ranch. Ill-suited to warm climates, the tahr survives only in small numbers in the vicinity of the ranch.

Introduced Species included in the text:
Wild Pig (p. 50)
Horse (p. 52)
House Mouse (p. 191)
Norway Rat (p. 192)
Black Rat (p. 193)
Eastern Fox Squirrel (p. 263)
Eastern Gray Squirrel (p. 263)
European Rabbit (p. 285)
Virginia Opossum (p. 334)

Burchell's Zebra

Extirpated Species

Habitat loss and intentional population reduction are the main reasons why some of California's mammal species are extirpated (no longer found in California but still found elsewhere in the world) and why many more mammals are listed as endangered (facing imminent extirpation or extinction if measures are not taken immediately to reverse the decline of the populations). The following species are no longer found in California:

GRAY WOLF (*Canis lupus*)

The Gray Wolf once inhabited all of North America, but because of misconceptions about its nature, extermination programs resulted in the near-total eradication of the Gray Wolf from the contiguous states. Although infrequent reports of wolves occur in states north of California, this species no longer exists in our state.

White-Tailed Deer

GRIZZLY BEAR (*Ursus arctos*)

Walking in the wilderness of California can still invoke a sense of the fearsome power of the Grizzly Bears that once lived here. Like wolves, Grizzlies were exterminated; in California, no records of them have occurred since the 1920s.

JAGUAR (*Felix onca*)

The Jaguar is the largest native cat in North America, and it too is a creature regarded with both fear and fascination. Jaguars are shy creatures that are wary of people, but over-hunting and intentional extermination has pushed them out of California.

WHITE-TAILED DEER (*Odocoileus virginianus*)

In the past, small numbers of White-tailed Deer were reported in extreme northeastern California, and remains of antlers support this claim. It is extremely unlikely that these deer exist in the region today. Why they are absent from this and neighboring areas but inhabit most of the rest of the continent is unknown, but it may be attributable to natural population fluctuations.

Grizzly Bear

Glossary

altricial: describing offspring that are almost totally helpless at birth, usually born without fur, with their eyes closed and unable to walk.

bovid: a member of the cattle family (Bovidae).

cache: a place in which food is hidden for future use; the food hidden in such a place.

calcar: in bats, a small projection from the inner side of each hindfoot into the membrane between the hindlegs.

canid: a member of the dog family (Canidae).

cervid: a member of the deer family (Cervidae).

cetacean: a member of the whale order (Cetacea); a whale, dolphin or porpoise.

dewclaw: a small toe, usually paired, located high on a hoofed mammal's leg, so that it typically touches the ground only in mud or snow.

diurnal: active during the day (compare *nocturnal*).

dormancy: a state of inactivity, with greatly slowed metabolism, respiration and heart rate.

drey: a spherical tree nest made of leaves, twigs and moss.

echolocation: the ability of some animals (including bats and cetaceans among mammals) to detect objects by emitting sound waves and interpreting the returning echoes.

endangered: said of a species or subspecies that is facing imminent *extirpation* or *extinction*.

estivation: a state of summer dormancy that occurs in some mammals to conserve resources during very hot or dry periods (compare *hibernation*).

extinct: said of a species that no longer exists anywhere.

extirpated: said of a species that no longer exists in a given geographic area but still survives elsewhere in the world.

family: a biological classification that ranks below *order* and designates a group of closely related *genera*.

forb: a *herbaceous* plant other than a grass.

genus (pl. genera): a group of closely related *species* of organisms; if individuals from different species of a genus interbreed, their offspring are usually infertile.

gestation: the time of pregnancy, from conception to birth.

grizzled: said of mostly dark fur that is sprinkled or streaked with gray or another light color.

guard hairs: long, coarse hairs that help protect a mammal's *underfur* from the weather.

herbaceous: pertaining to plants that lack woody stems.

hibernation: a state of winter dormancy in certain mammals during which the body temperature is lowered and all body processes are greatly reduced, thereby conserving resources and allowing the mammal to sleep through much of winter (compare *estivation*).

home range: the total area in which an individual animal moves during its usual activities (compare *territory*).

insectivore: a member of the order Insectivora (moles and shrews); any animal that depends on insects as its primary food source.

interbreed: for individuals of different species to mate with each other.

invertebrate: an animal that lacks a backbone, such as an insect, spider, earthworm or snail.

lagomorph: a member of the order Lagomorpha (rabbits, hares and pikas).

membrane: a thin, flexible layer, such as the skin of a bat's wings.

migration: the journey that an animal undergoes to get from one region to another, usually in response to seasonal and reproductive cycles.

mustelid: a member of the weasel family (Mustelidae).

nocturnal: active at night (compare *diurnal*).

ochreous: an earthy yellow color.

order: a biological classification that designates a group of closely related *families* of organisms.

palmate: branching like the fingers of a human hand.

perianal: located around the anus.

pinna (pl. pinnae): a part of the external ear that projects outward; made mostly of cartilage.

pinniped: a member of the subgrouping of the order Carnivora that encompasses all seals, sea-lions and walruses.

precocial: describing offspring that are well developed at birth, usually having fur and opened eyes, and quickly being able to walk.

scat: a fecal pellet or dropping; feces.

species: a biological classification below *genus* that designates closely related organisms that are able to breed and produce viable offspring.

subspecies: a subcategory of *species* that designates a geographic population that is genetically distinct from other populations of that species, but is still able to successfully breed with them.

territory: a defended area within an animal's home range.

tragus: a lobe projecting upward from inside the base of the ears, as in bats.

underfur: a thick, insulating undercoat of fur.

ungulate: a hoofed mammal.

unicuspid: in shrews, any of the small teeth between the two front teeth and the large rear teeth.

vertebrate: an animal with a backbone, such as a mammal, bird or fish.

vibrissa (pl. vibrissae): one of the stiff hairs situated around the nostrils or on the face in many mammals; can serve as tactile organs; commonly called whiskers.

Index of Scientific Names

Page numbers in **boldface** type refer to the primary, illustrated species accounts.

341

Index of Common Names

Western Pipistrelle